COOK'S ENCYCLOPEDIA OF
WINE

COOK'S ENCYCLOPEDIA OF

WINE

STUART WALTON

BARNES & NOBLE BOOKS
NEW YORK

This edition published by Barnes & Noble, Inc., by
arrangement with Anness Publishing Limited

2005 Barnes & Noble Books

M 10 9 8 7 6

ISBN 0-7607-4220-0

Publisher: Joanna Lorenz
Senior Editor: Linda Fraser
Copy Editor: Jane Hughes
Designer: Sheila Volpe
Picture Researcher: Lynda Marshall
Special photography and styling: Steve Baxter with Roisin Neild pp. 6–7, 10, 11, 12, 13,
14, 15, 16, 17, 18, 19, 20, 21, 22, 23, 94–5, 200–1
Illustrator: Madeleine David
Maps: Steven Sweet

Photographs: With the exception of sources noted, all photographic
material supplied by Cephas Picture Library:
Bridgeman Art Library: p.8: Courtesy Pushkin Museum, Moscow, p.9: Courtesy
British Library, London; Eddie Parker: p.220; German Wine Information Service:
p.184; Jane Hughes: p.41 (right), p.96 (top), p.102 (bottom), p.177 (bottom),
p.205 (bottom), p.207, p.209, p.210; Morris & Verdin/Robert Wheatcroft: p.210
(top); Patrick Eager: p.51, p 231 (bottom); Sopexa (UK) Ltd: p.130 (top);
South American Pictures: p.223; Wines of Chile: p.217

Previously published as *The World Encylopedia of Wine*

Printed in China

CONTENTS

INTRODUCTION

Van Gogh's depiction of grape-harvesting at Arles in the 1880s (above) would still be recognisable today in parts of southern France.

At the heart of the enormous boom in wine consumption that has taken place in the English-speaking world over the last two decades or so is a fascinating, happy paradox.

In the days when wine was exclusively the preserve of a narrow cultural elite, bought either at auction or from gentleman wine merchants in wing collars and bow-ties, to be stored in rambling cellars and decanted to order by one's butler, the ordinary drinker didn't get a look-in. Wine was considered a highly technical subject, in which anybody without the necessary ability could only fall flat on his or her face in embarrassment. It wasn't just that you needed a refined aesthetic sensibility for the stuff if it wasn't to be hopelessly wasted on you. It required an intimate knowledge of what came from where, and what it was supposed to taste like.

Those were times, however, when wine appreciation essentially meant a familiarity with the great French classics, with perhaps a little sweet wine from Germany and a smattering of the traditional fortified wines - sherry, port and madeira. That was what the wine trade dealt in. These days, wine is bought daily in supermarkets and high-street chains to be consumed that evening, hardly anybody has a cellar to store it in and most don't even possess a decanter. Above all, the wines of literally

dozens of countries are available on our market. When a supermarket offers its customers a couple of fruity little numbers from Brazil, we scarcely raise an eyebrow.

It seems, in other words, that the commercial jungle that wine has now become has not in the slightest deterred people from plunging adventurously into the thickets in order to taste and see. Consumers are no longer intimidated by the thought of needing to know their Pouilly-Fumé from their Pouilly-Fuissé, their Bardolino from their Brunello, just at the very moment when there is more to know than ever before.

The reason for this new mood of confidence is not hard to find. It is on virtually every wine label from Australia, North America, New Zealand, South Africa and South America: the name of the grape from which the wine is made. At one time, that might have sounded like a fairly technical approach in itself. Why should native English-speakers need to know what Cabernet Sauvignon, Chardonnay or Sauvignon Blanc were? The answer lies in the popularity that wines made from those grape varieties now enjoy. Consumers effectively recognise them as brand names, and have acquired a basic lexicon of wine that can serve them even when confronted with those Brazilian upstarts.

In the wine heartlands of Europe, especially France, they are scared to death of that trend - not because they think their wine isn't as good as the best from California or South Australia (what French winemaker will ever admit that?) but because they don't traditionally call their wines Cabernet Sauvignon or Chardonnay. They call them Château Ducru-Beaucaillou or Corton-Charlemagne, and they aren't about to change. Some areas, notably the large swathes of the Midi in the middle of southern France, have now produced a generation of growers (not all of them French) using the varietal names on their labels and are tempting consumers back to French wine. It will be an uphill struggle, but there is probably no other way if France is to avoid simply becoming a speciality source of old-fashioned wines for old-fashioned connoisseurs.

Wine consumption was also given a significant boost in the early 1990s by the pioneering work of Dr Serge Renaud, a cardiologist based at Lyon, who has spent many years investigating the reasons for the uncannily low incidence of coronary heart disease in the south of France. One of the major findings to have emerged from his studies is that the fat-derived cholesterol that builds up in the arteries and can eventually lead to heart trouble by blocking the heart's supply of oxygen can be dispersed by the tannins in wine. Tannin is derived from the skins of grapes, and is therefore present in higher levels in red wines, because they have to be infused with their skins to attain their colour. The truth was out: wine is good for you.

That news caused a huge upsurge in red wine consumption in the United States when a television documentary about Dr. Renaud's findings was aired. It took a fair while to be accorded the prominence it deserves in the UK, largely because the medical profession still sees all alcohol as a menace to health, and is constantly calling for it to be made prohibitively expensive. Certainly, the manufacturers of anti-coagulant drugs might have something to lose if we all got the message that we would do just as well by our hearts, and be considerably happier, by taking half a bottle of red wine every day.

Wine is there to be enjoyed, and there is certainly a lot more good wine about today than there was a generation ago. This book is designed to help you get your bearings a little in the vinous jungle. It is not an academic textbook loaded with technicalities, nor is it an investor's guide for use in the salerooms by the seriously moneyed. It is instead aimed squarely at those who already enjoy drinking wine, but find themselves wanting a deeper knowledge of where it is made, what goes into it and what those often confusingly detailed labels are actually telling you.

The first part of the book deals with the practicalities of keeping and serving wine, what to drink it with and what to drink it out of. The second section takes a look at 12 of the most important grape varieties used in the making of wine internationally. I have tried to give an indication of the different regional styles each grape takes on, how the wines typically taste, and also an overview of what debates are currently taking place among wine professionals with regard to some of them, so that you can make up your own mind where you stand and not have somebody else's opinion foisted on you.

Finally, we take a globetrotting tour of the world's wine regions, exploring what grows where and why, and also shedding some light on the often arcane wine classification systems in use in most of Europe's vineyards. Summaries of the comparative quality of recent vintages should enable you to buy with confidence in both the wine-shop and the restaurant.

Wine possesses a virtually limitless ability to surprise. No two wines are alike; some say no two bottles are alike. It all depends on the context, the company, the bottle and you. I hope you enjoy reading about it, but even more, I hope you will go on to find ever greater pleasure in the wines that await you. That is what this book is all about.

Stuart Walton

The vintage has traditionally been one of the ceremonial high points of the year in Europe's wine-growing regions, as this illustration from the medieval Book of Hours, c.1520 (above) vividly demonstrates.

PRINCIPLES *of* TASTING

All that sniffing, swirling and spitting that the professional winetasters engage in is more than just a way of showing off; it really can immeasurably enhance the appreciation of any wine.

THE WINETASTER'S ritual of peering into a glass, swirling it around and sniffing suspiciously at it, before taking a mouthful only to spit it out again looks like a highly mysterious and technical procedure to the uninitiated. It is, however, a sequence of perfectly logical steps that can immeasurably enhance the enjoyment of good wine. Once learned, they become almost second nature to even the novice taster.

Don't pour a full glass for tasting because you're going to need room for swirling, but allow a little more than the wine waiter in a restaurant tends to offer. About a third full is the optimum amount.

When pouring a tasting sample, be sure to leave enough room in the glass for giving it a good swirl (below).

Firstly, have a good look at the wine by holding it up to the daylight or other light source. Is it clear or cloudy? Does it contain sediment or other solid matter? In the case of red wines, tilt the glass away from you against a white surface and look at the colour of the liquid at the far edge. Older wines start to fade at the rim, the deep red taking on an autumnal brownish or tawny hue.

Now swirl the glass gently. The point of this is to activate the aromatic compounds in the wine, so that when you come to stick your nose in, the bouquet can be fully appreciated. Swirling takes a bit of practice (start with a glass of water over the kitchen sink) but the aim is to get a fairly vigorous wave circulating in the liquid. If you are nervous about performing the swirl in mid-air, there is nothing wrong with doing it while the glass is still on the table and then bringing it to your nose, but beware of scraping your best crystal around on a rough wooden tabletop.

When sniffing, tilt the glass towards your face and get your nose slightly inside it, keeping it within the lower half of the opening of the glass. The head should be bent forward a little with the glass tipped at a 45° angle to meet it. Inhale gently (as if you were sniffing a flower, not filling your lungs on a blustery clifftop) and for a good three or four seconds. The scents a wine offers may change during the course of one sniff. Nosing a wine can reveal a great deal about its origins and the way it was made, but don't overdo it. The sense of smell is quickly neutralised. Two or three sniffs should tell you as much as you need to know.

Now comes the tricky part. The reason that wine experts pull those ridiculous faces when they take a mouthful is that they are trying to spread the wine around all the different taste-sensitive parts of the tongue. At its very tip are the receptors for sweetness. Just a little back from those, saltiness is registered. Acidity or sourness is tasted on the sides of the tongue, while bitterness is sensed at the very back. So roll the wine around your mouth as thoroughly as you can.

It helps to maximise the flavour of a wine if you take in air while it's in your mouth. To reduce the risk of dribbling, make sure the head is now back in an upright position. Using gentle suction with the lips pursed, draw in some breath. It will only be necessary to allow the tiniest opening - less than the width of a pencil - and to suck in immediately. Again, practise over the sink. Close the lips again, and breathe downwards through the nose. In this way, the taste of the wine is transmitted through the nasal passages as well as via the tongue, and the whole sensation is more intense. And *think* about the taste. What messages is the wine giving you? Do you like it or not?

When you have tasted the mouthful of wine, you can either swallow it - much the best thing in polite company - or, if you are tasting a number of wines at a time of day when you wouldn't normally be drinking, then spit it out. At public tastings, there will be buckets or lined boxes for spitting into, or else at an outdoor fair or in a marquee at a wine show, spit it out on the ground, taking care not to spray the shoes of unsuspecting passers-by. Spit confidently, with the tongue behind the ejected liquid, so as to avoid it trickling down your chin, but spit downwards. You are not aiming to extinguish a fire.

There are five principal elements to look for in the taste of a wine. Learn to concentrate on each one individually while tasting, and you will start to put together a set of analytical tools with which to evaluate the quality of any wine.
Dryness/Sweetness From bone-dry Chablis at one end of the spectrum to the most luscious Liqueur Muscats at the other, through a broad range of intermediary styles, the amount of natural sugar a wine contains is perhaps its most easily noted attribute.
Acidity There are many different types of acid in wine, the most important being tartaric, which is present in unfermented grape juice. How sharp does the wine feel at the edges of the tongue? Good acidity is necessary to contribute a feeling of freshness to a young wine, and to help the best wines to age. In a poor vintage though, when the grapes didn't ripen properly, an excessive sourness or even bitterness can spoil a wine. Don't confuse dryness with acidity. A very dry wine like fino sherry can actually be quite low in acid, while the sweetest Sauternes will contain sufficient acidity to offset its sugar.

Tannin Tannin is present in the stalks and pips of fresh grapes, but also in the skins. Since the colour in red wine comes from the skins (the juice of even black grapes being colourless), some tannin is inevitably extracted along with it. In the mouth, it gives that furry, drying feeling that makes very young reds hard to drink, but it disappears gradually as they mature in the bottle.
Oak Many wines are matured in oak barrels, and may even have gone through their initial fermentation in oak, and the flavour imparted to them by contact with the wood is an easy one to appreciate, particularly in the case of whites. An aroma or taste of vanilla or other sweet spice such as nutmeg or cinnamon is a strong indicator of the presence of oak, as is an overall feeling of creamy smoothness on the palate in the case of the richer reds. If the barrels a wine was kept in were heavily charred (or "toasted") on the insides, the wine will display a pronounced smokiness like toast left under the grill a little too long or a match that has just been blown out.
Fruit Anybody who has read a newspaper or magazine wine column in which the writer describes wines as tasting of raspberries, passion fruit, melon and glacé cherries (often all at once) will have wondered if there isn't an element of kiddology in it all. In fact, there are sound biochemical reasons for the resemblance of wines to the flavours of other foods (and not just fruit, but vegetables, herbs and spices too). In the sections on the main grape varieties, I have suggested some of the flavours most commonly met with in the wines made from those grapes. Let your imagination run free when tasting. Bright fruit flavours are among the most charming features a wine can possess.

A gentle swirling action of the hand is sufficient to produce quite a vigorous wave in the glass (above).

Sniff lightly and long, with the nose slightly below the rim of the glass (above).

Take a good mouthful of the wine, in order to coat all surfaces of the mouth with it (above).

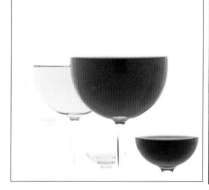

STORING *and* SERVING

Where is the best place to keep wine for maturation? Should it be allowed to breathe before being served? What does decanting an old wine involve? None of these questions is as technical as it seems.

NONE OF THE TECHNICALITIES involved in the storage and serving of wine needs to be too complicated. The following guidelines are aimed at keeping things simple. **Creating a cellar** Starting a wine collection requires a certain amount of ingenuity now that most of us live in flats or houses without cellars. If you have bought a large parcel of wine that you don't want to touch for years, you can pay a nominal fee to a wine merchant to cellar it for you, but the chances are that you may only have a couple of dozen bottles at any one time. Where to keep it?

The two main points to bear in mind are that bottles should be stored horizontally and away from sources of heat. You can pile them on top of each other if they are all the same shape, but it's safer and more convenient to invest in a simple wooden or plastic wine rack. Keeping the bottles on their sides means the wine is in constant contact with the corks, preventing them from drying out and imparting off-flavours to the wine.

Don't put your bottles in the cupboard next to the storage heater or near the cooker because heat is a menace to wine. Equally, don't leave it

A simple winerack is much the best way of storing bottles (right). This one allows enough space to see the labels too, so that they don't have to be pulled out to identify them.

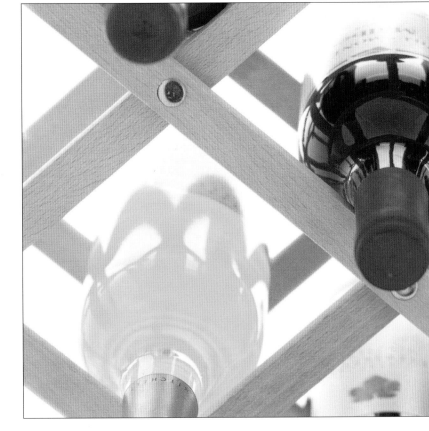

in the garden shed in sub-zero temperatures. Choose a cool cupboard that's not too high up (remember that heat rises) and where it can rest in peace in the dark.

Serving temperatures The conventional wisdom that white wine should be served chilled and red wine at room temperature is essentially correct, but it isn't the whole story.

Don't over-chill white wine or its flavours will be muted. Light, acidic whites, sparkling wines and very sweet wines (and rosés too for that matter) should be served at no higher than about 10°C (50°F) but the best Chardonnays, dry Semillons and Alsace wines can afford to be a little less cool than that.

Reds, on the other hand, generally benefit from being slightly cooler than the ambient temperature in a well-heated home. Never warm the bottle by a radiator as that will make the wine taste muddy. Some lighter, fruity reds such

as young Beaujolais, Dolcetto or the lighter Loire or New Zealand reds are best served lightly chilled - about an hour in the refrigerator.

Breathing Should red wine be allowed to breathe? In the case of matured reds that are intended to be drunk on release, like Rioja Reservas or the softer, barrel-aged Cabernet Sauvignons of Australia, the answer is that there is probably no point. Young reds with some tannin, or immature hard acidity, do round out with a bit of air contact, though. Either pour the wine into a decanter or jug half an hour or so before serving or, if you haven't anything suitable for the table, pour it into another container and then funnel it back into the bottle. Simply drawing the cork won't in itself make any difference because only the wine in the neck is in contact with the air. And remember the wine will develop in any case in the glass as you slowly sip it.

Here is an ingeniously designed winerack that ensures that the undersides of the corks are kept constantly in contact with the wine, thus preventing them from drying out.

Corkscrews The spin-handled corkscrew is undoubtedly the easiest to use because it involves one continuous motion and very little effort. The type with side-levers is less good because it often needs two or three attempts with longer corks. If you are good at displays of brute force, the Wine Waiter's Friend is the model for you, but a particularly obstinate cork can make you look very silly. In theory, the object is to insert the corkscrew far enough into the cork to be able to draw it without piercing the underside and risking fragments of cork falling into the wine. A bartender once taught me a trick for removing bits of cork before pouring. It involved giving the bottle one sharp flick in the general direction of the sink. If your aim is accurate, try it. It wastes less wine than pouring it, cork lumps and all, into a glass and then discarding it.

Some corkscrews are equipped with a foil cutter (above), allowing you to remove a neat circle from the top of the capsule for uncorking.

The most basic type of corkscrew (top left) involves simple tugging; it is far easier to use the opener (bottom left) as it requires hardly any effort; the levered model (top right) isn't bad, but can break a large cork. The very chic Fish corkscrew (bottom right) works with a gentle spring action.

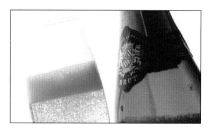

Opening fizz Many people are still intimidated about opening sparkling wines. Remember that the longer a bottle of fizz has been able to rest before opening, the less lively it will be. If it has been very badly shaken up, it may need a week or more to settle. Also, the colder it is, the less likely it will be to go off like a firecracker.

Once the foil has been removed and the wire cage untwisted and taken off too, grasp the cork firmly and take hold of the lower half of the bottle. The advice generally given is to turn the bottle rather than the cork, but in practice most people probably do both (twisting in opposite directions, of course). Work very gently and, when you feel or see the cork beginning to rise, control it every millimetre of the way with your thumb over the top. It should be possible then to ease it out without it popping. If the wine does spurt, put a finger in the neck, but don't completely stopper it again.

When pouring, fill each glass to just under half-full, and then go round again to top them up once the initial fizz has subsided. Pour fairly slowly so that the wine doesn't foam over the sides. Do not pour into tilted glasses: you aren't serving lager.

Decanting Decanting can help to make a tough young wine a bit more supple, but it is only absolutely necessary if the wine being served is heavily sedimented. In that case, stand the bottle upright for the best part of the day you intend to serve it (from the night before is even better) so that the deposits settle to the bottom. After uncorking, pour the wine in a slow but continuous stream into the decanter, looking into the neck of the bottle. When the sediment starts working its way into the neck as you reach the end, stop pouring. The amount of wine you are left with should be negligible enough to throw away, but if there's more than half a glass, then strain the remainder through a clean muslin cloth. Do *not* use coffee filter-papers or tissue as they will alter the flavour of the wine.

When opening sparkling wines, it is important to restrain the release of the cork (left). Control it every millimetre of the way once it begins to push out.

The quicker you pour, the more vigorous will be the foaming of the wine in the glass (left). Pour carefully to avoid any wastage through overflowing.

The Champagne Saver is a good way of preserving the fizz in any unfinished bottles of sparkling wine (left). Some swear, quite unscientifically, by inserting a spoon-handle in the neck.

GLASSES

Wine doesn't have to be served in the most expensive glassware to show it to advantage, but there are a few basic principles to bear in mind when choosing glasses that will help you get the best from your bottle.

Glasses these days come in all shapes and sizes (below). From left to right in the foreground are: a good red or white wine glass; a technically correct champagne flute; the famous "Paris goblet" much beloved of wine-bars, not a bad shape but too small; an elegant-looking but inefficient sparkling wine glass with flared opening, causing greater dispersal of bubbles; a sherry copita, also useful for other fortified wines.

ALTHOUGH I CAN scarcely remember any champagne that tasted better than the stuff we poured into polystyrene cups huddled in my student quarters after the examination results went up, the truth is that, certainly when you're in the mood to concentrate, it does make a difference what you drink wine from. Not only the appearance but the smell and, yes, even the taste of a wine can be substantially enhanced by using the proper glasses.

They don't have to be prohibitively costly, although - as with everything else - the best doesn't come cheap. The celebrated Austrian glassmaker Georg Riedel has taken the science of wineglasses to its ultimate degree, working out what specific aromatic and flavour components in each type of wine need emphasising, and designing his glasses accordingly. Some of

them are very peculiar shapes indeed, but they undeniably do the trick.

There are some broad guidelines that we can all follow, however, when choosing glasses. Firstly, always choose a plain glass to set off your best wines. Coloured ones, or even those that have just the stems and bases tinted, can distort the appearance of white wines particularly. And, although cut crystal can look very beautiful, I tend to avoid it for wines because it doesn't make for the clearest view of the liquid in the glass.

Look for a deep, wide bowl that tapers significantly towards the mouth. With glasses like that, the aromatic compounds in the wine can be released more generously, both because the deeper bowl allows for a more demonstrative swirling action than anything too small, and because the narrower opening channels the

scents of the wine to your nostrils more efficiently. A flared opening disperses much of the bouquet to the surrounding air.

Traditionally, red wine is served in bigger glasses than white. If you are serving both colours at a grand gastronomic evening, it helps to allot different wines their particular glasses, but the assumption is that reds, especially mature wines, need more space in which to breathe. More development of the wine will take place in the glass than in any decanter or jug the wine may have been poured into. If you are only buying one size, though, think big. A wineglass can never be too large.

Sparkling wines should be served in flutes, tall thin glasses with straight sides, so that the mousse or fizz is preserved. The old champagne saucers familiar from the films (and originally modelled, as the legend has it, on the breast of Marie Antoinette) are inefficient because the larger surface area causes higher dispersal of bubbles and flattens the wine more quickly. Having said that, I have to confess a sneaking fondness for them myself, at least for a more riotous occasion.

Fortified wines should be served in smaller, narrower versions of the ordinary wineglass in recognition of their higher alcoholic strength. The *copita,* traditional glass of the sherry region, is a particularly elegant receptacle and will do quite well for the other fortifieds too. Don't use your tiniest liqueur glasses, though; apart from looking spectacularly mean, they allow no room for enjoying the wine's aromas.

These three glasses (left) are all perfectly shaped for tasting. The one on the right is the official international tasting-glass.

DRINKING WINE *with* FOOD

Matching the right wine to its appropriate dish may seem like a gastronomic assault course but there are broad principles that can be easily learned. And very few mistakes are complete failures.

AT ONE TIME, the rules on choosing wines to accompany food seemed hearteningly simple. It was just a matter of remembering: white wine with fish and poultry, red wine with red meats and cheese, with sherry to start and port to finish. In recent years, that picture has become much more complicated, although its essential principles were mostly fairly sound. Today, magazines frequently run tastings to find wines that match a variety of increasingly exotic dishes, often created specifically for the article in question. One must not be surprised to find oneself, as I once did, trying to find a partner for a dish of sautéed duck livers sauced with strawberries and balsamic vinegar.

The exceptions to the original rules continue to multiply. Port is fashionable as an aperitif in France, the meatier types of fish, such as sword-fish and tuna, are often found to go well with

Pre-dinner nibbles with strong flavours such as Parma ham, olives and asparagus (below) are best served with a chilled fino or manzanilla sherry.

light reds, while it has now become almost a cliché to observe that most cheeses are happier with white wines than with reds.

Some abdicate all choice and happily drink champagne throughout a meal - fine for the goat's cheese salad and the turbot, not so great with the roast lamb.

The following are rough guidelines that incorporate some less obvious suggestions that you may not have thought of. At best, a particular partnership of wine and food adds up to something greater than the sum of its parts. At worst, a strongly flavoured food might strip the wine of some of its complexity, and make it taste rather ordinary - a phenomenon that becomes more distressing in direct proportion to the cost of the wine. But on the whole you can afford to be bold: very few combinations actually clash.

APERITIFS

The two classic (and best) appetite-whetters are sparkling wine and dry sherry. Choose a light, non-vintage champagne (blanc de blancs is a particularly good style to start things off with) or one of the lighter California or New Zealand sparklers. If you are serving highly seasoned canapés, olives or nuts before the meal, dry sherry is better. Always serve a freshly opened bottle of good fino or manzanilla. Kir has become quite trendy again: add a dash of cassis or other blackcurrant liqueur to a glass of crisp dry white (classically Bourgogne Aligoté) or to bone-dry fizz for a Kir Royale.

FIRST COURSES

Soups In general, liquidised soups are happier without wine, although thickly textured versions containing cream can be successful with richer styles of fizz, such as blanc de noirs champagne. A small glass of one of the nuttier-tasting fortified wines such as amontillado sherry or Sercial madeira is a good friend to a meaty consommé. Bulky soups such as minestrone may benefit from a medium-textured Italian red (Chianti or Montepulciano d'Abruzzo) to kick off a winter dinner.

Fish pâtés Light, dry whites without overt fruit are best: Chablis, Alsace Pinot Blanc, Muscadet *sur lie*, German Riesling Kabinett, young Viura from Navarra. But serve something more robust such as young white Rioja or fino sherry with the oilier fish like mackerel.

Chicken or pork liver pâtés Go for a big, pungently flavoured white - Alsace Gewurztraminer, California Fumé Blanc, Hunter Valley Semillon - or a midweight, soft red such as Valpolicella, Valdepeñas, a light *cru* Beaujolais like Brouilly or Chiroubles with a couple of years' bottle-age or red Sancerre.

Smoked salmon Needs a hefty white such as Gewurztraminer or Pinot Gris from Alsace, or an oak-fermented Chardonnay from the Côte de Beaune or California.

Melon The sweeter-fleshed aromatic varieties require a wine with its own assertive sweetness. Try noble-rotted Muscat or Riesling from Washington or California, or even young Canadian Ice Wine.

Prawns, shrimps, langoustines, etc Almost any crisp dry white will work - Sauvignon Blanc is a good grape to choose - but avoid heavily oaked wines. Go for high acidity if you are serving mayonnaise.

Deep-fried mushrooms Best with a medium-bodied simple red such as Côtes du Rhône or one of the lighter Zinfandels.

Asparagus Richer styles of Sauvignon, such as those from New Zealand, are perfect. Subtler wines will suffer.

Pasta dishes These really are best with Italian wines. Choose a concentrated white such as Vernaccia, Arneis or good Soave for cream sauces or those using seafood. Light- to medium-bodied reds from indigenous grape varieties work best with tomato-based sauces. Or you could try a Barbera or Sangiovese from California.

FISH AND SEAFOOD

Oysters Classic partners are champagne, Muscadet or Chablis. Most unoaked Sauvignon also makes a suitably bracing match.

Scallops Simply poached or sautéed, this most delicate of shellfish needs a soft, light white - Côte Chalonnaise burgundy, medium-dry German or New Zealand Riesling, Chardonnay from Alto Adige - becoming correspondingly richer, the creamier the sauce.

A crisply flavoured salad, such as this one with langoustines and avocado (above) needs an equally crisp, dry white wine to accompany it.

Chardonnay, dry Rieslings from Alsace or Germany. Equally, it is capable of taking a lightish red such as *cru* Beaujolais or Pinot Noir.

Tuna Go for a fairly assertive red in preference to white: well-built Pinot Noir (California or Côte de Beaune), mature Loire red (Chinon or Bourgueil), Washington State Merlot, Australian Shiraz, Chilean Cabernet, even Zinfandel.

MEAT AND POULTRY

Chicken If the bird is roasted, go for a soft-edged quality red such as mature burgundy, Crianza or Reserva Rioja or California Merlot. Lighter cooking treatments may mandate one of the richer whites, depending on any sauce.

Turkey The Christmas or Thanksgiving turkey deserves a show-stopping red with a little more power than you would serve with chicken. St-Emilion or Pomerol claret, Châteauneuf-du-Pape, Cabernet-Merlot or Cabernet-Shiraz blends from the USA or Australia will all oblige.

Rabbit As for roast chicken.

Pork Roast pork or grilled chops are happiest with fairly full reds with a touch of spice: southern Rhône blends, Australian Shiraz, California Syrah or the bigger Tuscan reds such as Vino Nobile or Brunello.

Lamb The meat that Cabernet Sauvignon might have been invented for, so go for the ripest and best you can find - from Bordeaux to Bulgaria, New Zealand to Napa.

A delicate white fish dish such as paupiettes of sole (above) is best with a lightly oaked dry white wine.

Lobster Cold in a salad, it needs a pungent white with some acidity, such as Pouilly-Fumé, dry Vouvray, Chablis, South African Chenin Blanc, Australian Riesling. Served hot as a main course (eg. Thermidor), it requires an opulent and heavier wine - Meursault, Chardonnay from California or South Australia, Alsace Pinot Gris, or perhaps one of the bigger Rhône whites like Hermitage.

Light-textured white fish Sole, trout, plaice and the like go well with any light, unoaked or very lightly oaked white from almost anywhere.

Firm-fleshed fish Fish like sea bass, brill, turbot or cod need full-bodied whites to match their texture. *Cru classé* white Bordeaux, white Rioja, Australian Semillon, California Fumé Blanc and most oaked Chardonnays will all fit the bill.

Monkfish Either a heavy, alcoholic white such as Hermitage or Condrieu or the biggest Australian Chardonnay, or - if cooked in red wine - something quite beefy such as Moulin-à-Vent, young St-Emilion, or even California Cabernet.

Salmon Goes well with elegant, midweight whites with some acidity such as *grand cru* Chablis, California, Oregon or New Zealand

The classic partner for coq au vin *(right) is a soft, mature burgundy - the region from which the dish originated.*

Beef A full-flavoured cut such as rump or sirloin can cope with the biggest and burliest reds from anywhere: Hermitage, Côte-Rôtie, the sturdiest Zinfandels, Barolo and Barbaresco, Coonawarra Shiraz. Fillet steak needs something a touch lighter such as Bordeaux or a midweight Châteauneuf. Peppered steak or sauces containing mustard or horseradish call for an appropriate bite in the wine, either from Syrah or Grenache varietals or from the high acidity of Italian blends.

Duck A midweight red with youthful acidity to cut any fattiness is best: Crozes-Hermitage, Chianti Classico, California or New Zealand Pinot.

Game birds Best of all with fully mature Pinot Noir from the Côte d'Or, Carneros or Oregon, or - at a pinch - an aged Morgon.

Venison Highly concentrated reds with some bottle-age are essential. *Cru classé* Bordeaux or northern Rhône are the reference points. Cabernet, Shiraz and Zinfandel from hotter climates work well.

Offal Liver and kidneys are good with vigorous young reds such as Chinon, Ribera del Duero, Barbera or New Zealand Cabernet. Sweetbreads are better with a high-powered white such as a mature Alsace varietal.

DESSERTS

Fresh fruit salads are best served on their own, as there is generally too much acidity in them to do wine any favours. Similarly, frozen desserts like ice-creams and sorbets tend to numb the palate's sensitivity to wine. Anything based on eggs and cream, such as baked custards, mousses and *crème brûlée,* deserves a noble-rotted wine, such as Sauternes, Barsac, Monbazillac, Coteaux du Layon, the sweetest Vouvrays, or equivalent wines from outside Europe. Chocolate, often thought to present problems, doesn't do much damage to botrytised wines, but think maximum richness and high alcohol above all. Fruit tarts are best with a late-picked rather than rotted style of dessert wine, such as one of the lighter German or Austrian Rieslings, Alsace Vendange Tardive or late-harvest Muscat or Riesling from North America or the southern hemisphere. Meringues and creamy gâteaux are good with the sweeter styles of sparkling wine, while Asti or Moscato d'Asti make refreshing counter-balances to Christmas pudding. Sweet oloroso sherry, Bual or Malmsey madeira and Liqueur Muscat from Victoria are all superb with rich, dark fruitcake or anything nutty such as pecan pie.

Choose an assertively spicy red, such as a Syrah or Grenache, to accompany the peppery hotness of steak au poivre *(left).*

The chocolate sauce in poire belle-Hélène *(below) doesn't have to present problems for wine if you go for a big, rich noble-rotted dessert wine.*

LABELLING

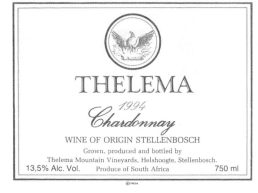

A BOVE THE VINTAGE DATE on this German label, we see the rather complicated name of the estate proprietor, and below it the individual vineyard the wine comes from: Badstube in the village of Bernkastel. Below that is the grape variety, Riesling, and then the style, Kabinett - the least sweet of the QmP quality categories. Mosel-Saar-Ruwer is one of Germany's finest wine regions. To the left, the word *Erzeugerabfüllung* means "bottled by the grower". Note the typically low alcohol - 7.5%.

Wine labels from outside the European appellations have made a virtue of simplicity, so this South African wine simply tells us the name of the estate (Thelema), the vintage year (1994), the grape variety (Chardonnay) and the region of the country in which it was grown and produced (Stellenbosch). "Wine of Origin" is the rough equivalent of the French *appellation contrôlée*. Like many another hot-climate Chardonnay, the alcohol is high - 13.5%, reflecting the ripeness of the grapes.

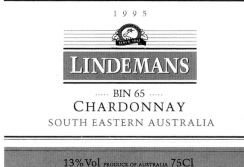

Here is a wine intended to serve as an everyday brand from the portfolio of Lindemans. The label is as simple as can be. Australian winemakers often use bin numbers on their labels to refer to particular batches of wine, sourced perhaps from specific vineyards. Bin 65 is Lindemans' formula for an established blend of wines sourced from quite diverse regions, hence the geographically vague South Eastern Australia, which includes most of the country's grape-growing areas.

This California label has opted to put the regional and varietal identifiers higher than the name of the producer, since those will communicate most immediately to consumers (although there can't be many Californians who haven't heard of Robert Mondavi's wines). In the United States, a wine labelled with one variety like this has only to contain a minimum 75% of that grape, so there may in theory be other ingredients in it, but they must all have been grown in Napa.

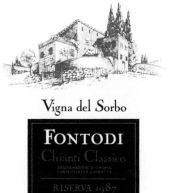

Vigna del Sorbo

750 ml ℮   12,5% vol.

L. 691

The information on this Italian label is not substantially different from that on the German one. Reading down, we have the name of the individual vineyard (Vigna del Sorbo), then the producer (Fontodi) and then the appellation or denominazione (Chianti Classico, the heartland of Chianti). Then comes the quality level, or equivalent of AC - in this case Italy's highest, DOCG. Riserva here denotes a wine that has been aged for at least three years before release. Below that is the information that the wine has been bottled at the estate by its producer.

The practised eye begins to discern similarities between the labels of different European countries. On this Spanish label, we see the name of the producer (La Rioja Alta SA), then the brand name (Viña Ardanza), used to denote a particular blend in this case rather than an individual vineyard. *Embotellado en la propriedad* means "bottled on the estate". In the case of Rioja, Reserva denotes a wine that has been kept for three years before release, of which at least one must be spent in oak. The appellation is Rioja, below which appears the AC formula, DOC.

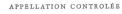

Champagne labels are rarely complicated. The house name will always dominate, since it is a form of brand, in this case Billecart-Salmon at Mareuil-sur-Ay. Above is the style, Brut being virtually the driest, and this one is pink. Champagne is the only AC wine that doesn't require the words *appellation contrôlée* to appear. Beneath the alcohol, the reference number of this house denotes that it is an NM (*négociant-manipulant*), a producer that buys in grapes and makes its own wine.

Burgundy labelling can be a minefield to the uninitiated. The merchant's name (Drouhin) is followed by the appellation. Clos de la Roche is one of the *grand cru* vineyards of the Côte de Nuits. This label at least tells you this is a *grand cru* wine, but doesn't have to state which village it belongs to (Morey-St-Denis, in fact). Note that *mis en bouteille* is not followed by *au domaine*, because it has not been bottled on an individual estate, but by a négociant or merchant based elsewhere.

GRAPE VARIETIES

Soil is furrowed the ancient way to catch winter rain (above), in the sweltering south of Spain.

S uch is the mystique and reverence attached to the appreciation of wine that it is easy to forget just what a simple product it is.

Visiting a modern winery today, with its acres of carefully trained vines, the giant tanks of shining stainless steel, the automated bottling line and perhaps the rows of oak barrels resting on top of one another in deep, cavernous cellars, you might think this was the end product of centuries of human ingenuity.

To the extent that the techniques for making good wine have been steadily refined through succeeding generations, indeed it is. Unlike beer, though, which had to await the discovery of malting grains before it could be produced, wine has always been there, for it is nothing other than spoiled grape juice.

Any substance that is high in natural sugars - whether it be the sticky sap of palm trees, or honey, or the juice of ripened fruit - will sooner or later start to ferment if it comes into contact with yeast. Wild yeasts, transported by insects and falling on to the fruit that they hover around, feed on its sugars and create two by-products in the process.

One is carbon dioxide gas, which is the reason why anything that has accidentally start-ed fermenting creates a fizzy sensation on the tongue, and the other is alcohol. And we know what that does to us.

Long before the earliest human societies had begun to live settled existences in one place, and thus to cultivate land, a type of alcoholic liquid could be made relatively quickly by allowing fresh fruit to ferment.

One particular species of wild vine that origi-nated in the area around the Black Sea that today takes in the modern states of Georgia, Armenia and eastern Turkey proved especially well-suited to quick fermentation, owing to the naturally sweet berries it produced. It is in fact the only vine species native to Europe and the Near East, and because it came to play such a pre-eminent role in the development of wine-making all over the world, it was later given the botanical classification *Vitis vinifera* - "the wine-bearing grape".

Within that one species, however, there are as many as 10,000 different sub-types, known as varieties. Some of these would have developed by natural mutation; many have been created by deliberate cross-fertilisation. Only a very small percentage of those 10,000 varieties are impor-tant in the commercial production of wine today, and many of those are fairly obscure. A mere handful, almost exclusively French in origin, now constitute the international language of wine, and it is these that this section deals with.

Not all of the 12 varieties we shall look at in detail are grown throughout the world, and the

A breathtaking springtime scene (right),with flower-ing mustard seed growing in the vineyards of Sonoma, California, the state that has become a major player on the world wine scene.

last of them - Gamay - is of no real viticultural significance outside its ancestral home, the Beaujolais region of France. But these are the 12 varieties - six white and six red - whose flavours it is most useful to become familiar with. They are responsible between them for producing all of the most famous French wine styles, from sparkling champagne in the north to the richly heady reds of the sweltering south, and thus they provided the original models when serious winemaking first began to be pioneered beyond the shores of Europe.

All sorts of other factors influence the taste of a wine than the grape variety or varieties from which it is made. The climate in which the grapes are grown determines the balance of sugar and acid in the harvested berries. In some still inadequately defined way, the type of soil the vines are planted in also has a crucial effect, in the opinions of many growers.

Then there are the many variables at work in the winery. At what temperature does the juice ferment? What does it ferment in - stainless steel or wood? How long, in the case of red wines, is the juice left in contact with the grape skins, from which it derives its colour and also the tannin that helps to preserve it? Is it kept in oak barrels after the fermentation? If so, are they new or used or a mixture of both, and how long does the wine spend in them before bottling?

There are as many styles of wine as there are winemakers, an equation multiplied by the number of different vintages each practitioner will make over the course of his or her career. But the identity of the grapes in the fermenting vat is the first and foremost indicator of style.

If you want to make a delicately crisp, simple white, it doesn't make sense to use Gewürz-traminer. Similarly, if you're after a featherlight fruity red for drinking young, Cabernet Sauvignon may give you more than you bargained for. The most commonly met grape varieties have innate characteristics that can be teased out of the wines they are made into in wholly diverse parts of the globe.

As we are introduced to each of these 12 VIPs of the wine world, we shall also take a look at the different regions they have travelled to, and explore the typical flavours to be found in each of them.

The impressive vaulted cellars of Ch. de Meursault, in Burgundy's Côte de Beaune (above), filled with wine ageing in oak barrels.

CHARDONNAY

From its homeland in Burgundy, Chardonnay has travelled the world to become the most fashionable and sought-after of white varieties. This chameleon of grapes bows to the whim of the winemaker, offering a diversity of styles to appeal to all palates.

AS SOMEBODY once (nearly) said, if Chardonnay didn't exist, it would be necessary to invent it. No other grape, white or red, has achieved quite the degree of international recognition that Chardonnay has. In some consumers' minds, it stands as a synonym for dry white wine in general, and the reason is not hard to see. It is grown in some proportion in virtually every wine-producing country on the planet; within France itself, Bordeaux and the Rhône are about the only two regions that it has not yet penetrated.

No grape could have colonised the vine-growing world so effectively had it not possessed the adaptability of a chameleon. Given reasonably competent winemaking, it can usually produce something worth drinking, whether grown in the smouldering heat of South Australia or the precarious summers of the English Home Counties. In terms of the amount of land planted with it, Chardonnay is effectively the house white in the United States, Australia and New Zealand, not to mention the pays d'Oc in southern France.

The adaptability on which its huge commercial success is founded is twofold. In the first place, compared with most other grape varieties, it is something of a cinch to grow. Not only can it tolerate climatic conditions at either extreme of the viticultural spectrum, but it can make itself at home in a wide diversity of soil types without too much fuss. It is a fairly reliable ripener and gives a good crop in most harvests. Very fine wines, it is true, are almost invariably produced from vines that only give low yields, but as much of the Chardonnay that is sold around the world is intended for everyday drinking at economical prices rather than ageing in cellars, the vine's capacity to bear a lot of fruit makes it a winner.

Secondly, just as Chardonnay is everybody's flexible friend in the vineyard, so it proves similarly malleable in the winery. Unlike some of the other white grapes we shall encounter,

Chardonnay matures in the warm vineyards of California (right). A vigorous vine, relatively unfussed by climate or soil, this golden grape is neutral in character and has a natural affinity with oak. It is as suited to classic white burgundies as to Australian sparkling wines.

Chardonnay is not a naturally aromatic variety. Vinified very simply in stainless steel, and bottled early for drinking young, it doesn't possess a great deal of obvious personality. If it has any fruit aroma at all, it is generally a very faint appley quality, backed up perhaps by a refreshing streak of lemony acidity, but nothing more exotic than that. But it is precisely that neutrality that enables it to produce some of the world's most sought-after dry white wines.

Possibly more than any other white grape, it has a natural affinity with the flavour of oak. Matured in small new barrels, or even a mixture

of new ones and others that have been used for two or three vintages already, it begins to take on those richly creamy, buttery scents and tastes that we associate with really good Chardonnay. If the wine undergoes its initial fermentation in the barrels, in addition to being matured in them, it can derive a powerfully pungent smokiness from the charred inner surfaces of the wood that may remind you of anything from toast that's just beginning to burn to smoked bacon crackling in the frying-pan.

It is that ability to absorb the flavours of oak that originally made the top wines of Burgundy so esteemed, and accounts for the desire in other wine-making regions to imitate the full-blown oak opulence of Chardonnay *à la bourguignonne*. There is a feeling, however, in some quarters that the mania for oak flavours (which has resulted in small producers in less wealthy wine regions dunking bags of oak chips into

their wines to satisfy consumers' craving for that telltale taste of vanilla) is getting out of hand. The truth is that only the best-quality fruit from low-yielding vines represents a suitable case for the oak treatment. Grapes from younger, more vigorous vines will tend to produce less concentrated juice, so that oak fermentation leads to a wine that tastes of wood and nothing more.

As well as making the most popular styles of white table wine, Chardonnay is also indispensable to the production of sparkling wine the world over. With its two red partners, Pinot Noir and Pinot Meunier, it forms the triumvirate of grape varieties used in champagne, and nearly all attempts to produce classic sparklers outside that region use a healthy proportion of Chardonnay in their blends.

Once again, it is the grape's inherent neutrality of flavour that bestows elegance and finesse on the best fizz.

FRENCH ORIGINS

Almost all of the white wines of Burgundy, from Chablis down to Beaujolais. Champagne (where it makes up 100 per cent of wines labelled *blanc de blancs*). May appear as varietally labelled *vin de pays* across the south, especially Languedoc, and also in the Loire.

WHERE ELSE IS IT GROWN?

Wherever the vine will grow.

TASTING NOTES

Light and unoaked (eg. Chablis) - tart apple, lemon, sometimes pear. Lightly oaked (eg. Rully, St-Véran) - melting butter, baked apple, nutmeg, oatmeal. Heavily oaked (eg. Meursault, classic Australian Chardonnay) - vanilla, lemon curd, butterscotch, praline, bacon fat, woodsmoke.

Burgundy

If Chardonnay represents the monarch among white wine grapes, then the Burgundy region in eastern France is its official residence. From isolated Chablis in the *département* of the Yonne down to the wide swathes of vineyard known as the Mâconnais to the west of the river Saône, Chardonnay is the predominant white grape variety.

The entire gamut of styles is produced. There are easy-drinking everyday whites of honest simplicity as well as powerfully complex wines intended to be aged in the bottle. There are wines that rely on youthful acidity and freshness alone for their appeal, while others mobilise the fat, buttery opulence imparted by oak.

Co-operatives and négociants (merchants who buy in grapes or even finished wine from other growers and bottle the resulting blend under their own brand name) tend to be the sources for much of the commercial white burgundy seen in national drinks outlets, while the many individual producers who operate entirely self-

The rich, golden colours of a Burgundian autumn (below) spread through the sloping grand cru *vineyards of Vaudésir (nearest) and Grenouilles, in Chablis.*

sufficiently are responsible for some of the world's most extravagantly rich - and extravagantly expensive - dry white wine.

Chablis in some ways deserves to be considered as a region in itself, because it is not geographically part of Burgundy proper, lying as it does slightly nearer to the most southerly of the Champagne vineyards than to the northernmost tip of the Côte d'Or. Its climate is cool and fairly wet, its winters often severe, and late frosts in spring are a regular occurrence. As such, the Chardonnay grown there ripens quite late, and tends to produce a wine of high acidity, to which the adjective "steely" is often applied.

At their best, these are squeaky-clean, bone-dry wines that are crisp to the point of brittleness in their youth. Those used to warmer-climate Chardonnays may find them almost too acidic, but as they age, they lose some of that sharp edge and become mellower. That said, there is a general tendency to make softer wines these days.

The great majority of the wines are made without oak, Chablis being the reference for unwooded Chardonnay the world over. Some producers, however, do use a certain amount of oak on their best *cuvées*, particularly those with land in one or more of the seven *grand cru* vineyards - Blanchots, Bougros, Les Clos, Grenouilles, Preuses, Valmur and Vaudésir - that sit at the top of the quality tree. Even without oak, Chablis from a good producer in a fine vintage (such as 1995, '96, '99 or 2000) can develop its own inherent richness with a few years in the bottle.

Southeast of Chablis, white wines from the Côte d'Or - and in particular the Côte de Beaune, its southern section - represent the pinnacle of Burgundian Chardonnay. It is here, in the exalted appellations of Corton-Charlemagne, Puligny-Montrachet, Meursault and others, that oaked Chardonnay really began.

The top wines, often produced in tiny quantities which helps to ensure they sell for dizzyingly elevated prices, are sumptuously rich and concentrated, usually deep golden in colour from months of ageing in oak barrels, and generally high in alcohol (13-13.5 per cent is the norm). Many possess an intriguingly vegetal flavour, like French beans or even cabbage, that is something of a shock to those used to

fruitier-tasting Chardonnays. The Burgundians argue that this is their famous *goût de terroir* - the unique taste of the limestone soils in which the vines are grown.

It is still fair to say that wherever winemakers are aiming to produce premium-quality oaked Chardonnay, it is the top wines of the Côte d'Or that provided the original inspiration, however much they may since have diverged from that earliest model.

The Côte d'Or is connected to the Mâconnais by a strip of land called the Côte Chalonnaise, so called because it lies to the west of the town of Chalon-sur-Saône. Its Chardonnays, from appellations such as Montagny, Rully and Mer-curey, are considerably lighter in style than those from further north, but can possess their own lean elegance. They tend to have corre-spondingly less oak than the Côte d'Or wines, and are thus suitable for more delicate white fish dishes.

In the south of Burgundy, the Mâconnais is the largest of its sub-regions. Here is where most of the everyday quaffing wine is made, much of it of rather humdrum quality, often vinified without oak. A couple of appellations stand out from the generality. Pouilly-Fuissé

can have something of the depth and ageability of lesser Côte de Beaune wines, although quality across the board fails to justify the ambitious price it commands. St-Véran is cheaper but lacks that extra dimension of flavour that the best Pouilly-Fuissé has.

Certain villages within the overall appellation of Mâcon Blanc-Villages are considered to pro-duce wines of sufficiently distinctive quality for their names to be added to the label; hence you may see Mâcon-Lugny, Mâcon-Viré and so forth on the labels. In most cases the quality differ-ence from the catchall "Villages" designation is barely perceptible.

The white wine of Beaujolais, the most southerly of Burgundy's regions, is made from Chardonnay. Rarely seen outside its region of production, it tends to be hard, dry, and unoaked, somewhat like a less graceful version of Chablis.

Burgundy's sparkling wine - Crémant de Bourgogne, made by the champagne method - relies heavily on the Chardonnay grape. The grapes can theoretically come from anywhere in the region so styles vary from delicate, even slightly floral fizz to heavier wines that can have more than a tinge of that old green vegetable in the flavour.

Hand-picked Chardonnay grapes are loaded on to a trailer at Fuissé (above) in the Mâconnais, the largest sub-region of Burgundy.

United States

Wineries in New York State, especially those on Long Island (above), are increasingly producing elegant, complex Chardonnays.

Madonna Vineyards in the cool Carneros region of northern California (right), a region that produces some of the state's finest Chardonnays, eerily similar in style to certain top burgundies.

Undoubtedly Chardonnay's most important home outside Europe is in the United States. Indeed, towards the end of the 1980s, the state of California alone had more extensive plantings of the grape than the whole of France, where its growth has not exactly been stagnant. No group of winemakers beyond the ancestral heartland of Burgundy has taken greater pains with the variety than the Californians, and the transformations that the wines have undergone in the last two decades have been a fascinating barometer of Chardonnay philosophy.

Twenty years ago, the fashion was for a massively overblown style of rich golden wine, with dollops of sweet new oak all over it, not dissimilar to the textbook Australian mode. When the backlash came, it sent the pendulum hurtling in the other direction, so that it suddenly seemed as if everybody was competing to produce West Coast Chablis, so lean and green and biting were many of the wines.

By the mid-1980s, the picture was beginning to even out, and there is now a much greater diversity of styles, each representing a more relaxed expression of its microclimate and the orientation of the individual winemaker.

The very best Stateside Chardonnays - such as those from the cooler areas of California like Carneros and Sonoma Valley, from Oregon, even from New York State - can sometimes achieve an almost eerie similarity to certain top burgundies, partly because of the comparable levels of acidity, and partly because of the sensitive use of French oak.

A lot of work has been done in researching types of oak, and the different levels of flame treatment the cooper can give the barrels, to find out what best suits American Chardonnay. Some producers, veterans of trips to Burgundy, put their faith in the supposedly more sophisticated flavours of French oak, but others are now beginning to look once again at native American woods and are starting to disprove the theory that you can't make a subtle Chardonnay in US oak.

Another French habit that has taken root among many of the premium producers is the avoidance of the filtration procedure whereby tiny solids that are residues of fermentation are cleaned out of the wine. While filtering a wine certainly results in a crystal-clear, stable product, many feel that it also strips it of some

of its flavours and some of its richness of texture. As the debate has grown in intensity, the anti-filtration brigade has often proudly inscribed the word "Unfiltered" on its labels.

Despite the studious awareness in the States of how things have traditionally been done in Burgundy, there is increasingly less dependence on that region as a role model. American winemakers have carved out a niche in the world market for their Chardonnays to the extent that they no longer need the reflected glory of comparison with the Côte d'Or.

It is no more possible to generalise about a typical California style than it is to talk about a French style. The state contains a multitude of different microclimates: Calistoga, at the northern end of Napa Valley, is one of the hotter areas, as is the inland San Joaquin district; Santa Barbara, one of the more southerly grape-growing regions, is relatively cool.

Most of California's coastal regions are affected by the Pacific fog drifts that can take until mid-morning or later to clear. Cool nighttime conditions help to ensure that the ripening grapes don't become heat-stressed, so that acidity levels at harvest time are not too low.

Good California Chardonnays have the same sort of weight in the mouth as a wine like Puligny-Montrachet, and with a carefully

defined balance of oak and fruit. Acidity is usually fresh, though with perhaps not quite the same tang as young burgundy. The fruit flavours are altogether more overt, California wines often having a riper citrus character, even a tropical element like fresh pineapple. By and large, despite what some producers intend, they are not particularly susceptible to improvement in the bottle. Most will never be better than they are at one to two years old.

In the Pacific Northwest, Oregon Chardonnay tends to be crisper and slightly more austere on the palate than the wines of California, and the characteristic style is leaner and less ostentatious. Washington State is improving all the time, with the earlier tendency to slight flabbiness now being erased in favour of some attractively balanced wines, though again with somewhat less flesh than California examples. Idaho has a more extreme climate, and tends to produce wines with high acidity, though they can be rounded out by gentle oak treatment.

New York State has a much cooler climate than the West Coast, and the Chardonnays it produces are in a correspondingly more bracing style, but the best wineries - notably on Long Island - are capitalising on that to turn out some elegant and complex wines with some ageability.

Chardonnay is also gaining in importance in Texas, where it makes a broad, immediately approachable style with plenty of ripe fruit.

Chardonnay ageing in new oak barrels (above). A lot of research has been carried out in the US to find out which oak best suits American Chardonnay, leading to a trend among certain producers away from French oak to native American oak.

Australia

Carpets of purple flowers surround Mountadam Estate (below) on the High Eden Ridge, in South Australia. Eden Valley, part of the Barossa Range, shares the soils and climate of Barossa Valley, the source of richly concentrated Chardonnays.

Such was the soaring popularity of Australia's Chardonnays on external markets in the 1980s that, at one stage, it began to look as if the country might not be able to produce enough to cope with the worldwide demand for them. One consequence is that there is now more Chardonnay planted across the continent than any other white grape variety.

With the advent in this decade of the "flying winemakers" - travelling wine consultants who flit between the hemispheres working as many vintages as they can fit into their schedules - the success of Australian wine had received the global endorsement that it was due.

Many of the flying winemakers came from Down Under and, though it often involved a great swallowing of cultural pride on the part of the natives, they were instrumental in revolutionising winemaking practices in the viticultural backwaters of southern France. It was their skill with Chardonnay that, more than anything, served to create the demand for their services.

Australia taught the wine world that Chardonnay could be as unashamedly big and ripe and rich as you wanted it to be. Since the climate in most of the vineyard regions, the majority of which lie in the southeast of the country, is uniformly hot and dry, the fruit grown there regularly attains sky-high levels of natural sugar. Winemakers thus generally have to sharpen their wines up by controlled additions of tartaric acid to prevent them from tasting too sweet.

Nonetheless, the benchmark style of Chardonnay is a sunshine-yellow, extraordinarily luscious wine that, married with the vanilla and butterscotch flavours of new oak, is quite a way off being fully dry. High sugar means high alcohol (up to 14 per cent in some wines) so that, at the end of a generous glassful, you certainly know you've had a drink.

As British wine consumers (and many American ones too) discovered an almost insatiable thirst for Australian Chardonnay, it became the habit in some quarters to start calling into question whether these wines really possessed true balance.

In Australia, there is a long-established system of regional wine shows, where wines are judged with scrupulous attention to detail by experts from the industry, and lessons and inspiration are drawn from the results. It has been suggested that, under the conditions of having to taste many similar wines over a number of days, tasters will inevitably be most easily won over by those wines that make the boldest impact on the palate - ie. those with the heaviest oak influence, the most alcohol, and therefore the ones that linger longest on the palate after tasting.

The response to this can only be a personal one. Undoubtedly, classic Australian Chardonnay is a commercially popular style, and it is always hard to argue with that. But it should be remembered that framing the debate in those terms also gives a conveniently simplistic view of the matter.

In latter years, trends in Chardonnay have begun to diversify in Australia just as they have in California. There is a desire on the part of many winemakers, notably in Western Australia, in South Australia's Coonawarra region and in the Yarra Valley in Victoria, to make a subtler, more European - or perhaps more Californian - style of Chardonnay.

While that move to greater refinement may represent the future, I suspect it will be a long while before wine-drinkers grow tired of the blockbuster Chardonnays that put Australia on the wine map. They constitute, after all, one of the world's truly unique white wine styles.

Much of Australia's wine is made from grapes grown in different areas, blended to get the best balance of attributes in the final wine, so regional characteristics can only be significant to the extent of their proportion in the bottle. However, an increasing number do bottle wines that are the produce of particular vineyard areas, vinified separately so as to give a true expression of what the French would call their *terroir*.

In the state of South Australia, the Barossa Valley is one of the most important regions, producing broad-beamed, richly concentrated Chardonnays that make a dramatic impact on the palate. McLaren Vale and Padthaway are responsible for wines with perhaps a touch more finesse. The Clare Valley is distinctly cooler, and its wines are correspondingly lighter and less upfront in style.

Chardonnays from the Goulburn Valley area of Victoria often possess hauntingly tropical fruit characters, while the cooler-climate Yarra Valley wines can resemble those of the cooler parts of California. In Western Australia, the Margaret River region is producing some unashamedly Burgundian wines that sometimes have that pungent whiff of green vegetable found on the Côte d'Or.

On the island of Tasmania, Chardonnay can be more austerely European still in its orientation, owing to the cool and fairly wet climate. Levels of grape acidity comparable to Chablis are not unheard of.

Stormy skies at first light (above) over the high ridges of the Barossa Range, South Australia.

New Zealand

Like its northern neighbour, New Zealand now has more Chardonnay planted than any other white wine grape. Grown in what is a considerably cooler and damper climate than Australia, the wines it produces tend, on the whole, to be noticeably lighter and more acidic.

That doesn't mean to say that Chardonnay lacks anything in terms of character because, in common with the even more fashionable New Zealand Sauvignon Blanc, it nearly always possesses a positively unearthly degree of juicily ripe fruit. It is quite the norm to find pineapple and mango, grapefruit and apple chasing each other around the glass, almost as if the wine had

(Above) Montana Estate, Marlborough, South Island. New Zealand Chardonnay is light, with juicily ripe fruit.

set out to confound the notion that Chardonnay isn't an aromatic variety.

About the richest styles come from the Gisborne and Poverty Bay regions on the eastern tip of the North Island, and these are the ones that respond best to oak-ageing. A little to the south, the wines of Hawkes Bay have more of a tang to them, and require a correspondingly more delicate touch with the wood.

Hopping over to the South Island, edging in the direction of the Antarctic Circle, the typical style becomes snappier and more citric in Marlborough, and then quite taut and austere from Canterbury and Otago.

South Africa

When South Africa began to play a full part on the international wine scene at the beginning of the 1990s, many consumers were surprised to discover that Chardonnay was not the major force that it is elsewhere in the southern hemisphere. It played second fiddle to the much more widely planted Chenin Blanc. It still accounts for only a very small percentage of the vineyard land planted with white varieties, although that will presumably increase as it has done just about everywhere else.

Although South Africa remained largely isolated from world trade while the wine boom of the 1970s and 1980s was gathering momentum, it did profit in one respect. It was able to observe

The lush green vineyards of Stellenbosch wineries Warwick Estate (above), and Thelema Vineyards (right), producers of rounded, golden Chardonnays. Coastal Stellenbosch is home to many of South Africa's finest producers.

the trend for the galumphing, heavily oaked style of Chardonnay (at first inextricably associated with so-called New World winemaking) as it fell from favour among forward-looking winemakers, and simply pass that fad by.

How the wines will taste depends inevitably on how far the vineyards lie from the southern coast. Those from further inland have the hotter climates. Thus, the Robertson Valley - over 100km (63 miles) away from the cooling maritime influence of the Indian Ocean - is home to some of the Cape's biggest and brassiest Chardonnays, while those from Walker Bay achieve a subtler style with the emphasis on fruit and more sharply defined acidity.

Rest of the World

SOUTH AMERICA

Chile's Chardonnays, as with its Cabernet
Sauvignon wines, occupy two pigeonholes.
Some are made in a recognisably French vein,
with pronounced acidity, light appley fruit and
carefully judged oak maturation. Others go the
whole hog, with full-blown charred oak flavours
and a high-extract, alcoholic feel. It all depends
on the producer. Argentina's wines, made
largely in the province of Mendoza in the
foothills of the Andes, occupy a midway point
between those two extremes.

EUROPE

Increasing concentrations of Chardonnay are
cropping up across northern Italy now, from
Piedmont in the northwest to the Veneto in the
northeast. Although some rugged individualists
are aiming for top-flight barrel-fermented wines
(and charging energetically for them), the basic
style - best typified by the wines of Alto Adige
on the Austrian border - are delicate, very lightly
creamy wines made without the use of wood.

Northern Spain is getting in on the act too,
with plantings of Chardonnay vines in Penedés,
Lerida and Navarra, where it is often blended
with local varieties to make clean-cut, nutty,
dry modern whites.

Chardonnay is of increasing importance in
central Europe, particularly in Hungary where
the flying winemakers have been regular
visitors. The wines tend to be made in the
straightforward neutral style, clean and sharp
for everyday drinking. When they do have
some oak on them, it is only to add a gentler,
rounder feel to them.

Further east, Bulgaria has been making
Chardonnays for export since its heavily state-
subsidised entry into western markets in the
1980s. A little on the clumsy side, they often
don't taste especially fresh, although the odd
wine from the Khan Krum region in the east of
the country can be palatable in a sour-cream
sort of way.

*Chardonnay is taking root in
northern Italy, especially in
Piedmont (above), in the
foothills of the Alps, where it
produces delicate, lightly
creamy wines.*

*Harvesting Chardonnay
grapes (left) in Blatetz,
Bulgaria. The quality of
Chardonnay, one of many
wines produced for the export
market, varies, some of the
best coming from Khan Krum.*

CABERNET SAUVIGNON

Its pedigree is firmly founded in the gravelly soils of the Médoc, in the heart of Bordeaux. The king of red grapes, Cabernet Sauvignon has conquered vineyards across the world without losing the classic character that brought it such renown.

THE RED HALF of that hugely successful partnership that has come to dominate international winemaking is the Cabernet Sauvignon grape. Alongside Chardonnay, it strode imperiously through the world's vineyards in the 1980s, often insisting that native varieties get out of its way wherever serious red wine was to be made. Although the example held up to Cabernet growers - the classed-growth clarets of the Médoc in Bordeaux - is an illustrious one, it isn't immediately easy to see why Cabernet came to be perceived as the pre-eminent red counterpart to the crowd-pleasing Chardonnay.

Its adaptability to different soils and climates is certainly quite as impressive as that of Chardonnay, yet the number of berries the vine typically yields, even in the warmest climates, is relatively low. Since that obviously means it can provide less wine than many of those native varieties that ceded precious vineyard land to it, it bore a heavy responsibility to earn its keep.

In many regions, particularly those subject to marked climatic variation from one year to the next, Cabernet Sauvignon was basically a loss-leader. For the sake of having its name on the label, many winemakers simply tightened their financial belts and allowed their higher-volume wines to subsidise it.

What the sacrifices were about was achieving that heady mixture of pure blackcurrant fruit, density of texture and substantial ageing capacity that the best Cabernet Sauvignon wines combine, and that seems to many consumers the essence of all that is noble in a red wine. The greatest productions of the Médoc - Lafite, Latour, Margaux, Mouton-Rothschild - are among the most famous names in wine, and if some of the class of those wines could be seen, however distantly, in a Cabernet Sauvignon from Chile, Italy or Bulgaria, then the winemaker behind it might have a fair chance of making the big time.

Like Chardonnay too, Cabernet responds supremely well to oak ageing, when the vanillin in new wood helpfully serves to soothe some of the natural ferocity of the young wine. That ferocity is basically tannin, the substance in youthful red wine that furs up the drinker's mouth and can obscure the natural flavours of the fruit. It is derived from the pips and skins of the grapes, and Cabernet Sauvignon is particularly well-endowed with regard to those parts of its anatomy. The small berries the vine puts forth mean that the pips constitute a higher proportion of the grape than in other varieties, and it is famously - notoriously, some have found - thick-skinned.

Indispensable for producing handsome, deeply-coloured red wine, those thick skins do however mean that vinifiers of Cabernet need to make some finely detailed decisions in the winery about how to treat their wine. Allow the crushed skins to soak for too long in the juice, and you can end up with fearsomely tannic, merciless morning-after stuff, and there isn't much point in advising customers to keep it for a decade if that is not what your market positioning is about.

What many producers of Cabernet wine have gradually learned, and the lesson was there in the original Bordeaux model, is that Cabernet Sauvignon is much better off in company; that is, blended with at least a small proportion of one or two other grapes. Left to its own devices, it too often comes out tough and brutal, whereas a carefully judged admixture of (classically) Merlot and/or Cabernet Franc, or (innovatively) Shiraz in Australia, can soften and civilise it without in the least lessening its austere beauty.

The holy grail is a wine capable of acquiring distinction from long cellaring. Cabernets or Cabernet-based wines react in fascinatingly various ways as they age, depending on the quality of the fruit prior to fermentation, on the type of wood used for the maturation and on the length of time the wine spends in barrel (and perhaps subsequently in bottle in the winery) before being released. As the initial tannins start to loosen up and dissolve into the wine, the first

The small, dusty-blue Cabernet Sauvignon grape (right), produces wines of good tannin, body and aroma. It adapts easily to differing soils and climates, and in its finest form, with warm, late summer sun to ripen it fully, Cabernet creates complex, deeply coloured reds, packed with juicy blackcurrant fruit.

FRENCH ORIGINS

Bordeaux, specifically the left bank of the river Gironde, from the north of the Médoc down to the Graves. (On the right bank, it tends to play second fiddle to Merlot.)

WHERE ELSE IS IT GROWN?

Just about everywhere, although it has not made significant inroads into the cooler climates of northern Europe.

TASTING NOTES

In warm climates, almost any of the purple-skinned fruits - classically blackcurrants (perhaps most startlingly so in the best wines of Chile), but also black plums, brambles, damsons, etc. Often has a distinct note of fresh mint or even eucalyptus, especially in parts of Australia and Chile. Cooler climates can create a whiff of bitterness in it, often uncannily like chopped green pepper. Oak treatments generally emphasise a mineral austerity in the wine, likened in Bordeaux to the smell of cigar-boxes, cedarwood or - most recognisably - pencil shavings. With several years' bottle-age, it can take on aromas such as well-hung game, plum tomatoes, warm leather, dark chocolate, even soft Indian spices like cardamom, while the primary fruit begins to taste more like preserved fruit.

fresh flavours of the grape - known to tasters as primary fruit - begin to take on other aromas and tastes that may be reminiscent of dried fruits, savoury spice or gamey meat. Even at quite advanced stages of development, though, the telltale mineral purity of Cabernet Sauvignon still shines through.

It is this potential for gathering complexity that explains the high prices paid for top Cabernet Sauvignon around the world, and that also explains the enormous pains taken with the variety by all sorts of winemakers who might be able to turn a faster buck growing something more mundane.

Bordeaux

A landmark in the Pauillac vineyards of first growth Château Latour (above), one of the five great premier cru châteaux of the Médoc.

The chai *at Château Mouton-Rothschild, Pauillac (below). The four famous communes of the Médoc - St-Estèphe, St-Julien, Margaux and Pauillac - are where the reputation of red Bordeaux is founded.*

Although Cabernet Sauvignon occupies far less vineyard land in its home base of Bordeaux than its traditional blending partner Merlot, it is nonetheless widely considered the pre-eminent variety in the region. This is because it plays a major part in the wines on which the reputation of Bordeaux is founded - the *crus classés*, or classed growths, of the Médoc and Graves. When the classification system for Bordeaux was drawn up in 1855, it was not that the judges ignored the Merlot-based wines of Pomerol and St-Emilion on the right bank; they simply didn't consider them to be in the same class.

That classification (which we shall look at in further detail in the chapter on Bordeaux) is now considered seriously outdated by many commentators, but the general perception that the majority of Bordeaux's most illustrious wines derive the greater part of their authority from the presence of Cabernet Sauvignon has never really changed.

Cabernet contributes those austere tannins that give the young wine the structure it needs to have a good chance of ageing. Its pigment-rich skins endow the wine with full-blooded depth of colour. When claret-lovers refer to their favourite wine as having a profoundly serious quality that appeals first and foremost to the intellect rather than the senses, it is Cabernet Sauvignon they have to thank.

If Cabernet enjoys such an exalted status, you may ask why more châteaux don't simply produce an unblended Cabernet wine instead of making it share the bottle with Merlot and other varieties. The answer is partly that the grape works better in a team. Solo Cabernet, as some winemakers in California have found, is not necessarily an unalloyed blessing. In hot years, it can just be too much of a good thing, the resulting wines having colossal density and concentration, but not really seeming as if they are going to be ready to drink until the next appearance of Halley's comet.

The other reason for blending in Bordeaux is that, even though its southerly position makes this one of the warmest of France's classic regions, the summers are still highly variable. In problem vintages (and it is worth bearing in mind that, despite its phenomenal run of luck in the 1980s, Bordeaux did not have an overall success in any of the years 1991, '92, '93 or '94) Cabernet Sauvignon is the grape that suffers most. If the end of summer is cool - and, what's worse, wet - it simply doesn't ripen properly, resulting in those vegetal green-pepper tastes that make for harsh, depressing wine.

Since Merlot has much better tolerance for less-than-perfect vintage conditions, it makes sense for the growers to have the option of blending in some of the lighter Merlot to soften an overly astringent or green-tasting Cabernet. In the great vintages, however - such as 1989 and '90 - the richness and power of Cabernet is worth celebrating, and the Merlot will only play a discreet supporting role, just smoothing the edges a little so that the full glory of ripe Cabernet can be shown to maximum advantage.

Most of the wines that occupy the five ranks of the 1855 hierarchy come from four vineyard areas to the west of the river Gironde: St-Estèphe, Pauillac, St-Julien and Margaux. From top to bottom, collectively, they extend over not much more than 40km (25 miles), but there are subtle differences in the styles of Cabernet-based wine they produce.

St-Estèphe generally makes the fiercest wine, with typically tough tannins that may take years to fall away, and a very austere aroma that is often compared to fresh tobacco. Pauillac - the commune that boasts three of the five first growths in Lafite, Latour and Mouton-Rothschild - is a little less severe, even when young. Its wines have more emphatic blackcurrant fruit than those of St-Estèphe, and a seemingly more complicated pot-pourri of spice and wood notes as they age.

St-Julien, which adjoins Pauillac, displays many of the characteristics of its neighbour, although its wines somehow display a softer fruit - more like dark plums and blackberries than blackcurrants - as they begin to mature. The best wines of Margaux are noted for their extravagant perfume, although in general the

underlying wine is lighter than anything from further north, the exception being first-growth Château Margaux itself.

South of the city of Bordeaux, the large area of the Graves makes wines that vary in character. These range from featherweight reds that constitute some of the region's lightest reds, to those that have a mineral earthiness to them, thought to derive from the gravelly soils that give this part of Bordeaux its name. Elsewhere, the quality becomes gradually more prosaic until, at the lowest level of AC Bordeaux, the wines can be hard red jug-wine of no great appeal.

In Bordeaux, it is the name of the property rather than the name of the producer that goes on the label. Much time and attention is devoted to studying the relative form and fitness of the most famous estates as each new vintage appears on the market. Those planning to buy even a single bottle of top-flight Bordeaux would do well to consider the present reputation of a château as well as the quality of the vintage.

Cabernet Sauvignon vines (above) planted in the poor, gravelly soils of St-Estèphe, in the Médoc, on the right bank of the Gironde river.

United States

Cabernet Sauvignon was introduced to California in the 19th century in the form of cuttings from Bordeaux. The readiness with which it took to the fertile soils in which it was planted is evidenced by the fact that it already had something of a reputation among the American wine cognoscenti before the century was out. The best was held to come from the Napa Valley, north of San Francisco, where the late, hot summers resulted in strapping great wines of swarthy hue, thickly textured and capable of delivering a hefty alcoholic blow to the unsuspecting drinker.

Some might facetiously say that not much has changed. Certainly, in many consumers' minds, the benchmark style of California Cabernet has been fiercely tannic, often virtually black wines that potentially took a decade or two to unravel into anything like a state of drinkability. It would be grossly simplistic to characterise all California Cabernets in that way today, but it was undeniably the predominant style of the wine as recently as the 1970s, and there are undoubtedly some wineries that still nail their colours to that particular mast.

The winery at top Napa Valley producer, Robert Mondavi (below). Napa Valley, in Sonoma County, is renowned for the world-class Cabernets it can produce.

It is not as if, however, there are not perfectly good antecedents for it. Most classed-growth Bordeaux in the hot years like 1989 and 1990 would answer that description - or something very like it - when first released. The wines are not intended to be drunk straight away, however much the French predilection for youthful red wine seems perilously close to infanticide to other wine-drinking cultures. California's winemakers were aiming high after all, and Cabernet Sauvignon doesn't come much higher than Château Latour, still black as sin and guarded by snarling tannins at ten years old.

The problem lay in the fact that most consumers did not wish to drink wine that tastes like that, even if they could readily afford the exorbitant price the achievement of such concentration demands. Producers realised a middle way had to be found between the extremes of budding West Coast Latours and insipid commercial jug wine.

Thus the 1970s saw a huge upsurge in plantings of Bordeaux's most celebrated variety in all sorts of diverse microclimates across the state, as Cabernet fever took hold.

Picking Cabernet Sauvignon grapes in vineyards south of Prosser, Washington State (left). Despite the fairly cool climate, some fine Cabernets have been made in the Pacific Northwest.

Statue at sunset (above) in the gardens of the Robert Mondavi Winery, Napa Valley, California.

Some of the resulting wines, notably those from the cooler areas, have more than a touch of the familiar bell-pepper/asparagus/French bean vegetal quality that the grape is prone to when its juice has not had sufficient ripening time. Maturation times in oak barrels have sometimes been excessive, giving wines an exaggeratedly woody taste.

But without a doubt, California - and especially the Napa Valley - has also turned out some wonderfully sleek, opulently fruit-filled Cabernets of world-class status, many of them blended with others of the Bordeaux varieties.

In the Pacific Northwest, the climate is generally a little too cool for producing great Cabernets, although Washington State has come up with some fine examples. The tendency is to compensate for less than generous fruit flavours by applying fairly heavy oak maturation, which can run the risk of creating top-heavy wines. Oregon is a much safer bet for cool-ripening Pinot Noir than sun-seeking Cabernet.

Texas, on the other hand, is proving itself to be highly Cabernet-friendly, although as yet the grape only accounts for a relatively small proportion of total plantings there. The state style - exemplified by wineries like Fall Creek and Pheasant Ridge - is of big, rich, upfront fruit, some savoury herb character and good weight, but with the tannins kept in check. In time, this could emerge as the best American Cabernet territory outside the Napa Valley.

Australia

Australia's approach to Cabernet Sauvignon has arguably been much more straightforward than that of California. The aim among its growers is all about emphasising the kind of ripe, juicy drinkability that wins friends even among those who don't consider themselves fans of rich red wine. In the ultra-reliable climates enjoyed by most of Australia's wine-growing regions, Cabernet more often than not attains levels of ripeness Bordeaux's producers would give their eye teeth for.

Oak barrel ageing is used enthusiastically by the great majority of Cabernet growers. When your wine is as rich and dense and blackcurranty as most Australian Cabernet is, you can afford to be generous with the oak flavours. At the same time, however, the familiar style aims to maximise fruit characters without extracting too much tannin from the grapeskins. Thus, although an intensely concentrated wine, it doesn't necessarily scour your mouth with harsh astringency when it's young.

The chances are that, even if you are unfamiliar with the winery, a Cabernet from practically anywhere in Australia will deliver plump, soft, cassis-flavoured wine with an engaging creamy texture and no hard edges. That is not to say

Endless rows of Cabernet Sauvignon vines under an endless Australian sky (below), in Clare Valley, South Australia. The hotter, drier climate encourages rich, dense Cabernets.

that there aren't wineries intent on producing wines in a more austere style that are built to age, but even these will come round far sooner than most California Cabernets or Cabernet-based clarets made in the same idiom. A classic example is South Australian winery Wynns' top Cabernet, John Riddoch, a ferociously dark wine of massive concentration. Even tasted in its infancy, the tannins on it are nowhere near as severe as the colour may lead you to expect.

The John Riddoch that Wynns' best Cabernet is named for was the wine-grower who, in the last decade of the 19th century, first planted grapes in a part of South Australia called Coonawarra. Coonawarra's chief distinguishing feature is a narrow strip of red soil the colour of paprika known as *terra rossa*. It is here that Cabernet Sauvignon produces its most gorgeously distinctive performances in Australia.

The wines often have a chocolatey richness to them, tinged with hints of coffee bean like mocha. Some, noting the relatively cooler climate the region enjoys, have compared the region to a southern-hemisphere Bordeaux, but Coonawarra stands in no need of such vicarious honour. Its wines are nothing like claret; they have their own uniquely spicy style.

South Australia is the most important state for Cabernet Sauvignon wines. In the heat of the Barossa Valley, they tend to be richly coloured and thickly textured, with an intensity like bottled fruits. From McLaren Vale, the wines are often more delicately proportioned, with slightly higher acid levels. In the Eden Valley, Cabernets of almost European profile are being produced, with aromatic spice notes in them, and often a dash of mint.

Coonawarra, discussed above, takes that spice component a little further, and there is a lean elegance to the wines that full-fleshed Cabernets from hotter regions can lack. Riverland is a much less distinguished bulk-producing region where the wines are made in an easy-drinking, uncomplicated style.

Victoria makes Cabernet in the leaner, mintier style. The vineyards are mainly located in the centre of the state, especially in the increasingly fashionable district of Bendigo. Despite its notably cool climate, Yarra Valley has been responsible for some of Australia's most talked-about Cabernets.

Cabernets from the Margaret River area of Western Australia also tend to the subtly scented end of the spectrum, rather than the blockbuster fruit-essence idea. Acidity is particularly good and the wines are consequently quite long-lived.

Tasmania's cool, damp climate is better suited to other varieties, but the large-scale Heemskerk winery has scored some successes with lighter, more sharply angled Cabernets than are found on the mainland.

The famous terra rossa *soil of Coonawarra, South Australia (above). Vineyard land here is highly prized for the quality of grapes it yields.*

Other Non-European

NEW ZEALAND

Most of New Zealand's vineyard land has proved to be too cool and damp for Cabernet Sauvignon, which is notoriously bad-tempered if it doesn't get enough sun. Some varietal Cabernet has achieved a refreshing fruitiness, more loganberries or even raspberries than the textbook blackcurrant, but the telltale green-pepper flavours of cool-climate Cabernet have marred too many wines. Acidity tends to be high, but at least tannin is usually low. They are generally wines for short-term drinking, rather than the long haul.

New Zealand's most conspicuous successes have been with Bordeaux blends, where real complexity and depth in a midweight style not a million miles from the softer wines of Bordeaux can be very attractive. Te Mata Coleraine and the Cabernet-Merlot blend from Cloudy Bay are the two obvious show-stoppers.

SOUTH AFRICA

Cabernet Sauvignon became, in the early 1990s, the most widely planted red grape variety in South Africa. Although many winemakers are lavishing all the care and attention on the grape to which it is accustomed elsewhere, the results have so far not been an unqualified success. Many of the wines have been marred by a muddy, not particularly fruity character. This is partly due to the specific variant of the Cabernet mostly grown on the Cape, and partly to the grapes suffering heat stress in some of the world's hottest vineyards.

In the right hands, though, there are some convincingly classy wines that have proved capable of ageing. Nederburg, Stellenryck and the Reserve wines of Avontuur stand out from the crowd. The best regions so far have been coastal Stellenbosch and inland Paarl. As with New Zealand, wines made from the Bordeaux blend, using Cabernet Franc and Merlot to soften some of Cabernet Sauvignon's severity, tend to be the best: Warwick Farm Trilogy and Meerlust Rubicon are just a couple of noteworthy examples.

CHILE

During the course of the 1980s, Chile was a kind of southern-hemisphere epicentre for European wine consultants, and no variety was more consulted on than Cabernet Sauvignon. When no less an eminence than Gilbert Rokvam of Château Lafite arrived at the Los Vascos winery, it seemed pretty clear that Chile had made its entrance on the world wine map with a vengeance, at least as far as Cabernet was concerned.

What has happened since is that Chilean Cabernet has diverged into two broadly identifiable styles. One is what Europeans love to think of as the benchmark New World style, ripely blackcurranty Cabernet of sumptuous, velvety texture with low tannins and plenty of oak. The Montes winery's top Cabernet, Montes Alpha, and some of the Reserve bottlings of Caliterra are typical examples.

The other style is much more austere, cedary wine of high acidity and more pronounced tannins, vinified in a way that is intended to help it to age in the bottle, and owing much to the taste of classic Médoc claret. Prime movers here are Los Vascos, Cono Sur and the celebrated Antiguas Reservas wines of Cousiño Macul.

The towering Drakensteinberg mountains form a stunning backdrop to the higher and cooler district of Franschhoek in coastal Stellenbosch, South Africa (below), source of classy Cabernets capable of ageing.

At its best, Cabernet Sauvignon wine from Chile can possess some of the most intensely pure essence of blackcurrant found in any red wine produced anywhere. Too often, though, that fruit quality is obscured by over-extraction of tannin, or it is simply rendered dilute by allowing the vines to bear too many grapes, resulting in unfocused flavours. Despite such aberrations, Chile is slowly but surely on the way to becoming a world-class producer of some pedigree Cabernets.

ARGENTINA

On the other side of the Andes, the Mendoza province of Argentina is beginning to show its own potential as a major runner in the Cabernet stakes. Strangely enough, it is a red grape called Malbec - one of the bit-part players in red Bordeaux - that is the star of the show, with Cabernet still very much its understudy.

Initially, varietal Cabernets were rather sternly tannic, and dominated by wood flavours as opposed to fruit on account of their having been aged for too long in old oak casks. Far less outside investment poured into Argentina compared with what was happening in Chile in the 1980s, and so the wines, Cabernet Sauvignon in particular, have taken time to find the right style to make the rest of the world take note.

Led by the quality-conscious Trapiche, Norton and Weinert operations, Cabernet is now being made in a generally French-oriented style, with the rich plum and cassis fruit backed by savoury herb flavours and a judicious amount of tannin. Cabernets from the recently established Cateña Estate could turn out to be the best of all.

Harvesting Cabernet Sauvignon at Los Vascos (above) in the hot Colchagua Valley, Rapel, Chile. Los Vascos produces Cabernets moulded in the classic Médoc style.

Old Cabernet Sauvignon vines owned by the grand 19th-century bodega, Cousiño Macul (left), in Maipo, Chile. The vines date back to the 1930s.

Other European

Pickers on the Marqués de Griñon's estate near Toledo, in the hot centre of Spain (above). The estate has drawn attention for its structured, long-ageing Cabernets.

The Torres Mas la Plana vineyard in Penedés, planted solely with Cabernet vines (below). Torres and Jean León set a precedent for Cabernet in Spain in the '60s.

FRANCE

Just outside Bordeaux, in appellations such as Bergerac and Buzet, the permitted grape varieties are the same as in Bordeaux itself, and from certain producers (notably the large co-operative at Buzet) the wines can rival middle-of-the-range claret. Cabernet Sauvignon has now made inroads into the experimental zone of Languedoc-Roussillon, on France's warm south coast, where it appears as varietal Vin de Pays d'Oc, with very patchy results to date.

SPAIN AND PORTUGAL

Cabernet Sauvignon established a bridgehead on the Iberian peninsula when it was planted in Penedés by the Torres family and Jean León in the 1960s. Although the León wines have tended to the mellow and approachable axis, both the Black Label wine of Torres and - even more so - the Marqués de Griñon Cabernet, from near Toledo, are made in the opaquely concentrated, towering style for long keeping.

Many producers, in regions such as Ribera del Duero and Costers del Segre, are experimenting with blending amounts of Cabernet Sauvignon in with Spain's indigenous superstar grape, Tempranillo - often with exciting results.

The same philosophy towards blended wines has tended to be followed by those Portuguese growers who have planted Cabernet, although there are some accomplished varietal wines

produced on the Setúbal Peninsula south of Lisbon, notably from José Maria da Fonseca. Quinta da Bacalhoa is a noted Bordeaux blend made in an unmistakably Portuguese idiom.

ITALY

Italy's growers have traditionally tended to be a little cavalier, particularly in the northern regions, in distinguishing Cabernet Sauvignon from its Bordeaux sibling Cabernet Franc. Thus, a Trentino wine labelled "Cabernet" may be one or the other, or both. Yet these two grapes are quite different and produce distinct styles of wine.

Less confusion arises in Tuscany, where Cabernet Sauvignon is allowed to make up a minor part of the blend in Chianti, and in lesser-known reds such as Carmignano. A revolution in Italian wine was effected in the 1970s by a group of Tuscan innovators, led by the highly respected family house of Antinori. They began working outside the Italian wine regulations to produce monumental reds that made free use of Cabernet Sauvignon, either blended with the Chianti grape Sangiovese - such as Piero Antinori's Solaia - or with the other Bordeaux varieties, as in the case of his brother Lodovico's Ornellaia.

Cabernet has also gained a foothold in Piedmont in the northwest, with trailblazer Angelo Gaja producing an ostentatious unblended Cabernet called Darmagi.

CENTRAL AND EASTERN EUROPE

The cheap red wine boom in the 1970s and 1980s was sustained almost single-handedly by the state-subsidised exports of Bulgaria. For a supposedly marginal wine-making culture, Bulgarian Cabernets generally offered the sort of easily lovable, softly plummy fruit flavours that producers of cheap Bordeaux can only dream about. The wines were smoothed with plenty of oak and were often released as "Reserve" bottlings after several years' ageing in the state cellars.

At their best, these wines managed to combine enough depth of character to grace a serious dinner table, with the sort of instant drinkability that made surefire party wines. Sadly, the break-up of the old state monopoly immediately resulted in wild inconsistencies in quality but, with a little investment, Bulgaria may well come back into contention.

Hungary, Moldova and Romania are all capable of producing good Cabernet at a price the wine-drinker wants to pay. Hungary's Villany and Romania's Dealul Mare look the most promising regions so far.

Other Cabernet-based one-offs include the legendary Chateau Musar of Lebanon, a blend of Cabernet with Cinsaut made in the Bekaa Valley by the indefatigable Serge Hochar. Where other winemakers worry about problems like spring frosts, Hochar has had to contend with the siege conditions imposed on swathes of the Middle East by war, invasion and rocket attacks. That the fruit of his labours is a magnificently long-lived and powerful wine is a due tribute to his determination.

Chateau Carras, from the foothills of Mount Meliton in Thrace, is Greece's convincing attempt at a claret-style blend, aided and abetted by Bordeaux wine professor Emile Peynaud.

Bulgaria's vineyards, like these overlooking the village of Ustina, near Plovdiv (above), were the source of much commercially successful Cabernet in the 1980s.

SAUVIGNON BLANC

The grape of the famous Loire whites, Sancerre and Pouilly-Fumé, Sauvignon also brought New Zealand to the attention of the wine world, with a fruit cocktail of a wine, that proved the versatility of this variety.

IF CHARDONNAY is the first white wine grape that consumers get to know, then Sauvignon Blanc tends to be the second. In many ways, that is because its characteristics can be seen as diametrically opposed to those of Chardonnay. Whereas Chardonnay is typically seen as a golden-hued, fat-textured, oaky white wine with whatever aromatic personality it possesses being derived from the influence of wood, Sauvignon is a pale, relatively light and acidic wine most often vinified without oak and endowed with a piercingly distinct perfume.

A well-made Sauvignon performs its role as light refreshment almost too well. The simplicity of this style has led some to treat the variety with mild contempt. This undoubtedly does the grape a great injustice - it is in fact capable of impressive complexity. Sauvignon is responsible for two of France's most celebrated dry white wines - Sancerre and Pouilly-Fumé; when the vine's yields are controlled, it displays a wealth of uninhibited ripe fruit flavours, one of the most pleasing attributes a white wine can boast, as shown by the great success of New Zealand Sauvignon.

In addition to its upfront fruit, Sauvignon grown on certain flinty soils in the upper Loire valley in the centre of France can take on an inexplicable but oddly powerful smoky quality that deceives many into thinking it must have had some oak treatment. At its most pungent, it can resemble the savoury fume of woodsmoke; in a gentler vein, it may remind you of the wisps of steam from an espresso machine. This attribute is celebrated in the second half of the name of Pouilly-Fumé (although it only makes its presence felt in a minority of the wines), and it came to be much imitated in the California of the 1970s when Napa Valley winemaker Robert Mondavi renamed his Sauvignon wine Fumé Blanc.

Wines labelled Fumé Blanc made outside France generally tend to rely on some oak fermentation and/or maturation to achieve the elusive smokiness. If a hot climate and excessively high yields have reduced some of the natural varietal intensity of Sauvignon, then the influence of charred oak can seem a handy, if expensive, way of putting it back. Whether Sauvignon responds well to ageing in oak has become one of those debates that periodically convulses the wine world. The California trend for making an almost sweet-seeming, though

The green Sauvignon Blanc grape (right), here in Pessac-Léognan where it is destined for blending with Sémillon for the dry white Bordeaux. A prolific vine, but when yields are controlled it is capable of massive fruit character.

technically dry, style of oaked Sauvignon has since been imitated in Bordeaux, where the grape almost certainly originated, so the issue can't be presented as a straightforward scrap between Europe and America.

Just as Cabernet Sauvignon finds its compatible bedfellow in Merlot, so the Sauvignon Blanc often gets on famously with Sémillon - a grape that, as we shall see in due course, is rapidly assuming an individual reputation of its own. Nearly all white Bordeaux, whether dry or sweet, contains some Sauvignon, and the proportions are likely to increase since the region has seen a tremendous upsurge in plantings of the variety as it has become internationally trendy.

More than any other region outside France, it is New Zealand that has done wonders for the worldwide status of Sauvignon. It may very well be that, across the board, New Zealand's winemakers now have a better understanding of the grape than the French. Nor do their Sauvignons necessarily sell at dissuasively high prices on the export markets as many of the French versions do. Mouthful for mouthful, New Zealand Sauvignons offer more ecstatically happy fruit flavours than practically any other dry white wines in the world.

In general, Sauvignon Blanc is lost without a decent level of good crisp acidity, which is why, in very hot areas, it results in a rather flabby and fruitless wine. Many Australian Sauvignons have suffered from precisely this problem.

FRENCH ORIGINS

Bordeaux, where it is nearly always blended with Sémillon (and perhaps a drop of Muscadelle). The upper Loire valley is where France's top varietal Sauvignons are based, and less exalted wines are made further west along the Loire in Touraine.

WHERE ELSE IS IT GROWN?

Fairly widespread, but particularly important in New Zealand, and somewhat less so in the United States, Australia and South Africa. Isolated plantings in the warmer Languedoc and northern Spain are beginning to prove surprisingly successful.

TASTING NOTES

Practically the whole gamut of fruit flavours, ranging from sour green fruits like gooseberry and tart apple or pear to astonishingly exotic notes such as Charentais melon, passion fruit and mango. It very often has a precise nose of blackcurrants. Vegetable flavours can loom large too. Green peas, asparagus and sweet red peppers often crop up in New Zealand examples. Then there is a curiously pungent animal quality in many cool-climate, especially Loire, versions that is often compared to cat's pee, or even to male sweat. If you're lucky, that fugitive wisp of faintly acrid smoke is there as well.

France

Early-morning mist (above) over Sauvignon vines in the Loire's famous Pouilly-Fumé appellation.

LOIRE

In the vineyards around the upper reaches of the river Loire, in the centre of France, unblended Sauvignon Blanc reigns supreme. It wasn't that long ago that these crisp, scented dry white wines, designed to be drunk within a couple of years of harvest, were not especially highly regarded even within France itself. As fashion shifted momentarily away from the richer and oakier styles of white in the 1960s, Loire Sauvignon - Sancerre in particular - found itself catapulted to the height of popularity.

Pouilly-Fumé and Sancerre are the two most famous appellations for Sauvignon. They are situated on opposite sides of the river, on the east and west banks respectively. It is a very accomplished taster indeed who can spot one from the other, both capturing, as they do at their best, the combination of refreshing green fruit flavours, snappy acids and distant smoky aromas that typify the grape in these parts.

The fashionability of the wines elevated their prices in the 1970s, and they have never really come down again. For wines of such great cachet, it has to be said that there are too many indifferent producers, notably in Pouilly-Fumé. Gitton, Mellot and Bourgeois are reliable names in Sancerre, Dagueneau and de Ladoucette in Pouilly-Fumé.

To the west of Sancerre are three minor appellations for the Sauvignon grape. They offer something of the flavours of their more exalted neighbours while possibly just lacking that final dimension of concentration. The best, and closest to Sancerre, is Ménétou-Salon (where Henry Pellé is the outstanding grower). Further west, across the river Cher, Quincy and Reuilly produce brisk, assertive Sauvignon in a clean but less elegant style than the others.

In the heartland of the Loire region, the Touraine district - more famous for its Chenin Blanc wines - also has a lot of Sauvignon. A fair amount of it gets used as blending fodder, but some varietal wines are bottled under the label Sauvignon de Touraine. In good years, they too can offer a glass of cheerfully fruity white, without anything like the intensity of the wines of the upper Loire.

The village of Sancerre (right) that gives the appellation its name stands on a hilltop close to the river Loire, overlooking the vineyards.

BORDEAUX

The dry white wines of Bordeaux were dragged kicking and screaming into the modern world during the 1980s. Too often stale and dispiriting creations based on over-produced Sémillon, they have benefited hugely from the trend towards colder fermentations using temperature-control equipment.

As Sauvignon wines from further north gained in modishness and therefore retail value, it dawned on the Bordelais that perhaps they could cash in on the Sauvignon mania by vinifying more of what was after all one of their own main grapes. The percentage of Sauvignon in many of the blends has accordingly noticeably increased, bringing in its train a greater freshness and zip to the wines.

Top of the quality tree is the region of Pessac-Léognan at the northern end of the Graves, where a healthy scattering of wines from properties such as Domaine de Chevalier and Châteaux Haut-Brion and Laville-Haut-Brion show true class. Some producers use only Sauvignon in their whites: Couhins-Lurton, Malartic-Lagravière and Smith-Haut-Lafitte can be magnificent. The smart operators have used barrel-ageing (and even fermentation in oak as well) in order to achieve a rich, tropical-fruit style that is far more opulent than the unoaked Sauvignons of the Loire.

The large production of the Entre-Deux-Mers region is generally more humdrum stuff, although the occasional wine can shine. Château Thieuley, in the west of the region, makes an oaked and unblended Sauvignon to rival the best of Pessac-Léognan. Sauvignon also plays a supporting role in the great sweet wines of Bordeaux, to lend a flash of balancing acid to the noble-rotted Sémillon.

ELSEWHERE

The Bergerac appellation, on the river Dordogne, has the same grape varieties as Bordeaux and can turn out some light, refreshing Sauvignon-based blends, as can the Côtes de Duras to the south. White wines labelled Vin de Pays des Côtes de Gascogne, from further down in southwest France, may be made from any of a number of grapes, and there is a smattering of varietal Sauvignon among them.

Although it may seem inauspiciously hot, the increasing plantings of Sauvignon in the Languedoc are yielding some attractively crisp, fruity Vins de Pays d'Oc that owe their super-

fresh quality to cold fermentation in stainless steel. Chais Baumière and La Serre have made two of the better wines seen in recent years.

Finally, there is a lone outpost of Sauvignon in the far north of what is technically the Burgundy region, near Chablis. Sauvignon de St-Bris is an historical oddity, best described as tasting like Sauvignon made in a Chardonnay style, with the recognisable green fruit but smoother contours than are found in the Loire versions. Because the traditional white grape around here is Chardonnay, the wine is only accorded VDQS status, one rung down the ladder from *appellation contrôlée*.

In the Sauternes region, as here at Château Suduirat (below), Sauvignon Blanc brings a streak of fresh acidity to balance the sweetness of noble-rotted Sémillon.

New Zealand

Sauvignon devotees weaned on the exhilarating flavours of New Zealand's finest efforts may be surprised to learn that it is only the third most widely planted grape in the country. It is easily outnumbered by Chardonnay and the common-or-garden German variety Müller-Thurgau. New Zealand Sauvignon shot to prominence in the 1980s on the back of the wine made by the bulk-producing Montana winery in Marlborough on the South Island. The commercial success of its Sauvignon Blanc - always a harvest festival of pure raw-fruit ripeness - was founded on its sheer exuberance of flavour, and shored up over the years by the fact that its export price has hardly moved. This despite the fact that few wines have further to travel to the international marketplace than those of southern New Zealand.

Having sparked a trend, Montana's example was quickly followed by a host of other wineries. That surge of abundant fruit is present in nearly all of the wines of the Marlborough

The Cloudy Bay winery in New Zealand's Marlborough district (below), one of the country's greatest success stories with the Sauvignon grape.

region, although occasionally the acidity can be out of focus, or - as in the troubled vintages of 1992 and '93 - just a little too aggressive. Some of the most sensationally concentrated fruit of all has been seen on the wines of Jackson Estate, Wairau River and the Oyster Bay range from Delegat's, while Hunters Estate and the famed Cloudy Bay (which is blended, Bordeaux-style, with a dash of Sémillon) achieve a textural depth as well that renders the wines unbelievably lush.

That slightly softer style of Sauvignon really comes into its own in the North Island region of Hawkes Bay. The fruit seems less green and more peachy, and there is a correspondingly greater readiness to use oak in the vinification, though by no means universally. Vidal's Sauvignon is one of the more opulent Hawkes Bay examples, with Castle Hill from the Te Mata winery also showing well. Villa Maria, although not based in the region, makes a fine, competitively priced Sauvignon from fruit grown there.

Other Regions

AUSTRALIA

The hotter the wine region, the less likely it is to be capable of producing the appetising fruit and natural crispness that Sauvignon wines need. Australia has consequently made some of the least sharply defined Sauvignons around. One of the best - Cullens - comes, not unexpectedly, from the cooler Margaret River region of Western Australia, while Mount Hurtle, in McLaren Vale, makes an appealingly fruity version.

UNITED STATES

Robert Mondavi's attempt to elevate the status of California Sauvignon by renaming it Fumé Blanc has still not managed to persuade other growers to take the variety to their hearts. Dry Creek Vineyards in Sonoma makes an impressively ostentatious one, as does Ferrari-Carrano. Sterling Vineyards is gradually moving towards a steelier Loire-like style of Sauvignon, albeit using a small percentage of barrel fermentation in the wine. Many other growers, if they have Sauvignon at all, try to disguise what they see as an embarrassing herbaceousness in the flavour of the grape by ageing in oak or else leaving a distracting quantity of residual sugar in the wine.

CHILE

There was a large, and for the time being intractable, problem with Sauvignon Blanc in Chile, which is that a lot of it wasn't. Quite a few growers planted a grape called Sauvignon Vert or Sauvignonasse thinking it was the Loire variety, whereas it is in fact the dullish, neutral-tasting relative of a grape native to northeast Italy. Despite the confusion, those wines were still likely to be labelled Sauvignon Blanc, but the picture in recent years has improved. One of the best, and most definitely the real thing, is Casablanca Santa Isabel, from one of Chile's cooler growing regions. The Carmen winery's Reserve Sauvignon is also good.

SOUTH AFRICA

As elsewhere, it is the cooler areas that do best with Sauvignon, and there are some brilliantly aromatic, concentrated wines being produced now. That said, some co-operative wines from the hotter Swartland district can be surprisingly crisp, if not exactly a riot of fruit.

The Cullens winery in the Margaret River area of Western Australia (above) has consistently produced one of the country's more sharply defined Sauvignons.

Chile's cooler Casablanca Valley (left) is proving a good spot to grow characterful Sauvignon Blanc.

PINOT NOIR

Difficult to grow, difficult to vinify but still producers across the globe are attracted to this temperamental grape variety, tempted to try matching the classic style of Burgundy's greatest red wines.

O F ALL THE French grape varieties that have migrated around the viticultural world, this is the one that excites the greatest passions. More tears are shed, greater energy expended, more hand-wringing despair engendered over it than over any other variety.

Almost every serious grower outside those areas where plantings of the grape aren't permitted (and even some within) would like to produce a fine Pinot Noir at some stage in their careers, and such is the challenge involved in it that many would settle for only ever producing one. It is not, by and large, an endeavour for those who relish a quiet life.

In the beginning, it was all so simple. Pinot Noir is the only grape permitted in the great majority of red burgundy (the only exceptions being at the bottom of the quality ladder). At the summit of Pinot ambition sit the *grand cru* wines of Vosne-Romanée on Burgundy's Côte d'Or, wines of positively exotic complexity that offer a once-in-a-lifetime experience of sumptuous richness at a once-in-a-lifetime price. All the red-wine appellations of the Côte d'Or, however, are capable of producing great Pinot at one time or another - they don't call it the Golden Hillside for nothing.

So there is the model for the world to emulate. Why all the heartbreak?

Initially, the almost insuperable obstacle seemed to be that Pinot Noir just couldn't be coaxed into producing the same sorts of flavours that it is able to achieve in Burgundy. It most emphatically doesn't take to hot climates. Grown in the kinds of conditions that Cabernet Sauvignon loves, it results in horribly muddy wines, often with the flavour of sub-standard fruit being boiled up for jam.

Burgundy itself is cool and wet, prone to spring frosts and even hailstorms. The lesson seemed simple enough. Plant it in similar environments elsewhere and maybe it could be persuaded to yield up its charms.

The first attempts in the cooler areas of the United States, Australia and New Zealand, however, didn't seem to suit it either. Now it came over all green and bitter, full of off-putting vegetal pungency and a streak of hard, spiteful acid that made it a powerful repellent to consumers. Pinots produced in these conditions were among the feeblest red wines in the fine wine sector, and the labour of love that had been lavished on them with so little reward meant that they had to be sold for stupidly high prices.

What was being discovered was that Pinot is much more choosy about where it will grow than those other cosmopolitan vines, Chardonnay and Cabernet. Not only does it want the right weather, but it has a distinct partiality for soils with some limestone in them. Even at its

Ripe, healthy bunches of Pinot Noir grapes (right). A thin-skinned grape that is highly sensitive to climate and soil, and notoriously difficult to nurture, Pinot Noir can make ripely fruity reds of great class. It is also invaluable in the production of sparkling wine.

ripest, it is a thin-skinned variety - physically as well as temperamentally - which means that it is more prone to vine diseases than most, and rots very easily if the vintage has to take place in persistent rain.

The potential pay-off, if conditions are exactly right, is that, because of those thin skins, Pinot produces a generally lighter wine than Cabernet. Because there is less tannin to be extracted, the wines tend to be approachable earlier in their development (although it pays to wait for the naturally high acidity to settle down a bit) and they mature faster. Good Pinot can be a memorable experience at six or seven years old - although the best will continue to improve for substantially longer - whereas the finest Cabernets are still clenched shut and full of sulking tannins.

Increasingly, producers outside Burgundy have got the hang of it in recent years. In California and the Pacific Northwest of the US, the dedication and viticultural intelligence of a hard core of growers has demonstrated more conclusively than anywhere else that Pinot can thrive

outside its native Burgundy. After all, once the overall conditions are established, it should be possible to produce more good Pinot more often than in climatically chaotic Burgundy, where the conservative estimate is that two vintages in every three are not really suitable for the production of decent wine.

As a result, the emphasis of the Pinot debate has now shifted to what the optimum style of the wine should be. Put simply, there are two schools of thought: one school opts for deeply coloured, ripely scented wines full of red fruit but possessed of fairly big beefy texture, while the other wants to achieve the lighter, earthier-smelling brews liable to turn gamey with age. This latter wine is associated with the old-fashioned style of the Côte d'Or. Don't think of this as a straight fight between Americans and Burgundians, though. There are examples of both styles in each camp.

Additionally, Pinot Noir plays an important role in the production of champagne and other sparkling wines, where it adds depth and longevity to the Chardonnay and colour to the rosés.

FRENCH ORIGINS

Burgundy and Champagne. Also used in some of the light reds and rosés of the Loire, and the red wine of Alsace.

WHERE ELSE IS IT GROWN?

California, Oregon, Australia, New Zealand, a little in South Africa. Quite important in central Europe - southern Germany, Switzerland, and points east - but still fairly rare along the Mediterranean. Anybody making sparkling wine by the traditional champagne method is likely to use some Pinot.

TASTING NOTES

In youth, it can possess light aromas of red fruits, typically raspberry, strawberry, redcurrant, cherry. In parts of California and Australia, it also has a faint note of coffee bean or mocha. Nearly always has an element of meatiness - beef stock in young wines, shading to well-hung game as it ages, overlaid in the very best with the other-worldly pungency of black truffle. Classically (or notoriously, depending on your tastes) mature wines can also display a distinctly rank smell, politely described as "barnyardy", but really referring to what you might accidentally put your foot in as you walk through the barnyard

France

Levelling Pinot Noir grapes in the traditional wooden press at Champagne Bollinger (above).

Harvested Pinot Noir grapes resting in traditional wicker baskets (below) at Louis Latour, in Aloxe-Corton on the Côte d'Or, the home of most of Burgundy's famous names.

Betting on vintage conditions in Burgundy as harvest-time approaches makes for slightly more peace of mind than playing Russian Roulette - but not much more. In most years, the region's white grape variety, Chardonnay, fares reasonably well: only torrential rain during the picking can really ruin it at the eleventh hour. Pinot Noir, the only runner in the red wine stakes, is a different kettle of fish.

It is no exaggeration to say that, more often than not, Pinot Noir yields disappointing results. Precisely because out-and-out successes are so hard-won, great red burgundy has come to be valued by many as the most precious wine of classical France, consort to Bordeaux's monarch, but held in special esteem because of its rarity.

The Pinot grape reaches the apex of its potential on the Côte d'Or, the narrow escarpment running southwest of the city of Dijon, and home to most of Burgundy's famous names. The narrower northern strip, the Côte de Nuits, which includes such appellations as Gevrey-Chambertin, Nuits-St-Georges and Morey-St-Denis, tends to produce the weightiest style of Burgundian Pinot, with all sorts of meaty notes ranging from the singed skin of roasted fowl to gravy bubbling in the dish. Further south, the Côte de Beaune, which takes in Aloxe-Corton, Pommard and Volnay among others, specialises in a lighter, gentler Pinot, smelling of soft summer fruits and sometimes flowers as well.

The further south of the Côte d'Or you travel, into the Côte Chalonnaise and then the work-horse region of the Mâconnais, the more ordinary the Pinot Noir wines become. At the bottom of the scale, wine labelled Bourgogne Rouge may be a blend of grapes from different sources in the region and covers a multitude of sins, as well as the occasional happy surprise.

If the vintage has been particularly chilly, or worse doused with rainfall as in 1991, the resulting wines can be extremely light, both in colour as well as in texture. When a red wine is full of hard acids and bitterly unripe fruit, and feels no richer on the palate than a heavyish rosé, then consumers have a tough time seeing why they should pay the inflated prices.

On the other hand, if burgundy is noted for one thing, it is a resistance to generalisations. Some producers - Joseph Roty in Gevrey-Chambertin, to take one random example - managed to make densely concentrated wine in 1991, while others were wringing their hands. It pays to know who the high fliers are.

Because Pinot often lacks adequate natural sugar to ferment into a full-bodied red that will stay the distance, producers are permitted to add ordinary cane sugar to the freshly pressed juice. The process is known as chaptalisation, after its inventor Jean-Antoine Chaptal. By giving the yeasts more sugar to work on, the potential alcohol content of the finished product is raised. The average strength of red burgundy is a stiffish 13 per cent. Sometimes, especially when young, it can give off a telltale whiff of burnt sugar, a probable indicator that the winemaker has resorted to fairly heavy chaptalisation.

In the best vintages, however, such as the happy trio of 1988, '89 and '90 - known in France as *les trois glorieuses* - when the Pinot Noir has attained full ripeness, the wines it is turned into are richly perfumed, exquisitely elegant creations that go some way at least to justifying the heart-stopping prices they sell for.

Although it is a red grape, Pinot Noir is hugely important in the making of champagne. The colourless juice is vinified without its skins so that the resulting wine remains white, although if you compare a blended champagne with one that has been made entirely from the region's only white grape, Chardonnay, you will notice a deeper, nuttier hue in the one that contains Pinot

Autumnal Pinot Noir vines (left) running down towards to the town of Aÿ, in Champagne. The inclusion of Pinot in champagne lends it a nuttier, darker hue, and gives the wine depth and good ageing potential.

The beginnings of a red burgundy - Pinot Noir gently fermenting in an open wooden vat (above).

Noir. Champagne producers consider that Pinot gives their wines depth and the ability to age well. Some champagne, labelled "blanc de noirs", is made entirely from Pinot Noir and the region's other red grape Pinot Meunier, but is still a white wine. A small amount of still red wine, vaguely Burgundian though even more crisply acidic in style, is made, and may be added to white wine to make rosé champagne. Tiny quantities of pink champagne (such as Laurent-Perrier rosé) are made by the painstaking method of infusing the red grape skins briefly in the white juice to tint it to the desired shade.

In the eastern Loire, Pinot Noir is used to make the red and rosé versions of Sancerre and Ménétou-Salon. These are much lighter in style than top burgundy, often with a slightly vegetal hint like cabbage leaves. They are not intended for ageing but, served slightly chilled, can make good summer drinking.

Pinot Noir also makes the only red wine of Alsace, again in a typically featherlight not overly fruity style, although attractive, perfumed examples from the likes of Zind-Humbrecht and particularly Marcel Deiss provide the exceptions that prove the rule.

United States

CALIFORNIA

This has undoubtedly been the most successful region across the board for Pinot Noir outside Burgundy itself. Although they are extremely unlikely to admit it, Burgundy's producers could profitably learn a fair bit from the approach of the most conscientious growers of Pinot Noir in America.

The most successful area to date has been Carneros, a cool district straddling Napa and Sonoma Counties and benefiting from the coastal fogs that waft in from San Francisco Bay. The afternoons and early evenings in Carneros are sufficiently warm to endow the developing grapes with the exciting flavours of ripe red fruits that are characteristic of the best Pinot wines. At the same time, the cooling influence of those thick mists that often hang around until mid-morning ensures adequate levels of fresh acidity, so the wines are impeccably balanced and capable of ageing.

Its ripe fruit intensity means that California Pinot Noir is generally ready for drinking earlier than traditional burgundy, although it does benefit from keeping for a year or two after release just to allow the nervy edge on those acids to calm down. If it had a noticeable problem during the 1980s, the period when the wine

Terracing a new Pinot Noir vineyard in Oregon (below). The grape of Burgundy is making itself at home in the Pacific Northwest.

world was beginning to abandon its presumption that Pinot Noir was not a suitable occupation for a non-European winemaker, it was that the levels of alcohol were a touch high. That often resulted in wines that were very attractive until you swallowed them, whereupon they left a slight smouldering at the back of the throat. Today, the balance is a lot better.

In addition to Carneros, where producers like Saintsbury and the low-profile Kent Rasmussen have scored some considerable triumphs in recent vintages, parts of Santa Barbara County south of the Bay have proved promising for Pinot Noir. Au Bon Climat and Sanford are both wineries to watch here. The mountainous inland region of San Benito is home to the pace-setting Calera Winery, whose Pinot is regularly among the most stunning from California.

OREGON

Because of its cooler, damper climate, this Pacific Northwestern state was seen as ideal Pinot territory when the search for appropriate vineyard sites began to gather momentum. Climatically, it is undoubtedly much closer to Burgundy than most of California, and yet the results have not so far been an unqualified success. It remains to some extent a tale of unfulfilled potential.

In some cases, yields from the vines have been allowed to go too high, a vice that Pinot Noir is very unwilling to forgive. Mainly, though, the problem has been that the fruit just hasn't quite attained the state of ripeness conducive for good wine. If you emulate Burgundy's environment too closely, after all, you may end up duplicating the same handicaps that spoil too many of its wines.

That said, Oregon enjoyed a succession of great vintages in the late '80s and early '90s, and some wineries are now beginning to show just what thrilling Pinots Oregon is capable of making. The Reserve wines of Bethel Heights have been sublime, while Domaine Drouhin - an Oregonian outpost of one of the great Burgundy merchants, where the wine is actually made by a member of the Drouhin family - broke into the super-league with its 1991 Pinot Noir. The style is generally lighter than in most of California, less meaty but with more accentuated strawberry fruit.

Other Regions

NEW ZEALAND

The coolest wine climate in the southern hemisphere should be nicely hospitable for Pinot Noir. Although there are not many superstars as yet, New Zealand should soon be well on the way to producing some top-flight wines from this grape. Best so far have been Martinborough Vineyards, Palliser Estate and Ata Rangi, all displaying the savoury intensity that adds complexity to the familiar red fruits.

AUSTRALIA

As with other cool-climate grapes, it is crucial to find the right site for Pinot Noir in Australia, in order to avoid the muddy or jammy characters that can so easily spoil it. The Yarra Valley in Victoria fits the bill because of its altitude (Yarra Yering and Coldstream Hills have both made richly satisfying Pinots in this area). In the centre of Victoria, the Bendigo district is home to a winery called Passing Clouds, which has made some fine, thickly-textured Côte de Beaune-style wine. Moss Wood, in Western Australia's cool Margaret River region, is making great strides, while on Tasmania, Piper's Brook produces some of the most Burgundian Pinot Noir outside France.

SOUTH AFRICA

As in Australia, much of the country is simply too hot to achieve great elegance in wines made from Pinot Noir, and the grape is not that important in South Africa. The coastal Walker Bay region, however, boasts two world-class producers in Hamilton-Russell and Bouchard-Finlayson (the latter a joint venture with one of the major Burgundy companies).

GERMANY

In Germany, they call it Spätburgunder, and it has long been a traditional grape for the very small amount of red wine the country is able to produce. The typical style is light as a feather and not much further on from rosé. Although the northerly region of Ahr somehow contrived to get itself a reputation for red wines, Baden in the south seems considerably more auspicious for wines of decent fruit. Some of the young, innovative producers are beginning to coax some concentration and depth out of German Pinot Noir, but the quantities involved have so far been very modest.

A layer of plastic sheeting is used to insulate Pinot Noir grapes growing in the Hollenburg vineyard in Germany's Rheingau region (above).

Hand-plunging the grape skin cap on a tank of Pinot Noir (left) at the Yarra Yering winery in Victoria.

SEMILLON

To many producers, Sémillon suffers a lack of individuality that has destined it to be blended with more fashionable varieties. Yet as the source of rich, golden, honeyed Sauternes, and the unique, aged dry white of Australia, Sémillon is second to none.

WHILE IT IS undoubtedly one of the world's foremost grape varieties, Sémillon has a surprisingly low profile. In the northern hemisphere, it was traditionally not seen very much as an unblended varietal wine. This is largely because, in its native Bordeaux, it is always mixed with Sauvignon Blanc.

However, its highly prized susceptibility in the right conditions to botrytis, the so-called noble rot that concentrates the sugars of overripe grapes by shrivelling them on the vine, makes Sémillon a surefire bet as a dessert-wine producer. The lofty reputation enjoyed by sweet Sauternes and Barsac - in which Sémillon typically represents around four-fifths or more of the blend - has been such that the grape's role in the production of dry white wine has been largely eclipsed.

In Bordeaux today, producers of dry white wine are in the business of pulling out a lot of their Sémillon vines and replacing them with further plantings of its partner Sauvignon. (As we saw when we looked at Sauvignon Blanc, some of the trendiest dry whites of Bordeaux use no Sémillon at all.) That said, it still accounts for far more acreage in the vineyards than Sauvignon, so if it is in decline, the process will be a lengthy one. Many producers frankly consider it to have far less character than its brasher stablemate, being short of aromatic appeal and general *joie-de-vivre*.

To which one can only reply, tell that to the Australians. Semillon (as it is commonly spelt outside France) has been used to produce a varietal dry wine in southern Australia since the 19th century. Its homeland Down Under is the Hunter Valley in New South Wales. True, many growers weren't sure what the variety was, and its traditional (and misleading) name was Hunter Riesling. It does share some of the aromatic characteristics of real Riesling, most notably a minerally aroma of lime-zest, but it almost always gives a fatter, oilier wine than Riesling.

The most peculiar trait a dry Sémillon wine can have is to smell and taste as if it has been wood-matured when it hasn't. Often, there is a distinctly toasty quality to the wine that becomes steadily more pronounced as it ages. Its colour darkens rapidly too, making old Hunter Semillon one of the strangest but most memorable experiences in the world of white wine.

In areas where a lot of cheap bulk wine is produced, Sémillon's easy-going temperament in the vineyard has made it the grape of choice for those who haven't yet caught the Chardonnay bug. Much of South America's vineland, especially in Chile, is carpeted with the variety. An indication of the status in which it is held here is that these are not the wines Chile chooses to boast about on the export markets.

For many, Sémillon provides a relatively trouble-free source of blending material for more fashionable varieties. Although the Bordeaux precedent is to blend it with Sauvignon, Sauvignon is too much in vogue currently to be thought by many producers to need a partner in the bottle. That is why many winemakers, in Australia particularly, have taken to blending Semillon with Chardonnay.

The resulting wines have become bargain-basement alternatives to neat Chardonnay. The lowish prices of these wines indicate how seriously we are being asked to take them. In a hot vintage, where both grapes have yielded similarly rich, fat, silky-textured wines, it is difficult to see what they are supposed to be doing for each other in a blend.

On the other hand, the Sémillon-Sauvignon partnership is nearly always a happy one. The acidity of the latter gives definition to the textural opulence of the former.

The blend makes particular sense in the production of sweet wines. What makes great Sauternes, Barsac and Monbazillac so sought-after, and so extremely long-lived in the bottle, is that a good balance of sugar and acid is present in the wines to start with. Compared to lesser dessert wines from other wine regions, they are hardly ever cloying, despite their massive, syrupy concentration.

Sémillon, a golden-coloured grape with markedly deep green leaves (right) is often used to blend with Sauvignon or Chardonnay. When affected by botrytis (noble rot), it creates the world's finest dessert wines.

FRENCH ORIGINS
Bordeaux.

WHERE ELSE IS IT GROWN?
Australia, Chile, Argentina,
a little in South Africa and
California, and isolated pockets
of southern France.

TASTING NOTES
When dry, lime-peel, exotic
honey, sometimes has a little of
Sauvignon's gooseberry too.
Often has a hard mineral purity,
even slightly metallic. In the
Hunter Valley, deceptive
woodiness even when unoaked,
turning to burnt toast with age.
Blended with Chardonnay,
lemon-and-lime squash seems
to be the main flavour. When
subjected to botrytis for sweet
wines, can take on a whole
range of exotic fruit characters,
but classically has overripe
peach or apricot flavour, barley-
sugar, honey, allied to a
vanilla-custard, *crème brûlée*
richness from oak ageing.
Australian sweet Semillon can
have an emphatically medicinal
tinge to it as well.

Bordeaux

*Sémillon grapes left on the
vine that have been affected
by botrytis (right). The shrivelled, blackened grapes will
yield a lusciously sweet, concentrated juice.*

Sémillon's most glorious display in its home
region is in the wines of Sauternes and Barsac.
At the top of the tree, with a classification to
itself, is the legendary Château d'Yquem, the
most expensive sweet wine in the world. The
late-summer and autumn climate in Bordeaux
provides perfect conditions in many years for
the development on Sémillon of the noble rot,
botrytis, that causes the berries to moulder and
dry out on the vines. As the liquid proportion of
the grapes drops, so the sugar in them comes to
represent an ever higher percentage, and the
result is lusciously sweet, alcoholic, sticky
wines of enormous longevity.

If the top wines are so expensive, it is in large
part because the more conscientious châteaux
take great pains over the harvest. They will
hand-select only those berries that are fully
rotted, so labour costs are accordingly very
high. Most of the wines are aged in at least a
proportion of new oak, adding further dimen-
sions of richness to them. These wines have for
long been the inspiration for the production of
botrytised Sémillon the world over.

*The elegant Château La
Louvière in Pessac-Léognan,
Graves (below), owned by
the Lurton family. Dry white
Bordeaux from the Graves is
often the best of its style.*

Elsewhere in Bordeaux, in the making of dry
wines, Sémillon rather hangs its head these
days. The finger of blame for the old-style
flabby, fruitless dry whites of the region has
been pointed its way. But this style is on the
wane as fresh young Sauvignon Blanc, with its
tangier fruit flavours, shows it the door. As a
result, consumers may get the idea that Sémillon is incapable of making great dry wine in
Bordeaux, but it ain't necessarily so.

In the northern Graves region of Pessac-
Léognan, close to the city, some of Bordeaux's
most illustrious names in dry white wine pro-
duction still use a greater percentage of
Sémillon than Sauvignon Blanc in their wines.
These include Châteaux Olivier, Laville-Haut-
Brion and La Tour-Martillac.

New Zealand is beginning to have better success with Sémillon now that the particular strain
(or clone) of the grape they had planted there is
being replaced with better ones. For the time
being, it is best in the Bordeaux-blend style, as
exemplified by the oak-fermented Sauvignon-
Semillon of North Island producer Selaks.

Australia

Dry Semillon is one of a handful of unique styles of wine that Australia has contributed to the world. Nor is it a product of some antipodean search for novelty, conceived in a struggle to find ways of doing things that escape the eternal French archetypes. Australia was making Semillons like this in the late 19th century, even though it may have been calling them Hunter Riesling or - even less convincingly - White Burgundy.

The classic Hunter Valley style can be quite austere, as typified by the wines of Tyrrells. Crisp and acerbic in youth, they age to a wonderful roasted-nuts complexity, all achieved without recourse to the expense of oak barrels. Some producers do actually use a modicum of oak to emphasise that natural toastiness. With the tendency now for consumers to drink most wines young, greater stress is being laid on primary fruit flavours - sharp green fruits, usually lime, being the main reference point. Other good Hunter producers are Rothbury, Brokenwood and Lindeman's.

The grape pops up in most Australian regions, though, and fares equally well in areas that are considerably cooler than the Hunter. In the Clare Valley, for instance, Semillon produces a less oily version. As a rough guide, producers who make good Riesling are likely to be reliable for Semillon too: in a cool part of the Clare called Lenswood, Tim Knappstein makes fine, bracingly tart but certainly ageworthy wines.

Western Australia's Margaret River region makes some generously fruity, distinctly smoky Semillons in a style hugely reminiscent of Sauvignon. Evans & Tate is a prime example here.

Although unblended Sauvignon can too often be a disappointment from many parts of Australia, when it is blended with Semillon in the Bordeaux fashion it can produce impressively ripe-fruited wines capable of gaining real complexity with ageing. Cape Mentelle in Margaret River and even St Hallett, in the broiling Barossa Valley region of South Australia, make good blends.

Botrytised, or noble-rotted, Semillon has a long and distinguished tradition here, too. The style may be big and obvious when compared with the top wines of Sauternes, but then there is no particular reason to compare them to Sauternes. De Bortoli in New South Wales was among those who blazed this particular trail, while Peter Lehmann makes a textbook orange-barley-sugar version in the Barossa.

The de Bortoli winery in New South Wales, Australia (below), complete with irrigation canal.

The verdant landscape of South Australia's Clare Valley (below), with Lenswood Vineyard in the foreground. A cool upland district, it can produce bracingly tart but ageworthy Semillons.

SYRAH

Whether recognised as the French grape of the northern Rhône, Syrah, or in its popular guise as Shiraz, in Australia, this grape remains one of the noblest red varieties, fabled for its ability to age majestically for decades.

SUCH IS the success of this grape in Australia that many may know it only by its southern-hemisphere name of Shiraz. More of it is grown there than any other red wine grape, and it appears in the bottle either alone or in the company of Cabernet Sauvignon - a highly successful partnership for which there is no French precedent.

Although a fair amount of Shiraz is of no more than ordinary, every-day quality, it is without doubt among the first division of interna-tional grape varieties, as witness the fact that the most fabled red wine of Aus-tralia - Penfold's Grange - is overwhelmingly composed of Shiraz, with the merest dash of Cabernet to season it.

Shiraz produces some of the world's deepest, darkest, most intense red wines, full of liquorice richness, hot spice and alcoholic power. Then again, it can be used to make the kind of sweet-ly jammy, oak-smoothed nursery wine that can lure confirmed white wine drinkers on to red once in a while.

As Syrah, as we should call it when in France, it blends well with a number of other grapes, and hangs around with a very mixed gang of rough diamonds and ne'er-do-wells in the wines of the southern Rhône and Languedoc-Roussillon.

The Rhône valley is the ancestral home of Syrah. In viticultural terms, the valley divides into two zones - northern and southern - and represents two very different approaches to the grape. In the south, it makes its way among a large coterie of minor varieties, from the rough-and-ready reds of Côtes du Rhône and Côtes du Ventoux up to the twin stars of Châteauneuf-du-Pape and Gigondas.

Producers of red Châteauneuf may choose from a menu of no fewer than 13 grapes (although hardly anybody uses all of them), of which Syrah may play only second or third fiddle. The northern Rhône is where Syrah really comes into its own.

Hermitage is the most celebrated wine of the north; like the other northern appellations, its reds must be constituted from 100 per cent Syrah. (The one exception to that is Côte-Rôtie, where the wine may idiosyncratically contain up to 20 per cent of the white variety Viognier, although by no means all the growers use it.)

These monumental, classic reds can age for at least as long as the very greatest Bordeaux, on account of their precise and complex balances of hugely concentrated fruit, acidity and mas-sive extract. Generally, they are not remotely approachable until around six or seven years old, and the best need perhaps twice as long as that to begin to uncoil into the exotically seductive beauties they can be.

At the most accessible end of the scale, and not to be confused with Hermitage itself, is Crozes-Hermitage, whose wines can be drink-able at a mere three or four years old. They may not be anything like as dazzling as the best Hermitage and Côte-Rôtie but, across the board, they do offer a genuine insight into the unique flavours of Syrah.

One of the most commonly encountered descriptions of Syrah wines is "peppery", and even a simple Crozes from a co-operative can display something of that characteristic, although it may vary in intensity from a mild suggestion of spiciness at the back of the throat to the exact and inescapable smell of freshly milled black peppercorns, as if the winemaker had given the wine a few twists of the grinder before bottling it.

In Australian Shiraz, that pepperiness is distinctly more muted. The fruit flavours are generally riper and more obvious, and the wines rarely have that sharp edge of tannin that north-ern Rhône examples do. In youth, the softer contours of Shiraz are derived from the overt influence of creamy oak flavours, so that the wine can be drunk sooner than can Syrah.

The stylistic differences between the French and Australian manifestations of the grape are therefore comparable to those of Cabernet Sauvignon. From some regions, especially South Australia's Barossa Valley, Shiraz can

The vibrant blue of the Syrah grape variety (right). Syrah has a unique character most often described as "pep-pery", and responds well to oak. In its classic form as the grape of northern Rhône's finest reds, and in Australia as Shiraz, it can make wines that will age for decades.

FRENCH ORIGINS
Northern Rhône.

WHERE ELSE IS IT GROWN?
Australia. A little in California
and South Africa. Is of some
significance in Switzerland.

TASTING NOTES
Can smell of almost any dark
purple fruit - blackberries,
blackcurrants, black cherries,
damsons, plums. Freshly ground
black pepper in the northern
Rhône. Exotic flavours can
include liquorice, ginger, dark
chocolate, often a distinct floral
note, too, like violets. Cool
topnote of mint characteristic in
parts of South Australia.
Aged wines can take on
something of the gaminess of
old Pinot Noir.

take on a surprisingly delicate aromatic range, so that the leather and tar and pepper the grape traditionally rejoices in may be overlaid with a refreshing waft of eucalyptus.

Australians have also used some of their Shiraz to make a thoroughly innovative thick red sparkling wine that tastes of frothing blackcurrant juice - a quickly acquired taste to most who come across it. Those whose vinous memories go back to fizzy red Lambrusco should abandon their trepidation: sparkling Shiraz is a hedonistic mouthful of purple southern sunshine.

France

The greatest names in Rhône Syrah are now ranked up with Bordeaux's and Burgundy's finest. It is still a very recent phenomenon, though. While the burly red wines of Hermitage had always had a lofty reputation among British wine connoisseurs, the production of the region as a whole was not held in particularly high regard. When the esteemed American wine critic Robert Parker began, in the 1980s, to rate some of the best wines of Marcel Guigal (one of the northern Rhône's superstars) as the equals of great vintages of Mouton-Rothschild, the international wine trade was persuaded to take notice.

The chapel and vines on the famous hill of Hermitage (below), overlooking the river Rhône and the towns of Tournon and Tain l'Hermitage.

That development inevitably allowed the producers to put up their prices, but it has to be said that the best had certainly been undervalued in the past. These are wines with the same sort of structure and ageing capacity as Cabernet-based clarets (often even more muscularly built, in fact) and their flavours resemble no other red wines in France.

Of the northern Rhône appellations for varietal Syrah, Hermitage is traditionally the biggest and beefiest. Although solidly constructed, the wines are not without grace and elegance, and the fruit flavour can be surprisingly lighter than the norm - more raspberries than blackberries. Chave is a fine producer, while the Hermitage La Chapelle of Jaboulet, whose wines crop up all over the Rhône, is a densely textured, ferociously dark stunner.

Côte-Rôtie is the appellation that has created all the excitement in recent years. Guigal's top three wines from single vineyards (La Mouline, La Landonne and La Turque) are mind-blowingly concentrated expressions of pure Syrah that sell for sky-high prices, but there are other growers such as Jamet, Delas and Vidal-Fleury whose formidable talents have helped shore up the reputation of this area.

St-Joseph makes slightly lighter wines, with piercingly ripe fruit in the good years, while the bottom-line appellation of Crozes-Hermitage is well worth trying as an introduction to the flavours of Rhône Syrah. (A stunning exception is the Crozes of a grower called Graillot, whose wines are as opaquely black and intense as some Hermitage.)

The final appellation of the northern Rhône, Cornas, is an odd one; its Syrah is the least immediately recognisable. The wines are often rather tough without the benefit of youthful fruit, or they can simply taste more like blended wines from areas further south like Châteauneuf-du-Pape. That said, Colombo, Clape and Voge are three of the better producers making some exciting Syrahs in Cornas.

In the southern Rhône, and down into Languedoc, Syrah is blended with many other red grapes, the most important of which is Grenache, which we shall meet shortly. Unless a producer has used a particularly high percentage of Syrah, the grape may not be individually perceptible in these wines.

Australia

Shiraz has been *the* pre-eminent red grape variety in Australia for as long as anyone can remember, but it is only in the last 20 years or so that there has been a significant impetus towards producing world-class wine from it. At its most humdrum, Shiraz is a rather gloopy plum-jam sort of wine with too much heavy oak flavour in it, so that the toffee sweetness of its aftertaste can quickly become cloying. Thankfully, there are more than enough accomplished Shiraz producers to make for a brighter picture.

It's all a question, as so often, of microclimate. In the hotter parts of the country, such as the Hunter and Barossa valleys, Shiraz is responsible for the thickest, most opulently fruity of all Australia's reds. Charles Melton and St Hallett Old Block Shiraz (so-called because it is made from a particularly venerable plot of vines) are emblematic of the Barossa

style; Rothbury offers a leaner, but still intensely aromatic Hunter Valley alternative. In the hotter northeast corner of Victoria, the Goulburn Valley is home to some especially concentrated Shirazes, notably from Chateau Tahbilk.

The red soil of Coonawarra is as distinguished a hotbed of Shiraz as it is of Cabernet Sauvignon. The Penfold's range of reds draws extensively on plantings in this area, as do the subtly spiced Shiraz-based wines of the Penley Estate and the accessibly fruit-filled offerings of Wynns, not all of which use oak.

Along with Penfold's Grange, one of the most majestic of all Australian Shiraz wines comes from the Henschke winery's Hill of Grace vineyard in the Barossa. The vines planted here are over a century old, and produce small amounts of extraordinarily deep, resonant and complex wine that lasts for years.

The Hill of Grace vineyard, owned by Henschke (above), in the Barossa Valley, South Australia. The Shiraz vines planted here are over 100 years old.

Other Regions

SOUTH AFRICA

As in Australia, it took a while for Shiraz to persuade its growers that it was worth taking seriously as a grape variety. Inspired by success elsewhere, however, some impressive Shiraz is now beginning to emerge from the Cape. It should work, after all, given that most of South Africa's wine regions enjoy just the sort of sultry climatic conditions that Shiraz loves. Hartenberg in Stellenbosch and Fairview in Paarl are just a couple of the more conspicuously successful Shiraz producers to date.

CALIFORNIA

Despite the fashion in recent years on the West Coast for Rhône grape varieties, Syrah - as it tends to be known in the United States - has not really established itself as a particularly important grape. The trend so far has been to make a wine with French levels of acidity and memorably aromatic fruit, but not quite the degree of extract of the most well-bred Hermitage and Côte-Rôtie. Two wineries setting the pace have been Qupé in Santa Barbara and Joseph Phelps in the Napa Valley.

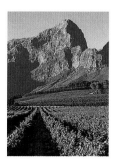

Orderly rows of Shiraz vines at Franschhoek's Bellingham Vineyards, Paarl, South Africa (above).

Vineyards of Joseph Phelps, (left), a trend-setter for quality Syrah in California, in springtime Napa Valley.

RIESLING

Germany's noble white grape variety, Riesling, is a versatile performer. It is prized in northern Europe and the southern hemisphere for its ability to produce classic sweet whites as well as impeccable dry wines.

THE ONLY FINE wine grape of international importance not to have originated in France, Riesling is the great speciality of German winemaking. Its only base in France is in the Alsace region, a sheltered northeastern enclave between the Vosges mountains and the Rhine valley that was a geopolitical part of Germany for much of its history. Like the Sémillon we looked at earlier, Riesling is capable of making impeccably dry wines of surprising longevity, as well as lusciously sweet dessert wines affected by the noble rot, botrytis, but unlike Sémillon it also runs the whole gamut of styles in between.

In recent years, Riesling has come to be considered the most underrated of all the top grapes. Why this should be so when it is such a versatile performer might seem a mystery until one bears in mind the baleful influence of a certain sweet wine produced in huge quantities, and which wrongly came to be seen as virtually synonymous with the whole German wine industry. No matter that there is no mention of Riesling on labels of branded Liebfraumilch (although most brands do actually contain an insignificant proportion) - Liebfraumilch was German, and so was Riesling.

The great problem German wines have to overcome is that nearly all wine drinkers - except those who grow up within spitting distance of a vineyard and are weaned on the local wine - cut their teeth on products like Liebfraumilch. It's sweet, it's not noticeably alcoholic and it doesn't seem to contain the tart acids that drier white wines have. When tastes become more sophisticated, meaning drier, an important part of the rite of passage for the budding wine enthusiast is to shun such wines as "kids' stuff", and the more serious German wines get swept aside in that process.

If only Liebfraumilch had its own peculiar bottle. But it sits proudly on retail shelves next to top-quality Rhine Rieslings in identically tall, narrow flute bottles of dark brown glass (wines from the northerly Mosel valley, where Liebfraumilch may not be made, are bottled in similarly shaped green glass). Attempts to persuade customers to look for the word "Riesling" on the label amid the thicket of polysyllabic Gothic lettering may still run aground on the fact that, even when newcomers do try these wines, the twin qualities they dismiss in the cheap branded wines are still there more often than not: lightness and some degree of sweetness.

Because Germany's vineyards are at the northern extremity of where vines can be grown and still produce crops of fermentable fruit, its quality classification system developed along the lines of assessing just how ripe the grapes were when harvested and therefore how potentially sweet the resulting wine would be.

Historically, before it was feasible to maintain stable conditions in the winery, the severely low temperatures of the northern winter would bring the fermentation to a halt. This would leave plenty of natural sugar (as opposed to an added sweetener, as in Liebfraumilch) in what was a low-alcohol wine. Up until the early years of this century, this was precisely the style that connoisseurs prized above all in German wines. Many consider these are still Germany's greatest claims to fame today.

Driven by international taste trends, a movement gathered pace in Germany in the 1980s and '90s to ferment the wines - Rieslings and others - all the way out to dryness, resulting in bone-dry wine that reached the kind of alcohol level (around 12 per cent) that white wine drinkers were more familiar with. The experiment ended in tears for some, as consumers rejected the searingly acidic, sour-grapefruit flavours these wines possessed. The compromise style was *Halbtrocken* - half-dry, or off-dry.

Riesling always gives a high-acid wine, which is perhaps best balanced in Germany by some level of natural sweetness, so that even those at the lower end of the classification have a softening edge on them, akin to sprinkling a grapefruit with at least a pinch of sugar. In warmer climes, there is enough ripeness and

The Riesling (right) is a hardy, frost-resistant vine, which makes it ideal for the cool vineyards of northern Europe. Riesling can produce long-lived wines of intense aroma and character, ranging in style from bone-dry to lusciously sweet.

ORIGINS
Germany.

WHERE ELSE IS IT GROWN?
Alsace. Australia and New Zealand. Austria and northern Italy. Some in the United States and Canada.

TASTING NOTES
Nearly always has both the scent and taste of fresh lime, whether bitter zests or sweetened juice. Riper German ones can have softer fruit like ripe peach or apricot, as well as a gentle floral aroma. In Alsace, there is a very austere mineral quality in the wines and a texture on the palate like sharpened steel. The whiff of petrol (or gasoline) flowing from the pump generally comes with age, although some Australian wines can display it quite young.

alcohol to offset the high acidity, so that the wines feel perfectly balanced when fully dry.

This is the case in both Alsace and Australia, where the vine is as highly prized as it is in Germany. One useful attribute of pronounced acidity is ageing potential, and even the lightest German Rieslings have the capacity to keep well and improve for many years, their first flush of tart citric fruit turning into an extraordinary, and powerfully spellbinding, pungency that has classically (and accurately) been compared to the heady fume of petrol before combustion.

Germany

Riesling is grown in nearly all of the wine regions of Germany, although it is by no means the most widely planted variety. It is in many ways particularly well suited to the cold climates it encounters there, because the tough stems of its vines enable them to cope with the worst the winters can throw at them.

The drawback comes at the other end of the annual cycle, when ripening the grapes is something of a gamble against the elements. Picked too early, Riesling can be full of hard, unripe acidity. Waiting for the right levels of ripeness can often mean leaving the bunches hanging into November, when French growers have long since picked, pressed and fermented, and when the weather is so bitter that it can be hard to get a natural fermentation going.

With all that in mind, much effort and funding has gone into crossing Riesling with other German varieties, or producing crosses with no Riesling in them, and then crossing the crosses with Riesling and others. The aim has been to

The famous steep vineyards of the Mosel region (below) where the Riesling vines tumble down towards the Mosel river. Such steep sites means hand-picking is the only option at harvest-time.

try to perfect a grape that will give the fresh fruit flavours of Riesling, as well as its invaluable susceptibility to botrytis, but with a more reliable ripening pattern. A handful of these have yielded goodish results, but no one seriously believes they can take the place of Riesling as Germany's premier performer.

The top classification for German wines, their equivalent of the French *appellation contrôlée*, is *Qualitätswein mit Prädikat* or QmP (literally quality wine with distinction). Within this class, there are five types of wine, measured according to the amount of sweetness in them. In ascending order, they are: *Kabinett, Spätlese, Auslese, Beerenauslese* and *Trockenbeeren-auslese*. The "-lese" means "picked", and the time of picking is indicated in the prefix, from Spätlese (late-picked, ie. just after the normal harvesting time) to Trockenbeerenauslese or TBA (meaning berries picked outside or after the main harvest that are dried and shrivelled with sugar-concentrating rot).

Any of the first three styles may be fermented out to total dryness to become Trocken (dry) wines, or halfway in the case of Halbtrocken. Some super-sweet berries are left on the vines until nearer Christmas, in some vintages even into the New Year, and are picked at the crack of dawn when they are frozen solid. During the pressing, some of the crystals of ice that represent the water content of the grapes are removed and the very sweet juice that hasn't frozen is then fermented. This style is known, for obvious reasons, as *Eiswein*.

The fullest, most concentrated Rieslings have traditionally come from the Rheingau, where there is more of this grape planted than any of Germany's other varieties. It is also where the best producers make wines that are as expressive of their particular vineyard locations as any Burgundy *grand cru*.

History insists that the Rheingau was the region where the first noble-rotted wines were accidentally produced, years before the technique was exported to Sauternes. A non-Trocken Riesling from the Rheingau is generally around 10 per cent alcohol, quite heady in German terms, and

there is a rounded, often honeyed feel to the best of them. Leading estates are Schloss Johannisberg, Balthasar Ress and Robert Weil.

To the west of the Rheingau, the Nahe also has a preponderance of Riesling, although here it is a more recent development as a result of the region's standing having risen considerably in the last few years. Anheuser is one of the growers' names on everybody's lips.

The other two neighbouring Rhine regions are Rheinhessen and Pfalz (the latter originally known in English as the Palatinate). Riesling has made great strides in the Pfalz. The stars of the show are the wines of Müller-Catoir, where an almost tropical intensity is the house style. Lingenfelder's offerings are in the more delicate, traditional style, but quite as accomplished.

To the northwest, and centred on the city of Trier, the Mosel-Saar-Ruwer region produces the lightest, most exquisitely subtle and refined versions of Riesling anywhere in the world. Alcohol levels may be as low as 7 per cent, and the aromatic profile of the wines so astonishingly rarefied that a sniff at the glass can be like breathing in pure mountain air. The vineyards are planted on vertiginously steep slopes on either side of the river, so any thought of harvesting by machines is out of the question. Fritz Haag, Dr. Loosen and J. J. Prüm are among the finest winemakers of the Mosel.

Vineyards looking down to the village of Ungstein, in the Pfalz region of Germany (above). The traditional style of Riesling wines here is both aromatic and tremendously delicate.

Schloss Johannisberg, looking down over its Riesling vineyards (left), in the Rheingau. Rheingau Rieslings are traditionally the fullest, most concentrated in style.

Alsace

The 15th-century church in the midst of vineyards at Hunawihr, Alsace (above).

Those familiar with the wines of Alsace may tend more readily to associate them with the highly perfumed, positively decadent flavours of Gewurztraminer and Pinot Gris than with the steely austerity of Riesling. It is, however, an open secret in the region that Riesling is considered the noblest of them all, partly because the acidity levels it usually attains mean that the resulting wines have a good long life ahead of them. About a fifth of all Alsace vineyard land is planted with this variety, and the total is steadily mounting.

It is in the hilly Haut-Rhin district of Alsace that most of the Riesling is concentrated. The best plots are those that are protected from the wind so that the ripening of the grape is not inhibited, although the climate of this particularly sheltered region is much more benign than German growers have to contend with. Unusually for a fine wine grape, the amount of fruit the vines are permitted to yield under the appellation regulations is quite high, without the wines themselves necessarily lacking anything in intensity.

Most Alsace Riesling is made in an assertively bone-dry style, with quite powerful alcohol and rapier-like acidity. They are the only Alsace wines that are not especially enjoyable if drunk

young, most requiring at least five years to begin to settle down. In their youth, they have a highly strung, quite taut feel on the palate, leavened with some bracing citric fruit, comparable to freshly squeezed lime juice.

In addition to the basic dry wines, there are two designations for sweeter styles. The lighter of the two is *Vendange Tardive* (meaning late harvest); in a warm, late summer the grapes are left on the vines to achieve higher sugar levels that convert to a delicately sweet wine. If conditions are right, ie. damp misty mornings giving way to mild sunny daytime weather, Riesling will botrytise, just as it does in Germany. The hugely concentrated syrupy wines that result are called *Sélection de Grains Nobles* - among the most appealingly balanced nobly-rotted dessert wines in all of France.

Certain of the best vineyard sites in Alsace have been designated *grands crus* since the mid-1980s. Only four of the grapes permitted in Alsace, Riesling included, may be planted in these areas. The wines should have a noticeable extra dimension of intensity in the flavour, and are inevitably sold for higher prices.

Among the foremost producers of Alsace Riesling are Zind-Humbrecht, Hugel, Schlumberger, Trimbach and Louis Sipp.

Steeply shelving vineyards form the backdrop to the typically alsacien *architecture of Trimbach's premises at Ribeauvillé, Alsace (right).*

Other Regions

AUSTRALIA

There was once more Riesling in Australia than there was Chardonnay, which may come as a sobering thought to a wine world obsessed with the sun-drenched oaky flavours of Aussie Chardonnay. Because it needs a certain amount of acidity in order to define its flavours, the variety is much more successful in the cooler areas of the country, such as the Clare Valley of South Australia and parts of Western Australia such as Mount Barker.

The Australian style is richer and fatter than the European models. In youth, they have pungent lemon-and-lime fruit and oily texture. Sometimes, most notably in wines from Clare Valley, they also display those heady petrol fumes that German and Alsace Rieslings only tend to take on with bottle-age. Despite their smoother angles, the most sensitively made Australian Rieslings still show good acid balance to maintain that sense of freshness without which Riesling wines are lost.

Because they used to call their Semillon grapes Hunter Riesling, there was once a risk of some confusion in Australian consumers' minds about the identity of the true Riesling. This is why some of the wines are still labelled Rhine Riesling, but that doesn't mean to say that those labelled simply "Riesling" are not the real thing: they are.

Among the top producers of Australian Riesling are Tim Knappstein, Tim Adams, Petaluma, Hill-Smith and Frankland Estate.

Harvesting Riesling grapes in the depths of winter, (above) in Ontario, Canada. The frozen grapes are destined for Canada's fabled Ice Wine.

NEW ZEALAND

Across the Tasman Sea, New Zealand's cooler climes should be ideally suited to the production of good dry Riesling. In fact, there was a tendency until fairly recently to make an indeterminate medium-dry sort of wine. The South Island has since led the way in producing fresh, clean, impeccably lime-flavoured Rieslings of great promise. Redwood Valley in Nelson and Wairarapa's Martinborough Vineyards, in the north of South Island, are two of the outstanding examples. When vintage conditions permit, many producers also make a botrytised Riesling (as they do in Australia).

UNITED STATES

Cooler parts of California and particularly Washington State have seen tentative plantings of Riesling, but it is fair to say the grape has not so far proved the hottest property commercially in the USA. The Kiona winery in Washington makes an excellent late-picked Riesling. Further north, in Canada, Riesling is turning out some convincing wines in the province of Ontario. Some of Canada's fabled Ice Wines use Riesling; the top ones can challenge the best of German Eiswein.

Checking the progress of bunches of ripening Riesling (left), in South Australia's Clare Valley, one of the grape's best growing areas.

MERLOT

Historically used in the blended reds of Bordeaux, Merlot's fame is founded on its partnership with Cabernet Sauvignon. Its reputation as a solo performer has been earned more recently.

FOR WINEMAKERS all over the world, Merlot is the significant other of Cabernet Sauvignon, its best blending friend and truest partner. Whereas Cabernet, rightly or wrongly, came to be seen as capable of performing in its own right, Merlot was not generally thought to have the wherewithal to produce great things alone - at least not at first.

Merlot may have been used alone for industrial quantities of everyday quaffing wine in the northern half of Italy, but in its homeland of Bordeaux, where it made its name, the red wines are always blended.

In Bordeaux, Merlot is considered very much the junior partner. This is because the five levels of *crus classés* that constitute Bordeaux's aristocracy are concentrated on the left bank - the Cabernet Sauvignon side - of the Gironde, in Médoc (and at Château Haut-Brion, lower down in Cabernet-dominated Graves). In fact, there is far more Merlot planted than there is Cabernet, largely because it plays a significant part in the red wines made in the less illustrious parts of the region.

But Merlot does have a starring role to play in Bordeaux, in the two best areas of the right bank, Pomerol and St-Emilion. Although Pomerol and St-Emilion were both left out of the celebrated 1855 classification that created the *crus classés*, they too have their famous names and their own individual styles. Some Pomerol properties use virtually all Merlot in their reds; the leader of the pack, Château Pétrus, is all Merlot down to the last five per cent, which is accounted for by the less widespread Cabernet Franc. Since no red wine in Bordeaux commands anything like the stratospheric price of Pétrus, it is clear that Merlot has no need to hide its light under a bushel of Cabernet Sauvignon.

In fact, as in most regions where the foremost wines are blends of two or more grape varieties, Bordeaux growers mix and match their propor-

The plump, blue Merlot (right), an early-ripening grape, produces soft, rich wines - often described as "fleshy" - that harmonise well with the more structured Cabernet Sauvignon.

tions of Cabernet, Merlot and the others, according to what nature has bequeathed them that year in the way of vintage conditions. Merlot tends to ripen a little earlier than Cabernet, so if late rain or a sudden cool snap at the end of the growing season spoils the chances of great Cabernet, at least there may have been some good-quality Merlot to draw on.

Even in the better years, Merlot can often produce healthier, more concentrated grapes than its colleague, the fine vintage of 1990 being a notable example.

Stylistically, what Merlot does for Cabernet in the wines of the Médoc is to smooth away some of its harder edges. Since Merlot is a thinner-skinned variety than Cabernet, it produces a less tannic wine, thus mitigating some of the astringency of prickly young Cabernet. (It may also, for the same reason, lighten the colour of the wine.) A claret that uses, say, 35 per cent Merlot will have a noticeably softer feel than one where it is limited to a mere 10 per cent.

Outside Bordeaux, Merlot really started to branch out on its own during the 1980s in California. Varietal Merlot had been produced in California before this, but the tendency was towards inky, fierce and tannic wines - not a mode that Merlot takes to particularly well. In the latter half of the '80s, the style began to change and a kinder, gentler Merlot emerged that has found great favour with consumers looking for a softer type of red for everyday drinking. West Coast Merlot-mania is such that plantings of the grape in California increased fivefold in the decade from the mid-'80s to the mid-'90s, and are still on the increase.

Growers in Washington State have also discovered that their climate is rather good at producing the kind of concentrated but velvet-soft red that newcomers to red wine especially appreciate. In the USA, at least, Merlot is a grape whose time has come.

In the southern hemisphere, it is only lately beginning to gain ground in the same way. Argentina has a fair amount of Merlot planted, and more Chilean winemakers are now producing it as a varietal wine. In Australia and New Zealand, it has so far been seen mainly as a blending partner for Cabernet à la Bordeaux, but there are signs that solo Merlot is finding its feet.

FRENCH ORIGINS
Bordeaux, especially the Libournais on the right bank of the Gironde, which includes St-Emilion and Pomerol.

WHERE ELSE IS IT GROWN?
Throughout central and eastern Europe, from Switzerland to Bulgaria. United States. Argentina. Some in Chile, Australia, New Zealand, South Africa.

TASTING NOTES
At its ripest, soft purple fruits such as blackberries and black plums. In cooler climates, it can have a distinct vegetal streak in it, like green beans or asparagus. If the sun gets to it, there may be a suggestion of dried fruit such as raisins or even fruitcake. Rounded out with oak in the best wines of Pomerol and California, it can also take on a textural richness that has overtones of melted chocolate or possibly Turkish Delight.

France

The fairy-tale Château Ausone (above), in St-Emilion, set amid its vines.

The legendary Château Pétrus, Pomerol (below). Oil burners are still used in the vineyards as late as May to protect the early-ripening Merlot from frost damage.

Merlot's French fiefdom is on the right bank in Bordeaux. There it dominates the communes of Pomerol and St-Emilion. While red wines from the latter district are characteristically composed of around two-thirds Merlot with perhaps just a splash of Cabernet Sauvignon, in Pomerol the percentage may be more like nine-tenths Merlot, with no Cabernet Sauvignon at all.

Differences in character between the two communes are fairly subtle, but the top wines of Pomerol tend to have a seriousness and austerity about them, together with something of the dry, herbal flavour found in left-bank Cabernet. St-Emilion wines, on the other hand, for all that there may be less Merlot in them, are often softer and more approachable in their youth. Despite the popular assumption that Merlot-based wines mature more quickly than those dominated by Cabernet Sauvignon, St-Emilions and Pomerols can be quite as long-lived as the finest offerings of the Médoc.

In 1955, on the 100th anniversary of the Bordeaux classification system, St-Emilion endowed itself with a similar league table of quality. In contrast to the entrenched immutability of the left bank, however, the proprietors of St-Emilion undertook to update their classification every ten years. There may be little change from decade to decade, but perhaps that is precisely because they know their wines will be

rigorously re-assessed, and so the motivation to maintain standards is acutely compelling. Top spot is shared deservedly by two châteaux: Cheval Blanc and Ausone.

Alone among the premier communes of Bordeaux, Pomerol has never been subjected to the trials of classification, and there are no plans to do so. After the legendary Pétrus, its other high-performance names include Châteaux le Gay, Trotanoy, l'Evangile, le Bon Pasteur, Vieux-Château-Certan and Clos l'Eglise.

Less illustrious Merlot-based wines come from the "satellite" areas of St-Emilion, a group of small communes that form a northeasterly fringe to St-Emilion itself and are all allowed to append its name to their own - Montagne, Lussac, Puisseguin, St-Georges. In good vintages, when the grander properties can fetch dizzyingly high prices for their wines, some of these satellite wines can represent exemplary value. Bel-Air, in Puisseguin, and Lyonnat, in Lussac, are but two good examples.

Elsewhere, Merlot has made great inroads among the varietal wines being produced in the Languedoc under the catch-all Vin de Pays d'Oc designation, and it also has a part to play in some of the traditional appellations of the southwest. In Cahors, for example, it performs its time-honoured role, tempering the sterner attributes of the Auxerrois and Tannat grapes.

Rest of the World

UNITED STATES

Merlot is the red wine of choice for those California and Washington wine-drinkers who want the richness and structure of a good red, without having to age it until it is soft enough to drink. In that respect, it's very much Cabernet without tears. For once, fashion has proven a beneficial influence, because the Merlot craze has led many winemakers to look again at the most suitable ways of vinifying the grape. The benchmark style is now ripe red fruit with a lick of sweet oak and gentle tannins.

Good Merlots come from Duckhorn, Murphy-Goode, Ravenswood and Newton in California, and Chateau Ste Michelle and Hogue Cellars in Washington State.

ITALY

It's fair to say that Merlot does not enjoy a particularly exalted reputation in Italy, although large swathes of its wine industry - especially in the northeastern areas of the Veneto, Friuli and Piave - would be lost without it. The tendency is to make a light-toned, juicy red from it, such as the classic lunchtime thirst-quenchers served by the carafe in *trattorie*. In hotter years and from producers prepared to limit their yields, however, there can be a little meaty complexity to the wines.

In the hotbed of viticultural experimentation that is Tuscany, one or two of the smart operators are achieving fine results with Merlot. Producers such as Lodovico Antinori, with his varietal Merlot, Masseto, are showing that the variety can make full-blooded, age-worthy wines that are the equals of the monumental Cabernet and Sangiovese super-Tuscans that attracted all the attention in the 1980s.

SOUTHERN HEMISPHERE

Australia and New Zealand are only really starting out in the varietal Merlot stakes. The custom has been to blend it with Cabernet, although in Australia Shiraz is, as we have seen, the preferred partner to Cabernet. Delegats and Corbans are among those producing New Zealand's more characterful showings.

In South Africa again, the grape is mostly seen as a constituent of the classic Bordeaux blend, but the Fairview, Glen Carlou and Zonnebloem estates have all produced good varietal Merlots.

Merlot is the most widely planted red grape variety in Romania (left), making soft, easy-drinking reds.

The grape is gaining ground similarly in South America, particularly in Argentina, where it occupies the same extent of vineyard area as Cabernet. Chilean Merlot is now responsible for wines of stunning potential, probably even more so than Cabernet.

EASTERN EUROPE

Merlot was one of the mainstays of the Bulgarian wine revolution, and Reserve bottlings of it were (and are) often more pleasingly balanced wines than that country's Cabernets. In Romania, it turns out to be the most widely planted red grape, where it is responsible for many good, soft reds at keenly competitive prices.

Barrel cellars at Lodovico Antinori (below), Tuscany. Antinori is one of the band of top Tuscan producers creating stunning varietal Merlots.

CHENIN BLANC

Chenin Blanc's wide stylistic repertoire has made it the focal grape variety in the central vineyards of the Loire valley. Put through its paces in Vouvray, it runs the gamut of dry to sweet, and sparkling, wines.

PERHAPS THE most misunderstood of all the noble grape varieties, Chenin Blanc is the backbone of white winemaking in the Loire valley. While it undoubtedly has a very distinct and instantly recognisable profile in the wines it can produce, it has experienced difficulties in making friends among consumers for at least two reasons.

One is that, like Riesling, it has a wide stylistic repertoire, ranging all the way from the uncompromisingly bone-dry to luxurious botrytised dessert wines with decades of ageing potential. Nothing wrong with that, except that, in the past, the labelling on Chenin wines from the Loire has been low on information about the style of the wine.

The other hurdle for newcomers to clear is that the drier wines are not over-endowed with the sort of immediately obvious commercial appeal found in crisp, young fruit-filled Sauvignon Blanc. There is an aromatic character to Chenin, but after an initial burst of youthful fruit it turns into something quite different: a strange mixture of polished steel, old honey and damp. The classic tasting description often heard is "wet wool". Add to that the fact that Chenin is nearly always loaded with teeth-grinding acidity, and it is easier to understand why this is not a grape likely to be top of anyone's list of all-time favourites.

Learning to appreciate Chenin requires a slightly more precise knowledge of when to drink the different styles of wines than is the case with most other white wine varieties.

In the Loire, Vouvray is the most important appellation for Chenin. Its wines span the spectrum from dry to sweet, as well as a sparkling wine made by the champagne-method. The dry wines, increasingly labelled *sec* these days, can be delicious immediately on release, when they can display exhilarating fruit flavours, and that boldly assertive acid acts as a seasoning in the way that lemon juice does in a fruit purée. After a year, they seem to lose that fruit and slump into a prolonged sulk; tasted again at five or six years old, they have developed a honeyed softness that throws that dryness into relief.

In a hotter vintage, the winemaker may choose to leave some of the ripe natural sugars of the grape in the finished wine. This off-dry or medium-dry style is usually labelled *demi-sec*. It can be the most supremely refreshing example of its kind to be found anywhere in France. The delicate note of lingering sweetness tenderises the prickly acids in a hugely appetising way.

If the grapes reach a level of sticky-sweet overripeness that the French call *surmaturité*, then the resulting wine is known as *moelleux*. These are not quite the richest dessert wines - they still have that spiky streak of acidity running through the middle of them - but they do have a good coating of honey and caramel.

In years when botrytis has freely developed, some producers may make a fully botrytised wine. This will often be entitled *Sélection* because it involves selecting only the most extensively shrivelled berries from the vine, for maximum impact. Even then, the layers of concentrated sweetness have a discernible tartness at the centre, so that the overall effect is more toffee-apple than *crème brûlée*.

Elsewhere in the world, Chenin's malleability has made it something of a workhorse grape. That is certainly the case in the hotter regions of the United States and Australia, where its most widespread use has been as blending fodder, to add a tingle of acid and prevent basic white wines from tasting flabby. It is very extensively planted in South Africa, where it more often than not goes under the alias of Steen. While a lot of it inevitably disappears into the blending vats, some at least is turned into perfectly agreeable, fresh, simple whites of almost miraculous crispness given the warm climate.

Grapes with naturally high acidity are often a good bet for the production of champagne-method sparkling wine, where a thin, relatively neutral base wine gives the best results. In the Loire, there is, of course, Vouvray; Saumur is also a good source of such fizz, as is the wider regional appellation of Crémant de Loire.

Chenin Blanc (right) is a high-acid grape that favours the cooler climates of the Loire valley. Here, its acidity and susceptibility to botrytis are its keys to success, making fine sparkling wine and exquisite sweet wines that retain a thread of refreshing sharpness.

FRENCH ORIGINS

The central Loire valley - Anjou-Saumur and Touraine.

WHERE ELSE IS IT GROWN?

South Africa. Also California, Australia, New Zealand, and a little in Argentina.

TASTING NOTES

When young and dry, tart green apple and pear, occasionally something a little more exotic (passion fruit) in a good year. Mineral, even metallic, hardness on the palate, though often with paradoxical underlying hint of honey. Can have a dry nuttiness (walnuts) and an indeterminately damp smell, like old newspaper or wet woollens. Sweeter styles get progressively more honeyed without losing the tingly, appley acidity woven through them.

Loire

Despite its appearance in many areas outside Europe, no region makes more of Chenin Blanc than does the Loire. It is the most important white grape variety in the two central parts of the valley - Anjou-Saumur to the west, and Touraine in the east.

In Anjou, particularly, cultivating Chenin is something of a challenge. So far north, the grape is a notoriously slow ripener and, as summers in these parts are not exactly torrid, a lot of Anjou Chenin is very acerbic and raw-tasting - not at all a style that would find many imitators beyond France's borders. Then again, that is exactly how the locals like it.

Autumns, though, are damp and warm enough to permit the regular development of the noble rot botrytis. It is in Anjou that the premier appellations for botrytised Chenin are found: Coteaux du Layon, which encircles the tiny and

An unusually fine summer's day blazes down on the Chenin vines in the tiny AC of Bonnezeaux in Anjou (below), where some of the Loire's finest botrytised Chenins are produced.

very fine enclave of Bonnezeaux (an AC in its own right), and Quarts de Chaume. In the best years these wines are fully the equal of great Sauternes and Barsac because they have that nerve-centre of acidity that keeps them going into a well-balanced old age. Château du Breuil and Domaine de la Soucherie (Coteaux du Layon), Angeli (Bonnezeaux) and Baumard (Quarts de Chaume) are among the truly outstanding names.

The lesser-known appellation of Coteaux de l'Aubance makes some reasonably good, though much less rich, sweet wines.

In the west of Anjou is Savennières, the appellation that many consider to be the highest expression of dry Chenin anywhere in the wine world. In their first flush of youth, the wines make no concession to drinkability, tasting hard as nails and tightly clenched. Over maybe seven or eight years, they open out into an austere but profoundly beautiful maturity, full of minerals, bitter apples and bracing Atlantic fresh air. The word "racy" when applied to wine might have been coined just for Savennières. Domaine de la Bizolière, Baumard, and especially Joly at Coulée-de-Serrant (a single-ownership estate that has its own AC) are the names to conjure with.

Travelling eastwards into Saumur, we enter fizz territory. Sparkling Saumur is made by fermenting the wine a second time in the bottle to produce carbon dioxide, exactly as in champagne. Made only, or almost entirely, from Chenin, it usually has quite a snap to it, and is dead dry. Gratien & Meyer make a very typical one.

In Touraine, the most important appellation of all for Chenin Blanc is Vouvray. Together with its lesser-known and less distinguished neighbour to the south, Montlouis, Vouvray puts the Chenin through its paces, making it dry, *demi-sec, moelleux*, botrytised and fizzy. Quality is highly variable, and the wines - as elsewhere - are very vintage-dependent, but when it shines, it really shines.

The best growers in Vouvray, whose wines constitute an invaluable introduction to this underestimated grape, are Poniatowski, Champalou, Fouquet's Domaine des Aubuisières, Château Gaudrelle and Huët. The last makes a superbly rich and complex sparkling Vouvray that is probably the finest French fizz outside the Champagne region.

Other Regions

SOUTH AFRICA

Chenin, or Steen as it is more often termed, is put to the same sort of versatile use in South Africa as it is in the Loire. It is even used in some of the monumental fortified wines for which the Cape was once justly famous.

The difference is that the drier styles don't tend to be that remarkable. There is no South African Savennières to help the grape shine. Occasionally, they can fill the mouth with a gum-cleansing feel that's like biting into a just-picked apple, but they don't seem to have the sharper aromatic definition produced by the cool northerly climate of the Loire.

Much better wines are made from nobly-rotted Chenin, when the flavours of tropical fruit, honey, bitter orange peel and barley-sugar all seem to mingle in some of the world's most diverting sweet wines. Fleur du Cap Noble Late Harvest is a good, and very fairly priced, example of this style. Nederburg Edelkeur is perhaps more complex, but at around twice the price.

AUSTRALIA AND NEW ZEALAND

Not many other non-European producers have taken Chenin seriously yet as the base for a varietal wine. There is a tendency to make it too rich for its own good. In Western Australia, a plump, oak-enriched example is made by Moondah Brook in the sweltering Swan Valley. The cooler climate of New Zealand is a more likely setting for successful Chenins, although Collards Chenin Blanc from New Zealand is similarly high in extract to the Moondah Brook.

CALIFORNIA

One or two California wineries have produced successful varietal dry Chenin, some of it oak-aged. Those from Folie-à-Deux in the Napa, and Hacienda in Sonoma, are both good, but the bulk of the Chenin crop elsewhere goes into everyday blended whites to give added acidity.

Chenin Blanc, or Steen vines on the Klein Constantia Estate, South Africa (above). Chenin has been the backbone of the country's white wine production.

Widely spaced Chenin Blanc vines in the Temecula valley, California (left), where the variety is still a minority taste.

GRENACHE

Established as a vital ingredient to spice up the famous wines of Rioja and Château-neuf-du-Pape, the much-travelled, overworked Grenache is quietly developing a fashionable status. Discerning winemakers have recognised its worth as a varietal.

SEASONED WINE experts may raise a collective eyebrow at finding Grenache has claimed a place in my pantheon of great grapes. It is extensively planted around the world, to be sure, far more than any other variety we have met so far, but just because of that much-travelled, overworked reputation it is normally only accorded a fairly lowly status in the wine-drinker's league table. I say it is time to update that view.

As befits a grape that has been around quite a while, Grenache can turn its hand to almost any style of red wine, from darkly brooding behemoths, thundering with tannin, through sleek, svelte, spicy young things, to light-footed strawberry numbers with more than a dab of sweet oak scent. It's also quite good at fruity rosé.

There is some dispute as to precisely where the grape originated but, despite its common name, it isn't a native of France. It came to southern France from Spain, which is still its most likely provenance and where it goes by the name of Garnacha. Its pre-eminent role, in both countries, is as a versatile mixer, but it possesses enough innate character to play the lead in many a red blend.

Two historically renowned wines - Rioja from Castile, and France's very first *appellation contrôlée*, Châteauneuf-du-Pape, in the southern Rhône - would be nothing without Grenache, and its influence extends way beyond the confines of those two areas.

In Spain, its principal blending partner is the celebrated home-grown variety, Tempranillo. Experiments with unblended Tempranillo have often foundered for lack of the spicy depth of flavour that Garnacha can impart. Not just Rioja, but its neighbour Navarra to the east, Penedés in Catalonia and the huge central Spanish plain of La Mancha all rely on Garnacha to greater or lesser degrees. In the currently fashionable Ribera del Duero, it makes cherry-fruited rosé (or, properly, *rosado*) wines.

Grenache made its way into southern France sometime after the 13th century, when the Aragon kingdom expanded into Roussillon over the Pyrenees. From there, it spread northeastwards into Languedoc and then to the southern part of the Rhône valley. As it travelled, Grenache found itself bedding down with traditional French grapes such as Syrah, Carignan, Cinsaut and Mourvèdre. That assemblage now represents the bedrock of red wines made anywhere from Côtes du Roussillon, up through Fitou, Corbières and Minervois, the pays de l'Hérault and into the Côtes du Rhône backwaters.

At its most exalted, Grenache plays an integral part in the Rhône appellations of Châteauneuf-du-Pape and Gigondas. Most Châteauneuf has more Grenache in it than anything else, and the sheer diversity of styles from one producer to the next indicates something of the grape's adaptability.

Not the least reason for its ubiquity in these southern vineyards is that it responds to torrid growing conditions where there is little rainfall. It ripens without fuss, and can effortlessly attain sufficient natural sugar to give high alcohol: 14 per cent is quite the norm in Gigondas. In particularly ripe vintages, it also exhibits more than a little of the black-pepper aromatics traditionally associated with Syrah.

Down in the southwest of the central-southern swathe of France known as the Midi, Grenache pulls off some extraordinary tricks in the *vins doux naturels* of Roussillon. Here it is made into a sweet red wine by essentially the same method as port - that is, stopping the fermentation halfway through by adding spirit. This incapacitates the yeasts and results in a strong, soupy red with some of its natural sugar left unfermented.

Rivesaltes, Maury and the coastal appellation of Banyuls are the key areas for these rather rare wines; Rasteau in the southern Rhône makes something similar.

Outside Europe, Grenache is rapidly gaining ground as a constituent of the Rhône-style blends attracting attention in California, and as a densely concentrated varietal wine in Australia.

Grenache (right) is a hardy vine that thrives in hot, dry conditions. It produces good alcohol and plenty of spicy, rich fruit that makes it the ideal backbone to many red blends.

ORIGINS
Almost certainly Spain. (A Sardinian theory has its adherents, mostly in Sardinia.)

WHERE ELSE IS IT GROWN?
Throughout the Midi, southern Rhône and Provence. California, Australia, northwest Africa.

TASTING NOTES
Usually marries a lightish red fruit - redcurrants, strawberries, raspberries, morello cherries - to a spiciness like black pepper or, quite often, ground ginger. Sometimes a floral violet-like note as well. In its fiercest manifestations in the hotter parts of Australia, it can be tarry, chocolatey, liquoricey, like the most concentrated Shiraz, often supported by a distinct sweetness, so that the wines imitate the structure of vintage port.

France

The typical stony soils of the southern Rhône (above). On such poor soils, Grenache can yield crimson-coloured reds with spicy depth of flavour.

In Châteauneuf-du-Pape (below) the "galets" - large stones - that cover the soil retain heat at night and encourage the Grenache to ripen fully.

Travelling southwards through France, you will find Grenache first raising its head in the southern stretches of the Rhône valley, south of the town of Montélimar. Although other grape varieties - Cinsaut, Mourvèdre, Carignan, as well as the Syrah of the northern Rhône - play significant parts in the blended red wines from here on down, Grenache is so often the dominant partner that anybody who develops a taste for these wines has by definition developed a taste for Grenache.

Châteauneuf-du-Pape, the most famous name around these parts, is a confusing appellation to understand as far as its red wines are concerned. The chances are that most commercial Châteauneuf is not really made in the style that the textbooks tell you to expect. Big and beefy, massively structured, with galumphing tannins to ensure long life - that's the theory. In fact, much of the wine is made in a considerably more delicate style than that, with gentle red fruit, satiny lightness of texture and minimal tannic extraction. As such, these are wines that can be drunk at two or three years old - far sooner than the northern Rhône reds - and can fall apart if kept too long.

Domaine Père Caboche offers a textbook example of the lighter, fruitier style. Those in search of the bigger style, full of meaty richness, should seek out the wines of Château

Rayas, Chante-Cigale, Château de Beaucastel, Château St-André or Domaine du Grand Tinel.

The wines of Gigondas to the northeast should satisfy the most diehard devotees of big and burly reds. They are almost invariably hugely alcoholic and rigid with tannin, and seem to demand the sort of ageing that Hermitage requires, although you won't find anything like the same amount of fruit. Domaine de St-Gayan and Château de Montmirail are the stars. The latter also makes fine Vacqueyras, a good appellation that is one of the newer southern Rhône ACs.

Lirac, on the opposite side of the river Rhône to Châteauneuf, is an unfairly overlooked appellation that offers some pedigree reds from the likes of Domaine les Garrigues. Just south of Lirac is Tavel, which makes rosé wines only, again predominantly Grenache. Don't think of these as frivolous pink sippers for summer; they are pale in colour (often the shade of a faintly yellowed onion-skin) and loaded with alcohol. They can also reputedly age well, if ten-year-old rosé is your bag.

The preponderance of southern Rhône production is accounted for by Côtes du Rhône, a catchall appellation that extends through the whole Rhône valley, from north to south. It may include Syrah-dominated reds from the north, like the celebrated bottling from Guigal, to inoffensive house-red styles from any number of small growers, négociants and co-operatives. Of the various satellite areas, Côtes du Ventoux is a more reliable proposition than Côtes du Rhône, with the wines of Jaboulet and La Vieille Ferme showing plenty of spicy complexity in most years.

In the Midi, Grenache dominates most of the traditional appellations. Corbières, Minervois, Fitou, Faugères - these were once bywords for rough-and-ready red slosh. The widespread improvements in winemaking technology (not all of them home-grown, it has to be said) have brought with them a consequent upswing in quality with the result that these wines, Corbières especially, are now rivalling the best of the Rhône for character and ageability.

La Voulte-Gasparets and Château Les Ollieux in Corbières, Ste-Eulalie in Minervois and Mont Tauch in Fitou are the names to convince the cynics.

Other Regions

SPAIN

Garnacha crops up all over the northern half of Spain and in the flat, arid centre. It is used to add depth to the more refined Tempranillo in the reds of Rioja and Navarra. In the large southeastern portion of Rioja known as the Rioja Baja, it is particularly widely grown, to the extent that some varietal Garnacha is bottled here. Rosados, the Spanish name for rosé wines, are usually likely to be partly or wholly Garnacha. Many can be rather rustic, but very young ones can possess an appealing strawberry freshness.

In the Catalan region of Penedés, the cele-brated house of Torres makes a Garnacha-based red, Gran Sangredetoro, that is supple and rich, and usually has an appetising, slightly singed flavour, like spit-roasted meat. At the peak of achievement in Spanish Garnacha, though, sit the wines of Priorato, also in Catalonia but situ-ated further west. These are densely textured, inky, fiery reds with colossal alcohol and struc-ture (the regulations stipulate minimum alcohol of 13.75 per cent, higher than any other denom-inated table wine). If you're feeling brave, try the wines of Scala Dei.

AUSTRALIA

Talking of massively structured Grenache, some of Australia's growers are beginning to capitalise on the willingness of the grape to give big alcohol and strong colour in hot climates. They are making some of the most dramatic, muscle-bound reds the variety has yet produced. Rockford and Charles Melton in the Barossa produce some fine examples, the latter naming his Grenache-based blend "Nine Popes", in garbled homage to the name of Châteauneuf-du-Pape.

CALIFORNIA

The Rhône Rangers, that single-minded band of California growers inspired by the wines of the Rhône valley, have nearly all planted some Grenache, although as yet it is very much playing second fiddle to Syrah. The Bonny Doon winery in Santa Cruz has been the lead-ing light in this movement: its Clos de Gilroy is a fine varietal Grenache, while British consumers have for some years been able to enjoy a special ultra-peppery cuvée of Grenache called The Catalyst. The ability of the grape to produce fine rosé wines is ably demonstrated by La Rosé Sauvage from the Edmunds St. John winery in Alameda, just inland from San Francisco Bay.

The hilltop town of Laguardia in Rioja (above), with the Sierra de Cantabria towering behind. Grenache is an important ingredient in the historic reds of Rioja.

The hot climate of South Australia's Barossa Valley (left) is ideal for producing some of the world's most powerful Grenaches. These vines were planted in 1936.

GEWURZTRAMINER

Unique among the white varieties, Gewürztraminer is very much a love-it-or-hate-it grape. Once tasted, never forgotten, its ostentatious, scented, rich character has made it the grape forever associated with Alsace.

WHETHER YOU enjoy it or not, your first taste of Gewürztraminer will certainly make an impression. While a simple Chardonnay may seem shy and retiring in the glass, Gewürz comes screaming out at you with some of the most unearthly and downright bizarre scents and flavours to be found anywhere in the world of wine. So strange can it taste that those encountering it unsuspectingly for the first time may wonder whether it has had some other flavouring added to it.

The parent variety seems to be of north Italian extraction, and was originally known simply as Traminer. Its highly scented offshoot, first identified in the 19th century, took its prefix from the German word for "spiced". By this time the grape had acquired, by natural mutation, a deep pink rather than green skin and had begun to yield an extraordinarily perfumed juice. Popular in Germany, Gewürz was widely planted in Alsace, which was part of Germany on and off for much of its history, though it is now of course incontrovertibly French.

Alsace is now its first home. While there are increasingly impressive examples being produced elsewhere, particularly in Germany, they never quite seem to attain the uninhibited aromatic splendour of the greatest Alsace wines. In an especially ripe year, it may combine musky fruit notes like lychee and squishy apricot, with ginger, cloves, talcum powder and a whole florist's shop of roses, violets and jasmine. It is usually pretty low in acidity, which makes it drinkable quite young, but roaring with alcohol, so that a little - combined with those unsubtle flavours - goes an exhaustingly long way.

Because of its larger-than-life character, Gewürz is constantly in danger of not being taken terribly seriously by those who are used to more restrained flavours in a white wine. In the long, dry summers of Alsace, it ripens to a tremendous richness, which accounts for all that alcohol, but even when fermented up to around

The unmistakable livery of the Gewürztraminer grape (right). Unlike the green or golden colour of its fellow white grapes, Gewürz sports a dusky pink skin - a fitting outer expression of its flowery, highly perfumed character.

the 14-15 per cent levels I have seen on some, it still seems to retain a core of residual sugar that leads a lot of consumers to find it too sweet for a supposedly dry white wine.

Once the taste is acquired, however, it becomes clear that Gewürztraminer is without doubt one of the classic wine grapes. From a *grand cru* vineyard site owned by one of the top producers in Alsace, its peculiar intensity can be a mightily refreshing antidote to the container-loads of tell-'em-apart oaky Chardonnay that the wine market is awash with. The best Gewürzes will age, although they tend to be the ones that have unusually pronounced acidity to begin with, and there are not too many of these. You can bump up acid levels by picking the grapes earlier, but the less ripe they are, the less of that striking flavour you will obtain.

The dilemma over picking times is problem enough in Alsace. In warmer climates, it becomes a complete headache. Pick it too early, and you lose some of the flavour concentration that consumers expect to find in bottles labelled Gewürz; leave it too long, and it tastes unfocused and muddy. The difficulties of timing it right are largely why most efforts outside Alsace have so far failed to match the quality of the best wines produced in this little enclave of northeast France.

That said, some German growers are beginning to achieve convincing results with the variety, especially in the slightly warmer areas of the Pfalz and Baden. New Zealand is giving it its best shot, and there are isolated stars in South Africa and Chile.

For a grape that seems to be telling the wine-maker that it wants to be sweet, it comes as no surprise to find that many Alsace and German growers make a late-picked Gewürz, delicately flowery Spätlese and Auslese in Germany, and peach-scented Vendange Tardive in Alsace. When conditions are right, the grape can acquire noble rot, and a wine with full-blown botrytis is termed Sélection de Grains Nobles in Alsace. These are massively dense, opulent dessert wines, tasting like orange and ginger marmalade - one of the great taste experiences.

ORIGINS

For the Gewürztraminer specifically, possibly Alsace. For its less intoxicatingly scented forebear, Traminer, probably the south Tyrol area of northern Italy.

WHERE ELSE IS IT GROWN?

Apart from Alsace, it has important bases in Germany and Austria, less so in Spain and eastern Europe. Experimental plantings dotted around the southern hemisphere, and also the United States, particularly the Pacific Northwest.

TASTING NOTES

The list is well-nigh endless. Fruits are usually an eerily precise imitation of ripely juicy lychees, together with overripe peach or nectarine when the flesh is just starting to turn mushy. Some authorities dispute the spice connection evoked in the German word *Gewürz*, but there is nearly always a good sprinkling of ground ginger and often cinnamon, occasionally the scent of whole cloves and even a dusting of white pepper.

Flowers are very much in evidence too - violets and rose-petals (often reminiscent of attar of roses, as in Turkish Delight) - and then there is a whole range of scented bathroom products - aromatic bath salts, perfumed soap, talcum powder. Gewürz from regions other than Alsace may present a toned-down version of all that, which may come as a relief to some.

Alsace

Gewurztraminer (spelt without the *umlaut* in Alsace) accounts for about a fifth of total vineyard plantings in Alsace. It is considered to be one of the golden four varieties (along with Riesling, Pinot Gris and Muscat) that may be planted in those areas designated the *grands crus*. Although Riesling is unofficially thought of as the first among this top division by the growers themselves, Gewurz is cherished for the forthright character that has made it the grape most ineradicably associated in consumers' minds with the region as a whole. Blowsy, spicy, exotic Gewurz just *is* the taste of Alsace.

The grape does exceptionally well on the often rather claggy, clay-based soils found in the Haut-Rhin area of Alsace. Its willingness to ripen well in the generally dry vintages of this very sheltered region allows its personality to shine through in the finished wine. In many ways, it is the antithesis in Alsace of the Riesling we looked at earlier, giving more alcohol

and less acidity, resulting in a considerably more forward style of wine.

Another quality that marks Gewurz wines out from their counterparts is their very deep colour. They usually have a richly burnished golden tone, not dissimilar to the most heavily oaked Chardonnays, a characteristic derived in their case not from the use of wooden barrels but from the distinctive pigmentation of the skin. Whereas most white grape varieties come in conventional shades of green, Gewurz, as befits its gaudy nature, is turned out in a deep pink livery that lends some of its blush to the wine itself. Sometimes you may imagine you can see a faintly pinkish tinge behind the deep yellow.

In the cooler years in Alsace, Gewurztraminer can seem a rather pale imitation of itself, both in terms of colour and flavours. Neither 1991 nor '93 were particularly good, for example, and the wine's resulting balance can be seriously skewed, so that you end up with something

The Clos Windsbuhl vineyard at Hunawihr, owned by Zind-Humbrecht (below). The Gewurztraminer from this site is one of the finest examples of what Alsace Gewurz can achieve.

thick and heavy, but without the depth of flavour to carry it off with any grace.

The classification of the theoretically better hillside sites in Alsace as *grands crus* began in the 1980s. While dogged inevitably by controversy over what should be included and what should not, it is clear that much of the land that has been incorporated is of sufficiently good quality to inspire the producers to their greatest efforts. Some of the best sites for Gewurztraminer are Brand, Goldert, Hengst, Kessler, Sporen, Steinert and Zotzenberg, but there are many more.

Wines with those names on the label are undoubtedly worth the extra cost over a bottle of basic Gewurz. Many producers are in the habit of labelling their wines Cuvée Réserve, supposedly indicating notably successful batches of a particular vintage, but as the term has no legal force, it has inevitably been abused by

some, who get away with labelling their bottom-line productions as Réserve wines.

Co-operatives are an important part of the wine scene in Alsace, and vary enormously in quality. One of the most commercially significant, exporting substantial quantities, is also one of the most reliable - the Caves de Turckheim. Its Gewurztraminer from the Brand *grand cru* is generally intensely concentrated.

Any list of the greatest producers in Alsace invariably begins with Zind-Humbrecht. Its Gewurztraminers - especially the Herrenweg and Clos Windsbuhl bottlings, and some of the sweeter Vendange Tardive wines from *grand cru* sites like Hengst and Goldert - are unutterably exquisite, powerful essences of this most ostentatious grape.

Other good wines come from Hugel, Kuentz-Bas, Trimbach, Ostertag and Schlumberger.

Gewurztraminer grapes left on the vine until November, (above), destined for the peach-scented style of Alsace Vendange Tardive.

Other Regions

GERMANY

Although plantings of this grape in Germany are by no means extensive, some German growers have achieved notable successes with it in the light-textured, low-alcohol styles for which the country is renowned. It fares better in the warmer regions such as Baden, in the south, and the Pfalz, where its best exponent is the estate of Müller-Catoir, whose Gewürzes are full of expressive ripe fruit.

UNITED STATES

As others of the Alsace grape varieties, such as Riesling and Pinot Gris, have thrived in the states of the Pacific Northwest, so Gewürz has also done its bit. Success has come patchily and the results are not as yet much exported. In Washington State, Columbia Winery makes a reasonably tasty example, as does Kiona Winery with its late-harvest version.

NEW ZEALAND AND AUSTRALIA

The cooler climate of New Zealand is better for Gewürz than most of Australia, where the grape has often been used simply as blending material for dry Riesling. The North Island regions of Gisborne and Auckland have produced some convincing attempts, from wineries such as Villa Maria, Matua Valley and Morton Estate.

ELSEWHERE

Although "quiet" is the one epithet you don't expect to apply to this grape, the occasional quietly impressive Gewürz does crop up in other countries. There's Villiera from the South African region of Paarl, and Viña Casablanca from Chile. The Torres estate in Penedés in northeastern Spain successfully blends Gewürz with Muscat to make its Viña Esmeralda.

Matua Valley Winery, set amid its vineyards in the Auckland area of New Zealand's North Island (above). Matua Valley is one of New Zealand's most notable producers of characterful Gewürztraminer.

GAMAY

The one classic grape variety that has stayed close to home, Gamay is synonymous with Beaujolais, that light, fresh, strawberry-fruity red that is designed to be drunk young and lively.

LOOKING AT a map of the world distribution of grape varieties might seem to suggest that Gamay is something of an interloper among this exalted company of 12 noble grapes. A red blob shows a significant concentration of it in eastern France, with only the skimpiest of traces anywhere else. In fact, it gets in because that red blob constitutes one of the world's most individualistic red wine styles - Beaujolais.

Gamay is the only grape used in the making of (red) Beaujolais. Some is also grown further north, in the southern stretch of Burgundy known as the Mâconnais, where it is responsible for usually rather indifferent wines bottled as Mâcon Rouge. Elsewhere in Burgundy, it may be blended in a proportion of up to two-thirds with Pinot Noir to make Bourgogne Passetoutgrains. A fair bit is grown in the Loire valley to the west, some as Gamay de Touraine, some used in Crémant de Loire pink fizz. On the western flank of the central Rhône, in the Coteaux de l'Ardèche, it makes spicy reds to rival the Grenache-based wines of Côtes du Rhône.

It is on the stern, granite hillsides of Beaujolais, however, that the Gamay really comes into its own. In addition to basic Beaujolais and Beaujolais-Villages, there are ten villages that are theoretically capable of making the best wine (known as *cru* Beaujolais), and that are entitled to their own appellations within the region. Running north to south, these are: St-Amour, Juliénas, Chénas, Moulin-à-Vent, Fleurie, Chiroubles, Morgon, Régnié, Brouilly and Côte de Brouilly. The last is a peculiar little hill of blue granite that pops up in the middle of the larger Brouilly appellation.

There are some subtle stylistic differences among these ten, which we shall return to in the regional section on Beaujolais, but what links them is more important than what distinguishes them, and that is the sunny-natured Gamay grape. Gamay offers the lightest style of red

Gamay (right) offers the lightest style of red wine, full of simple strawberry fruit, fresh, sappy acids and very little tannin.

wine possible, full of simple strawberry fruit, fresh sappy acids and little or no tannin. It is meant to be drunk young and lively, not cellared for years like claret. Although the best growers do achieve a certain measure of complexity in their wines, and some of the best *cru* Beaujolais can age well for five or six years, most producers are content to turn out oceans of straightforward quaffing wine that reacts beautifully to chilling for summer drinking.

The light texture of Beaujolais derives from a method of vinification called carbonic maceration that is especially suited to the grape. Instead of pressing the berries in the normal way, which extracts some tannin from the skins and pips along with the juice, Gamay grapes are placed whole into fermenters from which the air has been driven out with carbon dioxide. The juice starts to ferment inside the whole grapes until the skins burst from the build-up of gas within them. The grapes at the bottom of the heap are crushed by the weight of those on top, and ferment in the normal way, but that is still gentler than pressing between metal plates.

Gamay's suitability for producing cheap, early-drinking, featherweight reds is what inspired the Beaujolais Nouveau race, which continues to this day. Those who feel like imbibing quantities of embryonic, just-fermented, acid-tingling red from the very latest vintage can indulge their passion freely in the third week of November.

There is a movement afoot in the region to introduce greater depth into the wines in an attempt to throw the happy-go-lucky, knock-it-back image of Beaujolais into some sort of relief. Some are using a proportion of normally fermented juice in order to introduce a little tannic kick; others are using new oak barrels in a region where such a thing was once anathema. Guy Depardon, in Fleurie, is an example of a producer swimming courageously against the tide. His top *cuvées* have the gingery, brambly concentration of northern Rhône Syrah.

External markets are still dominated by the wines of the powerful bulk producer Georges Duboeuf. For once, quantity does not preclude quality because most of his wines are good. Much debate was occasioned, for example, when Régnié was promoted to become the newest *cru* in 1988, with many commentators wondering whether the region deserved its elevation. Duboeuf is producing about the only one worth drinking so far.

Switzerland uses Gamay extensively, often in blends with Pinot Noir, and there are some producers in California doing their best with it (J. Lohr's Wildflower Gamay is a reasonable approximation of the style of young *cru* Beaujolais.) By and large, however, Gamay doesn't perform well on different soils, and the style of wine it is happiest producing has not been a noticeably fashionable one for red wines in recent years, so there is not the incentive that there is with a variety like Pinot Noir to compete with the best of France.

Misty autumnal scene in Brouilly (left), one of the ten crus of the Beaujolais region.

FRENCH ORIGINS
Beaujolais.

WHERE ELSE IS IT GROWN?
Burgundy, Loire, Rhône. Switzerland and other central European countries. Minute amounts in California.

TASTING NOTES
At its deliriously ripest, fistfuls of pulpy wild strawberries. When very young (as Nouveau, particularly) it can have a synthetic smell like boiled sweets, reinforced by the crunchiness of its acidity in the mouth. That, and related aromas like peardrops, banana flavouring and bubblegum, are all fermentation smells accentuated by the fact that no air gets into it while it is vinifying. Some of the richer, meatier *cru* wines can take on the attributes of mature Pinot Noir after five or six years.

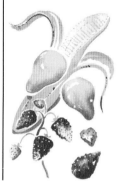

FRANCE

NOTES

NOTES

The Loire valley region is famed for its many riverside châteaux of great opulence, like this one (above) at Azay-le-Rideau on the Indre tributary, southwest of Tours.

France's appellation contrôlée regions (right), from the cool vineyards of Champagne to the hotter regions of the Midi in the south.

Why should we begin with France? More German wine is drunk in many countries than French, although most of that is artificially sweetened Liebfraumilch that the Germans themselves don't want. Is France perhaps the world's largest producer of wine? No, that honour it is – if honour it is – usually goes to Italy, as it has done for a very long time. Does it still make the best wine then? That, of course, has to be a matter for personal judgment, but certainly consumers in many parts of the northern hemisphere have been turning away from French wines in droves and embracing the produce of wine nations like Australia and South Africa as their export sectors have moved into top gear.

So what is it about France that makes it the logical starting-point?

The answer to that comes in two parts. One concerns historical pre-eminence, and the other is about quality control. The viticultural history of France is still the template for premium wine production wherever in the world individual grapegrowers and winemakers are seeking to make great wines - wines that are expressions both of their environments and of the personal passions and philosophies of those who made them. And, in its formulation of the *appellation contrôlée* system, the first of its kind in the world, France's wine industry established the concept of protecting the reputation of its best wines by circumscribing them within tightly drawn regulations.

To take the first of those two aspects, you may well ask - as many winemakers and consumers outside Europe do - why history should be so important. The fact that something was once great doesn't mean we should give it the benefit of the doubt forever more. That of course is true. The Greeks were once dab hands at making wine. It is they, indeed, who can take the credit for introducing vine-growing to France some time around the start of the 6th century BC. Sadly, it has not for a long time been possible to say that Greece is a leading light in the wine world. But, whatever individual attitudes people hold towards French winemaking, it is still - unlike Greece - a force to be reckoned with.

With a couple of exceptions, all of the major grape varieties we looked at in the preceding

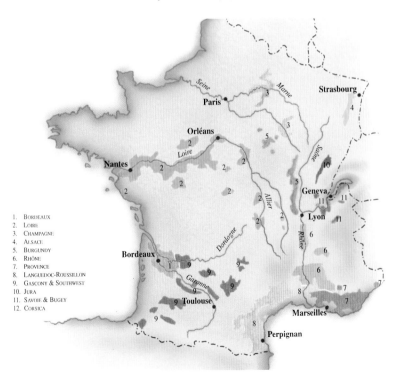

1. BORDEAUX
2. LOIRE
3. CHAMPAGNE
4. ALSACE
5. BURGUNDY
6. RHÔNE
7. PROVENCE
8. LANGUEDOC-ROUSSILLON
9. GASCONY & SOUTHWEST
10. JURA
11. SAVOIE & BUGEY
12. CORSICA

section of this book are French. They are grapes that are grown around the world. France has no particular monopoly on grape types - it has been estimated that commercially invisible Turkey, for example, has over 1100 indigenous varieties - but it is the Chardonnays, Cabernets, Sauvignons and Pinots that have travelled the world's vineyards most extensively. That is not to say that every Australian winemaker with a cellar full of Chardie is trying to make white burgundy, but the presence of the grape in the vineyard indicates that the original model was French. Otherwise, why not transplant some Austrian Grüner Veltliner or Spanish Verdejo?

In time, that may change. The spread of Italian grape varieties into California is one of the more intriguing phenomena of recent years. In order to plant Sangiovese, Dolcetto and Nebbiolo, some of those old cash crops, Cabernet and Chardonnay, are having to come out.

Secondly, the question of *appellation contrôlée* arouses much vexatious debate around the world. Americans, Australians and the rest say that the appellation regulations are what have held France's wine industry back from competing in the modern world. If a grower in Beaujolais is forced to replant, he or she can only put in more Gamay. It might be fascinating to see how Italian Dolcetto or Austrian Blaufränkisch fared on the granite hills of the region but, however it fared, the wine it made could not be called Beaujolais.

The French counter this argument by saying that, far from holding them back, the restrictions are precisely what has made their greatest wines possible. Once upon a time, for instance, a neutral-tasting, undistinguished grape, known as Melon because of its shape, was widely grown in Burgundy. Indeed, its full name is Melon de Bourgogne. Back in the 17th century, long before the creation of the appellation system, there were official moves to kick it out of the region as not being worthy of the best wines. Today, the heartland of Melon is Muscadet at the western end of the Loire, where it is the sole grape permitted under the appellation.

If there were no appellation rules, it would still be possible to put the high-yielding, high-acid, thin-tasting Melon grape into white wines of the Côte de Beaune. Now, Muscadet can turn out a clean, refreshing, zippy little wine in decent vintages, but Puligny-Montrachet it ain't. And the point is that Puligny-Montrachet itself would not have been what it has become if

Dusk descends over vineyards in Corbières in the Languedoc (above).

it had not been forbidden from using the inferior Melon de Bourgogne. The two wines are not ultimately easy to compare as they are so different in terms of style and the audience they appeal to, but we as consumers know what to expect from them because their names - Muscadet and Puligny-Montrachet - have been made to mean something legally.

Of course, even within the appellation regime, there are still good and bad winemakers. It is unfortunately not possible to legislate for talent. But what the regulations do set down, in terms of geographical demarcation, yields, grape types, alcohol levels and so forth, are designed to eliminate as much as possible the chances of sub-standard produce despoiling the hard-won reputation of each regional name.

It is that commitment to ensuring that everybody plays by the same rules for the greater glory of its wine industry, and the enshrining of it in rule-books that are minutely based on pinpointing the best grapes for the best sites and the best methods of growing and vinifying them, that sets the tone for the wines explored on the following pages. And it is because, in the light of that, some more or less rudimentary version of the controlled appellation concept is being instituted in every wine-producing country on the face of the earth, that we turn our attention first to the wines of France.

Ancient presses in the underground cellars at Gaston Huët (above), producer of fine sparkling Saumur, Loire.

BORDEAUX-*Red*

*Occupying a position at the pinnacle of world winemaking, the grand châteaux of
Bordeaux produce fine clarets and sweet whites in a landscape that could not have
been better designed for growing vines.*

BORDEAUX-RED

GRAPES: *Cabernet Sauvignon,
Merlot, Cabernet Franc,
Malbec, Petit Verdot*

*The Bordeaux region lies
within the Gironde département. The Médoc is a
narrow strip on the left bank
of the Gironde estuary.
Upstream, the river Garonne
provides the damp climate so
suitable for the botrytised
wines of Sauternes.*

THE RED WINES OF Bordeaux - or clarets,
as the British have called them for at least
the last four centuries - have long been synonymous with the popular image of fine wine. Any
major auction of vintage wines is likely to be
dominated by old bottles and cases of Bordeaux, since that is where most of the attention
of investors in wine was, and largely still is,
concentrated. In this respect, the profile of Bordeaux has always been higher than that of
France's other classic red wine region, Burgundy,
partly because the most magisterial clarets are
considerably longer-lived than most burgundy,
and partly because the annual production of the
Bordeaux region is incomparably larger.

Claret is not exclusively about well-heeled
bidders with private cellars to stock. Its wines
span the whole spectrum of status, from the
humblest and most *ordinaire* to the kind that
would require an uncommonly sympathetic

bank manager to allow you the merest taste. The
issue for the high-street consumer to confront is
that most of the wines require some degree of
ageing in the bottle, and most retail outlets only
trade in immature bottles. So, either you keep
them in your own cellar, or you go to an independent merchant who specialises in one-off
purchases of good mature vintages.

During the economic boom-time of the
1980s, a trend for buying claret directly from
the château in the spring following the vintage,
for delivery at a later date - a deal known as
buying *en primeur* - became the smart way to
invest. It was certainly cheaper than waiting
until the merchants had bought the wine themselves and then paying their mark-ups.
Everything went well until a run of mediocre to
poor vintages in the region, starting in 1991,
sent market values tumbling. Some investors
who had bought those wines either lost money
or else found themselves with rather a lot of
thin, insipid wine to drink up.

The result was that, by the mid-1990s, Bordeaux's cellars were awash with unsold wine.
Some châteaux would only sell wines from the
slightly better vintages on condition that their
regular buyers bought some of the produce of
the disaster years. As the chances for greatness
in successive vintages were rained off at the last
minute by inclement weather at harvest-time,
Bordeaux experienced its worst commercial
sticky patch since the early 1970s. Some relief
was at hand in the form of decisive intervention
by Japanese investors, as keen to buy a stake in
the alcoholic pinnacles of Western culture as in
its finest artistic achievements.

For all the torrid machinations of high
finance, Bordeaux remains at its best one of the
world's most irresistibly succulent red wines.
Opened in its youth, a good claret is really wasted, for all that the French themselves have a
taste for the juvenile article. They are tight and
tough in texture, and rigid with tannin. After
around five or six years, they can begin to soft-
en up a bit and display some of the blackcurrant
or plum fruit of the Cabernet Sauvignon or Merlot grapes more readily. Then, in a curious

1.	ST-EMILION	12.	GRAVES
2.	POMEROL	13.	PESSAC-LÉOGNAN
3.	LALANDE-DE-POMEROL	14.	SAUTERNES
4.	FRONSAC	15.	BARSAC
5.	CANON-FRONSAC	16.	CÉRONS
6.	ENTRE-DEUX-MERS	17.	LOUPIAC
7.	CÔTES DE BOURG	18.	CADILLAC
8.	CÔTES DE BLAYE	19.	STE-CROIX-DU-MONT
9.	PREMIÈRES CÔTES DE	20.	HAUT-MÉDOC
	BORDEAUX	21.	MÉDOC
10.	CÔTES DE CASTILLON	22.	ST-ESTÈPHE
11.	CÔTES DE FRANCS	23.	PAUILLAC
		24.	ST-JULIEN
		25.	MARGAUX
		26.	LISTRAC-MÉDOC
		27.	MOULIS

development that remains hard to account for, they seem to go into a sulky state of withdrawal, in which they taste rather flat and inert. You must now leave the rest of your bottles alone for perhaps three or four years, after which they will blossom again, still full of fruit hopefully, but with the scents and flavours now deepened into all sorts of seductive and complex modes. The infamous Bordeaux classification formulated for the Paris Exhibition of 1855 remains the principal determining factor in the pricing of these wines; the five-tier hierarchy is in fact based on the market values of the wines when the list was originally drawn up at the behest of Napoleon III. As we saw in the Merlot chapter, the league table for reds saw fit only to include the wines from the Haut-Médoc, plus Château Haut-Brion in the Graves. The Graves itself was then classified in the 1950s, along with St-Emilion. The other great red wine district, Pomerol, has never been classified.

Although much of the classification still holds good, properties do change hands, new winemakers are employed, different winemaking philosophies are explored, and the performances of individual châteaux inevitably fluctuate. Since the Bordelais themselves look likely never to amend the 1855 classification for fear of unleashing a vinous Armageddon, it is left to individuals to offer their own periodic reassessments. This is a practice positively encouraged by the president of the regional organisation for the top brass, the Syndicat des Crus Classés (what you might call Club 1855). Château names on the table below are followed by a star rating up to a maximum of five, based on the general consensus as to their performances over the last 20 years - a period that ranges in quality from the frost-devastated '91s and rain-soaked '87s and '93s to the trio of stunners that was '88, '89 and '90.

1855 AND ALL THAT

(Appellation shown in brackets - P = Pauillac, M = Margaux, P-L = Pessac-Léognan, *formerly Graves,* S-J = St-Julien, S-E = St-Estèphe, H-M = Haut-Médoc)

First Growth/1er cru

Lafite-Rothschild (P) ***** Margaux (M) ***** Latour (P) ***** Haut-Brion (P-L) ***** Mouton-Rothschild (P) *****

Second Growth/2ème cru

Rauzan-Ségla, *formerly Rausan-Ségla* (M)*****

Rauzan-Gassies (M) ** Léoville-Las Cases (S-J) ***** Léoville-Poyferré (S-J) *** Léoville-Barton (S-J) **** Durfort-Vivens (M) *** Lascombes (M) *** Brane-Cantenac (M) ** Pichon-Longueville, *formerly Pichon-Longueville Baron* (P) ***** Pichon-Longueville Comtesse de Lalande, *formerly Pichon-Lalande* (P) ***** Ducru-Beaucaillou (S-J) **** Cos d'Estournel (S-E) ***** Montrose (S-E) **** Gruaud-Larose (S-J) ****

Third Growth/3ème cru

Kirwan (M) ** d'Issan (M) *** Lagrange (S-J) **** Langoa-Barton (S-J) **** Giscours (M)*** Malescot St-Exupéry (M) *** Boyd-Cantenac (M) *** Cantenac-Brown (M) *** Palmer (M) **** La Lagune (H-M) **** Desmirail (M) *** Calon-Ségur (S-E) **** Ferrière, *not generally available outside France* (M) ** Marquis d'Alesme Becker (M) **

Fourth Growth/4ème cru

St-Pierre (S-J) *** Talbot (S-J) *** Branaire-Ducru (S-J) *** Duhart-Milon-Rothschild (P) *** Pouget (M) ** La Tour-Carnet (H-M) ** Lafon-Rochet (S-E) *** Beychevelle (S-J) **** Prieuré-Lichine (M) *** Marquis-de-Terme (M) ***

The hard way of transporting a barrel through the extensive chai, or cellar, of first-growth Château Margaux (above).

Ripe Cabernet Sauvignon grapes being harvested for first-growth Château Latour in Pauillac (below).

Fifth Growth/5ème cru

Pontet-Canet (P) ***   Batailley (P) ***
Haut-Batailley (P) ***   Grand-Puy-Lacoste (P)
****   Grand-Puy-Ducasse (P) ***   Lynch-
Bages (P) *****   Lynch-Moussas (P) *
Dauzac (M) *   d'Armailhac, *formerly Mouton-
Baronne-Philippe* (P) ***   du Tertre (M) ***
Haut-Bages-Libéral (P) ***   Pédesclaux (P) **
Belgrave (H-M) **   de Camensac (H-M) **
Cos-Labory (S-E) ***   Clerc-Milon (P) ***
Croizet-Bages (P) *   Cantemerle (H-M) ***

GRAVES/ST-EMILION/POMEROL

Graves This extensive sub-region, lying mostly south of the city itself on the west bank of the river Garonne, is named after the gravelly soils that predominate there. Many tasters insist that there is a gravelly, earthy taste in the red wines themselves, and certainly they tend to come clothed in much more austere garb than the lavish finery of the Médoc wines. However, they are quite as capable of ageing, notwithstanding the fact that many châteaux are attempting to make a more easy-going, early-drinking style of red.

The Graves was finally classified in 1959, for both red and dry white wines. Either a château in Graves is *cru classé* or it isn't; it's as simple as that. A superior swathe of land at the northern end of the region was separately demarcated as Pessac-Léognan in 1987, all of

the classed growths of 1959 falling within that appellation. (Château Haut-Brion is the only property that also appears in the 1855 classification.) For the reds, they are:

Bouscaut **   Haut-Bailly ****   Carbon-
nieux ***   Domaine de Chevalier *****   de
Fieuzal ***   d'Olivier **   Malartic-Lagravière
**   La Tour-Martillac **   Smith-Haut-Lafitte
***   Haut-Brion *****   La Mission-Haut-
Brion ****   Pape-Clément ****   La
Tour-Haut-Brion ***

St-Emilion Situated on the right bank of the river Dordogne, this is predominantly Merlot country - although not quite to the same degree as Pomerol to the north. The reds are supplemented largely by Cabernet Franc, with only a soupçon of Cabernet Sauvignon. The style is consequently leaner than in the Cabernet-dominated Médoc, but sharpened with a slightly grassier feel from the Cabernet Franc. The generality of wines are not that distinguished - many properties are guilty of overproduction - but the top names are worth the premium.

The classification of St-Emilion's reds was drawn up in 1955, but it is subject to revision every decade, the latest having been announced in 1996. At the humblest level, *grand cru* is so inclusive as to be meaningless. A step up is *grand cru classé* with around five dozen properties (among which l'Angélus and Troplong-Mondot stand out as worthy of ****)

and at the top is *premier grand cru classé*, which is subdivided into A and B. Class A consists of just two properties:

Ausone ****   Cheval Blanc *****

Class B contains nine:

Beauséjour (Duffau la Garrosse) ****
Belair ***   Canon *****   Clos Fourtet ***
Figeac ****   la Gaffelière ****   Magdelaine
****   Pavie ****   Trottevieille ***

Pomerol Immediately to the north of St-Emilion, and the only one of the top division of Bordeaux districts never to have been subjected to the indignity of classification, Pomerol's reds are as close to varietal Merlot as Bordeaux gets. Many have simply the merest seasoning of Cabernet Franc to add an edge of ageworthy sternness to what is essentially pure velvet-soft opulence, the sweetness of prunes coated in dark chocolate, and with a gorgeous creaminess that stays in the mouth for the longest time.

Anybody setting out to play the Pomerol classification parlour-game for themselves would have to start with the hyper-expensive Pétrus (*****) at the top, probably joined by Lafleur (*****). In the next rank (****) would come Bon Pasteur, Certan de May, Clinet, la Conseillante, la Croix de Gay, l'Eglise-Clinet, l'Evangile, la Fleur de Gay, la Fleur-Pétrus, le Gay, Latour à Pomerol, Petit-Village, le Pin, Trotanoy and Vieux-Château-Certan.

CRUS BOURGEOIS/PETITS CHATEAUX/SECOND WINES

Crus Bourgeois Immediately below the five layers of Médoc *crus classés* are a group of wines known, in an echo of 18th-century social stratification, as the *crus bourgeois*. For the purposes of this category, not only the Haut-Médoc but the bottom-line Médoc area to the north of St-Estèphe comes under consideration. Many of the properties would, if the 1855 document were to be redrafted, be included among the aristocracy, including a fair handful from the less well-known commune of Moulis.

Consistent reputations for reliably excellent wines over the last decade have been forged by the following (****): d'Angludet (M), Chasse-Spleen (Moulis), la Gurgue (M), Haut-Marbuzet (S-E), Gressier-Grand-Poujeaux (Moulis), Labégorce-Zédé (M), Lanessan (H-M), Maucaillou (Moulis), Meyney (S-E), Monbrison (M), de Pez (S-E), Potensac (Médoc), Poujeaux (Moulis) and Sociando-Mallet (H-M).

Next best (***) would be: Patache d'Aux (Médoc), Ramage-la-Batisse (H-M), Sénéjac (H-M), la Tour-de-By (Médoc) and la Tour-du-Haut-Moulin (H-M).

Petits châteaux and other districts Other important quality districts (with good unclassi-fied properties known as *petits châteaux*) are Lalande-de-Pomerol, adjoining Pomerol to the northeast (Bel-Air, Bertineau-St-Vincent), Fron-sac and Canon-Fronsac to the west of Pomerol (Canon-Moueix, Dalem, Mazeris, la Truffière) and the various satellite villages to the northeast of St-Emilion, such as Lussac (Lyonnat), Puis-seguin and St-Georges.

Many of the châteaux of Bordeaux have idiosyncratic architectural features, such as the pointed turret (above) after which Château la Tour-de-By is named.

Looking over the medieval rooftops of the City of St-Emilion (below) out towards the vineyards.

The huge area of Entre-Deux-Mers between the Garonne and Dordogne rivers tends to produce pretty rough-and-ready reds, which are only entitled to the most basic appellations of Bordeaux and Bordeaux Supérieur. On the right bank of the Gironde, directly opposite the *cru classé* enclaves of the Haut-Médoc, are the Côtes de Blaye and Côtes de Bourg areas. The latter is much the smaller of the two and is home to some rapidly improving properties. The long strip on the right bank of the Garonne, the Premières Côtes de Bordeaux, makes a mixture of simple sweet whites and some increasingly satisfying, firm-textured reds.

To the east of St-Emilion are two areas that are among the most unsung (and therefore good-value) sources of classy wine in the whole region: the Côtes de Castillon and Côtes de Francs. The style is lightish, depending significantly on Cabernet Franc for its appeal, but some châteaux (***) are turning out wines of impressive concentration. From Castillon:

Belcier, Moulin-Rouge, Parenchère and Pitray. From Francs: Puygueraud.

Second wines When the prices of Bordeaux began seriously inflating in the 1980s, much commercial attention came to be focused on the second wines of the principal châteaux. Most properties make a subsidiary wine to their main wine, or *grand vin*, to use surplus grapes that were not thought quite good enough for the main *cuvée*, or came from vines that were just too young to produce thoroughly concentrated fruit. A ready market was found for those who may not have been able to afford Château Margaux, but were interested in acquiring a broad impression of its style.

The point to remember when considering buying a second wine is only to buy from the best vintages. Top châteaux may be able to make a silk purse out of the sow's ear of a vintage like 1993, and it should be correspondingly cheaper, so you don't need the second wine - indeed, they probably shouldn't have made one. In a super-vintage like 1990, however, when the *grand vin* prices soar into the stratosphere, the second wines make economic sense.

These are regularly some of the best. They are not rated, as their quality should be in proportion to the ratings for the *grands vins*. The main château name is shown in brackets.

Les Forts de Latour (Latour), Carruades de Lafite (Lafite-Rothschild), Pavillon Rouge du Château Margaux (Margaux), Bahans Haut-Brion (Haut-Brion), Clos du Marquis (Léoville-Las Cases), Réserve de la Comtesse (Pichon-Longueville Comtesse de Lalande), Marbuzet (Cos d'Estournel), La Dame de Montrose (Montrose), Sarget de Gruaud-Larose (Gruaud-Larose), Lady Langoa (Langoa-Barton), Réserve du Général (Palmer), Haut-Bages-Avérous (Lynch-Bages), La Parde de Haut-Bailly (Haut-Bailly), Grangeneuve de Figeac (Figeac), La Gravette de Certan (Vieux-Château-Certan), La Petite Eglise (l'Eglise-Clinet).

VINTAGE GUIDE

The following is a broad overview of the most recent vintages, as represented by the best wines of each year, plus some earlier stars.
2001 ** Likely to be thin and mediocre on account of vintage-time rains.
2000 ***** A fabulous vintage, the best since 1990. Buy now and squirrel them away.
1999 **** Potentially very exciting. Good, concentrated, powerful wines across the spectrum.

1998 *** Pretty good, though not outstanding. St-Emilion and Pomerol are the safest bets.

1997 *** Much underrated at first, the '97s have turned out to be midweight but reasonably complex wines.

1996 **** Some classic, austere, ageworthy wines from the Médoc make this a vintage worth keeping.

1995 **** The first good one after 1990. The Cabernet-based wines of the Médoc in particular are very ripe and attractive.

1994 *** Potentially great but heavily spoiled by vintage-time rains. Pomerol and St-Emilion probably have the best wines.

1990***** Wonderful, superripe wines, full of richness and power and enormous ageing potential. Merlot was particularly good, so Pomerols are superb, but all districts made fine wine. Definitely one to keep.

1989 **** A long hot summer led to gloriously ripe Cabernet and some rather overripe Merlot. Most of the Médoc produced accessible wines of great charm that began to open out surprisingly quickly. The right bank is less great across the board but still made some outstanding wines.

1988**** Deeply classical wines with intensely ripe fruit and solid structure in pleasing balance. Exactly the sort of vintage to lay down. Most of the Médoc, Graves and St-Emilion produced fine wines.

1986**** A good vintage all in all, but the tannins in many wines are exceptionally severe. They still need time, but there is a real chance with a lot of them that the fruit may have broken up before the tannin disperses.

1985**** A warm year led to a large production of charming, fruit-filled wines, many of which drank well quite early on. The best will continue to hold.

1983**** Fine vintage of classically proportioned wines. There is a lot of tannin on the best ones, so they will need a few years longer yet.

1982 ***** One of the very greatest postwar vintages. Powerful, exotically rich and deeply beautiful wines by the score, most still needing several more years to show their true colours.

PICK OF THE OLDER VINTAGES: *1978 **** 1970 **** 1966 **** 1961 ***** 1959 **** 1955 **** 1953 **** 1949 **** 1947 **** 1945 ******

Despite its venerable history, Domaine de Chevalier, one of the Graves crus classés, has always kept abreast of the times, as witness its state-of-the-art cellars at Pessac-Léognan (above).

BORDEAUX-*Dry White*

The dry white wines of Bordeaux have enjoyed a remarkable renaissance in recent years, shaking off their image of being poorly-made and dull, and emerging with the kinds of flavours normally only found in America's finest.

BORDEAUX-DRY WHITE

GRAPES: Sémillon, Sauvignon Blanc, Muscadelle

IT IS ONLY IN THE last decade or so that the reputation of the dry white wines of Bordeaux has come once more into the ascendancy. Certain properties, such as Domaine de Chevalier, have always been highly valued for their white wines, and some of the *crus classés* showed themselves adept in both colours, notably Haut-Brion. The generality for a long time, though, was fruitless, stale-tasting rubbish, often loaded with too much sulphur dioxide (an antioxidant that helps to keep wine fresh, but that, used in excess, gives off an acrid smell and leaves a catch in the throat). These were the least prepossessing dry whites produced in any of France's classic regions.

The upturn came about via a handful of winemakers who began, in the early 1980s, to incorporate Californian and Australian ways of doing things. Denis Dubourdieu at Château Reynon, André Lurton at La Louvière and Peter Vinding-Diers, who consulted at a number of properties in the Graves, were among the pioneers who returned to Bordeaux a sense of pride in their wines. They achieved this through such obvious means as ensuring only impeccably ripe grapes are picked, that they are fermented at controlled temperatures and often given some judicious maturation in new oak to add an extra dimension to their flavours.

The Graves, and in particular Pessac-Léognan, have been the principal beneficiaries of the quality movement. Where it was most needed, in Entre-Deux-Mers, progress has been slower, partly because the soil contains quite a lot of clay, which inhibits drainage. (If it rains heavily, the vines' roots can become waterlogged.) Widespread use of a vineyard technique which originated in Austria, involving training the vines on high trellises for maximum heat absorption and therefore optimum ripeness in the grapes, has undoubtedly proved helpful.

Only the Graves has a classification for dry white wines, drawn up in 1959, with the white wine of Haut-Brion added the following year. As with its red wines, all of the properties come within the Pessac-Léognan AC in the northern Graves; in fact, all but three of them are dual classifications for red as well as white. The whites are:

Bouscaut ** Carbonnieux *** Domaine de Chevalier ***** Olivier ** Malartic-Lagravière

*** La Tour-Martillac **** Laville-Haut-Brion ***** Couhins-Lurton **** Couhins ** Haut-Brion *****

Unclassified fine dry whites from the Graves include de Fieuzal *****, Clos Floridène **** and La Louvière ****.

In the Entre-deux-Mers, the best property without a doubt is Thieuley (****). Elsewhere, the catch-all appellation of Bordeaux Blanc applies, and quality is all over the place. Some companies who make blended bottlings from all over the region can be reliable (for example, Coste, Dourthe, Mau and Sichel).

Down in the Sauternes region, the best makers of sweet wine make some dry white from the grapes that are not sufficiently shrivelled to be used for the Sauternes. Sometimes known as "dry Sauternes", they are in fact AC Bordeaux Blanc, and are named after the initial letter of the château - R from Rieussec, G from Guiraud and - best of all - Y from Yquem. Reputations make them expensive, but they are worth trying for some of the most majestically austere flavours in all dry white Bordeaux.

An ancient windmill presides over vineyards at Gornac, in the Entre-deux-Mers (above).

VINTAGE GUIDE

The simpler wines that use a high percentage of Sauvignon are best drunk on release. The top *crus classés* are intended for longer ageing.

2001 *** Not a great vintage at all, but the top properties will be fine.

2000 ***** Beautifully composed, concentrated wines for ageing.

1999 *** Initially underrated, but have turned out very attractive.

1998 *** Mostly leaner whites for early drinking.

1997 ** Early harvest of rather insipid wines.

1996 **** Some lovely creamy, tropical-fruited wines worth trying.

1995 *** Fairly rich, full-bodied wines still going strong.

1990 *** Some stunning wines from the top properties, but others found the sun just too hot for the Sauvignon, and the wines lack acid grip.

1989 *** Again, a very hot ripening period meant critically low acidity levels in many wines, so a lot will have had difficulty lasting this long. Only the very best (Haut-Brion, Laville-Haut-Brion and the like) made out-and-out classics.

1988 **** A good vintage of generally well-balanced wines, with the Graves *crus classés* still improving.

Top wines from 1987 *** and 1986 **** are still worth trying if you come across them.

The gently sloping vineyards of Château Benauge on the border between the Entre-deux-Mers and Premières Côtes de Bordeaux regions (left). Many of the dry whites made in these regions are now much improved.

BORDEAUX-*Sweet White*

Its lofty reputation founded on botrytis, a fungal disease that attacks ripened grapes in late summer and early autumn, the sweet wine of Bordeaux is the most celebrated of its kind in the world.

BORDEAUX-SWEET WHITE

GRAPES: *Sémillon, Sauvignon Blanc, Muscadelle*

The Sauternes region of Bordeaux contains some of the most valuable land in the world for producing sweet wines, none more so than at Château d'Yquem (below).

THE FINEST DESSERT wines in the world, whether in Bordeaux or elsewhere, are made from grapes infected by a strain of fungus called *Botrytis cinerea*, widely known as noble rot. Rot normally develops on grapes if the weather turns wet towards harvest time. This grey rot is the decidedly ignoble sort and, particularly with red grapes, can utterly shatter any hopes of making great wines. Botrytis, on the other hand, occurs in damp rather than drenching conditions.

Because of its proximity to the Atlantic Ocean, Bordeaux experiences increasingly humid, misty mornings as the autumn comes on, relieved by late sunshine during the day. This gentle process of dampening and drying off is the ideal climatic pattern for the encouragement of botrytis. (For an explanation of the vinification procedure, see the chapter on Sémillon.)

The most celebrated sweet wines on earth come from the southerly Bordeaux communes of Sauternes and Barsac. Although the technique was almost certainly discovered in Germany - by accident, of course, like many of the best inventions - it is here that it has been put to the most illustrious use. Not every vintage produces the right conditions, and the more quality-conscious châteaux simply don't bother making a wine in the off-years.

Quality depends on making painstaking selections of only the most thoroughly rotted grapes. In many cases, proprietors have decided the only way of doing that is by individual hand-sorting, picking only those berries that are completely shrivelled and leaving the others to moulder a little further on the vine before going through the vineyard again. Several such turns (or *tries*, as they are known in French) may be necessary to make the most concentrated wines possible. That, together with the long maturation in oak casks that the wines are generally given, explains the drop-dead prices that classic Sauternes sells for. It is an immensely labour-intensive wine.

A group of five villages in the southern Graves famous for their botrytised wines - Sauternes, Barsac, Bommes, Preignac and Fargues - was included in the 1855 classification. Together, they now constitute the Sauternes appellation, although Barsac is entitled to its own appellation as well, if an individual property so chooses. (Just for good measure, it can also be AC Sauternes-Barsac if it wants the best of both worlds.)

At the top of the classification, and with a category to itself like the duck-billed platypus, is the legendary Château d'Yquem, for many the supreme achievement in botrytised wine. Fantastically expensive and fabulously rich, its best vintages last literally for centuries.

Grand first growth/1er grand cru
Yquem *****

First growth/1er cru
La Tour Blanche **** Lafaurie-Peyraguey ****
Clos Haut-Peyraguey ** Rayne-Vigneau ***
Suduiraut **** Coutet **** Climens *****
Guiraud **** Rieussec ***** Rabaud-Promis
*** Sigalas-Rabaud ***

Second growth/2ème cru

de Myrat, *began replanting in 1988 after coming close to total extinction* Doisy-Daëne *** Doisy-Dubroca **** Doisy-Védrines *** d'Arche ** Filhot *** Broustet *** Nairac ** Caillou *** Suau ** de Malle *** Romer-du-Hayot ** Lamothe-Despujols * Lamothe-Guignard ***

Other good properties in Sauternes-Barsac, but outside the classification, are Raymond-Lafon (****), Gilette (****) and Bastor-Lamontagne (***).

In the immediate vicinity of Sauternes are four less well-known ACs for botrytis-affected wines. When the vintage is propitious, they can produce wines that give something of the flavour of their more exalted neighbours, while lacking those final layers of richness that make Sauternes so fabled. Given that, they are much more humanely priced. They are Cérons, Loupiac, Cadillac and Ste-Croix-du-Mont. Of these, all but Cérons, to the northwest of Barsac, are on the opposite bank of the river Garonne. The best properties are Cérons and Archambeau in Cérons and Loupiac-Gaudiet in Loupiac.

Sweet wines from the Premières Côtes de Bordeaux region, along the eastern side of the Garonne, are not invariably fully botrytised. However, one exception in recent years that has provided excellent value for money is Château de Berbec.

VINTAGE GUIDE

If a sweet white Bordeaux has been conscientiously made, it can easily last a good 20-30 years, and the very top ones are virtually indestructible. They turn from rich yellow to burnished orange and then the distinguished deep brown of dark sherry as they age, and go on selling for phenomenal sums.

2001 ***** Get ready. A sensational year for brilliant, complex, hauntingly beautiful wines.
2000 *** Very patchy, many wines lacking true richness for the prices.
1999 **** Highly appealing wines that began to show their class quite early.
1998 *** Overshadowed by its predecessor, but still a fine, dependable vintage.
1997 **** Potentially exciting year for full-fledged, creamy Sauternes.
1996 *** Plenty of noble rot about, resulting in a fine, ageworthy vintage.
1995 *** At the time the best since 1990, but many wines lack full richness.

1994 ** A limited amount of reasonable wine, though not for long ageing.
1990 ***** Virtual perfection - some say the vintage of the century. Unbelievable levels of concentration and intensity. No other vintage of recent years will demonstrate more conclusively what Sauternes is capable of.
1989 **** Generally ripe and rich, although some of the *crus classés* are unaccountably slender and may not age that well.
1988 **** The first of the three fine vintages known in France as *les trois glorieuses*. Huge, hefty stunners in which the influence of botrytis ran rampant.
1986 **** Beautiful vintage of properly botrytised wines, coming into its own at around ten years old.
1983 **** The equal of '86, '88 and '89, and beginning to drink well now, these are memorable, succulent, full-on Sauternes.
PICK OF THE OLDER VINTAGES: *1976* ****
1975 **** *1971* **** *1970* *** *1967* *****
1962 **** *1959* ***** *1955* **** *1953* ****
1949 **** *1947* **** *1945* *****

Pre-war vintages worth ***** would be *1937, 1929* and *1921.* I am told the *1899* and *1900* were rather good too.

Autumn vines resplendent beneath a clear blue sky at Château Rieussec (above), one of the best first-growth properties in Sauternes.

LOIRE

The river Loire flows through five wine-producing areas, from the Pays Nantais in the west, far inland to Sancerre in the east, each of them boasting very different styles of wine.

Château de Nozet (above) set in the upper Loire, where Pouilly-Fumé is produced.

PAYS NANTAIS

GRAPES: *Melon de Bourgogne (Muscadet), Folle Blanche (Gros Plant).*

The five wine regions of the Loire valley (below) lie along the banks of the river Loire.

WERE IT NOT FOR the unifying presence of the river itself, it would be difficult to see the various viticultural districts that the Loire valley encompasses as one single region. The Loire is the longest river in France, rising more or less in the centre of the country and flowing out into the Atlantic Ocean west of Nantes. To get a coherent view of it as a wine region, it makes sense to subdivide it into five areas. Running from west to east, these are: the Pays Nantais, Anjou, Saumur, Touraine and the Upper Loire (the last sometimes referred to as the Central Vineyards because they are in the centre of France).

Pays Nantais The main business of the area around the city of Nantes is Muscadet, France's most exported wine. The epitome of bone-dry, crisp, neutral-tasting white wine, Muscadet wouldn't seem to have a lot going for it in an era of oak-aged Chardonnay-mania, and yet it continues to find export customers for around half of what it produces each year.

There are four ACs. Muscadet de Sèvre-et-Maine, in the centre of the region, makes about 80 per cent of all Muscadet and is generally considered the best in terms of the character of its wines. Growers based in the villages of St-Fiacre and Vallet are particularly noteworthy. Muscadet Côtes de Grandlieu is the newest appellation, created in 1994. Centred on a large

lake, the district contains a fair amount of the sandy soil thought to impart more personality to the wines. Corcoués/Logne and St. Philbert de Bouaine are a couple of addresses to look for in the fine print on the label.

The small district of Muscadet des Coteaux de la Loire turns out a negligible quantity of undistinguished wine, and the rest is basic AC Muscadet, not by and large worth dwelling on.

About half of all Muscadets include the words *sur lie* on the label. This refers to a vinification technique whereby the finished wine is left on its lees (the dead yeast cells left over from fermentation), from which it picks up a gently creamy, slightly fuller feel than the unadorned version, as well as a touch of spritz. It is always worth buying a *sur lie* wine in preference to the alternative. Some producers have resorted to maturing their wines in oak casks, a risky technique for such a light wine, but the best improbably succeed in achieving some genuine complexity.

A more "natural" way of making Muscadet complex, however, is to age it for yourself in the bottle. At about five years old, it takes on a vaguely cabbagey pungency that is admittedly an acquired taste, but makes the wine a lot less spiky than the more conventional way of drinking it hot off the press as it were, screaming with raw young acid.

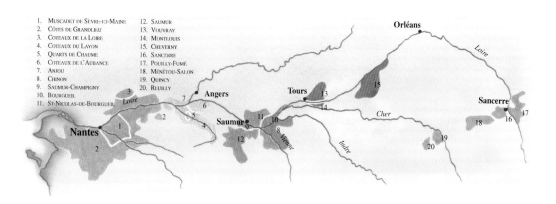

1. MUSCADET DE SÈVRE-ET-MAINE
2. CÔTES DE GRANDLIEU
3. COTEAUX DE LA LOIRE
4. COTEAUX DU LAYON
5. QUARTS DE CHAUME
6. COTEAUX DE L'AUBANCE
7. ANJOU
8. CHINON
9. SAUMUR-CHAMPIGNY
10. BOURGUEIL
11. ST-NICOLAS-DE-BOURGUEIL
12. SAUMUR
13. VOUVRAY
14. MONTLOUIS
15. CHEVERNY
16. SANCERRE
17. POUILLY-FUMÉ
18. MÉNÉTOU-SALON
19. QUINCY
20. REUILLY

PRODUCERS: Sauvion, Métaireau, Donatien Bahuaud, Luneau, Bossard, Guindon.

Talking of screaming acidity, there is a VDQS in this area (*vin délimité de qualité supérieure*, the intermediate quality stage between *appellation contrôlée* and *vin de pays*) called Gros Plant du Pays Nantais. This is the archetypal French "local wine", much beloved of the Nantais themselves, but not one they dare export to any great degree. It is so extraordinarily acidic that it can induce instant heartburn in the unwary. Served bone-chillingly cold with a platter of Atlantic shellfish, though - various species of prawn, tiny winkles, and slatherings of mayonnaise - Gros Plant is a winner.

PRODUCERS: Sauvion, Métaireau, Bossard.

Anjou The area south of Angers is the start of Chenin Blanc country, and it is here that the great sweet wines of the Loire are made. As we saw in the chapter on Chenin, the variety submits to botrytis with obliging regularity in these districts, producing some of France's most finely balanced dessert wines - full of mouth-coating sticky marmalade, but thrown into a state of nervous excitement by that lemon streak of acidity.

Coteaux du Layon is the largest area for sweet wines, and regularly produces liquorous but refreshing examples. Even in years when there is a lower concentration of noble rot, and the resulting wines have much less intense sweetness, these are generally pretty reliable.

PRODUCERS: Château du Breuil, Château de la Roulerie, Domaine de la Soucherie.

Within the Coteaux du Layon appellation is a small enclave answering to the name of Bonnezeaux, once neglected but now recovering its reputation for alcoholic, concentrated sweet wines of great class.

PRODUCERS: Château de Fesles, Angeli.

In the northwest of the Coteaux du Layon area, and likewise enclosed within it, is another small AC that scores highly for quality across the board - Quarts de Chaume. Growers here tend only to make wines when botrytis has been sufficiently widespread not to need to use non-rotted grapes. The result is almost unbearably intense sweet Chenin with all the majesty of top-flight Sauternes at considerably lower prices.

PRODUCERS: Baumard, Château de Bellerive.

Northeast of Chaume, the much larger Coteaux de l'Aubance makes medium-sweet, generally non-botrytised wines that offer a lighter option when full-blown rot is too daunting a proposition to accompany a lighter dessert.

Anjou is also the location of Savennières, the long-lived, brittle, bone-dry Chenin wine that achieves an impressive mineral purity in the best vintages and is always highly priced. Be warned that the wines positively command ageing, though, and should not be touched at less than seven or eight years old.

PRODUCERS: Domaine de la Bizolière, Baumard. Within the appellation, there are two superfine enclaves with their own ACs - La Roche-aux-Moines (Soulez makes a good wine) and Coulée de Serrant, which is wholly owned by one family. Here, Nicolas Joly makes his unearthly wine according to biodynamic principles, an abstruse practice involving much consulting of astrological star-charts.

Anjou Blanc Sec AC is the bottom line for everyday dry house white. It is allowed to mix in some Chardonnay and/or Sauvignon with the Chenin, and the best producers have generally availed themselves of the opportunity.

For reds, the two Cabernets - Sauvignon and Franc - may be used in the passable appellation of Anjou-Villages that covers the better village sites. Basic Anjou Rouge can be sandy-dry and charmless when made from the Cabernets, or lightweight and simple produced from the Beaujolais grape Gamay. (Varieties will be indicated on the label.)

Much rosé wine is made throughout the Loire, and quality is highly uneven. Cabernet d'Anjou can be appealingly creamy stuff, but simple Rosé d'Anjou is made from an unprepossessing variety called Grolleau (sometimes spelled Groslot).

Poplar trees break the skyline in vineyards near Vallet (above), Muscadet de Sèvre-et-Maine.

ANJOU
GRAPE: Chenin Blanc (whites)

Harvesting Muscadet grapes at Clisson (above), in the Sèvre-et-Maine AC.

The soaring turrets of
Château Saumur (above),
overlooking the Loire in
Saumur.

SAUMUR
GRAPE: *Cabernet Franc*
SPARKLING SAUMUR
GRAPES: *Chenin Blanc,*
Chardonnay,
Sauvignon Blanc
TOURAINE
GRAPE: *Chenin Blanc*

Saumur Two types of wine are important in Saumur - reds and sparklers. The Loire valley makes a speciality of the Cabernet Franc grape variety, one of the lesser players in red Bordeaux; the various red appellations of Saumur are permitted only that grape. In warm vintages, these wines have pleasant blackcurranty fruit, a lightish feel in the mouth (although by no means as light as, for example, Beaujolais) and gentle tannins. They can mature agreeably for several years. In less ripe years, though, they are pretty depressing, full of bitter green-pepper tannins and hard acids.

The best two appellations for reds are Chinon and Saumur-Champigny. At their best, these are attractive, juicy-fruited wines, their upfront flavours of summer berries underpinned by considerable structure. In the good years, they are worth ageing.

PRODUCERS: Couly-Dutheil, Domaine de la Tour, Raymond Raffault, Jean Baudry (Chinon); Filliatreau, Domaine des Roches Neuves, Sauzay-Legrand (Saumur-Champigny). Filliatreau also makes the best wines from the less distinguished area around Saumur-Champigny, designated straight AC Saumur Rouge.

In the north of Saumur, the ACs of Bourgueil and St-Nicolas-de-Bourgueil also make textbook Cabernet Franc reds, though in a distinctly lighter style to the others. The former is the better of these two, with some refreshing raspberry-fruited reds from the likes of Audebert and Domaine des Ouches.

Sparkling Saumur is made by the same method as champagne, and is mainly, but not exclusively, made from Chenin Blanc. From good producers such as Gratien et Meyer (who also make a sparkling rosé from Cabernet Franc) or Bouvet-Ladubay, they have a tart but thirst-quenching crispness that makes them a good choice for a summer aperitif.

Some producers do make a simple AC Saumur still white from Chenin Blanc that bears a not unexpected resemblance to the all-Chenin versions of Anjou Blanc Sec.

Touraine Chenin continues its sway into the area east of Tours, where its principal stamping-ground is Vouvray. Vouvray covers almost every stylistic manifestation that white wine can adopt - dry, medium-dry, semi-sweet, botrytised and sparkling. Confusingly, some producers are not always especially inclined to indicate the

style on the label, so that what you thought was going to be a snappy, bone-dry white can have a perplexing degree of residual sugar in it. However, the picture is slowly changing, and Vouvray - despite being very vintage-sensitive - is capable of making some of the most appetising Chenin wines of the Loire.

When the labelling does work, the designations are: sec, demi-sec, moelleux and 'Sélection' for the botrytis-affected *cuvées*.
PRODUCERS: Fouquet (Domaine des Aubuisières), Brédif, Champalou, Château Moncontour, Prince Poniatowski. Huët makes by far the best Vouvray fizz, a wine as deeply rich and complex as good champagne.

Montlouis is an AC to the south of Vouvray on the other side of the river. It makes Chenin wines in the same repertoire of styles as Vouvray, but with somewhat less finesse.

Cheverny, in the northeastern corner of Touraine, was promoted from VDQS to AC in 1993. Its whites may use Chardonnay, Sauvignon or Chenin, but there is also a separate appellation - Cour Cheverny - for wines made from the residual plantings of a high-acid local grape called Romorantin. Cheverny also makes a crisp-edged red wine that may use Cabernet Franc, Gamay or Pinot Noir.

The regional appellation, Touraine AC, is for basic reds and whites, usually labelled with the variety: Gamay or the Cabernets for reds, Sauvignon for whites that can sometimes offer a sanely priced alternative to Sancerre.

Upper Loire After a northerly detour, we follow the river Loire south again and Sauvignon Blanc comes into play for the most fashionable ACs of the entire region. The two most lauded of the Sauvignon appellations are Sancerre and Pouilly-Fumé, which face each other on the left and right banks of the river respectively. They are both capable of producing some of the world's most intriguing Sauvignon - full of intense green flavours of apples and asparagus, nettles and parsley, as well as wisps of beguiling smoke - but they do fall short of greatness uncomfortably often for the prices they command.
PRODUCERS: Gitton, Mellot, Roger, Vatan, Crochet, Bourgeois, Cotat (Sancerre); Didier Dagueneau, Châtelain, de Ladoucette, Château de Tracy (Pouilly-Fumé).

Travelling westwards from Sancerre, three less illustrious but noteworthy Sauvignon appellations are to be found. Ménétou-Salon,

bordering on Sancerre, is the best and its prices are beginning to climb as it establishes a reputation. Pellé is the best producer. Across the river Cher are Quincy and Reuilly, making lighter, much less piquant Sauvignon wines.

Many producers in Sancerre, Ménétou-Salon and Reuilly also make a red and/or rosé wine from Pinot Noir, perhaps with varying amounts of Gamay in the latter. These are nowhere near as powerful as the Pinots of Burgundy, but can be appealing in their grassy, cherry-fruited way.

Pouilly-sur-Loire is a little-seen dry white made from the humdrum Chasselas grape. South of the whole region, but north of the ancient town of Poitiers, is a VDQS area - Haut-Poitou - for good, simple whites and reds from Sauvignon, Chardonnay, Gamay, etc.

Any wine made outside the demarcated ACs, or using grape varieties not permitted within the specified AC (often fair-quality Sauvignon Blanc, Chardonnay, Chenin Blanc or Gamay) takes the rather florid regional designation of Vin de Pays du Jardin de la France.

VINTAGE GUIDE

The dry whites are not by and large intended for long ageing. *2001* is very patchy, with only the odd half-decent Sancerre, *2000* was much better, full of ripe, zingy fruit flavour, while '99 was reasonable without being at all special. Avoid *2001* Muscadet like the plague.

The best recent vintages for reds have been the juicily ripe *2000* and fine '96 and '95.

As with Sauternes, the Loire's best dessert wines will last for aeons. The very greatest recent vintages are *1988, '89* and *'90*, but *2000, 1997, '96* and *'95* are all good too.

UPPER LOIRE
GRAPE: *Sauvignon Blanc (whites)*
SANCERRE, MENETOU-SALON AND REUILLY
GRAPES: *Pinot Noir, Gamay (reds/rosés)*

Sparkling rosé, made from Cabernet Franc (left), resting in pupîtres *at Gratien et Meyer, Saumur.*

CHAMPAGNE

The name alone conjures an image of celebration, of romance. The most northerly of France's fine wine regions, Champagne is the source of the world's finest sparkling wines.

THE NIGHT THEY invented champagne was about 350 years ago. It didn't take place overnight, and they didn't actually invent it as such, but it was around the middle of the 17th century that the fashion for wines that frothed took hold of smart café society - in London.

Although it was the winemakers of the Champagne region itself who perfected the various techniques indelibly associated with producing quality sparkling wines the world over, they would not have done so had the metropolitan English not developed a taste for deliberately spoiled wine. For there were no two ways about it: effervescence in the wine was considered an exasperating liability in the cold northerly climate of Champagne.

The problem often arose when the slow fermentation of the delicate and high-acid wines was interrupted by plummeting cellar temperatures as winter came on. When the time came to bottle the wines the following spring, there was very often a certain amount of residual sugar left over from the uncompleted fermentation. As the weather warmed up again, the yeasts that

had lain dormant in the wine over the winter now came back to life in the bottle and began feeding on the sugars once more. This time, however, the carbon dioxide gas that the fermentation process creates had nowhere to escape, so it dissolved into the wine until such time as the bottle was opened, whereupon hearts would sink at the discovery of another wretchedly fizzy disaster.

Much of the highly regarded still wine of the Champagne region was exported to Britain at this time. It was shipped in cask and would be bottled soon after its arrival by the London merchants. The British trade had, for some time, been used to adding brandy and a little sugar to the wines it imported because it was the only way to save them from turning rank during the long sea voyages they had to endure. (This practice is the origin of the great fortified wines, as we shall see in the chapter on Portugal.)

Champagne was the only wine - with the possible exception of burgundy - not to undergo this treatment as a matter of course, for the simple reason that, being the closest fine wine

The four vineyard areas of the Champagne region (below), with the warmer Aube valley tucked away to the south.

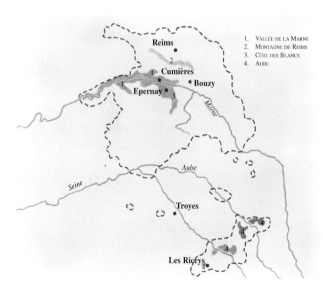

1. VALLÉE DE LA MARNE
2. MONTAGNE DE REIMS
3. CÔTE DES BLANCS
4. AUBE

region to the British Isles, the journey was nowhere near as arduous as that made, for example, by the wines of Portugal's Douro valley.

Since there was a marked British predilection, however, for sweetness and potency in wine, some merchants undoubtedly added a little sugar and a slug of spirit to the wines they brought in from Champagne as well. Given the fact that many of the wines were biologically unstable to begin with, this treatment, followed by early bottling, would have virtually assured anything from gentle pétillance to volcanic eruption when the bottle was broached.

Indeed, explosions in the cellar would have been quite commonplace and the injuries sustained thereby were viewed by the French as just desserts for the latest preposterous English fad. Not ones to be deterred by a bit of flying glass, the English responded by inventing stronger bottles.

Unbeknown to itself, the London *demi-monde*, having a rollicking good time drinking fashionable fizz in the cafés and playhouses, was assiduously developing the image that the champagne industry has traded on for most of the last three centuries. Fizzy wine is fun. All those little bubbles help it get right into the bloodstream without hanging about (which is why it "goes to the head" more quickly than whisky), and so champagne came to play a matchless role in partying and celebration.

Barrels holding unblended grape must (above). The markings show which area the grapes came from - VZY stands for Verzenay, on the Montagne de Reims.

Blanket of snow covers the walled Clos du Mesnil vineyard owned by Krug (left). Planted solely with Chardonnay grapes destined for Krug's prestige blanc de blancs.

Pinot Noir vines on the slopes of the Montagne de Reims (above). That puff of smoke in the distance is the prunings being burned.

Champagne going through the remuage *process (below) in traditional* pupîtres, *twisted and tipped by hand over many weeks.*

If you visit the headquarters of the largest and most famous champagne producer of all, Moët et Chandon, in Epernay, you will encounter a rather stern-looking statue in the forecourt. It stands in commemoration of Dom Pérignon, as does the wine at the top of Moët's range, which is named after him. Pérignon was a Benedictine monk who, in 1668, was appointed treasurer at the Abbey of Hautvillers near the town of Epernay, which is now the nerve-centre of the region as a whole.

Brother Pérignon's duties included overseeing the running of the cellars and the winemaking that was an important part of monastic life in the period. Among his formidable achievements were the perfecting of the technique of making a still *white* wine entirely from red grapes, refinement of the art of blending wines from different vineyards in the region to obtain the best possible product from available resources, and advances in clarification treatments to ensure a brighter wine than was the turbid norm at the time.

Dom Pérignon also devoted much effort to researching ways to avoid the dreaded refermentation that resulted in so many turbulent wines. His seminal place in the region's history is unquestionably merited, but not as the inventor of sparkling champagne.

As the process for making sparkling wines was rationalised, the inducement of the all-important second fermentation in the bottle was achieved by the addition of a little sugar solution to an already fully fermented wine. This then gave the surviving yeasts something more to chew over. The drawback to this was that the sediment of dead yeast cells then created remained trapped in the wine and gave it the cloudiness that Dom Pérignon had worked so sedulously to prevent. The house of Veuve Clicquot, founded in 1772, may take the credit for the solution to that particularly sticky problem.

Nicole-Barbe Clicquot-Ponsardin took over the running of the firm after her husband - the founder's son - left her widowed in her 20s. Her formidable promotional talents and encouragement of innovation in themselves would have made her one of the key figures in champagne history, but it was the development under her tutelage of the process of *remuage* that installed her unassailably in the region's hall of fame.

By this method, the bottles were placed in slots in wooden contraptions that look like large sandwich-boards. Over a number of weeks, cellar-workers would regularly give them a twist and a shake and in doing so gradually adjust their angles in the slots, until they were more or less upside down. As the bottles were slowly tipped, the sediment gradually sank towards the neck of the bottle until it all collected on the underside of the cap.

In time, the way to remove the accumulated deposit came to involve dipping the necks of the bottles in freezing brine so that the portion of wine containing the sediment is flash-frozen. When the metal cap is knocked away, the deposit flies out with it and the bottle is topped up and corked. All of this is automated now, of course, including the actual turning of the bottles, which is done by computer-programmed machines with the bottles packed in huge crates. Some houses make a virtue of the fact that they still painstakingly hand-turn all their wines. Whether this makes any noticeable difference in the finished wine is highly debatable, though great offence is occasioned if you dare to suggest otherwise.

The pre-eminence of champagne as the king of sparkling wines was well established by the end of the 18th century, but most of the world-famous houses we know today were founded in the first half of the 19th century. The region suffered horrendously during the Great War. The

rapid German advance through northern France in the early months of hostilities in autumn 1914 penetrated south of the river Marne. It was driven partially back by 1915 to a line north of the strategic city of Reims, where it was to remain virtually static until the Armistice.

With the coming of prosperity after World War Two, champagne began very gradually to trickle down the social scale and become less of a luxury. The industry lost its way somewhat in the 1980s when consumption in the UK reached unprecedented levels to coincide with relatively benign economic times. Some members of its controlling body felt that the wine was in danger of becoming too democratic and losing its aura of elite unaffordability. A more or less explicit attempt to ration consumption, using the sledgehammer of price inflation, was just beginning to work when the coming of severe recession did the job for them.

By the mid-1990s, champagne sales were once more on a gentle upward trajectory as prices moderated and a new quality charter came into effect to ensure that Champagne didn't just idly trade on its good name by selling wafer-thin, razor-sharp, watery wines as it had been tempted to do during the boom years. As a result, it is again possible to say that, when they play to the peak of their form, these are indeed the finest sparkling wines made anywhere.

THE WINES

Champagne production is dominated by members of the Club des Grandes Marques, the big houses such as Moët et Chandon, Bollinger, Mumm, Taittinger, Veuve Clicquot and Pol Roger. They have the highest profiles and their wines, in the main, sell for the highest prices. Additionally, there are a number of important co-operatives in the region who often make own-label champagnes for supermarket chains in the export markets. Increasingly, there are a number of go-it-alone growers who are making their own wines on an endearingly small scale.

The region divides into four broad areas, the Vallée de la Marne along the river at the heart of Champagne, the Montagne de Reims, a large hill overlooking the city where much of the Pinot Noir is grown, the Côte des Blancs where the concentrations of Chardonnay are found and - quite detached from the rest to the south - the Aube valley, with the most rustic wines. Throughout the region, the chalky soils are held to endow champagne with much of its finesse.

While most of the big houses own some vineyard land, they nearly all rely on buying in grapes from contract growers in the various vineyards. In the 1980s, the balance of power was radically shifted in the direction of the growers; previously bound by an annual price-fixing agreement, they are now free to negotiate for what they can get within much more discretionary guidelines. The initially dire impact on costs this entailed led to some swingeing price hikes, but things have lately moderated somewhat as the growers realise that champagne is their livelihood too.

Of the three grapes permitted in the wine, two are red, although most champagne is white. Pinot Noir brings weight and richness to a blend and helps it to age productively, while those who use a greater percentage of Chardonnay, such as Henriot, value it for the elegance and gracefully lighter feel it can impart.

Pinot Meunier is a less distinguished grape in itself, but does lend a distinct fruity immediacy to many blends. Some houses try to play down the influence of this grape; others, such as Krug, makers of expensive crème-de-la-crème champagne, openly celebrate the function it serves. (Its image isn't helped by the fact that it may not be planted on the best vineyard sites, designated *grand cru*.)

The aim for quality enshrined in the Chartre de Qualité that came into effect in the 1990s stipulates that only the first free-run juice of the harvested grapes, followed by the juice of one gentle pressing, may now be used in the wines of the charter's signatories. (Previously, the harsher, more astringent juice of a second pressing went in as well, and did a lot to coarsen the taste of many champagnes.)

Summer at Verzenay, on the Montagne de Reims (above). The sunny slopes of the Montagne are planted mainly with Pinot Noir.

CHAMPAGNE
GRAPES: Pinot Noir, Pinot Meunier, Chardonnay

Hand-harvesting ripe Pinot Noir grapes at Mailly on the Montagne (above).

Pruning vines in early March (above), and burning the cuttings on a portable fire.

Most champagne is labelled "Brut", which is the standard, bone-dry style. The dryness or sweetness of a champagne is determined at the last moment before the cork goes in, when a quantity of sugar in solution known as the *dosage* is added to create the final taste. Even the Brut contains some sugar, since unadorned champagne is naturally a very acidic wine. A very few wines receive no *dosage* at all, and may be labelled "Brut Zéro": the intrepid should look out for Laurent-Perrier's version for an acceptable taste of the style.

Alternatively, an above-average amount of sugar can be added to create a sweeter style - either medium-dry, labelled "demi-sec", or positively sweet, and labelled either "doux" or possibly "rich". Not many of these are especially attractive, although Louis Roederer makes a nicely balanced Rich.

Some still wine is made in the Champagne region, and goes under the appellation Coteaux Champenois. Red wines from the villages of Bouzy and Cumières may be good in a rasping, rustic sort of way. The rest are rather charmless. In the south of the region, in the Aube valley, is an appellation for still pink wines, Rosé des Riceys. Its tiny production constitutes one of the more arresting pink wines made anywhere in France, but the astronomical prices will act as a strong deterrent to the curious.

Non-vintage The benchmark style of champagne, and the brand that the reputations of the houses live or die by, is the non-vintage blend. Each year, a certain quantity of base wine is held back in reserve, and small amounts of this older, maturer wine, known as *vin de réserve*, is used to give a softer feel and more complex flavour to what would otherwise be very raw, acidic wine. When there has been a run of good vintages, as there was from 1988-90, the quality of the non-vintage (or NV) goes up significantly. Styles vary enormously from one producer to the next, but the ridiculous fluctuations in quality that were the norm in the 1980s seem to have been ironed out to a heartening extent now. BEST HOUSES: Charles Heidsieck, Billecart-Salmon, Bollinger, Henriot, Pol Roger, Mailly Grand Cru, Devaux, Bouché, Georges Gardet.

Vintage This is the produce of a single year's harvest, with the year stated on the label. The minimum ageing time it must spend on its sediment in the cellars is three years, although the better houses will give it longer. Like port, vintage champagne should theoretically only be made in the best years, maybe three or at most four times a decade, but it seemingly takes a spectacularly rotten vintage to dissuade everybody from producing a vintage wine.

On average, vintage wines are released at around five years old, although they don't really come into their own until after eight to ten years. In 1995, for instance, it was quite clear that the exceptionally good '88s, which had been on the market for some considerable time, still needed at least another three years. Bear this in mind when you buy it; these wines are too expensive to waste by drinking them immature. BEST VINTAGE PRODUCERS: Billecart-Salmon, Bollinger, Pol Roger, Henriot, Ruinart, Veuve Clicquot, Mailly Grand Cru, Mercier, Perrier-Jouët, de Venoge.

Rosé Pink champagne suffers somewhat from being seen as an unnecessarily frivolous wine, a little infra dig. Many could benefit, though, from a little frivolity, since in general they are nowhere near as attractive to taste as they look. Most of the wine is made by adding a little still red wine from the locale to the white champagne. A very small amount (Laurent-Perrier is the most famous example) is made by staining the white juice by allowing the red grapeskins to soak in it for a short while. At their best, rosé champagnes have an exhilarating strawberry or peachy fruit that makes them glorious for summer drinking. BEST: Pol Roger, Billecart-Salmon, Lanson, Laurent-Perrier, Jacquart and - among the arm-and-a-leg brigade - Krug and Roederer Cristal.

Blanc de Blancs Champagne that utilises only the Chardonnay grape. These are the lightest and most graceful wines of the lot. Many certainly do feel less mouth-filling than the blended champagnes, but vintage examples that are aged take on a gorgeous toasty richness that quite belies the lightness argument. BEST: Billecart-Salmon, Pol Roger, Drappier, Dom Ruinart, Salon, Taittinger Comtes de Champagne, Krug Clos de Mesnil.

Blanc de Noirs White champagne made from the black grapes, Pinot Noir and Pinot Meunier, usually with a noticeably darker tone to it, although it is never pink. Not an immediately attractive wine, certainly not beginner's champagne, too many of these wines taste muddy and leaden. When good, though, their richer style can be impressive. BEST: Bollinger Vieilles Vignes, de Venoge, Billiot.

Prestige Cuvée Most of the big houses make a top-drawer special bottling. These are usually - though not always - a vintage wine, produced just to show how good they can really get. They are often aged for longer than ordinary vintage wine or come from particularly favoured parcels of vineyard land. The packaging may be quite diverting, as witness Perrier-Jouët's Belle Epoque in its flower-painted bottle, or the multi-faceted crystal effect of Nicolas Feuillatte's Palmes d'Or. Even more than straight vintage wines, these champagnes have to be aged properly. If it's cost you a day's wages, the incentive should be there.

BEST: Bollinger RD, Roederer Cristal, Pol Roger Cuvée Sir Winston Churchill, Krug Grande Cuvée, Perrier-Jouët Belle Epoque, Gosset Grande Réserve, Veuve Clicquot La Grande Dame, Mumm René Lalou, Pommery Cuvée Louise, and Nicolas Feuillatte Cuvée Palmes d'Or.

VINTAGE GUIDE

The following vintages were currently available at the time of writing:

1997 *** Light, but convincingly ripe champagnes.

1996 ***** Shy at first, but will grow up to be exemplary wines of great stature.

1995 **** Quite forward but very charming vintage for drinking now.

1993 *** Initially underrated, but has turned out surprisingly well.

1992 *** Lighter wines that should be drunk up now.

1990 Very fine vintage that has matured into rich and full-flavoured champagnes.

1989 Intensely lush, honeyed wines that reached maturity sooner than the '88s.

1988 Extremely sturdy, full-bodied wines that needed ten years to assume their rightful majesty.

Earlier vintages worth trying if you see them, and if you can be assured the bottles have been stored carefully, are: *1985, '79, '76, '75.*

Autumnal glow of the Champagne region (below) with the golden-coloured vineyards spreading across the hills.

ALSACE

A richly endowed wine region that deserves greater recognition, Alsace is a unique blend of the best of Germanic and French culture and grape varieties, and offers some of France's most idiosyncratic wine styles.

The village of Hunawihr, Alsace (above), with its 15th-century church, and the grand cru vineyard of Rosacker on the slope beyond.

OF ALL OF FRANCE'S principal wine regions, Alsace is culturally the most distinct. Its political history has been a literal tug-of-war between the two great powers of continental Europe: since 1870, it has been run by France, Germany, France, Germany and France again. Now undeniably French in its cultural outlook, despite the Germanic names of its inhabitants, Alsace shelters between the Vosges mountains and the river Rhine and grows both French and German grape varieties.

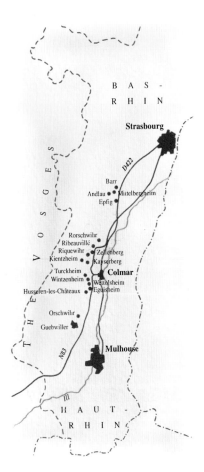

Alsace, bordered by the Vosges mountains and the river Rhine (right), has one overall AC, with specified grand cru vineyards. The marked villages are where the cellars of most of the region's top producers are located.

The wines it produces have no precise equivalents, however, in either the rest of France or Germany. They are among the most idiosyncratic styles made anywhere, and are greatly valued as such by those who know them. What Alsace is very bad at, unfortunately, is winning new converts. When people who have been introduced to wine via sugared-up German products like Liebfraumilch decide to branch out and try something more sophisticated, they tend to leave German wine behind. The wines of Alsace, bottled as they are in tall, Germanic green flutes by producers with Germanic names from vineyards with names like Pfingstberg, do not exactly make the novice customer think "France". When the grape variety is Riesling, the wine's fate is sealed. The assumption is that it will be sweet.

Ironically, Alsace should be just about the easiest French region to understand, because it is the only part of France where the wines have traditionally been named after their grape varieties, rather than villages (as in Burgundy) or the names of properties (as in Bordeaux). Furthermore, despite the demarcation of the *grands crus* in the 1980s, there is essentially one overriding regional appellation - AC Alsace - much as there is in Champagne or Cognac.

Although the location of these vineyards in a northeastern corner of France does mean that the growing season is relatively cool, it is also - because of the shelter of the mountains - particularly dry. Alsace has as little annual rainfall as parts of the broiling Midi down south (although vintages of the early 1990s were uncharacteristically damp). That means that, even when a harvest has been rather poor in much of the rest of France, Alsace tends not to take quite the caning that other regions suffer.

It is in these sometimes too arid conditions that clay-based soils, such as Alsace has in some of its lower-lying vineyards, are beneficial. Clay absorbs what moisture there is during wet spells and doesn't allow it to drain away as freely as other soil types - a nuisance if you have persistent rain, but a precious asset when summer drought is a real possibility.

Alsace's wines deserve a wider audience. Some producers border their neck labels in the blue, white and red of the *tricolor*, but short of actually changing the shape of the bottle - which there is no serious proposal to do - these wines will sadly continue to languish in mistaken identity. That could, in theory, be good news for those of us who have discovered the joys of Alsace wines and do want to drink them, but for the fact that the very lack of demand means that scarcely any mainstream wine merchants bother to list anything more than the lowest-common-denominator produce of the co-operatives.

THE WINES

Nearly all Alsace wine is dry to medium-dry varietal white, produced from one of the following varieties, and labelled as such. The first four listed here are considered the noblest of them all, and are the only ones permitted on the vineyard sites designated *grand cru*.

Gewurztraminer As outlined in the earlier section on this grape, this is the variety most readily associated in people's minds with the region's wines. Intensely aromatic, with a range of musky, floral scents underpinned with ripe fruit and sweet spice, Gewurztraminer is usually a deeply coloured wine with low acidity and rumbustious levels of alcohol. Despite its headstrong personality, it is a sympathetic partner to many foods but, perhaps best of all, the richly flavoured pâtés and terrines for which Alsace cuisine is famous. The wines can benefit from some bottle-ageing, although in very ripe years, such as 1989, the acidity level in the finished wine may be so low to start with that prolonged ageing will only turn it mushy.
PRODUCERS: Zind-Humbrecht, Hugel, Trimbach, Kuentz-Bas, Willm.

Riesling The starkest, most unnervingly pure dry Rieslings in the world come from Alsace. They are almost painfully austere in youth, and a period of bottle-ageing is mandatory for most examples. The fruit flavours are acerbic lime-peel and grapefruit, held together by exemplary levels of steely acid and noticeably higher alcohol than even Germany's driest Riesling Trocken tends to attain. They make an appetising accompaniment to simply prepared freshwater fish dishes. In their maturity, they can be overcome with a bewitching fume of freshly pumped petrol and damp earth, but never quite losing the outline of that nervy acidity. The buzzword for them is "racy".

PRODUCERS: Schlumberger, Louis Sipp, Trimbach, Hugel Cuvée Tradition, Zind-Humbrecht, Blanck.

Pinot Gris Once termed Tokay-Pinot Gris on the labels, after some misbegotten fable which had a soldier bringing back vines from the Tokaji region of Hungary (which doesn't have Pinot Gris), this is a much misunderstood variety. In some producers' wines, it can have all the spicy pungency of Gewurztraminer, with the fruit just a little sharper - orange perhaps rather than the mushy peach of Gewurz. Then again, it can have a fat, buttery texture to it and a layer of honey that can make it seem curiously like Chardonnay. Like Gewurz, the acidity is generally fairly low, and that should be taken into account when deciding how long to age a Pinot Gris.
PRODUCERS: Zind-Humbrecht, Beyer, Schlumberger, Kreydenweiss, Albrecht.

Husseren-les-Châteaux, a typical Alsace village, surrounded by vineyards (above), with the three ruined towers on the hill behind.

The steeply sloping grand cru *Rangen vineyard at the village of Thann (right), Alsace's most southerly grand cru.*

Muscat Muscat is the name of one of the oldest known grape varieties, in fact a many-membered family as opposed to a single variety. Two of its scions are present in Alsace, one of them not surprisingly known as Muscat d'Alsace and the other Muscat Ottonel. No distinction is made between them on the labels. Muscat is one of the great sweet-wine grapes, the only one by consensus to actually smell and taste of grapes. Vinified dry, it can be bracingly tart and much thinner in texture than the three grapes listed above. There is very little of it planted compared to the others, but in a good year, from low-yielding vines, it can make a pleasantly sharp, refreshing white with something of the musky spice the region rejoices in. PRODUCERS: Trimbach, Rolly-Gassmann, Weinbach, Schleret.

Pinot Blanc Not an especially aromatic grape, but definitely an underrated one. Pinot Blanc makes a creamy, slightly appley wine that provides an unstartling introduction to the region for those nervous of plunging headlong into the giddy waters of Gewurz. Sometimes it has a taste of bland tropical fruit like guava as well. Drunk young, these have far more character than many another unoaked dry white. Not for long ageing. (A minority of growers insists on calling the wines Klevner or Clevner.) PRODUCERS: Rolly-Gassmann, Hugel, Mann, Zind-Humbrecht, Weinbach.

Sylvaner The speciality grape of Franken, in western Germany, makes a pungently vegetal, often distinctly cabbagey wine in Alsace. Not the most attractive flavour in the world, but the odd one can have a honeyed quality and unexpected richness that makes it worth trying. PRODUCERS: Zind-Humbrecht, Becker, Weinbach, Domaine Ostertag, Seltz.

Auxerrois This is the grape variety that nobody really talks about, although there is certainly plenty of it about. An anomaly of the appellation regulations says that it can be considered as interchangeable with Pinot Blanc, so that a wine labelled simply Pinot Blanc may be blended with Auxerrois (or indeed in theory be nothing but Auxerrois). By itself, it gives very simple, though fairly full-textured wines with a vaguely soapy flavour. You won't see it mentioned on labels very often. PRODUCERS: Albert Mann, Rolly-Gassmann.

Chasselas Very rarely seen on labels, this undistinguished grape makes extremely light, neutral-tasting wine. Schoffit works miracles with it to produce an impressively lush-textured wine from old vines.

Edelzwicker The name used for blends of any of the above grapes (with the exception of Pinot Blanc and Auxerrois). Since the varietals are generally so sharply delineated, there seems little point in drinking one of these if you can have a single-grape wine.

Pinot Noir The only red grape in Alsace makes some exceedingly light reds and tiny amounts of rosé. Not a lot of it shows much pedigree, it has to be said. Perhaps it's the climate, perhaps it's the soils, but the variety just doesn't have the same class here as it does in Burgundy. There may be some sharp cherry fruit in the better ones, but in the cooler years it has an unpalatably green tinge to it that can be quite off-putting. Marcel Deiss makes about the only reasonably consistent one.

Crémant d'Alsace Alsace makes some of the most impressive sparkling wine in France outside the Champagne region - generally of higher quality than either of the two corresponding Crémants of Burgundy or the Loire. The principal grape used is Pinot Blanc, but the small plantings of Chardonnay found in the region go into the sparklers too. The method is the same as that used for champagne, with a second fermentation taking place in the bottle. The result is often attractively nutty, full-flavoured wines of considerable depth.

PRODUCERS: Wolfberger, Dopff au Moulin, Dopff & Irion, Turckheim co-operative.

Vendange Tardive This is the less rich of the two sweeter styles of Alsace wine. The name means "late harvest" to denote grapes that have been left on the vine to overripen, and thereby achieve higher levels of natural sugar. The designation applies only to the first four noble grapes mentioned above. They can be addictively delicious, perfectly balanced between the tang of ripe fruits and the lightest trickling of spicy syrup. In the great vintages of 1989 and 1990, they were particularly rich, honeyed and decadently creamy. In lesser years, they can be pretty close to the dry wines, but with a just perceptible extra depth to the texture.

Sélection de Grains Nobles The "noble" in the name of this category refers to the noble rot, botrytis, that stalks the vineyards in some years and allows the growers to make Alsace's richest and most unctuous wines. They are powerfully alcoholic and glutinously sweet, and should theoretically age beautifully. The only slight vitiating factor is that, particularly with reference to Gewurz and Pinot Gris, the acidity - low enough in the dry wines - plummets even further when the rotted berries are left on the vine for so long. Once again, only the big four grapes may be used, with Muscat by far the most seldom encountered.

Grands Crus Since 1983, a *grand cru* system has been in use in Alsace, covering the most prestigious vineyard sites of the region. In the mid-1990s, this was still being painstakingly argued and negotiated over, but there will almost certainly be somewhere between 50 and 60 names on the list by the time it is finalised. Yields permitted under the *crus* at the outset were fixed too high, but have now been reduced to the 60 hectolitres per hectare worthier of a *grand cru* wine. Eventually, the wines from these named vineyards should begin to justify the extra premium that such a badge of quality commands, and even those *grand cru* growers who currently feel they have no need of the classification, such as Hugel, may be won over. Riesling, Gewurztraminer, Pinot Gris and Muscat are the privileged quartet of grapes allowed on these specified sites, and since the individual vineyards are quite distinct from each other in terms of soil, exposure and microclimate, the *grand cru* wines should give us a beguiling insight into the versatility that Alsace is undoubtedly capable of.

VINTAGE GUIDE

2001 **** Late-summer warmth redeemed this vintage, and nearly all varieties (plus sweet wines) look great.

2000 **** Wines of powerful aromatic intensity and length.

1999 ** Generally very disappointing, wet vintage.

1998 **** Potentially very fine, with some great sweet wines.

1997 *** Reasonably ripe, but not hugely intense.

1996 *** Produced some attractive Gewurztraminer and Pinot Gris.

1995 ** Almost a straight repeat of '94.

1994 ** Very variable. The harvest was unusually wet for Alsace, resulting in some disappointingly dilute wines, though there is better stuff from those who picked later.

1990 ***** Great vintage of massively concentrated wines. Rieslings in particular are superb.

1989 **** Another dry, searing summer created the conditions for many splendidly intense wines. The late-harvest versions are sumptuous.

1988 *** Despite a good summer, this has not turned out as good as was first hoped. Too many wines seem to lack focus.

1985 ***** Excellent year that produced many monumental wines capable of long maturation.

The village of Riquewihr, dominated by its church spire (above), seen from the Schoenenburg grand cru.

Half-timbered Alsace building (below), Hugel's cellars in Riquewihr.

BURGUNDY

Lovers of great Pinot Noir and classic Chardonnay speak the name with reverence. Burgundy's vinous history dates back for centuries, tied up in the division of land and the role of the négociant.

The autumnal colours of the Charmes vineyard at Gevrey-Chambertin on the Côte de Nuits (above).

The great names of Burgundy (right) are concentrated in a line north-south between the towns of Dijon and Lyon; Chablis lies alone to the north.

1. CHABLIS
2. CÔTE DE NUITS
3. CÔTE DE BEAUNE
4. CÔTE CHALONNAISE
5. MÂCONNAIS
6. BEAUJOLAIS

BURGUNDY IS THE region that arouses the most passionate controversies within French wine. In times gone by, connoisseurs of French wine divided amicably into devotees of Bordeaux and Burgundy, the one traditionally seen as a cerebral, contemplative wine, the other as the stuff of hedonistic sensuality. In latter times, however, while claret has largely maintained its equilibrium, burgundy has been plunged into conflict - over how it should be made, whether the small growers are better than the big-time merchants, and whether it is now being consistently outstripped by producers from outside Europe.

What makes the debate all the more poignant is that the annual production of fine burgundy is microscopically small compared with the output of Bordeaux. Its premium wines - the equivalents of the classed growths of Bordeaux - come almost entirely from the narrow limestone ridge of the Côte d'Or, less than 48km (30 miles) from north to south and not more than 8km (5 miles) across at its widest point. (Most of the wines mentioned on the following pages are commercially unavailable, because the tiny production is snapped up immediately by contract customers, restaurants and hotels. Compare that with the oceans of unsold claret that built up in the Bordeaux region in the early 1990s.)

Furthermore, what land there is has been relentlessly subdivided over the generations. It is now quite common for a single proprietor to own no more vines than could be fitted into a decently sized back garden.

Before the French Revolution, large parcels of the land were owned by the nobility, as it had been when Burgundy was an autonomous ducal state in the 14th and 15th centuries, and the rest by the church. The Revolution saw that land sold to large numbers of the newly enfranchised bourgeoisie. The Napoleonic Code that was effected in the aftermath of the Revolution's demise decreed that, on the death of a landowner, property was to be divided equally among his offspring. Two hundred years later, where even a modest château in Bordeaux can put around 3000 cases of wine on to the market each year, a Burgundy grower may struggle to make two dozen.

It is hardly surprising, given this pattern, that the region came to be dominated by large merchant houses known as négociants. These would simply buy lots of wine, or even just harvested grapes, from the growers and blend what they bought to produce their own bottlings. The period since the Second World War, however, has seen the emergence of the *propriétaires-viticulteurs*, go-it-alone operators making infinitesimal quantities of wine from their own vineyard holdings and selling it independently. Some of these are unquestionably fine, indeed have a legiti-

mate claim to be the region's best wines. Others vary from the mediocre to the extremely ropey, often because they can't or won't invest in the kind of up-to-the-minute hygiene technology that the quality-conscious négociants have at their disposal.

This chapter moves from north to south to take in Chablis, historically considered a viticultural part of Burgundy, the two sections of the Côte d'Or (the Côte de Nuits and the Côte de Beaune), the Côte Chalonnaise and Mâconnais.

CHABLIS

The Chablis vineyards to the northwest of the main Burgundy region are geographically closer to the southern end of Champagne than they are to the Côte d'Or. As such, they represent one of the most northerly outposts of still Chardonnay wine in the world. Not surprisingly, the style that has come to be associated with the area is one of light-textured wines with scything acidity and either a very restrained use of or - classically - complete absence of oak.

Chablis's claim to fame is a geological formation of limestone and clay that it shares with parts of southern England, and which is known as Kimmeridgian after the Dorset village of Kimmeridge. This is held to endow the wines with their celebrated minerality, an austere hardness that makes them worth ageing for a few years.

The class structure of the wines of Chablis is much the same as in the rest of Burgundy. The top vineyard sites are designated *grand cru*, the next best *premier cru* and then come the wines of the basic appellation. In Chablis, this is supplemented by a basement category of Petit Chablis. This covers wines from land just outside the main appellation, and wines from within it where the vines have not attained the minimum age for Chablis proper.

Grands crus There are seven of these, all located on the same south-facing slope just to the north of the town of Chablis itself. They are: Blanchots, Bougros, Les Clos, Grenouilles, Les Preuses, Valmur and Vaudésir. (If you come across Chablis from a vineyard called La Moutonne, consider it *grand cru*, even though it officially isn't. It has the misfortune to straddle Les Preuses and Vaudésir and therefore escapes the classification.) These are the richest and weightiest Chablis, and quality is by and large very reliable. They should be at least five years old before drinking, and many will have had

their naturally more opulent flavours enhanced by oak ageing. If you are trading up from basic Chablis, go all the way up to *grand cru*.

Premiers crus There are around 40 vineyards specified for *premier cru*, although many of them shelter under larger collective names. The more commonly encountered of these are: Fourchaume, Beauroy, Vaillons, Montée de Tonnerre, Montmains and Côte de Léchet. The numbers of the *premiers crus* have gone on increasing steadily as consortia of growers in vineyards that hitherto came under straight AC Chablis have persuaded the appellation authorities to upgrade them. In far too many cases, it has to be said, these promotions were either very borderline or else wholly unjustified. The result is that a lot of *premier cru* tastes no different to normal Chablis, and can't therefore justify the extra premium it charges: 40-50 per cent on top of the price of AC Chablis.

CHABLIS
GRAPE: Chardonnay

Four of Chablis's seven grand cru vineyards (below): looking from Grenouilles towards Vaudésir, Preuses and Bougros beyond.

Chablis The basic appellation is the most extensive area of the total vineyard. At its best, it is a faintly appley, sometimes attractively vegetal wine, with fresh lemony acidity and powerful but not overwhelming alcohol - the essence of unoaked Chardonnay. It is a style that is often imitated elsewhere by picking the grapes earlier to attain higher acid levels, but good Chablis shouldn't ever be bitter or green. Indeed, at its centre, there is a paradoxical softness. As it ages, it often assumes a richer, more honeyed quality, as if it had spent some time in barrels on its way from vine to bottle, though it may have done no such thing.

Petit Chablis Just as a lot of simple Chablis was elevated to *premier cru*, so a lot of Petit Chablis has miraculously become Chablis, with the result that there is very little land planted in the Petit Chablis designation. The wines generally lack concentration and breeding, with the (very) occasional shining exception.

CHABLIS PRODUCERS: René Dauvissat, François & Jean-Marie Raveneau, Denis Race, Daniel Defaix, Robert Vocoret, Louis Michel, Jean Durup, la Chablisienne co-operative. For the best of the oak-influenced Chablis, go to William Fèvre.

BEST RECENT VINTAGES: *1992, 1990, 1989, 1988, 1986, 1985.*

COTE DE NUITS

GRAPES: Red - Pinot Noir; White - Chardonnay, small amount of Pinot Blanc

COTE DE NUITS

The northern half of the Côte d'Or, starting just south of Dijon, is the Côte de Nuits. The area is particularly noted for its red wines, although a small amount of white is produced in some appellations. For many aspirant red winemakers around the world, the Côte de Nuits is *the* true heartland of Pinot Noir. The majestic intensity (and scarcity) of the wines makes the highest among them - the legendary *grands crus* - among the most sought-after and highly-valued red wines on the planet.

This guide to the appellations runs from north to south. Some of the villages have individually designated vineyard sites within their appellations, *premiers crus* and (at the top of the tree) *grands crus*. I have listed here the names of the *grands crus* (GC) followed by the number of *premiers crus* (pc), where they are appropriate.

Marsannay An AC since 1987, Marsannay has always been famed for its light, strawberryish rosé, but it can come in all three colours. The reds are getting better. Good value.

PRODUCERS: Roty, Jadot, Bruno Clair.

Fixin Meaty reds with considerable depth and structure, if not always great finesse. Some humdrum white. (5 pc.)

PRODUCERS: Bruno Clair, Moillard.

Gevrey-Chambertin The first of the great appellations (reds only). Powerful, strongly scented, beefy wines with richness and ageability at their best. GC: Mazis-Chambertin, Ruchottes-Chambertin, Chambertin Clos-de-Bèze, Chapelle-Chambertin, Griotte-Chambertin, Charmes-Chambertin, Le Chambertin, Latricières-Chambertin. (28 pc.)

PRODUCERS: Rossignol-Trapet, René Leclerc, Joseph Roty, Roumier, Dom. Dujac, Jadot, Faiveley.

Morey-St-Denis Somewhat lighter than Gevrey, but still having that beef-stock character over fruit like dark-skinned plums. Tiny amounts of white. GC: Clos de la Roche, Clos St-Denis, Clos des Lambrays, Clos de Tart, Bonnes Mares. (20 pc.)

PRODUCERS: Groffier, both Lignier brothers, Roumier, Dom. Rousseau, Serveau.

Chambolle-Musigny Generally over-light reds with sweet strawberry fruit, atypical for the Côte de Nuits. GC: Bonnes Mares (overlapping with the above), Le Musigny (which can also be white). (24 pc.)

PRODUCERS: Roumier, Serveau, Hudelot-Noëllat, Faiveley, Drouhin, Prieur.

Vougeot Small production of sound wines from the basic AC, totally overshadowed by the *grand cru*. Also some fair whites. GC: Clos de Vougeot. (4 pc.)

PRODUCERS: Leroy, Méo-Camuzet, Mugneret.

Vosne-Romanée Superbly aromatic, gamey Pinot, intensely ripe raspberry fruit and huge structure. Demands ageing. The *grands crus* - famously from the celebrated Domaine de la Romanée-Conti - are the best reds in Burgundy, made in tiny quantities at prices to induce a blackout. No whites. The neighbouring commune of Flagey-Echézeaux has two *grands crus* but its village wine is labelled Vosne-Romanée. GC: Grands Echézeaux, Echézeaux, Richebourg, Romanée-St-Vivant, Romanée-Conti, La Romanée, La Grande Rue, La Tâche. (13 pc.)

PRODUCERS: Dom. de la Romanée-Conti, Leroy, Méo-Camuzet, Jayer, Gros, Grivot, Daniel Rion, Clerget, Confuron.

Nuits-St-Georges Famous for decades in the UK. At best, classically meaty, cherry-fruited reds with great depth and complexity, but can be patchy. Some rather solid whites. (27 pc.)

PRODUCERS: Leroy, Gouges, Dom. de l'Arlot, Chevillon, Chopin-Groffier, Moillard, Jadot, Jaffelin, Rion, Grivot.

Hautes-Côtes-de-Nuits A group of little villages in the hills to the west of the Côte de Nuits is bunched together under this appellation, a reliable starting-point for those wanting a gentle run-up to the more extravagant stuff. The fruit on the reds is generally excellent and the wines hint at the sinewy structure of the top Côte de Nuits. The whites are soft and hazelnutty, if unspectacular.

PRODUCERS: Jayer-Gilles, Verdet, Cave des Hautes-Côtes.

Côtes de Nuits-Villages An appellation that gathers in a handful of villages from the extreme northern and southern ends of the Côte de Nuits area itself. Usually well-made, if lightish reds.

PRODUCERS: Philippe Rossignol, Chopin-Groffier, Daniel Rion.

COTE DE BEAUNE

This is the southern stretch of the Côte d'Or, an area particularly famed for its white wines, although there are many good reds too. Burgundy's highly reputed oak-aged Chardonnays come mainly from the southern end of the Côte de Beaune, while the best reds from further north are fully the equals of those from the Côte de Nuits. They tend to be slightly softer and more immediately approachable, however, emphasising red fruit flavours first and the classic Burgundian meatiness second.

Once again, this is a north-to-south listing of the appellations, with the *grands crus* (GC) named and the number of *premiers crus* (pc) stated, where appropriate.

Pernand-Vergelesses Delicate whites and slimline reds can both be very attractive when a lighter style is required, but this is not generally the appellation to choose for the full-throttle Burgundy experience. Some of Burgundy's unsung alternative white wine, Aligoté (from the grape of that name), comes from around this village: expect lemon-sharp acids over a softer sour-cream base. GC: about a quarter of the *grand cru* Corton-Charlemagne lies within this appellation. (4 pc.)

PRODUCERS: Delarche, Pavelot, Rollin, Chandon de Briailles.

Ladoix Rarely seen appellation of the village of Ladoix-Serrigny, almost all lean, simple red. Now for the confusing part. GC: about one-

The château of Gevrey-Chambertin (above), the first of the great red Burgundy appellations in the Côte de Nuits.

eighth of Le Corton (nearly all red) and a tiny part of Corton-Charlemagne (white only) lie within Ladoix, although they are officially the *grands crus* of Aloxe-Corton (see below). Similarly, some of Ladoix's *premiers crus* are claimed by Aloxe-Corton, leaving it with 5 pc to call its own.

PRODUCERS: Ravaut, Chevalier, Capitain-Gagnerot.

Aloxe-Corton Good, muscular reds from the village appellation and a minuscule quantity of underwhelming white. GC: Le Corton (the only *grand cru* for red wines on the Côte de Beaune) may have any one of up to 21 vineyard names attached to it, eg. Corton-Bressandes, Corton-Perrières, Corton-Clos du Roi, etc. Corton-Charlemagne (the *grand cru* for whites only) is shared, as above, with Ladoix and Pernand-Vergelesses. (12 pc, some technically in the village of Ladoix.)

PRODUCERS: Chandon de Briailles, Bonneau du Martray, Remoissenet, Rapet, Louis Latour, Voarick, Tollot-Beaut.

COTE DE BEAUNE
GRAPES: *Red - Pinot Noir; White - Chardonnay, some Pinot Blanc and Aligoté*

The famous Hôtel de Dieu (above), glimpsed through the entrance to the Hospices de Beaune in the village of Beaune.

Savigny-lès-Beaune On the western side of the Côte, this was once considered rather rustic and forgettable, but improvements in winemaking have begun to alter that perception. Still relatively sanely priced. Good red-fruit Pinot. A very little decent white. (11 pc, on either bank of the Rhoin, a trickle of a river that runs through Savigny.)
PRODUCERS: Chandon de Briailles, Bize, Tollot-Beaut, Drouhin.

Chorey-lès-Beaune Underrated, and therefore generally affordable, reds (and tiny amounts of white). The best have the ripe red fruit of good Beaune Pinot, with some depth and ageability to boot. Worth looking out for.
PRODUCERS: Tollot-Beaut, Senard, Arnoux.

Beaune The village after which this part of the Côte is named. Famous for soft, strawberry-scented reds of great elegance. Also some initially hard but eventually impressive Chardonnay. (28 pc.)
PRODUCERS: Morot, Germain, Prunier, Hospices de Beaune (holder of Burgundy's annual wine auction in aid of several charities), Jadot, Drouhin.

Pommard Classy, long-lived red wines with as much authoritative weight as some Côte de Nuits reds. In the wrong hands, can be rather clumsy. Price-quality ratio not currently very favourable. (27 pc.)
PRODUCERS: Dom. de la Pousse d'Or, Comte Armand, Boillot, de Montille, Lafarge.

Volnay Top-drawer Beaune Pinot, at best perfectly capturing the combination of creamy red fruit (raspberries, loganberries) with underlying savoury depth. Arguably the finest red of the Côte de Beaune. Expensive, but overall standard of achievement very good. (35 pc.)
PRODUCERS: Dom. de la Pousse d'Or, Blain-Gagnard, Comte Lafon, de Montille, Lafarge, Ampeau, Hospices de Beaune.

Monthélie Suffers from its position between Volnay and Meursault, both of which are far more famous, this is nonetheless a good village for sturdy, if not noticeably elegant reds. (9 pc.)
PRODUCERS: Potinet-Ampeau, Doreau, Jadot.

St-Romain On the western flank of the Côte, St-Romain makes both white and red burgundy, its earthily dry Chardonnays distinctly better than its light and often inconsequential Pinot Noirs.
PRODUCERS: Thévenin, Gras, Germain.

Auxey-Duresses Quality for both reds and whites was on something of a roller-coaster in the 1980s, but things are looking up with some gentle, strawberryish Pinot and pleasantly buttery Chardonnay. (6 pc.)
PRODUCERS: Leroy, Diconne, Ampeau, Duc de Magenta, Prunier.

Meursault First of the important white-wine villages, and the only one with no *grand cru*. The wines of Meursault are hugely fat and rich, heavily oaked golden creations, full of honey and butterscotch. Increasing overproduction, however, has meant that surprisingly cheap-looking Meursault is likely to be poor value. (13 pc, two of which - Blagny and Santenots - are also for red wine, in which case they don't mention the name Meursault. Santenots then counts as a *premier cru* of Volnay.)
PRODUCERS: Comte Lafon, Coche-Dury, Boisson-Vadot, Roulot, Michelot-Buisson, Jobard, René Manuel's Clos des Bouches Chères (marketed by Labouré-Roi).

Puligny-Montrachet The village wines are leaner than Meursault, though still creamy and hazelnutty, and rounded with plenty of new oak. From here on in, all the wines bask to some degree in the reflected glory of the greatest white burgundy of them all, the *grand cru* Le Montrachet, which makes hauntingly powerful, smoky, palate-blasting Chardonnay at second-mortgage prices. There is a little fairly dull red Puligny. GC: Le Montrachet, Bâtard-Montrachet (both shared with AC Chassagne-Montrachet - see below), Chevalier-Montrachet and Bienvenues-Bâtard-Montrachet. (14 pc.)
PRODUCERS: Sauzet, Dom. Leflaive, Carillon, Drouhin and, for *grands crus*, Dom. de la Romanée-Conti, Amiot-Bonfils, Bachelet-Ramonet, Niellon, Lequin-Roussot and Drouhin's Montrachet Laguiche.

St-Aubin Out west, this up-and-coming appellation is making some fine, smoky, pedigree Chardonnay and a larger quantity of light, strawberry Pinot at very attractive prices. Should be on every shopping-list. Most of the appellation is *premier cru*. (10 pc.)
PRODUCERS: Thomas, Bachelet, Clerget, Albert Morey, Prudhon, Lamy.

Chassagne-Montrachet Last of the great white-wine villages, perhaps the least spectacular for its basic village wines - though they still have the imprint of fine Burgundian Chardonnay - but producing some memorable *grands crus*. Reds are pretty much run-of-the-mill. GC: Le Montrachet, Bâtard-Montrachet (both shared with AC Puligny-Montrachet), Criots-Bâtard-Montrachet (all its own). (16 pc.)

PRODUCERS: Blain-Gagnard, Dom. Ramonet, Bachelet-Ramonet, Duc de Magenta, Ch. de la Maltroye, Jaffelin.

Santenay In the south of the Côte, Santenay produces mainly reds of no conspicuous finesse. Can be a satisfyingly hearty glass of basic Pinot, though, from the better growers. (8 pc.)
PRODUCERS: Dom. de la Pousse d'Or, Lequin-Roussot, Girardin, Drouhin.

Maranges An AC created in 1988 that unites three villages - Dezize, Sampigny and Cheilly - each suffixed by -lès-Maranges, although the wines may simply be labelled Maranges. Production is overwhelmingly red, and fairly rustic stuff it is too, though scarcely overpriced.
PRODUCERS: Drouhin.

Hautes-Côtes-de-Beaune As in the Côte de Nuits, there is a scattering of villages among the hills to the west of the Côte de Beaune that take this appellation. Quality is generally very good, notably for the soft, cherry-fruited reds.
PRODUCERS: Mazilly, Joliot, Caves des Hautes-Côtes.

Côte de Beaune-Villages Red-wine appellation that covers most of the Côte, and may be used by any of the individual villages (with the big four exceptions of Aloxe-Corton, Beaune, Pommard and Volnay) or for any wine blended from two or more villages, a practice not much in evidence on the Côte de Beaune now.
PRODUCERS: Lequin-Roussot, Jaffelin.

Côte de Beaune The simplest appellation in the area takes in vineyards on the hill overlooking the village of Beaune itself - but not from anywhere else on the Côte, perplexingly. The wines may be red or white and are mainly of undistinguished quality.

CÔTE CHALONNAISE

The large bulk-producing area in the south of Burgundy, the Mâconnais, is separated from the southern tip of the Côte d'Or by a strip of vineyard called the Côte Chalonnaise. It takes its name from the town of Chalon-sur-Saône on the banks of the river Saône to the east. As well as producing some basic Bourgogne Rouge and Blanc, there are five important village appellations here. Because their reputation is nothing like as exalted as the villages of the Côte d'Or, these generally represent good value, although they don't have quite the class of their northern neighbours. This list runs north to south.

Bourgogne Aligoté de Bouzeron Although white wines from the enigmatic Aligoté grape

are made further north in Burgundy, the village of Bouzeron was granted its own appellation for such wines in 1979. The popular aperitif, Kir, is traditionally made from Aligoté with a slug of crème de cassis (blackcurrant liqueur) in it, but Bouzeron's Aligoté is considered a cut above that sort of treatment. Even so, it should be drunk fairly young to capture its challenging lemon-and-crème-fraîche character.
PRODUCERS: de Villaine, Chanzy, Bouchard père et fils.

Rully Increasingly fashionable lately, the whites and reds of this village have now eclipsed its erstwhile reputation as a source of cheap and cheerful fizz. Its whites are lighter and drier than from the Côte de Beaune, but well-made by and large, as are its simple, plummy reds. (19 pc.)
PRODUCERS: Jacqueson, Dom. de la Folie, Faiveley, Jaffelin.

Mercurey The lion's share of Chalonnaise production comes from this village, which is why you will sometimes see the whole region referred to as the "Région de Mercurey". Mostly well-balanced, concentrated reds, though whites

COTE CHALONNAISE
GRAPES: White - Chardonnay, Aligoté; Red - Pinot Noir

Dusk falls over the vineyards of the Hautes-Côtes-de-Nuits AC, in the hills of the Côte d'Or (below).

MACONNAIS/
OTHER WINES
GRAPES: *Red - Pinot Noir,*
Gamay, César, Tressot;
White - Chardonnay,
Aligoté, Pinot Blanc, Pinot
Gris, Sacy

Chardonnay grapes arriving
at the Caves de Buxy co-
operative (below) in the
Montagny AC, Côte
Chalonnaise.

have recently shown much improvement, and can be surprisingly rich. (29 pc.)

PRODUCERS: Ch. de Chamirey, Juillot, Sure-main, Chartron et Trébuchet, Faiveley.

Givry Predominantly red wines in an impressively scented raspberry style, with good structure. Small amount of intriguingly spicy white. (5 pc.)

PRODUCERS: Delorme, Chofflet, Lespinasse, Mouton.

Montagny Quality in this appellation for white wines only is decidedly patchy. Some possess convincing intensity; many taste pretty similar to anonymous Mâcon Blanc-Villages. Ridiculously enough, the designation *premier cru* applies not to specific vineyards in Montagny but - uniquely in France - to any wine that attains a minimum alcohol level of 11.5 per cent.

PRODUCERS: Caves de Buxy co-operative, Vachet, Roy, Louis Latour.

MACONNAIS

The southernmost region of Burgundy is the Mâconnais, opposite the town of Mâcon, which is in many ways the commercial hub of the region. The majority of Burgundy's co-operatives are found in the Mâconnais and further south in Beaujolais. Predominantly everyday whites, with one or two stars, the production is very much geared to bulk markets and is easily outshone in many instances by low-priced Chardonnays from elsewhere in the world. The following wines are listed in descending order of quality rather than geographically.

Pouilly-Fuissé A whites-only appellation that carries the quality torch for the Mâconnais as a whole, and prices its wines in accordance with its ambition. At their classiest, they are richly oaked and fleshy, and do display some pedigree. Neighbouring appellations of Pouilly-Vinzelles and Pouilly-Loché are not quite in the same class.

PRODUCERS: Forest, Manciat-Poncet, Ch. de Fuissé, Guffens-Heynen.

St-Véran In the dead south of the region, overlapping into Beaujolais and wholly enclosing the appellation of Pouilly-Fuissé, St-Véran is a somewhat underrated source of dry, chalky Chardonnay wines with a certain amount of Burgundian flair.

PRODUCERS: Lassarat, Dom. des Deux Roches, Drouhin, Duboeuf.

Mâcon-Villages The umbrella appellation for the Mâconnais covers a total of 43 villages, all of which have the right to append their names to the word Mâcon on the label. Otherwise, the wine is simply labelled Mâcon-Villages, red or white. Some of the more famous villages are Lugny, Viré, Prissé, Montbellet, Clessé, Uchizy, La Roche-Vineuse and - tantalisingly - Chardonnay. Red wine labelled Mâcon, rather than Bourgogne, is almost always likely to be made from the Beaujolais grape Gamay.

PRODUCERS: Lassarat, Manciat-Poncet, Guffens-Heynen, Josserand.

Below Mâcon-Villages are the basic appellations of Mâcon Supérieur (reds and whites) and simple Mâcon (reds only).

OTHER WINES

The basic appellation for the whole region, top to bottom, is AC Bourgogne - Blanc or Rouge. Some of the more northerly village wines, notably those from the Auxerre region near Chablis, should eventually receive individual ACs. Some, such as Chitry, Irancy and Epineuil, already have the right to add their names to the basic Bourgogne designation. In the whites, Chardonnay may be joined by leavenings of Pinot Blanc and Pinot Gris, while reds - generally unblended Pinot Noir - may also contain Gamay and even a couple of historical oddities from near Chablis - César and Tressot.

A little-seen label, Bourgogne Grand Ordinaire, is rock-bottom stuff under which a cocktail of ignoble grapes may be used for both red and white. Bourgogne Passetoutgrains is the AC for a blend of just Pinot Noir and Gamay, in which the former should account for not less than a

third of the *assemblage*. Pink wines from anywhere in the region are labelled Bourgogne Rosé or Bourgogne Clairet.

The champagne-method sparkling wine is Crémant de Bourgogne. Made from any of the region's grapes, but principally Chardonnay and Pinot Noir, it is entitled to use the terms Blanc de Blancs and Blanc de Noirs for white wines made from all white grapes or all black grapes respectively. There is also some Crémant rosé.

VINTAGE GUIDE

Vintage conditions in Burgundy affect the red wines far more than the whites. An off-year for Chardonnay may result in dilute but perfectly drinkable wines, whereas unripe Pinot Noir may be feeble in colour, flimsy in texture and hopelessly lacking fruit.

REDS

2001 ** Similar to 2000, very dependent on the individual producer. Côte de Nuits the safest bet.
2000 ** Distinctly underwhelming. Wet conditions resulted in a major letdown.
1999 *** A troubled vintage. Some good wines from the Côte de Beaune, but many lack flesh.
1998 *** Some harder, stalky flavours marred many of the wines. Côte de Nuits slightly better.
1997 **** Another lovely vintage that nearly rivals '88, '89 and '90.
1996 ***** The best since 1990. Expressive, aromatic wines that began developing early.
1995 **** Ripe, well-structured wines that are still showing their tannins. Will be great.
1990 ***** Superb, immensely rich and concentrated wines for the cellar. Most need a good few years to begin to acquire the bottle-aged complexity they deserve. The most stunning vintage of recent times.
1989 **** Very charming, supple wines that began to blossom quite early on in their careers, but will hold well and carry on developing.
1988 **** Big, chunky, often quite tannic, reds that should be kept until around ten years old.
1985 ***** A classic Pinot vintage of beautifully soft, supple and ripe-fruited wines, most still going strong but now horribly expensive.
EARLIER HIGHLIGHTS: *1982* *** *1980* *** *1979* *** *1978* ***** *1971* ***** *1969* **** *1959* *****

WHITES

BEST RECENT VINTAGES: *2000, 1998, '97, '96, '95, 92, 90.*

The rock of Vergisson (above) towers over the Pouilly-Fuissé vineyards, source of Mâconnais's finest white burgundies.

Barrels awaiting the new vintage (left) at Louis Latour's cellars in Aloxe-Corton, Côte de Beaune.

BEAUJOLAIS

Burgundy's southernmost wine region, the huge Beaujolais area, is devoted to the red grape Gamay and one of the winemaking world's most individual red wine styles. The winemakers here offer much more than just "Nouveau".

The hilly Beaujolais region (above), the most southerly of Burgundy's wine areas.

BEAUJOLAIS
GRAPES: *Red - Gamay; White - Chardonnay*

IT IS THE FATE OF Beaujolais never to be taken quite seriously. It is such a lightweight wine that few bother to age it, and certainly most retail outlets only ever sell the last couple of vintages. This means that the occasional pleasure that can be afforded by drinking a relatively mature Beaujolais with roast meats, or even a firm-textured fish like salmon, is denied to most. Then again, the fact that the regional industry happily sells about a third of its annual production hot off the presses as Beaujolais Nouveau doesn't exactly send out a message that this is a wine worth dwelling on.

All this is something of a shame, because when Beaujolais is on song - and it does fall woefully short of the mark too often - it is an incomparably charming wine. It can be as light-textured as the thinnest Italian reds such as Bardolino or red Lambrusco, and yet it still manages to have more substance than those because of its alcoholic weight and the easy, accessible ripeness of its juicy strawberry fruit. The drawback of very young Beaujolais is that it is extremely acidic, a trait the French themselves tend to be more relaxed about than most other wine consumers.

As we saw in the grape variety section on the Beaujolais grape, Gamay, there are moves in some quarters to give some of the *cru* wines more depth and power by varying the vinification method (traditionally *macération carbonique*, as explained under *Gamay*) to allow a little tannin into the wines. Those used to the chilled light reds of summer may find these wines something of a shock to the system. So, too, may those used to seeing Beaujolais as an oak-free zone when they first taste the barrel-matured wines of a producer such as Guy Depardon in Fleurie.

By and large, though, Beaujolais remains pre-eminently an unchallenging summer tipple, easily made and bottled early. In the light of that, it is hard to see why it should be priced quite as forbiddingly as it is, especially now that it has clear stylistic rivals from elsewhere in Europe.

The more basic the quality and the younger it is, the colder Beaujolais should be drunk. The best *cru* wines, however, when aged for six or seven years, can achieve a positively Burgundian gamey complexity. Négociants dominate the Beaujolais scene (most notably the excellent Georges Duboeuf) but there are many fine small growers to watch out for too.

The top wines, known as *cru* Beaujolais, come from ten villages thought to have the best vineyard sites. From north to south, they are:
St-Amour The one traditionally drunk on Valentine's Day, of course. Intensely fragrant, but with a hint of Burgundian structure to it as well, it is often one of the best-balanced of the *cru* Beaujolais.
PRODUCERS: Dom. des Ducs, Saillant, Ch. de St-Amour, Trichard.
Juliénas One of the less charming wines, often rather hard and insufficiently endowed with fruit, but made in a softer style by some.
PRODUCERS: Ch. de Juliénas, Pelletier, Perraud, Tête, certain of the Duboeuf cuvées.
Chénas At this point, the *cru* wines start becoming bolder and sturdier than the popular image of Beaujolais allows for. These are prime candidates for ageing, being clenched and dour in their first flush of youth but ageing to a meaty, sinewy richness.
PRODUCERS: Champagnon, Perrachon, Ch. de Chénas, Dom. des Brureaux, Lapierre.
Moulin-à-Vent The Beaujolais that seems to think it's a Rhône wine, Moulin-à-Vent is always the biggest and burliest of the *crus*. From a good producer, the wines can take ten years' ageing in their stride, but they can be just as enjoyable at three or four years, with ripe blackberry fruit and often a fair bit of tannin.
PRODUCERS: Janodet, Ch. des Jacques, Duboeuf's Dom. de la Tour du Bief, Siffert, Dom. Diochon, Dom. de la Rochelle.
Fleurie Still the best-loved of the *crus* - and therefore inevitably usually the most expensive these days. Classic Fleurie is summer-scented with strawberries and roses, light-textured and creamy and soft. A lot isn't. Depardon's atypical wines will shock the purists, but are masterpieces of violets-and-ginger-and-Turkish-Delight seductiveness, and need ageing for a decade.

PRODUCERS: Depardon, Duboeuf's Dom. des Quatre Vents and La Madone, Verpoix, Chignard, Berrod's Les Roches du Vivier.

Chiroubles Light and attractive wines, not much seen outside France, but worth trying if you come across one.

PRODUCERS: Passot, Méziat, Boulon, Ch. de Raousset, Cheysson, Dom. de la Rocassière.

Morgon Morgon's wines are famous for their capacity to age very quickly into a light, but interestingly meaty Burgundian maturity, an experience worth seeking out. To capitalise on this, some is released with the designation Morgon Agé - it is cellared for 18 months before it hits the market. Even in youth, there is a savouriness to them, and the fruit is often Cabernet-like blackcurrant rather than Gamay strawberry.

PRODUCERS: Janodet, Didier Desvignes, Duboeuf's Dom. Jean Descombes, Aucoeur, Ch. de Pizay.

Régnié The new *cru* on the block, since 1988 anyway. To put it charitably, Régnié was very lucky to be upgraded (there are other, more deserving villages such as Lancié).

PRODUCERS: Duboeuf, Rampon, Durand.

Brouilly Silky-soft, cherry-fruited charmers at their best, the wines of Brouilly are the most approachable of all *cru* Beaujolais. They don't generally need ageing, as their youthful fruit is too attractive to waste. Has by far the biggest production of the ten.

PRODUCERS: Large, Ch. de la Chaize, Jambon, Duboeuf's Ch. de Nevers and Dom. de Combillaty.

Côte de Brouilly Hillside vineyards in the middle of Brouilly, but possessing unique soil and exposure, and consequently making distinctive wine. Deeper cherry fruit and richer texture than Brouilly itself, and some have a touch of gingery spice to them. Underrated and not much exported, but this is definitely one to try.

PRODUCERS: Ch. de Thivin, Chanrion, Pavillon de Chavannes, Verger.

Wines from any of 39 villages in the northern part of the region may be sold as Beaujolais-Villages, with the village name mentioned if the wine comes solely from that vineyard. The rest is basic Beaujolais and represents a significant drop in quality. Buy a Villages wines if you are not in the market for a *cru*. There are small amounts of usually rather feeble Beaujolais rosé, and often pretty impressive, if austere, Beaujolais blanc made from Chardonnay.

As to Nouveau, it is the wine of the new vintage, released on to the market on the third Wednesday of November. In occasional years, it can be good, but it mostly stinks of fermentation and will make you queasy with acid-stomach syndrome. Yum.

BEST RECENT VINTAGES: *2001, 2000, 1999, '97, '95, '93, '91, '90.*

Gamay vines under an autumnal mist in the village of Juliénas (below), one of the more northerly of the Beaujolais cru *villages.*

RHONE

Overshadowed for centuries by Bordeaux and Burgundy, the Rhône Valley is nonetheless the source of formidable spicy, rich reds and intriguing whites from its two distinct areas - the Syrah-dominated north and the mixed culture of the south.

NORTHERN RHONE
GRAPES: *Red - Syrah;*
White - Viognier, Marsanne,
Roussanne

The Rhône river lends its name to the long stretch of the Rhône valley wine region (below), divided into two distinct viticultural districts - northern and southern Rhône.

THE RHONE VALLEY consists of two quite distinct viticultural districts about 50km (30 miles) apart, and referred to simply as Northern and Southern Rhône. Back in the 14th century, when the papacy was temporarily moved for political reasons from Rome to Avignon, in the southern Rhône valley, the local wines found immense favour with the papal retinue. Such was the wines' popularity that they ended up drinking more of them than the beloved and much prized burgundy.

Despite such lofty endorsement, however, the region never quite attained the premier status of Bordeaux and Burgundy. The odd wine, principally Hermitage from the northern Rhône and, to a lesser extent, Châteauneuf-du-Pape from the south, were known among British connoisseurs, but that was about it.

In the last 20 years or so, all that has changed. The Rhône has been "discovered", and deservedly so, since its finest red wines are as long-lived and opulent as top-flight claret, while its small production of dry white wines includes some quixotic and arresting flavours that can offer welcome relief to those suffering from Chardonnay-fatigue.

THE NORTHERN RHONE APPELLATIONS
(from north to south)

Côte-Rôtie What distinguishes the reds of the north from those of the south is that they are made purely from Syrah, whereas the southern wines are always a mix, with Syrah usually a fairly junior partner in the blend. Having said that, Côte-Rôtie is permitted to include up to 20 per cent of the white grape Viognier (see Condrieu, below). Not all producers use it, but those that do add a little - and it is hardly ever the full 20 per cent - produce perfumed wines of astonishing intensity.

The appellation's name, the "roasted slope", refers to its steep southeast-facing hillside on the left bank of the river, where the vines are sheltered from the worst the weather can do, and enjoy their own little sun-trap. In the hotter years, Côte-Rôtie is an uncommonly concentrated wine, crammed full of blackberry fruit and tannin, but with layers of spice and chocolate underneath, just waiting for a decade's maturation. It is arguably even more highly prized than Hermitage itself these days, with the inevitable consequence that prices for the wines of the best growers have shot through the roof. At the pinnacle of ambition are the wines of Marcel Guigal, who makes not only a straight AC Côte-Rôtie, but also three wines from single vineyards (La Landonne, La Mouline and La Turque) for which he charges the earth.
OTHER PRODUCERS: Jasmin, Jamet, Delas (especially the Seigneur de Maugiron), Rostaing, Gentaz-Dervieux, Champet.
Condrieu The sole grape of this white-wine appellation is Viognier, suddenly fashionable in the last few years as the wine world looks for a variety that can supply the broad textures of good Chardonnay with some distinctive aromatic personality. Condrieu is its true home, making wines that set the pace for all other growers of the variety. The wines initially seem rather heavy and creamy on the nose, but then a wonderfully musky scent of squashed ripe apricots comes through, followed by subtle spice notes that are often reminiscent of Indian cooking - cardamom pods, sticks of cinnamon,

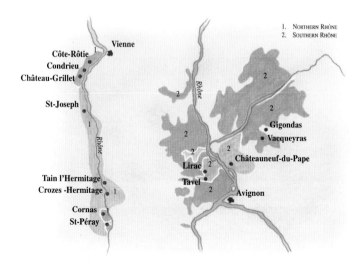

1. NORTHERN RHÔNE
2. SOUTHERN RHÔNE

Vienne
Côte-Rôtie
Condrieu
Château-Grillet
St-Joseph
Gigondas
Vacqueyras
Lirac
Châteauneuf-du-Pape
Tavel
Tain l'Hermitage
Crozes -Hermitage
Avignon
Cornas
St-Péray

ginger root - but all bound by that thick, clotted-cream feel. Many producers achieve this, moreover, without resorting to oak. Opinion tends to divide on the best moment to drink these wines. I think they are at their best fairly young, up to two years old. Once again, they are expensive, but worth trying at least once.
PRODUCERS: La Côte-Chéry, Vernay, Guigal, Dumazet, Cuilleron, Ch. du Rozay, Perret.

Château-Grillet Single-vineyard enclave of four hectares within Condrieu, wholly owned by the Neyret-Gachet family, awarded an appel-lation all of its own. The wine is aged in cask, and is intended to be far longer-lived than Con-drieu. Consensus is that its performance is patchy, often not as good as the top Condrieus.

St-Joseph Red and white wines. The reds may not be as distinguished as those of Côte-Rôtie or Hermitage, but do have a raspberry-fruited immediacy to them and some modest ageing potential. Some producers make a practically Beaujolais-like lighter red, but even the heavier ones are nothing like as dense as other northern Rhône reds. Whites are made from a pair of grapes often found together in these parts - Marsanne and Roussanne. There isn't much made in St-Joseph, but what there is is fairly chunky, walnut-dry in style.
PRODUCERS: Chave, Grippat, Trollat, Le Grand Pompée from Jaboulet (one the most important and reliable companies in the Rhône).

Crozes-Hermitage The largest output, mostly of red wines, of the north comes from this appellation. Usually considered to be at the foot of the ladder for quality, but in fact its wines are remarkably well-made, even at the basic co-operative level, and can therefore represent outstanding value. Peppery, plummy and firm-textured, they are capable of ageing for a few years. Up to 15 per cent white grapes (Marsanne and Roussanne) may be added to them, though rarely are. The white wines them-selves are rather hefty and uninspiring.
PRODUCERS: Graillot, Jaboulet's Dom. du Thalabert, Ferraton, Chapoutier's Les Meyson-niers, Combier, Pochon, Cave des Clairmonts.

Hermitage The great hill of Hermitage pops up in the middle of the Crozes appellation, and its steeply shelving vineyards form the famed AC of Hermitage itself. Often among the most majestically proportioned red wines made any-where in France, they are huge, powerfully concentrated, full-on Syrah, with tannin and extract to spare and demanding the best part of

a decade to begin to unwind. When they do, one of the causes of these wines' success is revealed: their fruit remains as vibrantly fresh as the day they were bottled, so that even at 12 years old they can gush forth blackberries and raspberries in abundance, backed up by dark chocolate and the most savoury herbs - thyme and rosemary. Whites, a blend of Marsanne and Roussanne, are rich and heavy, with flavours of roasted nuts and a twist of liquorice.
PRODUCERS: Guigal, Jaboulet's Hermitage La Chapelle, Chave, Delas, Sorrel, Ferraton, Vidal-Fleury, Chapoutier's La Sizeranne.

Cornas Enigmatic appellation for densely textured, tannic Syrah reds that never quite seem to open out into the fruit-filled glories of Hermitage. Tasted blind, they can often resemble the burlier versions of blended Châteauneuf-du-Pape, with roasting-meat aromas filling out the expected black-pepper character.
PRODUCERS: Clape, Colombo's Dom. des Ruchets, Verset, Voge, Jaboulet.

St-Péray Mainly noted for rather tough, unfriendly sparkling wine, made from the white Hermitage grapes (plus another, fairly rare variety, Roussette) using the champagne method, but lacking elegance. Some strangely cheesy but often likeable still white is also made.
PRODUCERS: Clape, Grippat, Juge.

Vineyards of Côte-Rôtie, "the roasted slope" (above), on the sunny left bank of the Rhône, overlooking the village of Ampuis.

Picking Viognier grapes at the four-hectare AC Château-Grillet (above), a single vineyard within Condrieu.

Vineyards of Châteauneuf-du-Pape (above), the most famous red wine of the southern Rhône.

SOUTHERN RHONE

GRAPES: *Red - Grenache, Cinsaut, Mourvèdre, Syrah, Carignan, Gamay; White - Clairette, Picpoul, Bourboulenc, Grenache Blanc, Roussanne, Marsanne, Muscat, Viognier*

THE SOUTHERN RHONE APPELLATIONS

Châteauneuf-du-Pape The most famous red wine of the southern Rhône, named after a palace built for one of the Avignon popes in the 14th century and flattened by Nazi bombers during the war, Châteauneuf is recognisable by the symbol of crossed keys embossed on its bottles. It embraces a wide stylistic range, from almost Beaujolais-light to fairly weighty, although these days it is never quite the blockbuster that old textbooks would lead you to believe. Principally Grenache, it can draw on 13 varieties, though most producers make do with three or four. It matures quite quickly too, and is perfectly drinkable at three years old, rarely possessing the fearsome tannins of young Hermitage. The white wines come from a cocktail of varieties led by such unlikely stars as Picpoul, Bourboulenc, Clairette and the white version of

Grenache. They tend to be fairly neutral in aroma, but appreciably fat, structured and alcoholic on the palate. Some exceptions, notably Ch. de Beaucastel, have real character and are worth keeping for three or four years. De Beaucastel also makes one of the very best reds.

OTHER PRODUCERS: Chante-Cigale, Dom. du Mont-Redon, Clos du Mont-Olivet, Ch. Rayas, Dom. du Vieux Télégraphe, Chapoutier's La Bernardine, Bonneau, Dom. de la Janasse.

Gigondas Seen as Châteauneuf's understudy, but a much fiercer, black-hearted wine, often rigidly tannic and head-clobberingly alcoholic. It needs plenty of time to soften up, but many of the wines are too austere to make the wait worthwhile.

PRODUCERS: Dom. du St-Gayan, Clos des Cazaux, Dom. Raspail, Jaboulet, Santa Duc.

Lirac On the opposite bank of the Rhône to Châteauneuf, this unfairly overlooked AC makes wines in all three colours - and all of them highly reliable. The reds have good fruit and considerable substance, the rosés are agreeably ripe and graceful and the whites are strong and flavourful. Good bargains.

PRODUCERS: Dom. les Garrigues, Dom. de la Tour, Maby, Ch. St-Roch.

Tavel An AC, unusually, for rosé wines only. They tend to look more beige than pink and have a lot of alcohol, but are not exactly overflowing with fruit. Most sit far too heavily on the palate to be considered refreshing summer quaffers. Try them with richly sauced shellfish and crustacean dishes.

PRODUCERS: Dom. de la Ginestière, Ch. d'Acquéria.

Vacqueyras Plucked from the mass of Côtes du Rhône-Villages in 1990 to become an appellation in its own right, Vacqueyras may be red, white or pink, although there is virtually no white to speak of. The reds are good spicy, gingery wines with a degree of rough-edged charm.

PRODUCERS: Dom. des Tours, Clos des Cazaux, Vidal-Fleury.

Côtes du Rhône-Villages A whole swathe of villages, from the Ardèche and the Drôme in the centre of the Rhône valley down through the southern section, are entitled to this appellation. Of those, 16 are allowed to append their names to the basic designation, among them Cairanne, Séguret, Sablet, Chusclun and Vinsobres. There are many conscientious winemakers, so quality across the board is quite dependable and the price is mostly right.

Côtes du Rhône This is the basic AC that covers all other villages, including those in the northern Rhône. Styles vary from light and fruity to tannin-driven reds, via some delightful rosé to a scant quantity of vaguely milky white. Quality, too, is all over the place, but at least the wines aren't costly. Reds to watch out for are Guigal's Côtes du Rhône, Dom. de Fonsalette and any wine labelled with the village name Brézème, from the area between the northern and southern zones, but which is made entirely from Syrah.

Other large areas around the southern Rhône make up a fair amount of the annual production, some of it at VDQS level (the next step down from AC), some of it not long promoted. Most of it is uncomplicated everyday stuff, but there are occasional stars. Côtes du Ventoux is a good area south of Vacqueyras (Jaboulet makes a fine red from there). Bordering it, the Côtes du Lubéron is less distinguished but quite acceptable. The Coteaux de Tricastin to the north makes reasonable wines, as does the VDQS Côtes du Vivarais. Costières de Nîmes is technically in the Languedoc, further south, but considers itself part of the Rhône, and its wines can be superb (look for those of the smartest producer, Paul Blanc).

In the central sector are two wine regions, the Coteaux de l'Ardèche and the Drôme, named after the one of the Rhône's tributaries. The former can be a source of good varietal wines (though not necessarily from the Rhône varieties - Mr Beaujolais, Georges Duboeuf, makes a good Gamay there).

The Drôme encompasses the small but good appellation of Châtillon-en-Diois, which makes Gamay reds and Chardonnay and Aligoté whites. There is also an interesting sparkling wine called Clairette de Die, made from the neutral Clairette grape, but often blended with grapey Muscat to make Clairette de Die Tradition - a dead ringer for sparkling Italian Asti to the uninitiated.

VINS DOUX NATURELS

These are sweet wine specialities of southern France. They are made naturally sweet by interrupting the fermentation of super-ripe grapes with the addition of spirit to produce a lightish fortified wine - basically the same method as is used for port.

Muscat de Beaumes-de-Venise The most celebrated of the fortified Muscats is a rich, golden dessert wine, tasting of ultra-sweet grapes and oranges, with a tongue-coating barley-sugar quality as well. They should be drunk young and fresh, and served very well chilled.
PRODUCERS: Dom. de Durban, Dom. de Coyeux, Jaboulet, Vidal-Fleury, Delas.

Rasteau This comes as either red or white, from the respectively red or white versions of the Grenache grape. The red can be good in a rough, young port-like style; the local co-operative makes a passable example.

VINTAGE GUIDE

For northern Rhône reds, the best recent vintages are *2001, 2000, 1999, '98, '97, '95, '91, '90, '89, '88* and *'85*.

In the south, the chance for blending means that more vintages are likely to produce something acceptable than if you have to pin all your hopes on the ripening of one grape variety.
GOOD RECENT VINTAGES: *2000, 1999, '98, '95, 94, '93, '90.*

Harvested Muscat grapes being taken to the local co-operative in Beaumes-de-Venise (below), to make the luscious, rich, golden sweet wine of the same name.

PROVENCE *and* CORSICA

Traditionally known for its pale rosés, the Mediterranean region of Provence now grows a wider and better choice of grape varieties that are bringing some fine reds and whites to market.

PROVENCE

GRAPES: *Red - Grenache, Mourvèdre, Cinsaut, Syrah, Carignan, Cabernet Sauvignon, Tibouren, Braquet; White - Clairette, Ugni Blanc, Grenache Blanc, Rolle, Sauvignon Blanc, Marsanne, Terret*

The broad sweep of the Provençal wine region, running from the cooler inland hills along the sun-soaked but Mistral-blown Mediterranean coast (below).

IT IS HIGHLY PROBABLE that the much-loved Mediterranean region of Provence, in southeast France, was the cradle of French viticulture. Its ancient seaport of Marseilles was founded around 600 BC by Greek settlers, who brought their own wines with them, probably sourced from their colonies in what was eventually to become Rome. Later, when France - as Gaul - had become a major component of the Roman Empire, cultivation of the vine spread slowly westwards and northwards.

Today, despite the fondness of European tourists, especially the British, for the region as a whole, Provençal wines remain largely unknown to the outside world, although a good quantity is exported. There is an unusually high production of rosé wine, and nearly all the wine is blended from a handful of grape varieties, some of them quite obscure, so that they don't have varietalism on their side. Provence has been the scene of much healthy experimentation and commitment to quality in recent years, however, and the region should soon see the greater prominence that it deserves.

Côtes de Provence By far the biggest appellation, covering the whole region, Côtes de Provence embraces a number of totally diverse areas in a broad sweep that runs from near

Aix-en-Provence down via the coast at St-Tropez and back up to a mountainous enclave north of Nice. The greater part of the production is pink wines - known locally as "little summer rosés" - targeted specifically at the tourist hordes. The wines are largely based on the Midi varieties Grenache and Cinsaut, but there is a good quality local grape, Tibouren, that is used on its own by some producers, and makes characterful rosés that are a cut above the basic slosh.

Reds have traditionally been based on that ubiquitous dullard, the Carignan grape. In an effort to raise the profile of Provence's reds, the regulations were amended in the 1980s to stipulate that a maximum of 40 per cent Carignan was allowed into any Côtes de Provence red. As the more forward-looking growers are ripping out their Carignan vines, and replacing them with Cabernet Sauvignon, Syrah and more of the much better Mourvèdre (one of the indigenous grapes), that 40 per cent will with any luck shrink still further. Only a small amount of white wine is made, but it can be unexpectedly good.

PRODUCERS: Dom. de Courtade, Ch. de Selle, Mas de Cadenet, Dom. Ott, Dom. Richeaume.

Coteaux d'Aix-en-Provence The area around the old university town of Aix-en-Provence produces wines in all three colours that are quite as varied as those from the main regional appellation, but at a higher overall standard of quality. It was demarcated in the mid-'80s, and its performance has since been on a steady upward trajectory. Again, Cabernet and Syrah are beginning to make their presences felt, and some of the reds from this westernmost part of Provence have a tantalisingly claret-like profile. Rosés account for about a third of the output, while whites are very few and far between.

PRODUCERS: Ch. Vignelaure and Ch. du Seuil are the two front-runners.

Les Baux de Provence This appellation was finally demarcated from the above in 1994. Situated at the western end of the Coteaux, it is a mountainous outpost of rare and highly individual red and rosé wines, some of them from relatively recently planted vineyards. Cabernet

1. COTEAUX D'AIX-EN-PROVENCE
2. LES BAUX DE PROVENCE
3. PALETTE
4. CASSIS
5. BANDOL
6. CÔTES DE PROVENCE
7. COTEAUX VAROIS

Nice

Aix-en-Provence

Marseilles

Cassis

Bandol

St-Tropez

and Syrah combine to do their stuff once more among the more traditional Provençal varieties, and there has been a widespread move towards organic viticultural methods (eliminating the use of pesticides and herbicides on the vines).
PRODUCERS: Dom. de Trévallon and Mas de Gourgonnier lead the pack.

Bandol Potentially the weightiest and most age-worthy reds in Provence come from this coastal appellation that also makes some good savoury rosé and a little crisp, appley white (some containing a good dollop of Sauvignon Blanc). The reds have to be cask-aged for a minimum of 18 months, and they include a generous proportion of the distinguished Mourvèdre grape to achieve a dense-textured wine full of black plum fruit and herbs. They are slowly but surely acquiring a reputation outside the region - largely thanks to the first-named producer below - and represent a serious alternative to Bordeaux on grand gastronomic occasions.
PRODUCERS: Dom. Tempier, Ch. Pibarnon, Ch. Pradeaux, Dom. de l'Olivette.

Cassis Nothing to do with the blackcurrant liqueur of the same name, this tiny appellation a little further westwards along the coast from Bandol makes mainly white wines from a fascinating grab-bag of southern Rhône varieties - Marsanne among them - and Sauvignon Blanc. Mainly sold locally, they can be quite sturdy, but often possessed of an uncommonly beautiful aromatic allure. Reds and pinks use proportionately about as much Mourvèdre as those of Bandol.
PRODUCERS: Dom. Clos Ste-Magdelaine.

Bellet Perched high up in the hills to the north of Nice, near the border with Italy, Bellet's wines are only very infrequently seen outside Provence. Because of its altitude, this is a cooler area and the small production of reds, whites and rosés reflects that in slightly higher acid levels. The grape varieties are shared with parts of western Italy, so that the Rolle of Bellet's whites is Vermentino to the Italians, while the Braquet used in its pinks is called Brachetto over the border. Outposts of Grenache and Cinsaut make their appearance in the reds.
PRODUCERS: Ch. de Bellet, Ch. de Crémat.

Palette An historic enclave near Aix-en-Provence, about 80 per cent of which is owned by one property, Ch. Simone. In addition to the usual southern grape varieties, there are some microscopic plantings of all-but-forgotten local grapes on very aged vinestock, producing reds,

Carefully tended vines at Dom. Clos Ste-Magdelaine (left), in the hot coastal hills of Cassis.

whites and rosés. Reds and rosés can both make quite an impact in the best years.

Coteaux Varois Named after the *département* of the Var in which it is located, the Coteaux Varois - once simple AC Côtes de Provence - was made an AC in 1993. The usual mixture of southern grape varieties is employed to mostly good effect, although the whites can be a shade dull. The wines of Ch. St-Estève are worth looking out for.

CORSICA

The Mediterranean island of Corsica may be French-controlled, but its vine culture owes much to neighbouring Italy. Once the source of basic slosh for the European wine lake, it set about radically improving its ways in the 1980s, with cautiously encouraging results to date.

Corsica has a wide range of grapes, principally the reds of the southern Rhône and Languedoc, as well as more fashionable international varieties. In the white Vermentino (known as Rolle in Provence) and two characterful reds (Nielluccio and Sciacarello), it has a handful of good indigenous grapes.

Only a small percentage of the island's production goes under one of the eight ACs available. They are Patrimonio, Ajaccio, Vin de Corse (making emphatic use of the local grapes), and five subdivisions of Vin de Corse (Coteaux du Cap Corse, Calvi, Figari, Porto Vecchio and Sartène). Coteaux du Cap Corse includes a *vin doux naturel*, Muscat du Cap Corse.

A fair proportion of the rest is made by powerful co-operatives as Vin de Pays de l'Ile de Beauté. Over half, though, is still simple table wine and can only hold back Corsica's ambitions as a quality region.

Houses tumble down the hillside (above) in the Corsican town of Sartène that gives its name to the local AC, Vin de Corse Sartène.

LANGUEDOC-ROUSSILLON

Better grape varieties and modern technology are assisting producers across Languedoc-Roussillon in their efforts to move away from vin de table *to greater quality, with clean, stylish varietal wines.*

Tradition bush-trained vines near Caramany in Côtes du Roussillon-Villages (above). Behind are the Pyrenees.

France's largest wine region (below), taking in Languedoc and the Côtes du Roussillon - once known as the Midi - that touches the Spanish border.

THE CENTRAL-SOUTHERN swathe of France that comprises the twin regions of Languedoc and the Côtes du Roussillon - often referred to by its old name, as the Midi - is where the most dynamic developments in the recent history of French wine have been taking place. This is the traditional grape-basket of France, source of the surplus production that came to constitute much of the European wine lake in the 1980s. Now it is the scene of frantic innovation, inspired in large measure by the arrival of wine technicians from other regions and countries.

A debate of gathering ferocity has been going on as to whether roving winemakers, with their technocratic ways, jetting in from Australia and elsewhere, and stopping just long enough to oversee the harvest, the grape-crushing and the juice becoming wine, are not guilty of standardising the taste of these wines. Consumers will have to vote with their purses eventually, but it should at least be acknowledged that the new wines being produced today in the Languedoc are certainly cleaner and more palatable than the old-fashioned stuff, for which the word "rustic" was the politest description.

Even before the advent of the so-called flying winemakers, the Languedoc's potential was only just beginning to emerge. Some of its key appellations were upgraded from VDQS only as recently as the mid-'80s, while a lot of the running has been made by growers working outside those regulations. They have been planting varieties that were not the norm in the region - Cabernet Sauvignon, Chardonnay, Sauvignon Blanc, even the odd outbreak of Pinot Noir. In consequence, the Languedoc is - with the exception of Alsace and its handful of traditional white grapes - the best bet for the varietally-minded wine lover starting out in France.

Vin de Pays d'Oc/de l'Hérault The Languedoc is doing a good job of turning wine tradition on its head (after the fashion of many Italian quality producers) by bottling much of its best wine under the catch-all generic designation of *vin de pays*. Theoretically inferior to wines of AC and VDQS status, these would-be "country wines" are, in many cases, putting the produce of the appellations to shame in terms of quality. Prices are rising too, as growers realise that an oaked Cabernet Sauvignon (whether country wine or no) has more cachet than the fanciest Fitou.

Furthermore, the fact that the climate in these southern parts is so much more reliable than in most of the classic French regions means that a relatively high success rate has been achieved by the conscientious operators. Deep, blackcurrant Cabernets are often far better than cheap claret, Chardonnays range from the lightly oaked and lemony to strapping young things full of smoke and butterscotch, and Sauvignon Blancs can be improbably crisp and fresh for such a warm climate, and yet still full of tempting gooseberry fruit. Soft, juicy Merlots, peppery, plummy Syrahs and - excitingly - some ripely apricotty Viogniers (half as good as Condrieu for a quarter the price) fill out the picture.

The prize for the *grand cru* of the *vins de pays* must go to an estate in the Hérault in eastern Languedoc called Mas de Daumas Gassac, producer of a powerful and complicated white, as well as thick, strong, mountainous reds of uncompromising intensity.

OTHER PRODUCERS: Fortant de France (especially Viognier), Chais Baumière (fine Chardonnay and Merlot), Dom. Virginie, Dom. de Condamine-l'Evêque, Dom. de Limbardié, Peyrat.

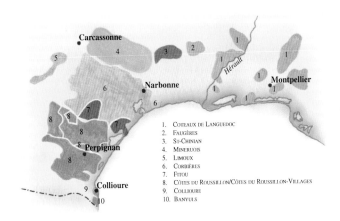

Carcassonne
Narbonne
Montpellier
Hérault
Perpignan
Collioure

1. COTEAUX DE LANGUEDOC
2. FAUGÈRES
3. ST-CHINIAN
4. MINERUOIS
5. LIMOUX
6. CORBIÈRES
7. FITOU
8. CÔTES DU ROUSSILLON/CÔTES DU ROUSSILLON-VILLAGES
9. COLLIOURE
10. BANYULS

Coteaux du Languedoc A rather sprawling designation for some of the best village wines of the Hérault, flanked by the eastern edge of the Aude and the western fringe of the Gard *départements*. In time, more of the villages that are currently only entitled to credits on the bottle label - such as La Clape, Pic-St-Loup, Vérargues and Montpeyroux - may come to attain their own ACs, as others did before them. There is still a lot of fairly undistinguished stuff - textbook red and white blends of southern grape varieties, with a bit of pale pink rosé thrown in for good measure. The overall picture is improving all the time, though, and with Grenache, Syrah and Mourvèdre staking a claim to a larger share of the red blends, at the expense of the humdrum Carignan, things can only get better. Meanwhile, the appellation boasts a white wine of extraordinary versatility in Clairette du Languedoc. It ranges in style from light, neutral and dry to heavily sweet and oxidised. Take your pick.
PRODUCERS: Mas Jullien, Pech-Redon, Dom. de la Roque, Dom. de l'Hortus, the co-operatives in the villages of St-Saturnin and Cabrières.

Working our way around in a southwestern arc from just north of Cabrières, the other appellations for unfortified wines are as follows:
Faugères An AC since 1982, Faugères preserves its distinction from the umbrella Coteaux du Languedoc tag by making big, rich reds from Syrah, Grenache, Mourvèdre and a proportion of Carignan that will have been edged down to a 40 per cent maximum by 1997. Small amount of fairly ordinary rosé. Excellent value.
PRODUCERS: Alquier, Vidal, Louison, Barral.
St-Chinian A little further west in the foothills of the Cévennes, St-Chinian shares the same history and grape varieties as Faugères, with light rosés and impressively long-lived reds.
PRODUCERS: La Dournie, Dom. Madalle, Ch. Viranel, the Berlou co-operative.
Minervois As for Faugères and St-Chinian, with the addition of a little white. Quality has steadily improved since it gained its AC in 1985. There are now some richly aromatic and age-worthy reds in particular beginning to shine.
PRODUCERS: Dom. Ste-Eulalie, La Combe Blanche, Villerambert-Julien, Ch. d'Oupia, Big Frank (a Polish-born ex-Bostonian!).
Cabardès/Côtes de la Malepère These two VDQS regions to the north and west of the city of Carcassonne are situated on the very cusp of Languedoc and the southwest. They have a

variety of different soils and microclimates and, not surprisingly, they are allowed to utilise both the Midi grapes and those from Bordeaux for their red and rosé wines. Some diverting wines are coming out of both, although only in small quantities, reflecting the fact that they are both aiming to become ACs before too long.
PRODUCERS: Ch. de la Bastide, Dom. Jouclary (Cabardès); Caves du Razès, Ch. de Festes (Malepère).
Limoux Created in 1993, this appellation for white wines represents a determined attempt to give the oaked-Chardonnay brigade a run for their money, so much so that oak-barrel treatment is compulsory. There are also plantings of the Loire grape Chenin Blanc and the interesting, crisply appley local variety, Mauzac.
PRODUCERS: Best so far is Sieur d'Arques.

The old farmhouse at Mas de Daumas Gassac (above), star of the Vins de Pays de l'Hérault.

LANGUEDOC-ROUSSILLON
(PLUS OTHER NATIVE VARIETIES)
GRAPES: Red - Carignan, Grenache, Cinsaut, Mourvèdre, Syrah, Merlot, Cabernet Sauvignon, Malbec; White - Clairette, Rolle, Terret, Bourboulenc, Picpoul, Muscat, Maccabéo, Marsanne, Viognier, Sauvignon Blanc, Chardonnay

Bush vines growing high in the hills of the Côtes du Roussillon (above), with the snow-capped Pyrenees and the Spanish border in the near distance.

Blanquette de Limoux/Crémant de Limoux The former is the traditional sparkling wine of the region, left to re-ferment in the bottle the spring after vinification, and claiming an older lineage than champagne. Blanquette is a synonym for the local Mauzac grape, although there has always been a little Chardonnay in the wine. Since 1990, any wine that contains up to 30 per cent of Chardonnay, Chenin, or both, goes under the Crémant appellation. Delmas and Collin make two of the more appetising examples.

Corbières One of the larger and more famous Languedoc appellations covers a range of good, sturdy, often spicy reds as well as small amounts of white and pink wine from southern varieties. Here again, the general picture has been of demonstrable improvement on the past, with sloppy, ropey wines being shunted aside by some of the more fascinating - and fairly priced - examples of modern French winemaking. Some of the less convincing reds are made with partial recourse to the Beaujolais technique of carbonic maceration (see Gamay section). PRODUCERS: Ch. les Ollieux, La Voulte-Gasparets, Ch. Cabriac, Dom. des Caraguilhes, Dom. du Révérend, Ch. de Lastours.

Fitou The oldest AC in the Languedoc makes red wines on the border of Languedoc and Roussillon, in two separate zones that are divided by part of Corbières. While the general pattern of improvement has certainly touched Fitou, a lot is still made in the rather indifferent, rough-old-red style beloved of students. EXCEPTIONS: Dom. du Mont-Tauch, Colomer.

Roussillon/Côtes du Roussillon/Côtes du Roussillon-Villages The area south of Perpignan, bordering on Catalan country, is home to some rather more run-of-the-mill offerings. By far the best of these three designations is the last, which is for red wines only, and comprises the northern section of Roussillon, nearest to Fitou. PRODUCERS: Vignerons Catalans, Ch. de Jau, Ch. Corneilla.

Collioure A beautiful coastal appellation of vertiginously steep vineyards, making some remarkable and thoroughly original reds in an ultra-ripe, expansive style, principally from Grenache and Mourvèdre. One to try. PRODUCERS: Dom. du Mas Blanc, Dom. de la Rectorie, Les Clos de Paulilles.

OTHER WINES

There are a number of *vins doux naturels* produced in this region, both white and red. Winemaking techniques are the same as those for Muscat de Beaumes-de-Venise (see entry, Rhône) and the whites here all use either of two strains of Muscat. Frontignan, together with three other Muscats suffixed respectively by de Mireval, de Lunel and de St-Jean-de-Minervois, all use the Muscat à Petits Grains grape, and produce lightly fragrant, barley-sugar sweet wines of varying degrees of intensity. The chunkier, less attractive Muscat d'Alexandrie is permitted as well in Muscat de Rivesaltes, made north of Perpignan. PRODUCERS: Dom. de la Peyrade (Frontignan); Dom. de Barroubie (Muscat de St-Jean-de-Minervois); Brial (Muscat de Rivesaltes).

Sweet red wines, usually made entirely from or heavily based on Grenache, are made in Rivesaltes, Maury to the west of Fitou, and Banyuls, down on the Roussillon coast and overlapping with Collioure. Of those, Banyuls is considered to be about the best, with sweet strawberry fruit and a heady perfume sometimes reminiscent of good ruby port, but much less aggressive on the palate. PRODUCERS: Dom. de la Rectorie, Mas Blanc (Banyuls); Mas Amiel (Maury).

GASCONY *and* THE SOUTHWEST

These small wine areas, scattered from Bordeaux down to the Spanish border, offer a diverse and exciting range of wines that have been little influenced by passing fashions. These winemakers are proud of their traditions.

WHEREAS MOST OF the appellations of the sprawling Languedoc region make use of the same basic collections of red and white grapes for their wines, a much more diverse picture prevails in the southwest. There is an umbrella organisation for the wines of the southwest, but each appellation retains its own fiercely guarded identity, and many have one or two local grape varieties they are proud to call their own.

They also have a culinary tradition to be proud of. After Burgundy, this is probably the most celebrated gastronomic corner of France, home of magnificent pork and poultry, chunky Toulouse sausages, foie gras, prunes and armagnac.

The producers have been considerably less susceptible to the influence of foreign technologists, the flying winemakers, around these parts than further east, and are consequently more fearful that their often little-known wines will continue to be swept aside in the varietal mania that has overcome the world markets. However, there is at least a sporting chance that a wine-drinking generation will discover Petit Manseng and Négrette, and then the southwest will have its day.

Wending our way circuitously down from just south of Bordeaux to the far southwest corner, the main appellations are as follows:

Bergerac/Côtes de Bergerac The first few ACs in the immediate vicinity of Bordeaux were once considered part of its overall catchment area. They use the same grape varieties (chiefly Cabernet Sauvignon, Merlot and Cabernet Franc for reds and rosés, Sauvignon Blanc and Sémillon for whites). Bergerac and the theoretically slightly superior Côtes de Bergerac are to the east of the Côtes de Castillon sector of Bordeaux, on the river Dordogne. There are a few stars here, though a lot of the wine is pretty basic stuff from the local co-operative.

PRODUCERS: Ch. la Jaubertie, Ch. Belingard, Ch. Court-les-Mûts, Ch. Tour des Gendres.

Montravel/Côtes de Montravel/Haut-Montravel White-wine appellation at the western end of Bergerac, mainly planted with Sémillon. The three designations refer to dry, semi-sweet and very sweet wines respectively. The dry Montravel wines are best, and much improved of late.

Château de Crouseilles peering majestically over its vineyard in the Gascon red-wine enclave of Madiran (above).

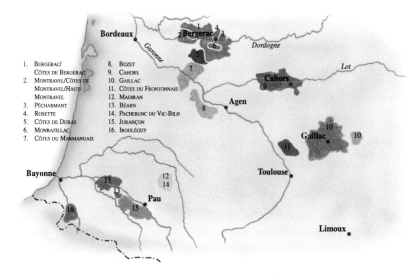

1. BERGERAC/ CÔTES DE BERGERAC
2. MONTRAVEL/CÔTES DE MONTRAVEL/HAUT-MONTRAVEL
3. PÉCHARMANT
4. ROSETTE
5. CÔTES DE DURAS
6. MONBAZILLAC
7. CÔTES DU MARMANDAIS
8. BUZET
9. CAHORS
10. GAILLAC
11. CÔTES DU FRONTONNAIS
12. MADIRAN
13. BÉARN
14. PACHERENC DU VIC-BILH
15. JURANÇON
16. IROULÉGUY

The scattered appellations of Gascony and the southwest (left), from Bergerac, close to Bordeaux, down to Irouléguy on the border with Spain.

GASCONY & SOUTH-
WEST

GRAPES: *the Bordeaux grape
varieties and a wide
collection of local varieties
further south*

Pécharmant Red wines from near Bergerac itself, using Bordeaux grapes with a preponderance of Merlot. Overall quality is high, with Ch. Tiregand the main exporter of reliably classy claret lookalikes.

Rosette Sweet-whites appellation overlapping into Pécharmant using Sémillon, but now sadly dwindling towards extinction.

Côtes de Duras South of the Dordogne, the Duras makes some passable wines in the style of simple Bordeaux. The best shots are the Sauvignon whites, which can be agreeably crisp and clean. Here, the co-operative makes a good range called Le Seigneuret, and Dom. Petitot is also good.

Monbazillac One of the secrets that escaped from the region in the 1980s was the potentially glorious botrytised wine of Monbazillac. While Sauternes prices soared, this appellation further east along the Dordogne suddenly looked a ringer for great dessert wines at affordable prices. Sensational vintages in 1988, '89 and (especially) '90 brought its name to a much wider audience. Made from nobly-rotted Sémillon, with Sauvignon Blanc and flowery Muscadelle, the best can hold their heads up in the company of Sauternes without embarrassment.
PRODUCERS: Ch. les Hébras, Ch. Haut-Bernasse, Ch. la Borderie, Ch. La Brie.

Saussignac Tiny appellation for sweet Sémillon-based whites, just west of Monbazillac. Of no great pedigree, though Ch. Court-les-Mûts produces an eminently passable one.

*The old face of Cahors, in
the Lot valley (below), an
area once renowned for its
"black wine".*

Côtes du Marmandais Elevated from VDQS to AC in 1990, the Marmandais appellation straddles the river Garonne, south of Bordeaux. It makes principally reds (with a smidgeon of rosé and white) in a no-nonsense, easy-drinking style. The Bordeaux varieties are allowed to constitute up to 75 per cent of the red blends, with the remainder made up by Syrah, Gamay, the rough-natured southwestern grape Fer Servadou and Marmandais speciality, Abouriou. A couple of co-ops make nearly everything the appellation produces.

Buzet Although south of Marmandais, Buzet returns once again to the Bordeaux varieties for all colours of wine. Once again, the co-operative predominates, but its versatile range (Cuvée Napoléon and Baron d'Ardeuil are particularly good) is of high quality. The austerely concentrated reds are often as good as *cru bourgeois* claret.

Cahors Situated northeast of Agen, the appellation of Cahors spans the river Lot. Historically one of the more famous southwest names, it was known as the "black wine" because the grape juice was boiled to concentrate its colour. Now more sensitively vinified, it is made from a minimum 70 per cent of the Bordeaux variety, Malbec (here known as Auxerrois, but nothing to do with the white Alsace grape of that name), backed up by Merlot and a fierce local grape, Tannat, used only in judicious dashes. Light red fruits and modest tannins are the hallmarks of the wines, but the best producers achieve an intriguing floral note as well - something like violets.
BEST: Clos Triguedina, Ch. de Haute-Serre, Dom. Poujol, Dom. de Quattre, Ch. des Bouysses from the Côtes d'Olt co-operative.

Gaillac A large appellation northeast of Toulouse, Gaillac makes a wide range of styles, from bone-dry as well as slightly sweet whites, some sparkling wine using the same method as nearby Blanquette de Limoux (see entry, Languedoc-Roussillon) to firm, full reds. Its proximity to Limoux means that Mauzac is an important variety and the dry whites and sparklers have the same sort of tart, Granny Smith bite to them. It is supplemented by local grapes Len de l'El and Ondenc, as well as a soupçon of Sauvignon. The fizzes may be either just pétillant (and labelled Gaillac Perlé) or fully refermented and released with the yeast sediment still sloshing around in them. Reds include the local Duras and Fer Servadou,

together with some Syrah and Gamay, as well as the big three Bordeaux varieties.
PRODUCERS: Plageoles, Cros, Dom. de Labarthe, Ch. Larroze.

Côtes du Frontonnais Distinctive reds made from the local grape Négrette, which has a deliciously savoury pepperiness to it, fleshed out with the two Cabernets and Fer Servadou. Some of these can give any other full-bodied country reds a real run for their money for sheer concentration and personality. Also makes a small amount of rosé.
PRODUCERS: Ch. Montauriol (very high-flying young grower who puts leather labels on his top *cuvées*), Ch. Bellevue-la-Forêt, Ch. Flotis.

Tursan VDQS producing roughish, everyday reds, mainly from the muscular Tannat grape, and an oak-matured white made from the local Baroque. (Three-star Michelin chef Michel Guérard at Eugénie-les-Bains makes most of the white!)

Côtes de St-Mont VDQS for all shades of wine, dominated by the very good Caves de Plaimont co-operative. Reds use Fer Servadou and Tannat among others, while indigenous white grapes include such delights as Ruffiac and Petit Courbu. Some highly interesting flavours and some oak experimentation are to be found.

Madiran The unforgivingly brutal Tannat grape comes into its own in these fiery reds that almost invariably need a few years to settle, but never quite lose the power to intimidate. When fully ripe, however, they can have a spicy elegance. The two Cabernets are used to provide some fruit relief.
PRODUCERS: Dom. Laplace, Ch. Montus, Ch. Peyros, Ch. d'Aydie, Dom. Capmartin.

Béarn To the west of Madiran, and using the same grapes for reds and rosés. These are softer than Madiran but not particularly characterful. A co-operative at Bellocq makes most of the wine on the separately demarcated land, but over half of Béarn's grapes are vinified within the districts of Madiran and Jurançon.

Pacherenc du Vic-Bilh A separate appellation within Madiran for generally sweet white wines made from the local grapes Ruffiac, Petit Courbu and Gros Manseng, together with Sémillon and Sauvignon. Depending on the vintage conditions, Pacherenc may be made dry, but its sweet offerings made from grapes that are left to shrivel on the vine can occasionally be as distinguished as the sweeter wines of Jurançon.
PRODUCERS: Ch. Boucassé, Ch. d'Aydie.

Jurançon Much underrated appellation south of the town of Pau, making white wines principally from a blend of the twin varieties Gros Manseng and Petit Manseng (the latter the better for its piercing pineapple and apricot aromas), together with some Petit Courbu. The wines may be refreshingly dry and full of exotic fruit ripeness, or lusciously sweet from raisined grapes, as in Pacherenc. Excellent-value wines that are definitely worth seeking out.
PRODUCERS: Dom. de Cauhapé, Clos Uroulat, Clos Lamouroux, Clos de la Vierge.

Irouléguy Practically on the Spanish border in the Pays Basque, this far-flung appellation takes in a number of newly established vineyards carved out of the Pyrennean rock by growers motivated by great regional pride. Tannat raises its brutish head in the reds and rosés, but is tempered by some Cabernet, while the whites use the Jurançon varieties. As elsewhere, the regional co-operative makes a fair amount of the wine, but Dom. Brana is also good.

Vin de Pays des Côtes de Gascogne Surplus grapes not used in the production of armagnac, the brandy of the southwest, go into white wines under the Côtes de Gascogne designation. Much comes from the Ugni Blanc grape, which makes nice brandy but yawningly dull wine, although there is also some Sauvignon Blanc and both Mansengs to add aromatic appeal, and even a little Chardonnay. Dom. de Tariquet and Dom. de Plantérieu are good wines, as are some of the offerings of the Caves de Plaimont co-operative and the crisp, green-fruited whites of Dom. St-Lannes.

The stunning Château de Monbazillac (above). The finest sweet wines of Monbazillac can rival those of Sauternes.

Cabernet Sauvignon grapes arriving at the Buzet co-operative (above). The Bordeaux varieties are used to make concentrated claret-style reds.

JURA, SAVOIE *and* BUGEY

To the east of Burgundy lie the three little-known regions of Jura, Savoie and the Bugey. Tucked up against the French Alps, the areas are dominated by white wines, and the unique styles of vin jaune *and* vin de paille.

THESE THREE EASTERLY regions are among the most obscure and insular of all France's wine-growing areas. Not much of their wine is exported, and what is makes few compromises to modern tastes.

JURA

The remote high-altitude vineyards of the Jura, not far from the Swiss border, harbour some of France's most individual wines. They do crop up in minute quantities on the export markets, but tend to be highly priced, and the house style of the region is not an especially fashionable one. That said - *vive la différence*.

There are two regional specialities - *vin jaune* and *vin de paille. Vin jaune*, "yellow wine", is made in a similar way to sherry in that it matures in cask for six years under a *voile*, or film, of yeast culture. As the wine oxidates, it turns yellow. About one-third also evaporates. The resulting wine is heavy-textured, dry as chalk-dust and alcoholic - rather like fino sherry to the uninitiated. *Vin de paille*, "straw wine", is equally rare, made from raisined grapes. These are rich, alcoholic wines, and again capable of some bottle-age. Both wines are only made in good years, and in small quantities, and are therefore pricey. Much of the *vin de paille* is found in Arbois, while *vin jaune* reigns supreme in L'Etoile and Château-Chalon.

Arbois The greatest volume of Jura wine is produced under this appellation in the northern part of the region, centred on the town of the same name. They may be red, white or rosé, and there are three important local grapes: two red varieties - Trousseau, which gives a deeply rich if unsubtle wine, and thin-skinned Poulsard, quite the opposite and good for rosés - as well as a white, the gloriously musky Gewürztraminer relative, Savagnin.

The Pinot Noir and Chardonnay grapes of Burgundy are also grown, the latter more extensively in recent years. Some of the wine is made sparkling by the champagne method, and labelled Arbois Mousseux, while wines from the best village, Pupillin, are allowed to add its name as a suffix. The most visible producer from Arbois is Henri Maire.

Côtes du Jura The central and southern parts of the region take this appellation, but make the same broad range of styles from the same grapes as Arbois. Ch. d'Arlay is one of the bigger names and a good producer of *vin jaune*.

L'Etoile Tiny appellation largely represented by the local co-operative and specialising in hazelnutty sherry-like *vins jaunes* made from Savagnin. There is also some straight red and white and some sparkling wine.

Château-Chalon The only AC which is entirely for *vin jaune* from the Savagnin grape. Château-Chalon sits on a little hilltop and remains completely aloof from the modern wine world. Wine is only made in years when the

The vineyards of Jura and Savoie (below) lie on the lower slopes of the French Alps, close to the Swiss border.

JURA:	SAVOIE:
1. ARBOIS	5. VIN DE SAVOIE
2. CÔTES DU JURA	6. ROUSSETTE DE SAVOIE
3. L'ETOILE	7. SEYSSEL
4. CHÂTEAU-CHALON	8. CRÉPY

The vineyards of Château-Chalon (left), the tiny AC in the heart of Jura that makes only vin jaune.

producers deem the harvest to be good enough to bother. Bourdy is one of the best growers.

SAVOIE

The region lies due south of Geneva. Home to some indigenous grape varieties, many of its wines have character but are not much exported.

Vin de Savoie The overall appellation for any wine produced within the *départements* of Savoie and Haute-Savoie. Most are whites and are made from the local Jacquère grape in a crunchy-fresh style, supported by Chardonnay, some of the Roussanne of the northern Rhône, and the neutral-tasting Chasselas much favoured in Switzerland. Reds use Pinot Noir and Gamay, as well as a local variety called Mondeuse, which makes something a little fleshier than the light-bodied norm. Certain privileged villages (17 of them) may add their names to the basic designation; they include Apremont, Abymes, Montmélian and Chautagne.

Roussette de Savoie The Savoyards consider the Roussette to be their best asset among white grapes. It has its own AC, though it covers the whole region, like Vin de Savoie. The wines have a diverting floral perfume and should be drunk young to catch their tingling acidity at its freshest. In four villages - Frangy, Marestel, Monthoux and Monterminod - the wines must be 100 per cent Roussette; elsewhere they can be up to 50 per cent Chardonnay.

Seyssel Small appellation taking in dry white wines from Roussette and the local Molette. There is also a sparkling version, Seyssel Mousseux, that is based on Molette, but has to contain at least 10 per cent of Roussette. Varichon & Clerc is the only exporter of note.

Crépy Chasselas makes the wines of this dry-whites appellation, and jolly dull they are too.

BUGEY

Just west of Savoie, in the Ain *département*, is the Bugey. Historically part of Burgundy, it now constitutes a mini-region of its own, its grape varieties marking its identity as a sort of cross between Savoie and the Jura. Finding any outside the region is something of a teaser, though it is reputed that some make it as far as Lyon.

Vin du Bugey One designation covers the whole region, although it only has VDQS status as opposed to full AC - a situation that may very well change before long. An entire range of styles is made, from aromatic, crisply textured dry whites, through delicate rosés, to lightish reds using Gamay, Pinot Noir and also some Mondeuse. There are additionally two styles of fizz - lightly prickly (*pétillant*) and fully sparkling (*mousseux*). Much praise has been heaped on the region's Chardonnay varietals. Cerdon is perhaps the best of the handful of individual village names that may appear on the labels.

JURA
GRAPES: White - Savagnin, Chardonnay;
Red - Trousseau, Poulsard, Pinot Noir

SAVOIE
GRAPES: White - Jacquère, Roussette, Molette, Roussanne, Chasselas, Chardonnay;
Red - Mondeuse, Gamay, Pinot Noir

The alpine town of Seyssel, in Savoie, on the river Rhône (left), that has given its name to the local white-wine AC.

VIN *de* PAYS

The vin de pays *designation was created to encourage production of higher quality, easy-drinking red, white, and rosé wines, "country wines" that display the character of their region.*

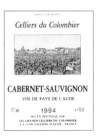

MANY FRENCH WINES - about one bottle in five - fall just below the two strictest categories for quality wine production, AC (*appellation contrôlée*) and VDQS (*vin délimité de qualité supérieure*). Vin de pays (literally "country wine") is a designation drawn up in the 1970s to denote wines that had some sort of regional identity, but for one reason or another, perhaps because the grower was using grapes not officially sanctioned in the locality, or perhaps because the vines were too young under the appellation regulations, didn't quite make it to AC or VDQS status.

The most basic quality category of all is straightforward table wine (*vin de table*). This is the generally insipid bulk production, mostly from the south, that did so much to swell the European wine lake in the last couple of decades. *Vin de pays*, intended in its way to be as representative of regional characteristics as the appellation wines, should therefore be several rungs up the quality ladder from *vin de table*, and most of it is.

There are three levels of *vin de pays*, depending on how specific the individual producer wants, or is able, to be. At the broadest, most inclusive level, the designation may cover a whole region, such as the commercially pre-eminent Vin de Pays d'Oc, the regional VdP for Languedoc-Roussillon (see the relevant section). Some are given slightly cloying, flights-of-fancy names that the authorities hope will prove marketable. The VdP for Corsica is Vin de Pays de l'Ile de Beauté (Island of Beauty), while the one that covers the whole of the Loire valley goes by the name Vin de Pays du Jardin de la France (Garden of France).

Then there are VdPs that use the name of the *département*, such as Alpes-Maritime in Provence, Gers in Gascony, or l'Hérault in the Languedoc. To use these, the wines must have been sourced from vines grown entirely within that *département*. Within the confines of those, there are named patches of vineyard land, particular hillsides, and so forth, that take the specificity of the VdP designation almost to appellation levels.

There are more than 100 such VdPs, including the following. Coteaux de l'Ardèche in the centre of the Rhône valley refers to a particular stretch of slopes within the departmental Ardèche VdP, Côtes de Thongue falls within the

Vins de pays that use the name of a département, *such as Ardèche (right), must contain grapes sourced only from within that district.*

Vin de Pays de l'Hérault, while Vin de Pays des Marches de Bretagne is a Loire VdP whose borders overlap three *départements* - Loire-Atlantique, Maine-et-Loire and the Vendée.

To qualify as a *vin de pays*, the wines must be made from certain grape varieties, and are not to be blended with grapes from other areas. With the exception of wines from the Alsace region, *vins de pays* are likely to be the only French wines you will come across that are labelled with the name of a grape, many of them being single varietals. (To be sure, some producers making basic AC Bourgogne Blanc are beginning to state the magic word Chardonnay on their labels in acknowledgement of varietal recognition among consumers, but they are still very much a minority.)

The *vin de pays* producers are obviously concerned to combat whatever inferiority complex they feel their wines may have in an appellation-dominated market-place, and varietal identification is one of the easiest routes to a higher market share.

Within the Vin de Pays d'Oc designation, there are many fine varietal wines - not all, as we have seen, made exclusively by French producers - and some of the bigger operators, such as Fortant de France, have established enough of a quality reputation to charge more ambitiously for their wines. Thus is born the anomaly by which a lightly oaked Chardonnay, officially styled "country wine", may sell for more than a white AC Coteaux du Languedoc made just up

the road. Whatever we may think about the encroaching international Chardonnisation of the world of white wine, there has undoubtedly been a certain payoff in terms of improving the general quality level of wines produced under some of the less distinguished ACs.

With lesser-known grape varieties, such as Marsanne or Viognier from the northern Rhône, the VdPs have introduced consumers to some important, slightly offbeat flavours that were previously only known to a handful of experts who could afford the white wines of Hermitage or Condrieu. Elsewhere, *vin de pays* has provided producers of cognac and armagnac with a handy outlet for surplus production of white grapes. (The respective VdPs are Vin de Pays Charentais and Vin de Pays des Côtes de Gascogne, with the latter representing distinctly better quality across the board.)

By the mid-1990s, production of *vin de pays* had risen to such a level that it had virtually matched the annual capacity of *vin de table*. That's fine as long as the wine is of distinctly more exalted quality, and the designation is not just being used as a way of getting higher prices for bottom-drawer plonk. About three-quarters of all *vin de pays* is red. At the bargain-basement end of the market, it is a long-established truism that it is considerably easier to produce a palatable red wine than it is to make a decent white within the same budget.

All in all, the *vin de pays* movement has been one of the more exciting developments within French wine in recent times, and one that offers a compelling opportunity for consumers to familiarise themselves with the tastes of some significant grape varieties.

These vineyards of Château Capion, in Hérault (above), grow Cabernet Sauvignon, Chardonnay and Merlot for Vin de Pays d'Oc.

Hand-picking of grapes near Reuilly in the upper Loire (above), destined for one of the region's comparatively rare red vins de pays.

Grapes growing in the spectacular Ardèche gorge for use in the region's highly regarded Vin de Pays des Coteaux de l'Ardèche (left).

EUROPE, AFRICA
AND THE EAST

The 11th-century Castillo de Milmanda (above), owned by the famous winemaking family, Torres, in Catalonia.

Picking grapes for Vinho Verde (above), on Portugal's "Green Coast".

As the winemaking cultures of North America and the southern hemisphere have emerged over the last 20 years to compete with their European antecedents, the struggle for supremacy (and it has been seen as nothing less in some quarters) has been billed as France versus the "New World". The countries included in that now outdated category - an illogical assemblage of the United States and Canada, South America, South Africa, Australia and New Zealand - are usually portrayed as storming the holy citadel of traditional wine production, falsely seen as an exclusively French preserve.

The plethora of French-inspired varietal wines from countries outside Europe has led many consumers to neglect the wines of the rest of Europe. In this respect, each of the European wine countries is saddled with its own particular image problem. When drinkers whose only previous knowledge of German wine is Liebfraumilch, or for whom Italy always meant fizzy pink Lambrusco in a screw-top bottle, graduate on to South African Chardonnay or California Merlot, they have little incentive to explore the *quality* wines of Germany, Italy and the rest.

As we have seen, the great majority of the internationally grown grape varieties are French in origin, and it is only recently that Italian and Spanish varietals have begun to be found outside their traditional homelands. If a wine like Chablis can suffer from the fact that consumers don't realise it is made from Chardonnay, what chance have wines from Ribera del Duero, Carmignano or Bairrada?

If the varietal trend were to continue unabated, it would eventually mean that Europe's traditional wines would find it extremely hard to gain market shares outside their immediate regions of production. Drunk solely by locals and holidaymakers, they would all come to occupy the same niche as many of the wines of Provence and eastern France (indeed, many have been quite happy to dwell in precisely such obscurity).

A handful of mainly southern European wines have actually established themselves as brand names. They include Spanish Rioja, Vinho Verde from Portugal, certainly Chianti, Valpolicella and Barolo from Italy. Beyond these, however, European wine represents an uncharted hinterland for most consumers.

It would be misleading to deny that a large part of the problem has been quality. Just as the poorer regions of southern France have been the last to drag themselves into the latter half of the 20th century, in terms of their vinification techniques and their understanding of what today's wine market expects of even a modestly priced bottle, so the countries of southern and central Europe languished for too long. They relied on the bulk production of indifferent wine made by frankly unhygienic and insensitive methods and sold at very cheap prices. What these areas were producing primarily was not wine but alcohol, a bottom-line commodity intended to be as roughly consistent from one year to the next as was humanly possible.

Consistency is, of course, a consideration. But, much more than this, wine is an expression of the environment and the conditions in which it is made, or it is nothing. That pride in the sense of place, a celebration of the flavours of native grapes, and what nature and the individual have combined to make of them in a particular vintage, should be reflected in every bottle of wine that a grower or merchant or co-operative sends out into the market. It isn't any longer just a question of keeping a few wine connoisseurs happy.

The fact is that, in commercial terms, there is no other way forward for the modern winemaker. Now that there is every chance that a Vin de Pays d'Oc may taste as excitingly fruit-filled and satisfying as something from South Australia or Chile, nobody wants ropey old reds and weary little whites from far-flung corners of southern Italy or the Iberian peninsula.

The signs are that the light of the quality revolution is at last penetrating some of Europe's dustiest cupboards. As the tendency gathers pace, and assuming that prices don't quickly

shoot through the roof, many of the old wines of Europe will be ripe for rediscovery.

If a renaissance in Italian wines turns out to have been nurtured in California, it won't be in the least surprising. What became known as Mediterranean cuisine, principally the olive oil, sundried tomatoes, balsamic vinegar and basil of Italian domestic cooking, spread from the West Coast of America rather than from the home country itself. Perhaps the wines will follow the same route. At any rate, there are California growers trying their hands at the Sangiovese, Nebbiolo, Barbera and Dolcetto grapes. The "home-grown" state speciality grape Zinfandel is actually southern Italian in origin (they call it Primitivo back home).

For red wines at least, there is certainly more untapped potential in Italy than in any other European wine country. Whites remain less than inspiring by and large, mainly because there is too great a dependence on the everyday Trebbiano grape. But Italy does have good white varieties, and we must hope to see more of them.

Spain is still struggling to emerge from its old image as a producer of dirt-cheap oily reds, more often than not aged for years in musty old casks until whatever fruit they possessed at the outset was completely bleached out of them. There is still a tendency to assume that great age equates with quality in Spanish wine, but producers in some of the more dynamic regions - notably Ribera del Duero, Navarra and even dear old Rioja - are beginning to produce some vibrant young reds and whites with gratifying levels of fruit that should unerringly point the way ahead.

Portugal too has been looking to its laurels. Although its production is only a fraction of Spain's, it has a broader palette of indigenous grapes to draw on, many of them of genuine quality. Its producers have so far been less go-ahead, however, in capitalising on the potential at their disposal.

Germany remains a prisoner of the structure of its export industry, which is still massively geared to producing commercial slosh for the unsophisticated end of the market. As long as that is unchanged, the efforts of its most prodigiously talented growers (by no means working exclusively with Riesling, either) will continue to be sold short. In central Europe, Austria is streaking ahead of Germany in overall quality terms. Where once its reputation rested solely

on dessert wines from the northeast of the country, it is now rapidly gaining ground as a producer of premium varietal wines, many of them from indigenous grape varieties that offer some challenging flavours.

The countries of the former Soviet bloc have had mixed fortunes since the break-up of the old state monopolies. Hungary and the Czech Republic are coming along in leaps and bounds, with tasty, inexpensive varietal wines often made by foreigners, while Romania probably always did have good wines that have only just started finding their way to a wider audience. Bulgaria, sadly, faltered when its vineyard land was re-privatised. During the communist era, its heavily subsidised varietals blazed some sort of trail for affordable quality, but the expertise has not always proved to be there now that the winemaking has returned into inexperienced hands.

Meanwhile, countries such as Moldova and Greece, benefiting from an influx of expertise and technology, are poised for promotion to Europe's second division. A willingness to absorb lessons from outside, together with enough internal investment to back up the more forward-thinking practitioners, should see some exciting results emerge over time. And as the volume of annual production inexorably grows, and assuming the summers continue to be benevolent, not even the UK need be left out of the European wine movement.

Autumn arrives in the vineyards of Germany's Mosel region (above), above the town of Piesport.

The dramatic modernist bodega (below), built in 1918 for Spanish producer Raimat.

ITALY

The invading Greeks called it "Oenotria", the land of wine. Italy has remained steeped in viticulture, and today usually produces more wine than any other country in the world.

VITIS VINIFERA, the wine-grape species, has been growing on what is now the Italian mainland since centuries before the birth of Christ. For a long time it was believed by archaeologists that cultivation of the vine was introduced to these parts by the Greeks in the centuries before the rise of the Roman Empire. It is now thought that some tribal cultures, notably the Etruscans whose domain extended along the western coast of the peninsula, already possessed viticultural knowledge and that the Greeks did little more than introduce new vine varieties when they arrived.

However that may be, the name the Greeks gave to the new territories in what was to become Rome was Oenotria, meaning literally "land of wine". That alone suggests what a centrally

important role wine has played in this part of the world since the very earliest civilisations. By the time the Roman Empire was at its height, the origins of wine connoisseurship were clearly apparent. Key texts of the period refer to particularly good vintages, while wines from specific regions, such as Lazio in the vicinity of Rome itself, Tuscany to the north and Campania, centred on Naples to the south, came to be especially highly valued.

The expansion of the Roman Empire into western Europe opened up busy trade routes, which not only kept the occupying armies supplied but also greatly expanded the practice of viticulture in such outposts as Spain and Gaul (in what is now France). Even Britain, with the relatively benevolent climate it enjoyed at the time, learned from the Romans how to tend vines and make wine. This was a habit Britain wasn't to lose until around the time of the dissolution of the monasteries.

Nowadays, in terms of volume, Italy remains in most years the most significant wine-producing country in the world, knocking France effortlessly into second place. Even more than in France, too, wine is an integral part of everyday life. The average Italian family consumes prodigious quantities of wine at both mid-day and evening meals, and it is a vital ingredient in traditional cookery.

Whereas there are whole swathes of France - notably northern parts such as Brittany and Normandy - that are climatically unsuited to wine production, there is no part of Italy at all that is a no-go area for the vine. From the Alpine border with Switzerland and the Tyrolean region abutting Austria, down to the tip of Italy's toe in Calabria - not to mention the islands of Sicily and Sardinia - Italian agriculture is about wine first and foremost.

What holds the country back is the lack of a coherent quality-control system that everybody can respect. The equivalent of the French *appellation contrôlée* is DOC, which stands for *denominazione de origine controllata*, and its upper subdivision DOCG (*denominazione de origine controllata e garantita*). These

Italy's foremost agricultural industry is grape-growing. Vines are planted across the country, from the northern borders to its heel in the south (below).

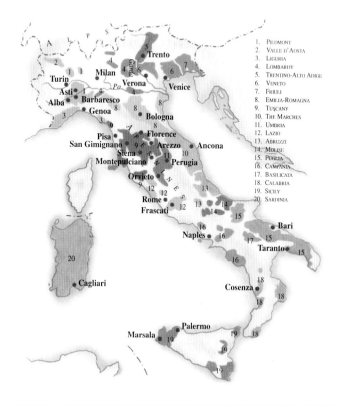

1. PIEDMONT
2. VALLE D'AOSTA
3. LIGURIA
4. LOMBARDY
5. TRENTINO-ALTO ADIGE
6. VENETO
7. FRIULI
8. EMILIA-ROMAGNA
9. TUSCANY
10. THE MARCHES
11. UMBRIA
12. LAZIO
13. ABRUZZI
14. MOLISE
15. PUGLIA
16. CAMPANIA
17. BASILICATA
18. CALABRIA
19. SICILY
20. SARDINIA

designations were created in the 1960s, but were rather randomly applied to whichever wines were of particular commercial value at the time. Consequently, as an overall indication of quality, they were at best useless and at worst positively misleading.

Since 1992, there has been a painfully slow campaign to redesign the system, known as the Goria Law after the former Agriculture Minister who instigated it. This should in theory tighten up on quality within the DOC and DOCG regions, by making all wines subject to approval by a professional tasting panel.

The Goria Law also made provision for classifying the best regional wines with a designation broadly analogous to *vin de pays* - IGT (*indicazione geografica tipica*). Everything else is *vino da tavola* (table wine), although it should be noted that some of Italy's very finest wines have been made with flagrant disregard for the regulations for their areas. These wines are defiantly labelled as humble VdT, in much the same way that the monumental Mas de Daumas Gassac of southern France is proud to be labelled as a mere Vin de Pays de l'Hérault.

PIEDMONT

The northwestern region of Piedmont, in the foothills of the Alps, is one of Italy's very best wine-growing districts. Styles made range from the lightest of whites through sweet sparklers to thundering reds of great longevity; they are listed here alphabetically.

Arneis DOC since 1989 for white wines made from the grape of the same name. They are more sternly constituted than many Italian whites, with a fruit like tart pears, often mixed with a discernible hint of almond. Grown in the Langhe hills around Alba, and also in Roero to the northwest of the town.
PRODUCERS: Castello di Neive, Voerzio, Giacosa, Vietti.

Asti Formerly known as Asti Spumante, the famous sweet fizz produced around the town of Asti is one of Italy's classic styles. Low in alcohol (usually about 7 per cent) and full of the flavours of ripe green grapes and sugared almonds, it is one of the most approachable sparkling wines in the world. Quality is extremely reliable across the board, although it has suffered from a certain vulgarity of image, presumably on account of its sweetness.
PRODUCERS: Fontanafredda, Martini, Sandro, most supermarket own-labels.

Barbaresco This and Barolo (see below) are the two most important reds produced from the brilliant Nebbiolo grape. Centred on the village of the same name, the Barbaresco DOCG is often held to produce slightly more elegant Nebbiolos than its longer-established sibling Barolo, but the difference is pretty subtle. These are huge, tannic, exotically scented wines, monstrously tough in youth, but ageing well to a savoury, chocolatey maturity.
PRODUCERS: Gaja, Giacosa, Pio Cesare, Marchesi di Gresy, Scarpa.

Barbera d'Alba/d'Asti/del Monferrato The Barbera grape variety, suffixed by any of these regional names in Piedmont, produces a sharply acidic, but agreeably cherry-fruited, red that is usually fairly light in both body and alcohol. Best drunk young and fresh, its undeniable potential is what has made certain California growers try their luck with it.
PRODUCERS: Viticoltori dell'Acquese, Guasti, Conterno, Borgogno.

Barolo King of the Piedmontese reds, Barolo is one of Italy's most travelled DOCG wines. Its supporters are among the most dedicated of wine fans, as it is often very difficult to know when to drink Barolo to catch it at its best. In its youth, it is absolutely rigid with tannin, although its colour starts to fade surprisingly quickly. It then begins to acquire an extraordinary range of flavours that includes violets, black plums, bitter chocolate and wild herbs, but even at 20 years old (when it may have gone quite brown), it obstinately refuses to let go of that heavyweight tannin. In the main, its growers have declined to compromise with contemporary tastes, so that Barolo remains one of the world's most gloriously unreconstructed red wines. Best vineyard sites may be specified on the label.
PRODUCERS: Aldo Conterno, Giuseppe Mascarello, Prunotto, Ceretto, Voerzio, Altare, Cavallotto.

The Barbaresco DO (above) in Piedmont, "the foothills" of the Alps.

Scything poppies in springtime (above) in Barolo.

PIEDMONT:
ARNEIS
GRAPE: *Arneis*
ASTI
GRAPE: *Moscato*
BARBARESCO
GRAPE: *Nebbiolo*
BARBERA D'ALBA/ D'ASTI/DEL MONFERRATO
GRAPE: *Barbera*
BAROLO
GRAPE: *Nebbiolo*

BRACHETTO D'ACQUI

GRAPE: *Brachetto*

DOLCETTO

GRAPE: *Dolcetto*

FAVORITA

GRAPE: *Favorita*

FREISA D'ASTI/
DI CHIERI

GRAPE: *Freisa*

GATTINARA

GRAPES: *Nebbiolo, Bonarda*

GAVI/CORTESE DI GAVI

GRAPE: *Cortese*

MOSCATO D'ASTI

GRAPE: *Moscato*

SPANNA

GRAPE: *Nebbiolo*

LOMBARDY:
OLTREPO PAVESE

GRAPES: *Red - Barbera,*
Bonarda, Croatina, Uva
Rara, Pinot Nero; White -
Riesling Italico, Pinot Bianco,
Pinot Grigio

VALTELLINA

GRAPE: *Nebbiolo*

FRANCIACORTA

GRAPES: *Red - Cabernet*
Sauvignon, Merlot, Pinot
Nero; White - Chardonnay

LUGANA WHITE

GRAPE: *Trebbiano di Lugana*

High on the alpine slopes of
Valle d'Aosta, vines are often
still trained up traditional
low pergolas (above).

Brachetto d'Acqui Oddball pink wine from the aromatic Brachetto grape, usually slightly pétillant.
Carema Tiny DOC for lighter Nebbiolo reds, in the far north. Look for Ferrando's wines.
Dolcetto Seven DOCs in Piedmont make red wine from the Dolcetto grape. They are Dolcetto d'Alba (the best), Diano d'Alba, Dogliani, Dolcetto d'Acqui, Dolcetto d'Asti, Ovada and Langhe Monregalesi. The wine is a bright purple, light-bodied, exuberantly fresh product for drinking young, crammed with a sharp berry-fruit flavour like blueberries. Compared to Beaujolais, young Dolcetto is nearly always a more attractive and more gently priced alternative.
PRODUCERS: Mascarello, Clerico, Vajra, Ratti, Viticoltori dell'Acquese.
Erbaluce di Caluso Light, fairly soft dry whites as well as a famed but rare golden dessert wine (Caluso Passito), made from the not especially distinguished Erbaluce grape.
PRODUCERS: Boratto, Ferrando.
Favorita White variety making pleasantly lemony varietal wine on both banks of the river Tanaro. Best grower is Malvira.
Freisa d'Asti/di Chieri A pair of DOCs, the latter very near Turin, for an intensely scented, floral red of appealing lightness, from the grape of the same name.
Gattinara Most important of the lesser-known red DOCs based on Nebbiolo. Gattinara's wines are intense and potentially long-lived.
PRODUCERS: Brugo, Travaglini.
Gavi/Cortese di Gavi Ambitiously priced dry whites from the herbaceous Cortese grape. Gavi (in particular its most illustrious manifestation Gavi di Gavi) is held in preposterously high esteem locally, which helps to explain its outlandish price. When all's said and done, the wine is not noticeably special.
PRODUCERS: Deltetto, Chiarlo, Arione.
Grignolino Light, quaffable varietal red made near Asti, only mildly less fruity than Dolcetto.
Moscato d'Asti Made in the same region and from the same grape as Asti, but much less fizzy than its more famous cousin, Moscato d'Asti is noted for its appetising citric freshness.
PRODUCERS: Chiarlo, Ascheri, Vietti, Gatti.
Ruchè Small DOC making full-bodied, herbal-scented reds in the Monferrato region. Not often seen.
Spanna Widely used synonym for the Nebbiolo grape, often seen on richly textured Piedmont reds from a number of localities. Travaglini makes a good example.

VALLE D' AOSTA

The far northwestern corner of Italy is occupied by a small river valley bordering on both France and Switzerland. Wines produced here are made from a number of native grapes, backed up by a smattering of Nebbiolo and Moscato and plantings of Burgundy and Alsace varieties. They are almost all consumed locally.

LIGURIA

An arc-shaped mountainous region that runs along the Mediterranean coast of northwest Italy, Liguria's main commercial centre is Genoa. In terms of exports, it is not a particularly significant winemaking district, and many of its traditional wines, such as the syrupy dessert wines made from raisined grapes, are dying out. Cinqueterre is a dry white based on the local Bosco grape, usually blended with Vermentino (known as Rolle in France, where it is a major player in the wines of Bellet in Provence). Rossese is an important native red variety, and has its own DOC, Dolceacqua, in the west of Liguria. Some Dolcetto is produced under the local name of Ormeasco.

LOMBARDY

The Lombardy region (or Lombardia) is centred on Milan, and runs from the alpine border with Switzerland down to the river Po, which forms its southern extremity. It is geographically the largest of Italy's wine regions, and has been in recent years one of the quality leaders.
Oltrepò Pavese In classic Italian fashion, this name covers almost any style of wine, from sparkling to sweet, only some of which qualifies for the DOC. The best is a good, sturdy red based on Barbera, while the dry whites from the Riesling Italico (nothing to do with the noble Riesling, confusingly) are largely forgettable. The champagne-method fizzes tend to use the various members of the Pinot family.
Valtellina The largest volume of Nebbiolo in Italy is produced in this DOC near the Swiss border. As well as basic Valtellina and the slightly better Valtellina Superiore, there are four recognised sub-regions that are responsible for the best wines - Inferno, Grumello, Sassella and Valgella. These are much lighter Nebbiolos than those produced in Piedmont, but the best do attain a purity of fruit and staying-power on the palate. Some powerful wine is made from shrivelled grapes fermented until fully dry, and bottled under the name Sforzato.

The castle of Soave (left), in the Veneto, that gives its name to one of Italy's most famous dry white wines.

Drying grapes for Amarone and Recioto (above) at the Masi winery, in Veneto's Valpolicella DOC.

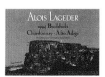

Franciacorta Created a DOCG in 1995 for potentially excellent champagne-method sparklers that are worth investigating. The still wines are labelled DOC Terre di Franciacorta, and tend to use classic French varieties and techniques. PRODUCERS: Ca' del Bosco, Bellavista, Cavalleri. Berlucchi is a benchmark fizz producer.

Lugana White DOC for dry wines based on a local variant of the dreaded Trebbiano grape - the Trebbiano di Lugana. The odd one has a little herbaceous snap to it. Zenato makes some half-decent examples. (Lugana overlaps into the Veneto region.)

TRENTINO-ALTO ADIGE

Hard by the Austrian border is Italy's northernmost wine region. The Alto Adige is known to the Austrians, as well as the many German-speaking Italians in these parts, as the Südtirol or South Tyrol. The lower half of the region takes its name from the city of Trento.

In the last couple of decades, producers here have made a name for the region by making some light but impressive wines from international varieties, most notably the Cabernets Sauvignon and Franc, Merlot and Pinot Noir, as well as Chardonnay, Pinot Gris and Pinot Blanc. The Australian winemaker, Geoff Merrill, has produced some outstanding wines here.

Some of the Chardonnay is barrel-aged and aims to carve itself a niche in the international market for oaky white wines, but prices for these wooded wines have tended to be too stiff for their own good. Local red varieties of particular note are the sour-cherry-flavoured Marzemino, the richly chocolatey Lagrein (which can make sinewy reds such as Lagrein Dunkel, as well as graceful rosés known as Lagrein Kretzer) and the blackcurranty Teroldego, which has its own DOC in Teroldego Rotaliano. PRODUCERS: Haas, Lageder, Tiefenbrunner, Walch.

VENETO

The Veneto is the major wine-producing region of northeast Italy, extending from east of Lake Garda across to Venice and up to the Austrian border. There are some important DOCs and commonly recognised names like Soave and Valpolicella, but overall quality is dragged down by excessive production and some ill-conceived matching of grape varieties to vineyard sites. However, the potential for improvement is clearly there, and some enterprising growers are showing signs of healthy impatience with the general level of mediocrity.

Cases of Soave leaving the packing shed (right).

VENETO:
BARDOLINO
GRAPES: *Red - Corvina, Molinara, Rondinella*
BIANCO DI CUSTOZA
GRAPES: *White - Trebbiano Toscano, Garganega, Tocai Friulano*
BREGANZE
GRAPES: *Red - Cabernet Sauvignon, Cabernet Franc, Merlot; White - Tocai Friulano, Pinot Bianco, Sauvignon Blanc, Chardonnay*
PIAVE
GRAPES: *Red - Merlot, Cabernet Sauvignon; White - Tocai Friulano, Verduzzo*
SOAVE
GRAPES: *White - Garganega, Trebbiano di Soave, Chardonnay, Pinot Bianco*
VALPOLICELLA
GRAPES: *Red - Corvina, Molinara, Rondinella*

Bardolino Featherlight reds from a trio of local grapes for drinking young and fresh but not for lingering over. Wines labelled Superiore should have a bit more oomph. The rosé version is called Chiaretto, but is rarely very nice.
PRODUCERS: Masi, Boscaini, Le Vigne di San Pietro.

Bianco di Custoza Mostly neutral dry whites from a cocktail of grape varieties, none of which seem able to contribute much character. Occasionally, a vague hint of tutti-frutti enlivens some wines, but not often.
PRODUCERS: Zenato, Le Vigne di San Pietro, Portalupi, Tedeschi.

Breganze One of those DOCs making waves by trying out international varietal wines, though there is plenty of humdrum stuff from local grapes too. The red wines made from the Bordeaux blend can be extraordinarily good in a genuinely claretty way. Maculan stands head and shoulders above other producers in the area.

Gambellara Dry whites that bear a marked resemblance to Soave, owing to their being made from the same grapes. Most are very bland indeed.

Piave The area immediately behind Venice produces large quantities of indifferent varietal wine, where the lion's share of it thin, grassy Merlot.

Prosecco di Conegliano/di Valdobbiadene Made near Piave, Prosecco can be a still dry white, but its more celebrated manifestation is as a simple sparkler, using the Charmat method in which the second fermentation is induced in a large tank before bottling. A lot of it is just off-dry and can be agreeably refreshing. In the bars of Venice, they mix it with peach juice to make the famous Bellini cocktail.
PRODUCERS: Collavini, Carpene Malvolti.

Soave One of Italy's most famous dry white wines, often synonymous with the bone-dry, totally neutral, flavour-free image of Italian whites that many wine-drinkers have. Increasing amounts of Chardonnay in the blend have added a little interest, even if we may be allowed some scepticism as to how traditional it is. If you're lucky, you may find a hint of almond paste on the nose that contributes some interest. Some producers are experimenting with ageing in oak - a difficult balancing-act to bring off. Recioto di Soave is a sweet but austere version made from raisined grapes.
PRODUCERS: Pieropan, Anselmi, Costalunga, Pasqua, Zenato, Tedeschi, Santi.

Valpolicella Red wine DOC that covers a multitude of styles, from very dilute pinkish wines of no discernible character to some deliciously concentrated, gamey, chocolatey reds of considerable ageing potential. As well as the basic style (and the slightly more alcoholic Superiore version), there are some high-octane traditional Valpolicellas produced from grapes that have been dried on straw mats.

Recioto is a silky-sweet version that can resemble port, while Amarone is fermented out to full dryness, is hugely alcoholic (often 15-16 per cent without fortification) and almost painfully bitter - its name coming from the Italian word for bitter, *amaro*. Ripasso is a sort of compromise, an ordinary Valpolicella that has been allowed to run over the skins of grapes used to make Amarone or Recioto.
PRODUCERS: Allegrini, Quintarelli, Tedeschi, Masi, Le Ragose, Dal Forno.

FRIULI

The easternmost wine region of Italy borders Austria to the north and Slovenia to the east, and forms part of the Adriatic coastline that extends down to Trieste. It is sometimes known as Friuli-Venezia Giulia. This is another region that has achieved some notable successes with international varieties, and the main production within DOC regions such as Collio or the Colli Orientali is of varietally named wines.

Best reds so far have been Cabernet Sauvignon and Merlot, particularly from the commercially important DOC of Grave del Friuli, Cabernet Franc from Collio, and local grapes Refosco, which makes a sharp-textured but appetising red, and spicy Schiopettino. Successful dry whites have been Pinot Grigio, the tantalisingly flowery Tocai Friulano, crisp

Sauvignon and even some subtly perfumed Gewürztraminer. The improving DOC of Isonzo has scored with most of these varieties too. There is also a very rare, austerely almondy, golden dessert wine that is made by the raisining method from a variety called Picolit: snap it up if you see it, but don't expect it to be cheap. BEST REGIONAL PRODUCERS: Collavini, Jermann, Puiatti, Schiòpetto, La Fattoria, Borgo.

EMILIA-ROMAGNA

A sprawling region south of the river Po, comprising Emilia in the west and Romagna on the Adriatic coast, and with the ancient city of Bologna at its heart, Emilia-Romagna is one of the bulk-producing wine regions of Italy. Very little of the wine is of DOC standard, and much of it is drunk in a slightly fizzy state, whatever the provenance. The epitome of this tendency is Lambrusco, which comes in all colours but is usually sparkling, high in acidity and often of little discernible quality.

A hillside district bordering on Lombardy, in the northwest of the region, the Colli Piacentini, is one of the better zones for quality wine. Gutturnio (made from Barbera and Croatina grapes) is a good, hearty red, and there are some refreshing white varietals, including Sauvignon Blanc. Down in the southern part of Romagna, Albana di Romagna is noteworthy only for being the first white wine to receive the exalted DOCG classification, a questionable choice for an unexceptional wine made from the workaday Albana grape. Some steadily improving red wine is made from Sangiovese, the great red grape of Tuscany. Labelled Sangiovese di Romagna, it is best drunk young while there is still a bracing acid edge to it.

TUSCANY

Along with Piedmont, Tuscany is the most significant part of Italy in quality wine terms, and occupies a special place at the cultural heart of the country. In addition to the beautiful old cities of Florence and Siena, the rolling landscape of olive trees and vines is one of the best-loved on the European tourist circuit.

For many newcomers to wine in the 1960s, Chianti - as often as not coming in straw-covered bottles like something from the tourist shops - came to be synonymous with Italian red wine. More than any other region, however, it was here that the Vino da Tavola revolution really took off, with the launch of a generation

of wines made without reference to the DOC stipulations. These proved once and for all that Italian growers are capable of producing genuinely world-class wines.

Bolgheri The Tuscan wine scene was transformed in the 1970s with the release of the first vintages of Sassicaia, the brainchild of the Incisa della Rochetta family. Blended from the two Cabernets, it was an explicit attempt to produce a premium wine in the image of a classed-growth Bordeaux. For all that there are no Italian varieties in it, it does still taste quintessentially Tuscan, the rich cassis-and-plum fruit always having a savoury edge like bitter herbs that proudly announces its provenance. It was a mere *vino da tavola* until 1994, when the Bolgheri DOC was drawn up to include it. Fiendishly expensive, but truly memorable wine.

Brunello di Montalcino Created single-handedly by the Biondi-Santi family in the late 19th century, Brunello is made from a particularly fine clone of the Chianti grape Sangiovese. It is only since the last war that any name other than Biondi-Santi has been involved in the production of this wine. Brunello is one of Tuscany's greatest red wines - deeper and richer than Chianti, full of sour black cherries and pungent herbs, and capable of long evolution. It has to be aged for three years in cask under the regulations, which many feel is too long, and prices are stratospherically high, but the quality is there. A separate DOC, Rosso di Montalcino, has been created for wines released at one year old; these represent much better value. PRODUCERS: Biondi-Santi, Val di Suga, Talenti, Il Poggione, Argiano, Castelgiocondo.

Merlot vineyard in the Bolgheri DOC (above), destined for the "super-Tuscan" Tenuta Ornellaia.

TUSCANY:
BOLGHERI
GRAPES: *Red - Cabernet Sauvignon, Cabernet Franc*
BRUNELLO DI MONTALCINO
GRAPE: *Red - Sangiovese*

CARMIGNANO

GRAPES: *Red - Sangiovese,*
Cabernet Sauvignon

CHIANTI

GRAPES: *Red - Sangiovese,*
Cabernet Sauvignon,
Canaiolo; White -
Trebbiano, Malvasia

VERNACCIA DI SAN
GIMIGNANO

GRAPES: *White - Vernaccia,*
Chardonnay

VINO NOBILE
DI MONTEPULCIANO

GRAPES: *Red - Sangiovese,*
Canaiolo; White -
Trebbiano, Malvasia

VIN SANTO

GRAPES: *White - Trebbiano,*
Malvasia, Pinot Grigio,
Pinot Bianco, Sauvignon
Blanc, Chardonnay

Grapes hanging from the
rafters (above) to dry out for
the sweet Tuscan wine, Vin
Santo.

Carmignano Cabernet was allowed into Carmignano before it gained admittance to any other Tuscan red, including Chianti. The proportion isn't great, but the Sangiovese is generally ripe enough not to need the extra dimension of intensity conferred by Cabernet. Impressive quality was rewarded in 1988 by elevation from DOC to DOCG. Capezzana is the major name on the export markets, and is highly reliable.

Chianti Inevitably for such a high-volume wine region, Chianti spans the quality range from heavenly wines of tremendous, often oak-powered concentration to vapid, thin apologies for red wine that have only helped over the years to undermine its reputation. Part of the problem is that the boundaries of the region are much too inclusive. It comprises seven sub-zones: Chianti Classico (the heart of the region between Florence and Siena), Chianti Rufina in the northeast, Chianti Montalbano, and four hillside areas named after the cities they adjoin - Colli Fiorentini (Florence), Colli Senesi (Siena), Colli Aretini (Arezzo) and Colli Pisane (Pisa).

Of these, only the first two are genuinely dependable for quality, and will always carry their regional names. Wines given longer in cask from any of the sub-zones are labelled Riserva, not necessarily an infallible indicator of a fine wine, since much Chianti is too frail to withstand long periods in wood. The traditional Sangiovese and Canaiolo blend has been joined by Cabernet, but the allowance of the white grapes Trebbiano and Malvasia has only hindered the production of quality wine, and many of the better producers don't bother with them.

Typically, Chianti is an orangey-red wine with an aroma of dried berry fruits, perhaps even a little plum tomato, and savoury herbs, feeling quite sharp on the palate from high acidity and a slight peppery edge. Modern production methods are now seeing wines with much richer colour, obvious Cabernet presence and longer finishes than has been the norm. PRODUCERS: Castello di Volpaia, Castello di Fonterutoli, Villa di Vetrice, Isole e Olena, Castello di San Polo in Rosso, Badia a Coltibuono, Berardenga, Fontodi, Selvapiana.

Galestro When the conscientious producers stopped diluting their Chianti with Trebbiano, something had to be done with this redundant, widely planted grape. Galestro, a water-white, low-alcohol, flavourless dry white, was the answer. Malvasia can add some interest.

Vernaccia di San Gimignano The local Vernaccia grape forms the base for this highly prized but low-volume white wine made within sight of the famous towers of the town of San Gimignano. It was actually the first wine to gain the new DOC classification in 1966, and was elevated to DOCG in 1993. Chardonnay may constitute no more than 10 per cent of the blend. At its best, it has an intriguingly waxy texture and attractive almond-paste character, but - as with many Italian whites - the generality is bland, anonymous quaffing stuff. PRODUCERS: Terruzzi e Puthod, Falchini, San Quirico.

Vino Nobile di Montepulciano There is an Italian grape variety called Montepulciano, but it isn't part of this DOCG wine, which is made in the hills southeast of Florence from the classic Chianti grape mix (minus Cabernet). Although the wines can be powerfully intense, with strong purple fruit and a dash of liquorice, they tend to stop just short of the pedigree of top Chianti or Brunello. Two years' cask ageing is required; again, the better producers ignore the white grapes. As with Brunello, younger wine may be released as Rosso di Montepulciano, under its own DOC. PRODUCERS: Avignonesi, Trerose, Boscarelli, Fattoria del Cerro.

Vin Santo Undoubtedly the best manifestation of the undistinguished white grapes of Tuscany is as Vin Santo, an often lusciously sweet *passito* wine. It is made from grapes that have been raisined by being hung up in the warmest part of the winery to lose their moisture. A small amount is fermented out to a nutty dryness like the driest sherry. There are two DOCs for Vin Santo - Val d'Arbia, and Colli dell'-Etruria Centrale. It is the latter that permits the use of the non-Italian varieties. Long cask ageing of the wines is the norm, and many are made in a deliberately oxidised style. PRODUCERS: Isole e Olena, Avignonesi, Selvapiana.

THE MARCHES

An eastern region on the Adriatic coast, with the city of Ancona its main commercial centre. Its best wines are a pair of red DOCs, Rosso Conero and Rosso Piceno, made from blends of the eastern Italian variety Montepulciano with Tuscany's Sangiovese. (In the case of Rosso Conero, the local grape predominates, while Rosso Piceno must be not less than 60 per cent Sangiovese.) Both are full-bodied, spicy reds

with notable ageing potential. Verdicchio is the regional white grape, most often seen in Verdicchio dei Castelli di Jesi, one of those infuriatingly neutral-tasting whites that Italy seems to specialise in (although a producer like Garofoli can coax some peanutty aromatic quality out of it). Verdicchio di Matelica is a superior version but not much of it is made. The house of Umani Ronchi makes good wines across the board.

UMBRIA

Wedged between Tuscany and the Marches, the small landlocked region of Umbria is centred on the city of Perugia. Its most famous wine is Orvieto, which lays claim to a distinctive local grape variety in Grechetto. Unfortunately it is swamped with admixtures of Trebbiano and Malvasia. It comes in three basic styles, a simple dry wine (*secco*) which often has the tartness of Conference pears, a medium-sweet, in-between version (*abboccato*) and a fully sweet, often rotted dessert wine (*amabile*). Overall quality is uninspiring; Barberani, Palazzone and Bigi make the best ones.

Torgiano is the best red wine, now classified a DOCG. It is made from Sangiovese in an almost improbably concentrated style (one producer, Lungarotti, has blazed this particular trail). Montefalco is a DOC for Sangiovese reds made near Assisi and blended with a little of the local variety Sagrantino. Vinified alone in this region, this latter grape also has its own DOCG, Sagrantino di Montefalco.

LAZIO

Lazio is the region surrounding Rome, chiefly responsible for large quantities of indifferent white wine, the most famous of which, Frascati, is - with Soave - virtually synonymous with Italian white on the export markets. The Trebbiano and Malvasia grapes hold sway here, so most Frascati is fairly dull stuff. Colli di Catone in the frosted bottle is about the best, having a bewitching tang of *crème fraîche*, but Fontana Candida is also good; both must be drunk as young as you can find them. The most overbearingly named white wine in Italy - Est! Est!! Est!!! di Montefiascone - is also Trebbiano-based, and rarely tastes as if it justifies one exclamation mark, let alone six. Some Cabernet Sauvignon and Merlot is grown in this region, but otherwise there are no particularly remarkable reds.

ABRUZZI

The reputation of this mountainous region on the Adriatic coast, south of the Marches, rests on a pair of DOC wines, one red and one white. The red, Montepulciano d'Abruzzo, is by far the more famous of the two. Made from the grape of the same name, it is always a softly plummy, low-tannin, easy-going wine with a strange but unmistakable waft of sea air about it. Despite its strong reliability, it has never become expensive on the export markets, and is often a surefire bet for a modestly priced Italian red with more depth than most of its equals. Umani Ronchi and Mezzanotte make fine ones.

The white wine, Trebbiano d'Abruzzo, is hampered by its name alone. It actually contains, in a typically Italian paradox, no Trebbiano at all, but is made from a southern variety with the rather splendid name of Bombino. A producer called Valentini has single-handedly made a name for this DOC with a hazelnutty dry wine of quite uncommon intensity.

Bottles of Montepulciano d' Abruzzo being packed at the Illuminati winery in eastern-central Italy (below). The wine is regularly one of the country's most reliable and reasonably priced reds.

Vines compete for space with houses on the coastal cliffs at Amalfi (above), in Campania.

MOLISE

Small and quantitatively unimportant region south of the Abruzzi, specialising in *vini da tavola* from international varieties such as Chardonnay and Riesling. Biferno is a regional DOC for wines in all three colours, the reds and rosés based on the Montepulciano grape, the whites on Bombino, Trebbiano and Malvasia.

PUGLIA

Puglia is the heel of Italy, incorporating the Adriatic port of Bari, and responsible for one of the largest annual productions of any of the country's wine regions. Only a small proportion of this is of DOC standard, however. The extreme southeastern province of Salento is where the finest reds come from. Here the spicily exciting Negroamaro grape is the claim to fame. Its best DOC is Salice Salentino, a richly plummy, often interestingly honeyed red wine of enormous appeal (Candida's Riserva is an especially good example). It also crops up in the wines of Copertino, Squinzano and Brindisi among others, sometimes given extra bite with another local grape, Malvasia Nera.

Primitivo di Manduria makes colossally alcoholic reds from the Primitivo grape, which has been identified as the Zinfandel of California. Castel del Monte is another red DOC with its own local grape, the intriguing Uva di Troia. Otherwise, the grapes of Abruzzi are relatively important for reds and whites, and there is the usual smattering of international varieties.

CAMPANIA

The Neapolitan southwest of Italy has the most venerable winemaking tradition of any part of Italy, but the lowest percentage of wine qualifying as DOC. That seems a shame because the DOC areas have undoubted potential. Taurasi is a fierce and exciting, if tannic, red made from a fine local variety called Aglianico. Falerno del Massico is a new DOC seeking to re-create the lost glory of Falernian, the much-revered wine of classical antiquity that is mentioned repeatedly in the literature of the period; it is a blend of Aglianico and the local Piedirosso with Primitivo and Barbera.

The main white DOCs are Greco di Tufo, a mildly lemony wine of some charm, and Fiano d'Avellino, which can have a haunting taste of ripe pears. Both are named after their grape varieties. Lacryma Christi del Vesuvio is one of the region's more famous wines, appearing in both red and white versions, both fairly unpalatable. Mastroberardino makes wines in most of the DOCs of Campania, and is certainly the best producer.

BASILICATA

This very poor southern region makes only minuscule quantities of wine, and indeed there is only one DOC, although it is a good one. Aglianico del Vulture is made from the red grape of that name also seen in Campania. Here it is grown in vineyards around the extinct Vulture volcano, and produces an astonishingly lush-textured wine with a strange coffee-like aroma, worth seeking out.

CALABRIA

Cirò is the only DOC wine you might see outside the region that forms the toe of Italy's boot. Based on the local Gaglioppo grape, it comes in red and rosé styles and may, as with many other Italian reds, be blended with some white grapes, inevitably including Trebbiano. On the south coast, a rather sophisticated DOC dessert wine is produced from semi-dried Greco grapes - Greco di Bianco - although, again, you'll be lucky to see it outside Calabria.

SICILY

The island of Sicily is one of the most copiously productive regions of Italy. Much of its produce is of no more than table wine standard, but there are isolated pockets of improving quality that suggest that, some time in the future, Sicilian wines could be among Italy's finest.

Its most celebrated product is the fortified wine Marsala, produced in the west of the island. Although it is of declining commercial importance now, in common with southern Europe's other classic fortified wines, it remains one of the great original wine styles, quite unlike any other. Various methods of fortification are used, including a rather clumsy one that uses cooked concentrated grape juice known as *mosto cotto*. The best grades of Marsala, however, are Superiore and Vergine, which are not permitted to use this method.

Styles range from the austerely dry (*secco*) to the liquorously sweet (*dolce*) but common to all of them is a smoky, almost acrid burnt-toffee tang that is Marsala's unique selling point. These days, most of it probably goes into zabaglione or tiramisu, but the best Marsalas, such as those from de Bortoli, deserve to be

appreciated on their own as stimulating alternatives to the more familiar after-dinner tipples.

Two of the white grapes used in Marsala make good dry table wines elsewhere on the island. They are Inzolia and Catarratto, both capable of producing lightly aromatic wines of some character. Nero d'Avola is about the best of the native red grapes, and blended reds with a healthy percentage of that grape are often among Sicily's best.

Regaleali is one of the leading Sicilian producers of quality wines. Its reds can be monumentally complex and ageworthy, as can Corvo Rosso, a long-lived, excitingly spicy red made by the house of Duca di Salaparuta. Settesoli, the main co-operative on the island, produces some well-made simple reds.

The tiny island of Pantelleria, halfway between Sicily and Tunisia, has revived one of the legendary dessert wines of history in Moscato di Pantelleria, made from dried Moscato grapes given delicious richness with extended oak-ageing.

SARDINIA

Sardinia's wine production continues to be hampered by its very insular approach to marketing, and the ridiculously high yields permitted under the DOC regulations for what could otherwise be quite interesting, characterful wines. Cannonau is one of the most important red varieties (claimed by some to be related to Grenache) and can make an inky, full-bodied red if yields are restricted. Monica produces a much lighter, almost Beaujolais-like red for early drinking.

Nuragus is one of the more significant white grapes, but its wines tend to the classic Italian neutrality, partly because of the massive yields obtained. Vernaccia di Oristano can be a diverting curiosity for those on holiday - a bone-dry, nutty, often oxidised white that may remind you of a basic fino sherry.

OTHER CLASSIC WINES OF ITALY

As the redesigning of Italy's wine classification system continues apace, one of its central concerns has been to draw into its embrace all of those quality wines that were being defiantly produced outside the regulations as *vini da tavola*, many of them selling for prices comparable to the most illustrious wines of France. The ground-breaking Sassicaia, as explained above, is now DOC Bolgheri, as is Ornellaia. The other wines listed here have all been designated IGT under the new rules. A lot depends on whether the individual producers care to play a part in the official system. Many don't as yet.

Balifico (Castello Volpaia): Sangiovese-Cabernet Sauvignon blend aged in French oak.

Cepparello (Isole e Olena): Attractively ripe varietal Sangiovese fleshed out with new oak.

Flaccianello della Pieve (Fontodi): 100 per cent Sangiovese similar in style to Cepparello, but with a slightly more obvious Tuscan bitterness to it.

Grifi (Avignonesi): Sangiovese-Cabernet Franc from the celebrated producer of Vino Nobile di Montepulciano.

Ornellaia (Lodovico Antinori): Massively concentrated blend of Bordeaux grape varieties, built for a long life.

Sammarco (Castello dei Rampolla): Three-quarters Cabernet, one-quarter Sangiovese.

Solaia (Piero Antinori): Cabernet-Sangiovese of great distinction, not as sweet and lush as some, but full of classical intensity.

Tignanello (Antinori): A Sangiovese-Cabernet blend from one of the finest houses in Tuscany, Tignanello is a hugely exciting, long-lived red that combines gorgeously ripe purple fruits with chocolatey richness.

RECENT VINTAGES

Piedmont: *2001 ***** 2000 ***** 1999 **** 1998 **** 1997 **** 1996 ***** 1995 *** 1994 * 1993 ** 1992 * 1991 ** 1990 ******
Tuscany: *2001 *** 2000 **** 1999 **** 1998 *** 1997 ***** 1996 * 1995 *** 1994 *** 1993 *** 1992 ** 1991 *** 1990 ******

Ancient farmhouse in the hills of Basilicata (above), surrounded by ploughed land ready for planting with new vines.

Sicilian vineyard (below) planted on black volcanic soils in the shadow of Mount Etna.

SPAIN

A proud winemaking tradition, and the producers' commitment to quality, are placing Spain at the forefront of Europe's great wine nations. Freshness and fruit are now the bywords for the best wines, rather than old-fashioned wood flavour.

The castle of Peñafiel (above) perches above the vineyards of the dynamic Ribera del Duero region.

Renowned for its sherries and oaked wines, the arrival on the map of new wine regions is bringing impressive still and sparkling Spanish wines to the market (right).

A S IN MUCH OF THE rest of southern Europe, vine-growing is a matter of considerable antiquity in Spain. The vine is known to have been cultivated on the Iberian peninsula since about the fourth millennium BC. By the time Spanish territory came to be fought over by the Romans and Carthaginians in the third and second centuries BC, a winemaking culture had long been established. Modern Spain has more land devoted to vine cultivation than any other country in the world, although its average annual production of wine is normally behind those of both Italy and France.

The viticultural industry has slowly but surely come to terms over the last 20 years with what the contemporary market expects of wine. Time-honoured practices such as the extended cask-ageing of both red and white wines, typified by the overwhelming oak flavour of classic Rioja, has gradually given way in many regions to a more sensitive approach that seeks to emphasise fruit flavours and youthful vibrancy over the desiccating impact of years in wood.

In addition to that, Spain's quality wine system, similar to that coming into operation in Italy, has been taken rather more seriously by the mass of producers than has been the case in Italy. The old DO designation (*denominación de origen*, the equal of *appellation contrôlée* in France) now has an upper level, DOCa (*denominación de origen calificada*) for the very best wines. Rioja was the first region declared a DOCa in 1991. Below those, an equivalent of *vin de pays* has been created - *vino de la tierra* - for wines that come from any of a series of large but geographically specific zones. After that comes a broader regional designation, *vino comarcal*, and then basic *vino de mesa*, or table wine.

As well as its rapidly improving reds and whites, Spain also boasts one of the world's

greatest fortified wines, namely sherry, together with the lesser-known Montilla and Málaga. Throw in some fine indigenous grape varieties, led by the ubiquitous but excellent Tempranillo, and it all adds up to a dynamic wine scene crammed with potential.

RIOJA

Spain's most visible export wines for years have come from the Rioja region surrounding the river Ebro in the northeast of the country. The red wine in particular, with its typically oily texture, strawberry-flavoured fruit and thick, creamy texture derived from ageing in oak, became a much-loved style in the 1970s, and remains the pre-eminent Spanish red for many wine-drinkers. When the new super-category of DOCa wines was created, Rioja was its first recipient, reflecting its pre-eminence in Spanish wine history.

The region is subdivided into three districts, the Rioja Alta west of Logroño (generally held to produce the wines of highest pedigree), the Rioja Baja southeast of the same town, and the Rioja Alavesa, which forms part of the province of Alava, in the Basque country. All three regions make reds, whites and rosés, the last known as *rosados* in Spanish.

The hierarchy of classification for the wines depends on the length of maturation in barrel and bottle they receive before being released on to the market. At the bottom of the pile, young new wine may be released as *joven* (meaning "young"). Not much is exported in that state, but it can have a delicious sweet-cherry appeal, and responds well to chilling.

Crianza wines must be aged for one year in barrel and a further year in bottle before release. Many commentators feel that this is probably the optimum period for those looking for an oaky red that still retains some decent fruit flavour. Reserva spends a year in barrel, but a further two in the bottle, while Gran Reserva is aged for at least two years in wood before being held in the bottle for a further three.

Traditionally, the type of wood favoured for the production of both red and white Rioja was American oak, which gives a much more pronounced sweet vanilla flavour to the wine than the softer French oak. More producers are now turning to French coopers, however, in order to achieve a subtler wood influence in their wines, and the innovation seems to be paying off in terms of yielding more balanced wines.

Tempranillo is the principal grape of the reds, contributing flavours of summery red fruits to young wines, but often turning fascinatingly gamey (almost like Pinot Noir) as it ages. It is supported mainly by Garnacha (Grenache), which usually lends a spicy edge to the softer Tempranillo fruit.

There are two distinct schools of thought in white Rioja. The traditional preference is for heavily oaked and deliberately oxidised wines of golden-yellow hue. They often smell tantalisingly like dry sherry, yet possess a bitter tang like dried citrus peel. Sipped in small quantities, they can be impressive wines to mull over, but "refreshing" is not one of the descriptions that springs to mind for them.

The newer style is all about squeaky-clean fermentation in stainless steel, at low temperatures, to maximise fruit flavours and freshness. Often made entirely without the use of oak, these light, lemony creations may not be as imposing as their barrel-fermented cousins, but they do chime more harmoniously with modern tastes in white wine. Rioja's white grapes are the relatively neutral Viura (often seen alone in the more modern-style whites) and the muskier, more headily perfumed Malvasia.

The rosados tend to be a little on the hefty side, rather in the manner of the rosés of the southern Rhône and the Midi over the border, but the odd one can be agreeably ripe and peachy. PRODUCERS: Marqués de Murrieta, CVNE, López de Heredia, Marqués de Cáceres, Campo Viejo, Bodegas Palacio, Montecillo, Amézola, La Rioja Alta SA.

Oak barrels piled up outside the winery at Rioja producer Bodegas López de Heredia (above).

RIOJA

GRAPES: Red - *Tempranillo, Garnacha, Mazuelo, Graciano*; White - *Viura, Malvasia*

Splashes of red mark the autumnal vineyards of Valde-orras (above), where increasingly characterful wines are being created.

NAVARRA

NAVARRA
GRAPES: Red - Garnacha, Tempranillo, Cabernet Sauvignon, Merlot; White - Viura, Chardonnay

RIAS BAIXAS
GRAPES: Albariño, Treixadura, Loureiro, Caiña Blanca

RIBEIRO
GRAPES: White - Treixadura, Torrontés, etc; Red - Garnacha, etc.

VALDEORRAS
GRAPES: White - Palomino, Godello, etc; Red - Garnacha, Mencía, etc.

EL BIERZO
GRAPES: Red - Mencía

TORO
GRAPES: Red - Tinto de Toro

NAVARRA

Just to the northeast of Rioja, but also on the river Ebro, is the increasingly trendy DO region of Navarra. While Navarra grows essentially the same grapes as neighbouring Rioja, its wines are quite different. There has also been increasing interest shown in incorporating some of the classic French varieties into the more ambitious oak-aged wines, so that it is not uncommon to see a white wine labelled Viura-Chardonnay. Unlike the traditional oaky wines of white Rioja, these wines are much fresher, with a gently buttery quality somewhat reminiscent of the lighter wines of Burgundy.

Navarra makes a much higher proportion of rosado than Rioja, and most of it benefits from attractively juicy strawberry fruit flavours and exemplary freshness. Red wines range from the relatively light in style, rather like Côtes du Rhône, to the seriously weighty and alcoholic.
PRODUCERS: Bodegas Ochoa, Chivite, Nekeus, Agramont from Bodegas Príncipe de Viana, and many of the co-operative wines produced under the auspices of the experimental research station EVENA.

RIAS BAIXAS

Rias Baixas has lately been one of the more talked-about wine regions of northern Spain. Situated in Galicia, in the northwest of the country, its reputation has been founded on some unexpectedly fragrant, positively floral dry white wines, mainly based on a fine local grape variety called Albariño. The DO is subdi-

vided into three distinct areas: Val de Salnes on the western coast, and O Rosal and Condado de Tea on the Portuguese border. As in much of the rest of Spain, the typical yields are low, and although other varieties are permitted in the wines under the Rias Baixas DO, they do not generally account for much of the blend. These are quite expensive but highly attractive modern white wines.
PRODUCERS: Lagar de Cervera from Lagar de Forlelos, Bodegas Morgadío, Codax.

RIBEIRO

The region's name means "riverside", and the vineyards occupy the land around the river Miño, which extends from northern Portugal. There is some fairly inconsequential red made here, but - as in Rias Baixas - the main business is white wine, and here quality is much improved of late. Some recently established plantings of Torrontés should add character to the whites in future. This is a florally aromatic grape with strong notes of orange blossom in it. Added to the Treixadura, the result is pleasantly fresh, fruity whites.

VALDEORRAS

Small wine-producing area in the east of Galicia that, in common with other regions, is progressing slowly but surely from making dull, bland plonk to wines of burgeoning character. Palomino, the sherry grape, has long been the scourge of northwestern whites, but is now being replaced by more appropriate varieties such as the local Godello, which gives good dry whites with a certain amount of aromatic personality. The ubiquitous Garnacha is responsible for many of the reds, but some attractively grassy, fresh-tasting reds are being made from the native Mencía grape in a style not dissimilar to the lighter reds of the Loire valley.

EL BIERZO

Just to the northeast of Valdeorras, El Bierzo is also beginning to explore its potential. The main focus of interest so far is good, ripe Loire-like reds made from the local Mencía grape. Watch this space.

TORO

The wines of Toro are produced in some of the most inhospitable conditions of any of Spain's vineyard regions, in a country that isn't short on climatic challenges for the vine. Planted at high

altitude along the river Duero, the grape responsible for the thunderously powerful Toro reds, Tinto de Toro, is a local mutation of Spain's main red variety, Tempranillo. Alcohol levels are typically around 13.5 per cent, and can go even higher, but the wines mostly wear it well, the thick, liquoricey flavours of the grape more than adequately supporting the almost spirity strength. One producer has dominated the region above all others - Bodegas Fariña. Fortunately, its wines - best exemplified by the darkly brooding, sweetly oaky Gran Colegiata - do not let the side down. Insignificant quantities of rosado and white are also produced.

RUEDA

A DO region since 1980, Rueda's regulations stipulate that it can produce white wines only. The old traditional style of wine was an oxidised fortified wine made from the Palomino grape that bore a passing resemblance to cheap, dry sherry. Nowadays, the region is carving out a reputation for producing some of Spain's freshest and most agreeable light dry whites. The native variety here is Verdejo, which gives generously full-textured wines. It is sometimes given a little citrus tang with a dash of the Rioja grape Viura, or increasingly brought into even sharper focus with a dose of nettly Sauvignon. Basic Rueda must be at least 25 per cent Verdejo, while wines labelled Rueda Superior have to contain a minimum of 60 per cent of the grape.
PRODUCERS: Marqués de Riscal, Marqués de Griñon.

CIGALES

North of the river Duero, Cigales is not much known to the outside world. It principally makes dry rosados and a little red from the two main red grapes of Rioja.

RIBERA DEL DUERO

For many, this dynamic, forward-looking region is now ahead of the Spanish pack. Across the board, its wines are increasingly more dependable than those of Rioja, and its producers appear to have absorbed more readily the lessons to be learned from current world tastes in red wine. Its principal variety is yet another local variation of Tempranillo, Tinto Fino, often making up 100 per cent of the wine. Controlled plantings of some of the Bordeaux varieties are permitted only in specific sections of the DO area, which was created in 1982. A proportion

of juice from the local white grape, Albillo, may be used to soften the intensity of the red wine, but the DO does not extend as yet to the production of white wines.

The best wines of Ribera del Duero have concentrated blackberry or plum fruit and usually a fair amount of oak influence. This is either the blowsy vanilla of American oak or the more muted, subtler tones of French oak. The system of ageing in cask and bottle is analogous to that of Rioja (from youngest to oldest: Joven, Crianza, Reserva and Gran Reserva).

In the west of the region is a property called Vega Sicilia that makes an enormously expensive, totally individual range of red wines, using Tinto Fino with the French varieties and a modicum of Albillo. Valbuena is a five-year-old oak-aged red with an astonishing and unforgettable mixture of perfumes - orange essence, loganberries and milk chocolate. Unico is its top wine, only made in the most promising vintages. The wine is released at about ten years old, after undergoing an elaborate ageing procedure in various types of wood (including large old casks that allow a fair amount of oxygen to seep into the wine) and in bottle. Vega Sicilia has been making wines in this way since modern Ribera del Duero was just a twinkle in an entrepreneur's eye, and has been fairly compared to the top classed growths of Bordeaux, in majesty if not in flavour.
OTHER PRODUCERS: Pesquera, Callejo, Arroyo, Torremilanos, Pago de Carraovejas.

RUEDA
GRAPES: White - Verdejo, Viura, Sauvignon Blanc, Palomino
CIGALES
GRAPES: Red - Tinto del País (Tempranillo), Garnacha
RIBERA DEL DUERO
GRAPES: Red - Tinto Fino (Tempranillo), Garnacha, Cabernet Sauvignon, Merlot, Malbec; White - Albillo

The church of Santa Maria la Mayor in Toro (left). On Spain's high central plain, the wine region of Toro makes big, powerful reds.

The 17th century castle of Raimat, in Catalonia (right), where the Raventos family has extensive high-altitude vineyards.

CHACOLI DE GUETARIA
GRAPES: White - Hondarrabi Zuri; Red - Hondarrabi Beltz
CALATAYUD
GRAPES: Red - Garnacha, Tempranillo, Mazuelo, Graciano; White - Viura, Malvasia
CAMPO DE BORJA
GRAPES: Red - Garnacha, Cariñena, Tempranillo; White - Viura
CARINENA
GRAPES: Red - Garnacha, Tempranillo, Cariñena; White - Viura, Garnacha Blanca, Parellada
SOMONTANO
GRAPES: Red - Moristel, Garnacha, Tempranillo, Cabernet Sauvignon, Merlot; White - Viura, Alcañón, Chardonnay, Chenin Blanc, Gewürztraminer
TERRA ALTA
GRAPES: White - Garnacha Blanca, Macabeo; Red - Garnacha
COSTERS DEL SEGRE
GRAPES: Red - Tempranillo, Garnacha, Cabernet Sauvignon, Merlot, Pinot Noir; White - Chardonnay, Parellada, Macabeo

CHACOLI DE GUETARIA

A tiny DO region (Spain's smallest) in the Basque country to the west of San Sebastian. Its mainly white wine is light and snappy and made in such minute quanitites that it is not viable as an export product. The equally light red is even rarer.

CALATAYUD

In the Aragon region on the river Jalon, Calatayud is dominated largely by co-operatives but not as yet geared for export. The varieties are essentially the same as Rioja and the wines come in all three colours, the unsubtle, alcoholic reds being the surest indicator of local taste.

CAMPO DE BORJA

Stunningly alcoholic reds are the speciality of Campo de Borja, near the town of Borja in the province of Aragon. Made mainly from Garnacha, they must attain at least 13 per cent alcohol to qualify for the DO. Again, co-operatives rule the roost, and again, most of the wine is drunk in the vicinity.

CARINENA

Much the most promising so far of the DO regions of Aragon, Cariñena - southwest of Zaragoza - is actually named after the grape variety that originated and once flourished there. (In its other guises, it is the Carignan of southern France, and is known as Mazuelo in Rioja.) Garnacha is star of the show currently for the big, opulent reds in which the region specialises, and, as in other parts of Aragon, they can attain spine-tingling levels of alcohol. Some Tempranillo is being blended in to soften the impact. Whites are largely fresh and clean, and some use a little of the Chardonnay-like Parellada grape more typically associated with the white wines of Penedés further east. A small quantity of champagne-method sparkling wine (known as cava in Spain) is made in Cariñena, although it too is more at home in Penedés. Monte Ducay from the Bodegas San Valero co-operative is a characteristic Cariñena red offered on the export markets.

SOMONTANO

A healthily outward-looking DO region in the Pyrennean foothills to the east of Navarra, Somontano makes reds, whites and rosados from a tempting mixture of local grapes (including the indigenous red Moristel and white Alcañón) and a catholic range of French varieties, including some convincingly perfumed Gewürztraminer. The Covisa winery in particular is finding its experimentation paying dividends. Espiral is another good name. As in Cariñena, a small amount of cava is produced.

TERRA ALTA

As its name suggests, Terra Alta is a high-altitude vineyard region in the west of Catalonia currently making the familiarly northern Spanish shift from heavy fortified wines to light, dry whites in the modern idiom. Reds are galumphing Garnachas in the jammy old style.

COSTERS DEL SEGRE

Split rather messily into four separated sub-regions, Costers del Segre has made waves outside Spain, despite its starting life as inauspicious desert land. These waves have been created almost exclusively through the efforts of the Raimat winery in Lerida, which makes a range of excellent varietals from softly velvety Tempranillo to densely meaty Merlot, as well as some Chardonnay fizz of impressive richness.

Some bottlings have successfully blended French and Spanish varieties in what has come to be characteristically Catalan fashion, notably Gran Calesa (Tempranillo-Cabernet) and Abadía (Cabernet-Tempranillo-Garnacha). Other producers are starting to enter the lists, and seem to be putting Costers del Segre on a vigorous upward trajectory.

PRIORATO

Practically a legend in its own right, Priorato makes one of the most uncompromising styles of red wine anywhere in Europe. Yields from the older vines in the region are minuscule and the rules specify a minimum alcoholic strength of 13.75 per cent for the wine to be true DO Priorato. The result is not hard to imagine - fiercely concentrated and heady wine, with a pugnacious peppery edge to it, capable of ageing for many years in the bottle. A Penedés producer, René Barbier, has planted some French varieties in the most promising vineyard sites, and may help to bring Priorato kicking and screaming into the modern wine world. The old-style stuff is still worth a flutter, though.
PRODUCERS: Scala Dei, Masia Barril, de Müller.

TARRAGONA

Tarragona once enjoyed a reputation for sweet, red, port-style fortified wines, but now contents itself largely with producing unambitious blending material for bulk producers elsewhere. Its limited local wine production, in all three colours but most of it white, is quite undistinguished.

CONCA DE BARBERA

Considered virtually a western extension of Penedés, Conca de Barberá produces some pleasantly fresh dry whites from the Catalan varieties (see Penedés below), as well as some hearty reds, but is mainly a source of sparkling cava. The region is a recently established DO that has benefited from substantial investment by the hugely important Penedés wine company of Miguel Torres.

PENEDES

Penedés, the largest of the DO regions of Catalonia, has two main claims to fame. It is the centre of the Spanish sparkling wine, or cava, industry, and it is the base of one of the most successful wine dynasties of Europe - the house of Torres.

Cava is a peculiarity in terms of its regulations, in that it can technically be made else-

where in Spain - the DO is not specific to Penedés. In practice, most of it is made in this northeastern region near Barcelona. The method used is the same as that in champagne, but the grapes are nearly all native varieties: Parellada, Macabeo and the rather assertively flavoured Xarel-lo. In addition to those, Chardonnay is being grown to a much greater extent than hitherto for cava production, and some cava (often labelled with the borrowed champagne term "blanc de blancs") is entirely Chardonnay.

Cava has to be aged on its yeast sediment for a minimum of nine months (two years in the case of vintage cava). A lot of it has a strangely leaden aroma, for which the description "rubbery" is often resorted to, but with more Chardonnay (or at any rate, less Xarel-lo) many producers are beginning to produce considerably more graceful examples. The small amount of cava rosado produced is not generally worth the price.
PRODUCERS: Codorníu, Freixenet, Segura Viudas, Mont Marçal, Condé de Caralt, Juvé y Camps.

The pioneering work of Miguel Torres, who died in the early 1990s, established Penedés as the most outward-looking wine region in the country. He planted international grape varieties alongside the indigenous ones, in many cases blending them together for certain wines, and created a formidable reputation for his company, and for Penedés.

Among the more successful Torres whites are the basic Viña Sol (made from Parellada, out of which Torres manages to tease more flavour than seemingly anyone else), Gran Viña Sol (a lightly oaked blend of Parellada and Chardonnay), Gran Viña Sol Green Label (Parellada with Sauvignon in a mouth-wateringly crisp, often slightly pétillant style), Viña Esmeralda (a honey-and-lemon, off-dry blend of Muscat and Gewürztraminer) and Milmanda (a highly opulent, uncannily Burgundian oaked Chardonnay).

The notable reds include Gran Sangre de Toro (earthy Garnacha and Cariñena), Atrium (a soft varietal Merlot), Mas Borrás (a classically cherry-scented, gamey Pinot Noir) and Mas la Plana, sometimes known as Black Label (a premium bottling of intensely dark, austerely tannic, unblended Cabernet Sauvignon).

Jean León is the other grower of note to have followed the international varietal trail here. His Chardonnay and Cabernet Sauvignon varietals are made in the thoroughly modern style, with lashings of ripe, vibrant fruit and unabashed levels of oaky richness.

PRIORATO
GRAPES: Garnacha, Cariñena
TARRAGONA
GRAPES: Red - Garnacha, Cariñena; White - Macabeo, Xarel-lo, Parellada, Garnacha Blanca
PENEDES
Numerous Spanish and French red and white varieties

Old Garnacha and Cariñena vines yield powerful, heady reds that have drawn attention to the small Priorato region in Catalonia (above).

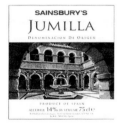

ALELLA

Alella is a tiny DO north of Barcelona, in which the Marqués de Alella co-operative is the pre-eminent producer. The output is light dry whites, in which the rather vegetal flavours of Xarel-lo (here known as Pansa Blanca) are frequently softened with a modicum of Chardonnay, and sparkling cava labelled Parxet, which may also contain a freshening soupçon of Chenin. A good varietal Chardonnay is also made.

AMPURDAN-COSTA BRAVA

This is a small DO situated on the opposite side of the border to the French Côtes du Roussillon. Nearly all the wine made here is drunk in situ - mostly simple rosados for the tourist market. There are also some rustic reds and, this being Catalonia, some cava made from the traditional Spanish varieties. A recent innovation was rush-released Vin Novell, an Iberian answer to Beaujolais Nouveau, although what the beach-bums on the Costa Brava make of it is anybody's guess.

MENTRIDA

A DO region immediately to the south and west of Madrid in central Spain, Méntrida's principal business is rough-and-ready Garnacha reds of no obvious pedigree. The excellent winery of Marqués de Griñon is also situated near here. As it is not within the DO boundaries, the wines - including an oaky Chardonnay and a pitch-black, awesomely concentrated Cabernet Sauvignon - are labelled as table wines of Toledo.

LA MANCHA

The largest DO region in Spain is also the largest individual appellation in Europe. La Mancha occupies the broiling, arid dustlands of the centre of Spain from Madrid down to Valde-peñas, about 200km (125 miles) from top to bottom. The pre-eminent grape variety grown here, the white Airén, is actually the most extensively planted wine grape in the world. Given that it is grown virtually nowhere outside Spain, that gives some idea of the sprawling vastness of La Mancha's vineyards.

Once seen as a workhorse area, dedicated as much to producing alcohol for industry as everyday table wines, La Mancha is now set on an upward course to quality. The Airén grape, previously dismissed as boringly neutral, turns out to make quite refreshing, simple, lemony whites in the right hands, and since the pre-

dominant red grape is Tempranillo (here adopt-ing another of its many pseudonyms, Cencibel), the prospects for classy reds too are good. They are generally somewhat lighter than those of Rioja, but have the pronounced strawberry fruit of the grape, together with appealingly smooth contours. The cosmopolitan duo of Cabernet and Chardonnay are beginning to make their presence felt in the vineyards of La Mancha too, reflecting the scale of ambition among many of the small proprietors.

In short, the region is set fair to prove that, even in the world of wine, big can be beautiful. It is expected, however, that sooner or later the region will have been broken up into a handful of more manageable chunks.

VALDEPEÑAS

Valdepeñas is the southernmost outpost of the huge central region of La Mancha. Its wines are thought sufficiently distinctive to merit a sepa-rate DO, and the growers have been quicker off the draw in penetrating the export markets than their neighbours to the north. Red wines from Tempranillo are the main business. Often given long cask-ageing, and labelled as Reserva or Gran Reserva, they can suffer from an excess of petrolly oak flavours on a basically rather light fruit base, but the better producers have man-aged to achieve good balance. (Señorio de los Llanos and Viña Albali are labels to look for.) Some straightforward, thin dry white is also made from the much-favoured Airén, but a fair amount of it, depressingly enough, goes into the red wines below Reserva level, reducing them to distinctly insipid specimens.

UTIEL-REQUENA

In the province of Levante, to the west of Valencia, Utiel-Requena's speciality is the Bobal grape - a good red variety that yields fairly meaty wine with a distinctive raisiny flavour. The reds can be a little clumsy, but the rosados are improving, and can be agreeably thirst-quenching on the right occasion.

VALENCIA

The eastern port of Valencia lends its name to a DO region inland from the city. White wines run the gamut from dullish dry wines, made from the less-than-inspiring local Merseguera grape, to the well-known sweet wine Moscatel de Valencia. The Moscatel doesn't undergo nor-mal fermentation but is made by adding grape

spirit to freshly pressed Muscat juice (a product known as *mistela* in Spanish). Red wines can be surprisingly thin and acidic when made from the Garnacha variant grown in these parts (rosados are better), but the Monastrell grape - Spain's second most widely planted red variety after Garnacha - produces a firmer, beefier style of red. Gandía is one of Valencia's better producers, making finely crafted reds as well as a very drinkable Moscatel de Valencia.

ALMANSA

A relatively unimportant Levantine DO that has concentrated much of its effort hitherto on making blending wine for other regions. When it does bottle its own red wines, they tend to the heavyweight end of the spectrum. Varietal Tempranillos are the best bets. Bodegas Piqueras is one producer intent on raising the reputation of the DO with some conscientiously made reds.

JUMILLA

Much the same applies in Jumilla as for neighbouring Almansa. A lot of blending wine is produced, alongside some strong-limbed Monastrell reds and Merseguera whites that lack excitement. Improvements seem to be afoot, though, particularly among the red wines. A huge co-operative, San Isidro - the second biggest in Spain - bestrides Jumilla like a colossus.

YECLA

Another DO making large quantities of blending wine, with a vast co-operative at the centre of operations. Big, beefy reds are the name of the game once more, supplemented by weedy Merseguera whites. Bodegas Castaño is one of the more reputable producers.

ALICANTE

The typical Levantine pattern of giant co-operatives producing mainly blending wine is repeated again in the Alicante DO that extends inland from the coastal city of the same name. A sweet fortified wine, Fondillon, using the same ageing method as in sherry, brightens the picture a little, and Tempranillo is beginning to make an appearance and lend some sophistication to the generally rustic reds.

BINISSALEM

The holidaymakers of the Balearic islands are kept well-supplied with wine by the Binissalem DO, the first to be created outside the Spanish mainland, on the island of Majorca. Two indigenous grape varieties, plus the white grapes of Catalonia, make some pretty rasping reds, simple, gluggable rosados and undistinguished whites. Nothing to get excited about in other words, but if the sun's shining and the price is right, who cares?

ALMANSA
GRAPES: Red - Monastrell, Garnacha, Tempranillo
JUMILLA
GRAPES: Red - Monastrell; White - Merseguera
YECLA
GRAPES: Red - Monastrell, Garnacha; White - Merseguera
ALICANTE
GRAPES: Red - Monastrell, Garnacha, Bobal, Tempranillo; White - Merseguera
BINISSALEM
GRAPES: Red - Manto Negro; White - Moll, Xarel-lo, Parellada

La Mancha, in the hot, arid centre of Spain (below left). This vast vineyard area is Europe's largest single appellation.

SHERRY

GRAPES: Palomino, Pedro Ximénez, Moscatel

The finest vineyards of the sherry region, as here at Osborne's Viña el Caballo west of Jerez (below), are planted on chalk-white albariza soil.

SHERRY AND OTHER FORTIFIED WINES

The province of Andalucía, in the south of Spain, is home to a range of traditional fortified wines, the most celebrated of which is sherry. At one time, fortified wines were produced all over Spain, but as the fashion in this century has gradually shifted towards lighter table wines, so the other regions have abandoned their frequently poor efforts, and Jerez and its satellites have cornered the market.

It is, to be sure, a dwindling market. Tastes have changed, and the image of sherry has suffered from its exasperating association with inferior products, such as the commercial pale and dark cream sherries that maturing tastebuds quickly grow out of. The profligate use of the word "sherry" to describe sub-standard sweet brown slosh from other countries has not helped. The latter problem was belatedly addressed by the European Union when, at the beginning of 1996, a ruling came into effect that rightfully reserved the word "sherry" for the produce of the Jerez region alone.

Sherry The wine takes its name from the city of Jerez de la Frontera in Andalucía, but the region also encompasses the major towns of Puerto de Santa María and Sanlúcar de Barrameda. These are the three principal locations for the maturation of the region's wines. Their quality rests fundamentally on the geology of the Jerez DO. The soil at the heart of the region is a mixture of limestone, sand and clay that looks deceptively like chalk, so blindingly white does it glare at you in the brilliance of a summer day. The local name for it is *albariza*, and most of the best

vineyard holdings are planted on this type of soil. Because of its proximity to the ocean, moreover, Jerez does not suffer quite the summer heat-stress that, say, La Mancha does. Although the summer months are relentlessly dry, cooling Atlantic breezes waft across the vines and the falling night-time temperatures mitigate the roaring heat of day.

Palomino is the main grape variety in sherry production. Nearly all of the wines, from the palest and driest up to the most liquorously treacly, are based on that grape. The variable element lies in how the producers decide which lots of the base wine will end up as which style.

After the light Palomino base wine has completed its fermentation, it is fortified with grape spirit up to anything from 15 to 20 per cent alcohol. Generally, the lighter fortification will be used for wines that are destined to be sold as fino, the palest, most elegant version of dry sherry. This is because fino sherries are matured in casks underneath a film of naturally forming yeast called *flor*, derived from wild yeasts that are present in the atmosphere of the cellars. The *flor* protects the developing wine from the influence of too much oxygen, and also imparts a characteristic nutty taste (like plain peanuts) to classic fino. Fortification above 15 per cent will inhibit the growth of *flor*, which is why fino sherries are lower in alcohol than darker and sweeter styles.

Sometimes the *flor* doesn't quite form a solid enough layer to produce fino. It breaks up and sinks to the bottom of the cask, and the more direct exposure to oxygen causes the wine's colour to darken. This becomes the style known as amontillado. (The best amontillados are still bone-dry, the popular conception of it as a medium-sweet style being derived from commercial brands that have been sugared up.)

The heaviest, darkest version of sherry is oloroso, which is fortified to the highest alcoholic degree of all, and is aged with maximum oxygen contact so that the colour is a deep burnished brown. Most olorosos are given a sweetening dose of juice pressed from raisined grapes, Pedro Ximénez (or PX) giving the best quality although Palomino may be treated in this way too. As with amontillado, however, there is a certain amount of totally dry oloroso made (labelled *oloroso seco*). Austere and intense, with a flavour of strangely bitter walnuts, it is one of the greatest taste experiences wine can offer.

Other sherry styles commonly encountered are *palo cortado* (which is a kind of naturally evolved median stage between amontillado and oloroso and is generally given some sweetening), Cream (sweetened, blended brown sherries, eternally symbolised by Harvey's Bristol Cream) and Pale Cream (a sweetened fino epitomised by Croft Original). Manzanilla is the official name of fino sherries matured in the town of Sanlúcar de Barrameda. They are popularly supposed to have a distinct salty whiff of the local sea air in them; on a good day, with a spanking-fresh bottle, it's possible to believe there is an element of truth to that.

Some houses make a speciality of bottling their raisined PX wine unblended. The result is an oleaginous, nearly-black essence of mind-blowing sweetness, so glutinously thick that it can scarcely be swirled in the glass. Everybody should try at least a mouthful, but it is admittedly hard to know what to do with a whole bottle of it. (The fashionable thing of late has been to pour it over vanilla ice-cream, which is indeed embarrassingly delicious.)

The traditional method of sherry maturation, now extensively abandoned by many houses, was in the so-called *solera* system. This consisted of massed ranks of barrels containing wines that went back a century or more. With each bottling, a third of the wine would be drawn off the oldest barrels, which would then be topped up with wine from the next oldest. This would in turn be replenished from the next oldest, and so on up to the youngest at the top of the pile, which would be topped up with newly made wine.

Given the painstaking labour involved in operating and maintaining such a system, it isn't entirely surprising that modern economics have decreed the abandonment of it in many cases. Wine that has been aged in a *solera*, however, will be labelled with the date of the oldest wine in it; there will of course be some 1895 wine in a bottle so labelled, but only a microscopic quantity sadly.

A note about serving the different types of sherry. Fino and manzanilla sherries *must* be served well-chilled, or they will taste hopelessly stale, but no other sherries should be. Equally as important with the paler sherries is to drink them as soon as possible after opening. Just treat them exactly as you would leftover white wine - they aren't that much more alcoholic, after all.

BEST SHERRIES: FINO: Tio Pepe, Don Zoilo, Hidalgo, Lustau, Williams and Humbert, Valdespino Inocente.

MANZANILLA: Barbadillo Príncipe, Hidalgo La Gitana and La Guita, Don Zoilo, Valdespino, Lustau Manzanilla Pasada (an older, darker version than the norm).

AMONTILLADO: Gonzalez Byass Amontillado del Duque, Valdespino Tio Diego and Coliseo, Hidalgo Napoleon, Lustau Almacenista.

OLOROSO: Gonzalez Byass Matúsalem and Apostoles, Valdespino Don Gonzalo, Williams and Humbert Dos Cortados, Lustau Muy Viejo Almacenista.

Montilla-Moriles A region to the northeast of Jerez that makes entirely analogous styles of fortified wine to sherry. However, it is generally somewhat behind the best sherries in terms of quality because of its inland location and less promising soils, and also the fact that the main sherry grape Palomino has not been able to make itself at home here. The wines can be good and are always cheaper than the corresponding sherry.

Málaga Made in the hinterland behind the Mediterranean port of the same name, the fate of Málaga stands as a salutary warning to what can happen to an original and inimitable style of wine when nobody wants to drink it any more. In the 19th century, it was highly revered, particularly in Britain where it was known as Mountain, owing to the steep hillside locations of its vineyards. By the 1990s, however, hardly anybody had heard of it and the last major producers in the region were close to shutting up shop. Málaga makes much more from tourism these days. This is a great pity, as the wine has a style all of its own, more often than not mahogany-coloured and full of a gentle raisins-in-caramel sweetness that is somehow never cloying.

Condado de Huelva A historically significant region for fortified wines situated to the west of Jerez towards the border with southern Portugal, Condado de Huelva is now sunk in obscurity as far as the outside world is concerned. It still makes some fortified wine, only very vaguely comparable to sherry; there is a kind of fino that develops under *flor* called Condado Palido, and a darker oloroso-type wine, Condado Viejo, that is aged in a *solera* system. Hardly any of it is exported, though. The emphasis is slowly shifting to the production of an unfortified table wine, Viño Joven. First impressions suggest it won't exactly set the world on fire.

MONTILLA-MORILES
GRAPES: *White - Pedro Ximénez, Muscat of Alexandria*

MALAGA
GRAPES: *White - Pedro Ximénez, Airén, Muscat of Alexandria, Palomino*

Fino sherry is matured in oak butts (above) under a film of flor, *a natural yeast that imparts a characteristic nutty taste to classic fino.*

PORTUGAL

Shaking off its old-fashioned attitudes, Portugal has rediscovered its greatest treasure - a range of exciting grape varieties - to prove that it can produce more than the world's top fortified wines.

At their best, traditional aged Portuguese reds (above) are liquoricey and spicy in character.

1. VINHO VERDE
2. PORTO/DOURO
3. DÃO
4. BAIRRADA
5. OESTE
6. RIBATEJO
7. BUCELAS
8. COLARES
9. PALMELA
10. ARRÁBIDA
11. ALENTEJO
12. ALGARVE
13. SETÚBAL.MOSCATEL
14. CARCAVELOS
15. MADEIRA .

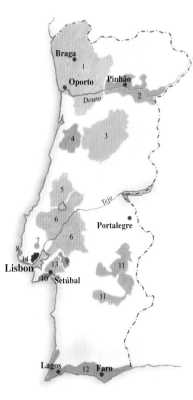

Portugal offers a striking range of wine styles (right), the two most renowned - port and Vinho Verde - coming from the north.

VINHO VERDE

GRAPES: *White - Loureiro, Trajadura, Arinto, Avesso, Alvarinho; Red - Vinhão, Azal, Espadeiro, etc.*

PORTUGAL'S ROLE IN the history of European wine is of an importance quite belied by the relative unfamiliarity of most of its table wines to today's consumers. Its reputation was founded primarily on the success of its fortified wines, port and madeira, in the lucrative markets of England and what was to become the United States. The 14th-century alliance between England and Portugal became significant when hostilities broke out between the English and French. Preferential tariffs for Portugal's wines were formalised in the Methuen Treaty of 1703, and drinking port rather than French wines became a matter of patriotic observance in English society.

In the centuries since then, Portugal's influence has declined as French wines once again became pre-eminent. Its economy was not easily able to support the kind of technological investment needed by every wine-producing country in order to make the wines the modern trade demands. For many years Portugal remained quite insular in its approach to wine, largely satisfying itself with the income generated by sales of port and, in Mateus Rosé, its own version of the semi-sweet sparkling wines usually guaranteed to be popular.

It is only in the last decade or so, since Portugal joined the European Union and the funds started to flow, that its other traditional table wines have begun to be appreciated across Europe. There is still a long way to go, and it is fair to say that the Portuguese have not been the most dynamically outward-looking among European winemakers. But they have a great asset in the broad range of high-quality indigenous grape varieties, many of which are capable of turning out some truly original wines at sharply competitive prices.

The classification of Portuguese wines follows the four-tier system that EU regulators have devised on the basis of the French model. At the top, the equivalent of *appellation contrôlée* is DOC (*denominação de origem controlada*). Then comes IPR (*indicação de proveniencia regulamentada*), a sort of Portuguese VDQS, *vinhos regionais* for regional wines like the *vins de pays*, and finally simple table wines, *vinhos de mesa*.

VINHO VERDE

This is Portugal's largest DOC region by far, up in the northwest corner of the country around Oporto. The sheer volumes produced and exported have made Vinho Verde one of Portugal's better-known wines internationally. At least, it is the *white* version that is popular; many consumers are unaware that just over half of all Vinho Verde is red, probably because the

Portuguese keep nearly all of it to themselves. The name means "green wine", but that doesn't refer to the greenish tinge in many of the whites, but to the fact that the wine, both red and white, is released young for quick consumption. Its youth means that there is usually a slight pétillance, even a positive sparkle, in many bottles (indeed some are deliberately carbonated before bottling), as well as generous dollops of raw, palate-scouring acidity.

Most wines are blends of various local grapes, and each sub-region has its own particular specialities, Loureiro and Trajadura for example being especially favoured in the central part of the DOC. The whites have a simple, bracing, lemony charm that can be appealing enough at the height of summer. Sensitive souls may gag on the reds, however, which are astringently dry as well as slightly fizzy, not a combination familiar from any other European wine (which is why they hardly ever leave the region). BEST WINES: Quinta da Tamariz, Terras de Corga, Gazela, Quinta de Aveleda Grinalda.

DOURO

Named after the river Douro, which has its origin in Spain (where they call it the Duero), the Douro valley's most celebrated product is port (see below), but the DOC for the region also encompasses some rapidly improving table wines. Growers here are not exactly short of choice when it comes to finding the right grape to grow on each particular patch - they have nearly 100 at their disposal, including all of the varieties used in port. A number of the port shippers have now diversified into the production of red and white unfortified wines.

Just as Spain has its premium red wine in Vega Sicilia, Portugal has one too, in Barca Velha, launched in the 1950s by the port house of Ferreira. It is a complex, subtly spicy wine made only in the best vintages and given long cask-ageing – a profound and inspired creation. Ferreira now belongs to the large wine combine Sogrape, which has itself pioneered many of the better Douro wines, and has achieved notable successes with international varieties such as Cabernet Sauvignon. The non-traditional grapes are not allowed DOC status, the wines taking the regional designation Terras Durienses. Quinta do Cotto is one of Sogrape's best labels for good, meaty reds, while its white Douro Reserva made from Portuguese grapes is an aromatic triumph. Raposeira is another company achieving results.

DAO

Dão, a large mountainous DOC just north of the centre of Portugal, makes one of the country's higher-profile red wines, as well as a small quantity of fairly undistinguished white. During the 1950s and '60s, it came to be dominated by co-operatives, whose regressive winemaking techniques were responsible for a corresponding drop in the quality of what had been a highly regarded wine. Extended ageing in casks of often dubious cleanliness robs a lot of the reds of their fruit, and they are often disappointingly dried-out before they even get to the bottle, let alone the market. When good, though, they can possess that spicy, liquoricey appeal that characterises the finest Portuguese reds. The whites were traditionally also over-aged and reached the consumer in an oxidised state, tasting flat and dull.

More conscientious small growers are slowly but surely elbowing the co-operatives and their outdated methods aside, and some fresher, more modern wines are emerging. Sogrape has a finger in the Dão pie as well, and makes good wines in both colours, its Grão Vasco white a real trail-blazer. Caves Aliança and the Terras Altas label of another large concern, José Maria da Fonseca, are also noteworthy.

The port house of Ferreira has gained a reputation for a fine red wine, from grapes grown on the steep hillsides (above) of the Douro valley.

DOURO

GRAPES: *Red - Touriga Nacional, Tinta Roriz, Tinta Cão; White - Gouveio, Malvasia, Viosinho*

DAO

GRAPES: *Red - Touriga Nacional, Bastardo, Tinta Pinheira, Tinta Roriz, Alfrocheiro Preto, etc; White - Encruzado, Bical*

A timeless scene outside the 19th-century bodega (above) at Bairrada's most innovative producer, Luis Pato.

BAIRRADA
GRAPES: *Red - Baga; White - Maria Gomes, Bical*
OESTE
GRAPES: *Red - Arruda*
RIBATEJO
GRAPES: *White - Fernão Pires, Arinto; Red - Periquita*

BAIRRADA

To the west of Dão, the Bairrada DOC shares some of the same problems as its neighbour in that its production is dominated by poorly equipped co-operatives using rather backward vinification methods. The picture will slowly brighten, however, as more of the small growers decide to cut out the co-ops and bottle their own wine. Three-quarters of Bairrada is red, and the major red-wine grape, Baga, is one of Portugal's more assertive red varieties. Sloppily vinified, it can be depressingly tannic and rough, but the smarter operators are managing to coax some ripe, plummy fruit out of it and show its potential. White Bairrada, given a gentle touch of oak by one or two producers, can be splendidly smoky and appley, but the majority is still fairly bland.

This is also the region in which Sogrape makes its famed Mateus Rosé. Sweetish pink fizz may not be the mood of the moment just now, and the wine has recently been relaunched in a drier version, its clean peachy fruit refreshing enough on a hot day.
PRODUCERS: Luis Pato (one of the region's great innovators), São João, Caves Aliança, Sogrape, Vilharino do Bairro.

OESTE

Quantitatively but not yet qualitatively important, Oeste is the collective name for a group of six IPR regions on the western coast of Portugal,

north of Lisbon. They are, from north to south, Encostas d'Aire, Alcobaca, Obidos, Alenquer, Torres Vedras and Arruda. European Union funds are showering on the region like winter rainfall, so things may improve, but so far, apart from the odd, rustically meaty Arruda red, not much of any note has braved the export markets. The presence of a little Chardonnay and Cabernet in the vineyards indicates one of the likely avenues of progress.

RIBATEJO

Inland from the Oeste, also north of Lisbon, Ribatejo is similar to Oeste in two respects. It is a huge volume producer, and it is subdivided into six IPR regions. Working downwards, these are Tomar, Santarém, Chamusca, Almeirim, Cartaxo and Coruche. The potential for better quality in the Ribatejo is quite distinct, however. Many of its wines have been sent to other regions to form the base for the long-aged reserve reds of Portugal known as *garrafeiras*. The main red grape, Periquita (locally called Castelão Frances) is a good one, giving deeply coloured, spicy wine, while the whites are based on Fernão Pires (the Maria Gomes of Bairrada). They can be enticingly fresh, and even lightly oaked from those with the resources.
PRODUCERS: Margaride, Bright Brothers (where the winemaker is Australian Peter Bright). The Almeirim co-op's Leziria label is pretty reliable too.

BUCELAS

A tiny DOC to the south of Oeste's Arruda, Bucelas came perilously close to extinction in the 1980s. Caves Velhas was its last producer in fact, although there are now one or two new estates determined to restore it to the lofty reputation it historically enjoyed. It is a white-wine region only, its light, crisply acidic wines based on Arinto, which crops up in white port, and Esgana, which - as Sercial - is one of the four noble grapes of Madeira.

COLARES

Another of the DOC minnows of Portugal, Colares perches high on the wind-battered clifftops above the Atlantic Ocean, northwest of the capital. Its claim to fame, the noble Ramisco grape, makes some fine, concentrated, age-worthy reds, both on the coast as well as further inland. Whites are less interesting. Overall production is sadly declining, largely because most of the vineyards are too inaccessible to maintain.

PALMELA

Palmela, in the northern part of the Setúbal peninsula, was made an IPR in 1990 and has gradually made a name for itself as one of the quality regions of Portugal. The fine red Periquita grape makes some intriguingly spicy and peppery wines with good plum and raisin fruit, as well as a small amount of fresh rosé. Some of the country's best large wine companies are based here - J. P. Vinhos (which makes a highly

acclaimed dry Muscat as well as some good savoury reds) and José Maria da Fonseca the two most notable. Sparkling wines are also becoming a speciality. This is a region to watch.

ARRABIDA

In the south of the Setúbal peninsula, the hilly Arrábida region is - like Palmela - producing some highly progressive wines from Portuguese grapes, as well as a handful of international varieties, which seem to have bedded in very well. The same big companies, Fonseca and J. P. Vinhos, are leading the way here too, and the region became an IPR at the same time as Palmela. Cova da Ursa, an intensely smoky barrel-aged Chardonnay from Peter Bright, is typical of the philosophy. Arrábida and Palmela form part of the Vinho Regional area known as Terras do Sado.

ALENTEJO

In the southeast of the country, not far from the Spanish border, the Alentejo region has become one of the hottest names on the Portuguese wine scene. Indeed, Alentejo was really where Portugal's latter-day wine revolution began. Much experimentation has taken place, and the evident quality of the predominantly red wines speaks for itself. The VR is divided into eight sub-regions, five of DOC status (Portalegre, Borba, Redondo, Reguengos and Vidigueira) and three IPR (Evora, Granja-Amereleja and Moura).

In addition to the co-ops, José Maria da Fonseca is once again playing a leading role, and the Esporão estate at Reguengos is also producing some impressively world-class wines. Tinto da Anfora, a Periquita-based red for the João Pires brand blended from various Alentejo sub-regions, took the British market by storm a few years ago. Cartuxa's wines, and those of João Portugal Ramos, are also top-drawer. Roupeiro is the favoured local white grape, showing particular promise in the scented dry whites of Esporão.

ALGARVE

The southern coastal strip of Portugal may be much-loved as a holiday destination, but it tends not to produce much in the way of quality wine. It consists of four DOCs - from west to east Lagos, Portimão, Lagoa and Tavira - mostly making burly reds of no particular charm. A long-forgotten pale, dry fortified wine is still made by the local co-operative.

BUCELAS
GRAPES: White - Arinto, Esgana Cão
COLARES
GRAPES: Red - Ramisco; White - Malvasia
PALMELA
GRAPES: Red - Periquita
ARRABIDA
GRAPES: Red - Periquita, Espadeiro, Cabernet Sauvignon, Merlot; White - Moscatel de Setúbal (Muscat of Alexandria), Arinto, Esgana Cão, Chardonnay
ALENTEJO
GRAPES: Red - Aragonez, Trincadeira, Moreto, Periquita; White - Roupeiro

Ripe bunches of Periquita grapes (left) destined for Tinto da Anfora, a blended red from the Alentejo region.

Taylor's Quinta da Vargellas,
source of one of the most
successful single-estate ports
(above).

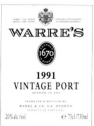

PORT, MADEIRA AND OTHER FORTIFIED WINES

The origins of port, as of all fortified wines, lie in the need to stabilise and protect light table wines from spoilage during long sea voyages. When the English merchants found themselves having to pay punitive tariffs to import French wines, as a result of the 17th-century wars with France, they turned to Portugal as their next best source. The thin white wines of northern Portugal (the modern Vinho Verde DOC) were not much to anyone's taste but, venturing into the Douro valley, the importers chanced upon the fiery red brews of what was to become port country.

Imported in barrel, the wines had inevitably spoiled by the time they reached England, and so the shippers learned to add a little brandy to them in order to preserve them. At this point, therefore, port would have been a potent but dry wine. It wasn't until some while later that the English systematically began adding the brandy *before* the red wine had finished fermenting. That stopped the yeasts dead in their tracks before all of the grape sugars had been consumed, and so port became naturally sweet as well as strong.

Today, the fortifying agent is a more neutral, colourless grape spirit rather than actual brandy, but the production process is otherwise not much changed since the 1600s. In the mid-18th century, in a drive to protect port from poor imitations from other regions, the Douro valley was demarcated as the only area that could produce genuine port. It was thus the first denominated appellation, predating the French system by about 180 years.

Of all the European fortified wines, port is the most confusing to the unsuspecting. The following is a summary of the range of port styles now made.

Ruby The most basic style of all, blended from the produce of several harvests and aged for no more than a couple of years. Many shippers produce a house brand that may or may not call itself Ruby - the term is somewhat debased now - but if it has no other description, that is what it will essentially be.

Vintage Character If ever a wine term were ripe for abolition, it is Vintage Character port. These are basic rubies, aged for longer (about five years on average), that theoretically have something of the depth of flavour of true vintage port. In practice, they simply never do, and if you are going to trade up from basic ruby, it is far more advisable to move on to the next category, Late Bottled Vintage.

Late Bottled Vintage (LBV) Unlike Vintage Character, these really are the produce of a single vintage which will be specified on the label. They are basically the years that are not quite deemed good enough to make true vintage port, but the quality is nonetheless generally good. They are aged for between four and six years, and the best ones will have been bottled without being filtered, so that the wine throws a sediment and requires decanting. Some companies filter their LBVs in order to avoid the need for that, largely because many consumers wrongly assume that decanting is more technical than it is (see the introduction for advice on the process). Buy an unfiltered LBV in preference to a filtered one; the flavours are far more resonant and complex.

Vintage port At the top of the pyramid, vintage port is the product of a single year, stated on the label as with ordinary table wine, that is bottled after two or three years' cask ageing. Each shipper must decide within two years of the harvest whether the wine of a particular year is going to be fine enough to be released,

unblended, as a vintage port. This is known as "declaring" the vintage. Good years such as 1985 may result in a universal declaration among the major shippers. Vintage port requires ageing in the bottle by the customer, and will always throw a sediment. Some, such as the relatively light 1980s, will only need a few years; other vintages, like the legendary 1977, may take a quarter of a century and more before they are ready for drinking (many were still nowhere near ready as the century turned).

Single Quinta Vintage wines made from the grapes of single estates or *quintas*. Since these grapes normally play a part in a shipper's best vintage port, the single-estate wines tend to be produced in the marginally less good years but quality is still good (and above LBV in most cases). Names to look for are Quinta do Bomfim from the house of Dow, Quinta da Vargellas from Taylor and Quinta da Cavadinha from Warre.

Crusted port So-called because it forms a crust of sediment in the bottle, crusted or crusting port is a kind of cross between vintage port and LBV. It is not the produce of a single year, but is treated like a vintage port and bottled unfiltered. The style is a creation of the British-owned port houses, and is intended as an economically kinder alternative to true vintage port.

Tawny port Traditionally a basic blended port that is aged for several years longer than ruby, so that its colour drops out and the flavour goes almost drily nutty with oxidation. Some tawny is now made by simply adding a little white port to a base of paler red wines to lighten the colour.

Aged Tawny These are invariably true tawny ports, aged for many years in cask. The difference from basic tawny is that the label will state the average age of the wines that have gone into the blend, calculated in multiples of ten. A ten-year-old tawny, such as the perennially superb example from Dow, may very well be the optimum age. Twenty-, 30- and 40-year-old wines will increase correspondingly in price, but may yield diminishing returns as to drinking pleasure.

Colheitas A *colheita* port is essentially a vintage tawny. The wines from a single year receive a minimum of seven years in cask, so that their colour fades. Many are only released at grand old ages, and the prices - compared to early-bottled vintage port - can look immensely attractive.

White port Among the cocktail of 80-plus grape varieties that are permitted in port are a handful of white ones. Some houses produce a port solely from white grapes (largely Arinto, Gouveio, Malvasia and Viosinho) that is fortified by the same method as the red. They may be dry or sweet and are not particularly great wines. The dry port has nothing like the pedigree of good fino sherry for instance, but can be refreshing served well-chilled in small quantities.

BEST NAMES IN PORT: Dow, Taylor, Graham, Cálem, Fonseca, Warre, Ferreira, Niepoort, Burmester. Quinta do Noval makes a famously brilliant vintage wine called Nacional from ancient vines, selling at a once-in-a-lifetime price. PORT VINTAGES: *2000* **** *1997* *** *'94* **** *'92* *** *'91* **** *'85* **** *'83* **** *'80* *** *'77* ***** *'75* **** *'70* **** *'66* **** *'63* *****

Back-breaking manual harvesting in the terraced vineyards of Quinta do Bomfim in the Douro (above).

A traditional barco rabelo *sails through Oporto (below), on the Portuguese coast. These boats were used to carry the pipes of port down the Douro to the port houses.*

MADEIRA

The history of madeira is perhaps the single most remarkable example of human dedication to the cause of fine wine. The island of Madeira is a volcanic tropical outcrop in the Atlantic Ocean, nearer to the coast of north Africa than to the Portugal of which it forms an autonomously governed province. Its soil contains a great quantity of ash from a conflagration that raged across the island many centuries ago, and its mountainous terrain means that its vineyards are among the most inaccessible in the world.

Like port, Madeira's wines were once light table wines that came to be fortified so that they might better survive long sea transportation. In the case of madeira, though, the shippers stumbled on an extraordinary discovery. Carried aboard the great trading vessels of the Dutch East India Company, the wine's voyage east was a more arduous matter than simply ferrying port from northern Portugal to the south of England. It was noticed that, when the wine arrived in India, it was unspoiled; in fact it was positively improved. So, just for good measure, the shippers left some to complete a round trip back to Europe, and that turned out even better.

No other wine has ever, before or since, proved so improbably masochistic. It sailed the heaving oceans in raging heat for weeks at a time, the barrels clattering around in the hold, and nothing could destroy it. For many decades, every bottle of madeira sold had been on this round-the-world cruise, until a way was found to simulate those conditions in its place of origin.

In the 19th century, a maturation system known as the *estufa*, or stove, was introduced. The *lagares* - the storage houses in which the wine is aged - were equipped with central-heating systems, hot-water pipes that ran around the walls (or occasionally through the vats of wine themselves) in order to cook it as it had been in its maritime days. Some wines, reputedly the best, were cooked by simple exposure to the tropical summer sun.

Simple blended madeira is often based on a grape variety called Tinta Negra Mole that used to find its way into any of the four varietal styles of madeira. Those must now, as a result of intervention by the European Union, be made up of no less than 85 per cent of the named varietal, and so Tinta Negra Mole is, at least in theory, in decline.

All of Madeira's agriculture, including its vineyards, is planted in terraces on sheer hillside land such as this (right). The fearsome gradients mean that any form of mechanised harvesting is out of the question.

The varietal wines are, from lightest and driest to richest and sweetest, Sercial, Verdelho, Bual and Malmsey, the last name being an Anglicised corruption of Malvasia. Even at its very sweetest, madeira always has a streak of balancing acid running through it to complement the amazing flavours of treacle toffee, Christmas cake, dates and walnuts. There is also often a telltale whiff of mature cheese about it, rather like old dry Cheshire, and just to complete its range of peculiar attributes, it generally has a distinct green hue at the rim.

Labels may state the age of the blend (ten-year-old is significantly more rewarding than five), or may use such vague-sounding but in practice fairly precise terminologies as Finest (about three years old), Reserve (five), Special Reserve (ten) or Extra Reserve (15).

A small quantity of vintage-dated madeira is made, which sells for a fraction of the price of vintage port. As the history of this fabulously unique wine suggests, it is virtually indestructible.

BEST NAMES IN MADEIRA: Blandy's, Henriques & Henriques, Cossart Gordon, Rutherford & Miles, Leacock.

SETUBAL

Three variants of the Muscat grape, the main one being Muscat of Alexandria, make a port-method sweet fortified wine on the Setúbal Peninsula. After the fortification, the skins of the grapes are left to infuse in the new wine for several months so that a particularly pronounced aroma and flavour of fresh Moscatel grapes is imparted to it. It is usually aged in cask for five years or so before bottling, though some premium wines are given up to 25 years' maturation, resulting in a nuttily oxidised, deep brown wine. Most examples taste fairly heavy on the palate, and don't quite attain the graceful balance of the best southern French fortified Muscats. José Maria da Fonseca is the main producer of note.

CARCAVELOS

Decreasingly important coastal DOC just west of Lisbon that once tried to rival port as a producer of quality fortified wine. The wines are made in much the same way, from both red and white grapes, and generally resemble basic tawny. Quinta dos Pesos is a recently established estate determined to keep the flame alive.

Traditional thatched A-frame houses, like this one at Palheiros (below), are a characteristic feature of Madeira's vineyards.

GERMANY

Germany's wines have struggled to earn respect abroad, yet the country's ultra-efficient producers can offer the very best of fine, light wines in a whole range of styles.

Germany's famous wine regions hug the river Rhine and its tributaries, along the southwestern borders (below). Saale/Unstrut and Sachsen are two additions since the fall of the Berlin wall.

IT MAY SEEM SOMETHING of an anomaly to today's wine-drinkers to reflect that Gemany once occupied a place in the connoisseur's hall of fame scarcely lower than that of France. In the Middle Ages, Rhenish - named after the river Rhine - was highly prized in the countries of northern Europe. Nor was it necessarily a white wine. Shakespearean references to it make it quite clear the wine was principally thought of as red; much of it would have been made from Pinot Noir. At this time, of course, Germany included all of the Alsace region, and many merchants held that the wines from that side of the Rhine were the finest of all.

A combination of factors, not least the ravages of the Thirty Years War in the early part of the 17th century, caused a general decline in German viticulture. That was thrown somewhat into reverse in the 1700s, but by the turn of the last century the country's vineyards were in wholesale retreat. Other forms of agriculture were more profitable, and the brewing industry generated considerably greater income than winemaking. The reparations demanded from Germany after the Great War in the Treaty of Versailles played their devastating part in the wine industry as much as any other sector. It was only by selling cheap blended wines, sourced from many regions and sweetened up to appeal to the broadest possible customer base (Liebfraumilch being the most famous, or perhaps notorious, example), that German wine survived at all as an export proposition.

Its principal problem ever since has been how to shake off the Liebfraumilch legacy. Seasoned wine-lovers may sniff at the very name, but the obstinate fact remains that sweetened German wine is still by far the largest sector of the British wine market. If consumers who develop a taste for those wines would just look towards Germany's premier varietal wines - best exemplified by Riesling - they would discover an unsuspected world of much subtler, and ultimately more rewarding, sweet wines.

Similarly, if those who have left German wines behind altogether because of the Liebfraumilch association, but who have learned to admire the Rieslings of Alsace or Australia, would give Germany another chance, they would find some of the most uncommonly beautiful, and stylistically unequalled, light white wines in the world in the best Riesling vintages of the Mosel or the Pfalz.

The German wine classification system has gone through a number of mutations this century, the most recent set of amendments being introduced in 1993. It was in 1971, however, that the foundations for a system comparable to that now used throughout the European Union were laid.

At the lowest level are the basic table wines, labelled *Deutscher Tafelwein*. This is only applied to a tiny fraction of Germany's annual production and may be blended from anywhere in the country. A step up is the *vin de pays*

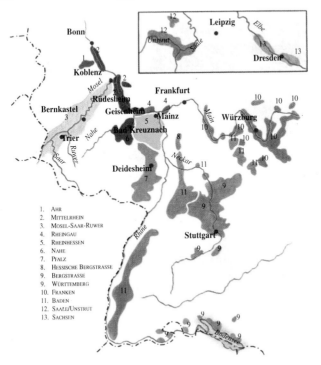

1. AHR
2. MITTELRHEIN
3. MOSEL-SAAR-RUWER
4. RHEINGAU
5. RHEINHESSEN
6. NAHE
7. PFALZ
8. HESSISCHE BERGSTRASSE
9. BERGSTRASSE
9. WÜRTTEMBERG
10. FRANKEN
11. BADEN
12. SAALE/UNSTRUT
13. SACHSEN

category, *Landwein*. This may come from any one of 20 large demarcated regions, and is used with greater frequency these days. Above that is QbA (*Qualitätswein bestimmter Anbaugebiete* or "quality wine from a specified region"). This is the volume category, in which the juice of underripe grapes may be sweetened to increase the final alcohol level, and the wine itself may be sweetened with unfermented grape juice before bottling to produce an easy-going commercial style.

At the top is QmP (*Qualitätswein mit Prädikat* or "quality wine with pedigree"). These wines are subdivided according to how much natural sugar the harvested grapes possess. In order of ascending sweetness, they are: Kabinett, Spätlese, Auslese, Beerenauslese and Trockenbeerenauslese. The separate category Eiswein ("ice wine" made from frozen ultra-ripe berries picked in the dead of winter) also counts as a *Prädikat* wine; it usually falls somewhere between the last two categories in terms of sweetness.

As important as the village it comes from, and the name of the grower, is the grape variety or varieties a German wine is made from. The varietal wines will always state the name of their grape on the label. It remains true that its Rieslings are still Germany's best shot, but there are other varieties to contend with, many of them grown in several different regions.

In an effort to find grapes that will ripen more dependably than Riesling in the cold, northern climate of Germany, viticultural researchers have worked at crossing varieties - and even crossing the crosses. The results have been decidedly mixed, and many of these new creations remain unheard of outside the country. We shall look first at these other grapes, and then at the wine regions.

Silvaner Particularly valued in the Franken region around Würzburg, Silvaner is one of the best of the uncrossed grapes after Riesling. Ripening much earlier than Riesling, it gives wines with a whiff of cabbage leaves when young, but that can age to a silky, honey-laden maturity.

Müller-Thurgau A Riesling-Silvaner mix, this was the first of the crossings, developed in the 1880s by a Swiss scientist working in Germany. So grateful were the growers for its early-ripening properties that they fell upon it with unconfined zeal - so much so that it became the most widely planted grape in Germany, a

position it still occupies. Indeed it could have been the Holy Grail were it not for the fact that the wines it produces almost invariably taste watery and flat.

Kerner One of the more successful new varieties, Kerner is a crossing of Riesling with a red grape called Trollinger. Although it was only conceived in the late 1960s, it is now planted on more German vineyard land than Riesling itself. One of the higher-quality crosses, it makes a crisply lime-zesty wine, without quite having the elegance of properly ripened Riesling.

Scheurebe Here is another Riesling-Silvaner cross, but a much more refined one than Müller-Thurgau. When properly ripe, Scheurebe has a distinct flavour of grapefruit, with the corollary that, if the summer hasn't been kind, Scheurebe wines are agonisingly tart. In the right conditions, it gives excellent noble-rotted dessert wines.

Rieslaner Probably the best Riesling-Silvaner crossing of them all, the clumsily named Rieslaner can be stunning, full of almost tropical fruit from the best growers. Rieslaner occupies only a tiny percentage of vineyard; it is a shame there isn't more planted.

Among more internationally known white varieties, Germany also grows Weissburgunder (aka Pinot Blanc), Grauburgunder or Ruländer (Pinot Gris), Gewürztraminer and even a little Chardonnay (see grape variety section).

The sundial (above) that gives the terraced Wehlener Sonnenuhr vineyard, one of the Mosel's premier sites, its name.

A misty winter morning dawns over the vineyard of Schwarzerde, near Kirchheim, Pfalz (above). German wines have to survive some of the severest cold-weather conditions anywhere in the world.

The village of Zeltingen (above), caught between the Mosel river and the steeply rising vineyards.

Dornfelder A fine red variety produced from two other crossed red grapes, Dornfelder is making inroads into various German regions, particularly along the Rhine. Its wines can be light and cherryish, a little like young Beaujolais occasionally but without the high alcohol. Some producers are attempting to coax a fuller, richer style from it suitable for oak-ageing.

Portugieser Not a Portuguese grape despite the name, it gives rather coarse reds with high acidity and is generally in decline.

Limberger Known as Blaufränkisch in neighbouring Austria, this is a good, characterful red grape that produces light, but appetisingly spicy, even violetty wines, with plenty of fresh acidity.

There are also significant quantities of Pinot Noir planted in Germany, where they call it Spätburgunder or Blauburgunder. A bit thin in the northerly Ahr region, it is beginning to produce impressively fuller-bodied wines along the Rhine and in the southerly Baden region.

THE REGIONS

Ahr This small northerly wine region, lying just south of the city of Bonn, specialises in red wines, mostly from Spätburgunder (Pinot Noir). They are inevitably light, in both texture and colour, as a result of being asked to ripen in such a marginal climate, but there are a few good examples - notably from late-picked grapes that retain a gentle natural sweetness. The region's production is overwhelmingly dominated by co-operatives. There are also some good Ahr Rieslings, but the grape is losing ground as a percentage of total plantings.

Mittelrhein A small production area that extends from Bonn to south of Koblenz, the Mittelrhein is three-quarters Riesling - a high proportion for any German region. Vineyards are planted on both banks of the Rhine, often on steep hillsides. Müller-Thurgau makes up most of the non-Riesling wine. Quality is good, but most of the wine is drunk in situ by the locals, or by tourists, as this is one of the most unspoiled parts of Germany. Toni Jost is a fine Mittelrhein winemaker, who is exporting some of his sharply defined, exciting Rieslings.

Mosel-Saar-Ruwer The Mosel valley runs southwest of Koblenz, down past the city of Trier, and stops short at the intersection where Germany borders Luxembourg and France. The region's full name includes two small tributaries of the river Mosel, the Saar and the Ruwer. It includes some of the most historically celebrated vineyards in German wine history, many of them located in the Bernkastel district in the centre of the valley. These are some of the world's more dramatically sited vineyards, clinging vertiginously to sheer hillsides on either bank of the river, completely inaccessible to any form of

machine-harvesting. Here the Riesling achieves some of its great glories, wines that are almost miraculously subtle expressions of the variety, extremely low in alcohol and yet possessed of a fragile purity all their own.

The best vineyard sites (preceded by their village names) have been Erdener Treppchen, Wehlener Sonnenuhr, Graacher Himmelreich, Bernkasteler Doktor, Brauneberger Juffer and Piesporter Goldtröpfchen. Some of these, notably Piesport, have suffered by association with bland, mass-market products that are blended from the general district (or *Bereich* in German). Always choose a single-estate wine in preference to anything else.

Around the Saar, Wiltinger Scharzhofberg, Ockfener Bockstein and Ayler Kupp are the leading vineyards, while Maximin Grünhaus and Eitelsbacher Karthäuserhofberg are the jewels in Ruwer's crown.
PRODUCERS: Haag, Dr Loosen, von Schubert, J J Prüm, Dr Thanisch, Schloss Saarstein.
Rheingau The Rheingau mostly occupies the right bank of the Rhine to the east of the Mittelrhein region. In some ways, it represents the nerve-centre of German winemaking. Rheingau boasts some of the most highly regarded wine estates in the country, growing a great preponderance of Riesling. At Geisenheim, the viticultural research institute has been responsible for so much of the work in creating new vine varieties.

A range of disparate vineyard conditions makes up the Rheingau. Around Rüdesheim, steeply-shelving slaty soils produce some ethereally light Rieslings, while more robust wines, known and much favoured in history as "hock", come from the more gently contoured land around Hochheim.

At the heart of Rheingau production is a group of about four dozen winemakers, calling itself the Charta Association. To qualify for the Charta seal of approval, wines must pass a rigorous tasting examination; only Rieslings are allowed to enter. It is a quality initiative that other German regions would do well to imitate.

The two most famous wine properties are the ancient castles of Schloss Vollrads and Schloss Johannisberg. In a region dominated by small producers rather than co-operatives, the names of outstanding individual growers are a better guide to quality than the vineyard sites themselves. They include Weil, Ress, Breuer and Künstler.

Rheinhessen South of the Rheingau, the Rheinhessen is where a lot of the mass-market wines of Germany originate. Half of all Liebfraumilch is made here, and there are other regional names that will be familiar to British and American consumers, such as Niersteiner Gutes Domtal. Much of Germany's acreage of crossed grape varieties is planted in the Rheinhessen too, with Müller-Thurgau leading the way. Production is much larger than the neighbouring Rheingau, and this is not by and large a quality region. There are, however, some exceptions, increasingly in the production of surprisingly sturdy reds from Spätburgunder (Pinot Noir) and Dornfelder. Silvaner also makes good wine, although somewhat less of it than hitherto.
PRODUCERS: Villa Sachsen, Guntrum, Heyl zu Herrnsheim.
Nahe The Nahe region, named after its river, lies to the west of the Rheinhessen. It is a fine, and considerably under-recognised, player on the German wine scene, its best estates as good as those in the Rheingau or Mosel. Some astonishingly concentrated Rieslings are made within the vicinity of the town of Bad Kreuznach, with Silvaner and Müller-Thurgau making up most of the rest of the plantings. A concerted campaign to raise the profiles of the best growers is under way, which will inevitably lead to a rise in prices, but for the time being, the Nahe represents one of the best-value regions in Germany.
PRODUCERS: Dönnhoff, Diel, Crusius, Plettenberg.

A tiny patch of red earth at the foot of the towering Rotenfels cliff (above) at Bad Münster, in the Nahe, yields intensely flavoured wines.

Assmannshausen, at the western end of the Rheingau (below). This wine region, like Burgundy, can trace an unbroken history back to the early days of the Benedictine and Cistercian monks.

Decorative architecture typical of Germany's wine villages (above).

Looking down over the town of Würzburg on the river Main in Franken (right), from the Marienberg vineyard.

Pfalz Formerly known as the Rheinpfalz, and before that the Palatinate, the Pfalz is a fast-improving and dynamic region to the south of Rheinhessen. The range of grapes grown is very broad. Not only Riesling, but Grauburgunder, Gewürztraminer, Scheurebe, Spätburgunder and Dornfelder are all producing good things. Among the more famous wine villages are Deidesheim, Ruppertsberg and Wachenheim, but good wine is proliferating all over the Pfalz now. Some of the new-style Pinot Noir reds could give some négociant burgundy a run for its money these days; not only do they have richness and body, but they can often match Burgundian Pinot for alcohol too. Decent sparkling wine, known in Germany as Sekt, is also becoming something of a speciality.

The very best Pfalz estate is Müller-Catoir, whose range of varietals is frankly world-class. Not only does it make breathtaking Rieslings and Rieslaners, as well as some convincingly spicy Gewürz, but the estate has even been known to cajole some display of personality from that old dullard Müller-Thurgau.
OTHER PRODUCERS: Bürklin-Wolf, Bassermann-Jordan, Lingenfelder, von Buhl, Köhler-Ruprecht.

Hessische Bergstrasse This small region, to the east of Rheinhessen, does not export much of its wine, but quality is impressively high. About half the vineyard is Riesling, and the better growers manage to achieve levels of concentration similar to those around Hochheim. This has been one of the sectors of Germany that has most wholeheartedly embraced the latter-day trend for fermenting wines of QmP standard to a dry (Trocken) or semi-dry (Halbtrocken) final style. The vineyards owned by the state of Hesse are producing some of the best wine.

Württemberg A large region centred on Stuttgart, Württemberg is not greatly renowned beyond its own boundaries. Riesling, Kerner and Müller-Thurgau are the principal white varieties, Trollinger the main red. The region specialises in red wines (some made from Pinot Noir) that are so light in both colour and body that they don't seem appreciably far from the style of other producers' rosés.

Franken Otherwise known as Franconia, the region through which the river Main runs was traditionally famous as the mainstay of the Silvaner grape, although this grape now accounts for only about a fifth of the area under vine. The local taste is for austerely dry wines, the best of which come in a flat, round bottle called a *Bocksbeutel.* Nowadays, Müller-Thurgau has made inroads into the vineyards, but there are some delicately floral wines from a crossing called Bacchus. The wines are exported to some degree, but the prices tend to be off-putting.
PRODUCERS: Wirsching, Ruck, the church-owned Juliusspital.

Baden The principal region of southwest Germany, just over the border from Alsace, Baden

has been on most people's lists as one of the more exciting European wine areas of recent years. It encompasses a long stretch between Franken and the border with Switzerland, with some vineyards situated in the vicinity of Lake Constance (or the Bodensee in German). Although there is a fairly high percentage of Müller-Thurgau in the vineyards, there is also some fine, boldly delineated Riesling, musky dry Weissburgunder, spicy Gewürztraminer and - perhaps most promising of all in these warmer southern climes - some intensely ripe, deep-flavoured Spätburgunder.

PRODUCERS: Johner, Huber, the Königschaff-hausen co-operative.

Saale-Unstrut One of two small wine regions that fell within the boundaries of the old GDR, or East Germany, Saale-Unstrut is named after two rivers at whose confluence it lies. Müller-Thurgau, Weissburgunder, Silvaner and others are used to make dry, relatively full-bodied wines, but the region wasn't much blessed with investment by the old state authority and it can still only be considered emergent as yet.

Sachsen The most northerly, the most easterly, and also the smallest wine region in Germany, Sachsen (known in English as Saxony) is cen-tred on the old city of Dresden, its vineyards planted along the banks of the river Elbe. Like Saale-Unstrut, it makes dry white wines from good varieties, but the prospects for quality wine are noticeably higher. Müller-Thurgau

rules the roost, but Riesling, Weissburgunder, Gewürztraminer and Ruländer all play their parts. The wine is mostly made by a single large co-operative of numerous small growers.

SPARKLING WINES

German sparkling wine covers a multitude of sins. It comes in four basic categories, the best of which is *Sekt bestimmter Anbaugebiete* or Sekt bA. The grapes are sourced from one par-ticular district, indicated on the label (eg. Pfalz Sekt); some of the wine is even made by the champagne method. The sparkling Rieslings from producers like Dr Richter are wonderfully fresh, like sparkling alcoholic limeade.

Deutscher Sekt is a step down, and may be blended from anywhere in the country. Lila, from the large wine company Deinhard, is a good, tasty Riesling. Basic *Sekt*, the great majority of German fizz, does not have the adjective "Deutscher" for the simple reason that it will contain wines shipped in from other countries, mainly Italy and France's unwanted slosh. Lowest of the low is the unbelievably atrocious *Schaumwein,* a term that covers virtually anything else that fizzes.

RECENT GERMAN VINTAGES: *2001 **** 2000 ** 1999 *** '98 *** '97 *** '96 **** '95 *** '94 *** '93 **** '92 *** '91 ***

Netting keeps birds off the sweet shrivelled Riesling grapes left on the vine after harvest to botrytise (above), in the Ungeheuer vineyard at Forst, in the Pfalz.

UNITED KINGDOM

In the relatively short period of the last 30 years, the UK's wine industry has developed dramatically. It may not ever become prolific but when the weather is kind, the quality is there.

A mechanical harvester at work at Denbies, in Surrey (above), the UK's largest producer at 250ha.

Most of the UK's vineyards (below) are clustered in the southeast, and are tiny, averaging less than one hectare.

IT WOULD BE EASY TO believe that wine-making in the British Isles is an innovation of the 20th century, a belated attempt to get in on the act in the face of stiff climatic odds. In fact, England once boasted a small but thriving viticultural sector, thanks - almost certainly - to the Roman invasion in the 1st century AD. Some have suggested that winemaking may even have predated the Romans, but as yet there is no firm evidence to support the contention.

What is certain is that, by the time the Venerable Bede came to write his *Ecclesiastical History* in the 8th century, he was able to note that there were vineyards in various parts of England. The advent of Christianity provided an impetus for the production of wine for use in church ceremony, and many of the monasteries established their own vineyards. Not all of the wine was for religious use, though. Much was drunk, and warmly praised, in secular life.

A number of factors contributed to the wholesale decline of English viticulture. The first was the marriage of Henry II to Eleanor of Aquitaine, which brought tracts of southwest France under English jurisdiction, thus providing a ready pipeline of reliable and cheap bulk wine. That was followed, in the 14th century, by a dramatic cooling in the British climate. Until this time, the average summer temperatures had been conducive to vine cultivation, but the cooler, damper weather that was to stay at least until the era of global warming made ripening grapes a much trickier proposition. The final nail in the coffin was the dissolution of the monasteries under Henry VIII, and the consequent abandonment of the vineyards.

Nothing much then happened between the 16th and 20th centuries, except that the United Kingdom, as it came to be, became the epicentre of the international wine trade. A culture of connoisseurship developed that could afford to be expansively broad-minded precisely because all the wine being drunk was imported. It is only in the years since the Second World War that English viticulture has been speculatively revived.

Volumes produced are still microscopic compared to the European countries we have so far looked at, although some sort of milestone was reached in 1992 when that year's output exceeded 25,000 hectolitres. That is the magic figure above which the European Union rules state that an appellation system has to be brought into being. So far the only two designations have been England and Wales, which are used for the Quality Wine category. Anything else is UK Table Wine, or if it contains any non-*vinifera* grapes, Regional Counties wine.

Britain's cool northerly climate is such that the range of grape varieties that can be successfully grown, in even relatively hot summers, is pretty narrow. Conditions being roughly comparable to those of Germany, England and Wales have, not surprisingly, had to rely on Germanic grapes, including some of the crossed varieties

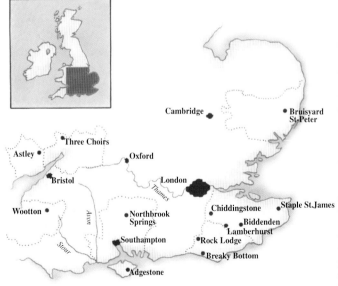

Cambridge

Bruisyard St-Peter

Three Choirs

Astley

Oxford

Bristol

London

Thames

Wootton

Northbrook Springs

Chiddingstone

Staple St.James

Biddenden

Lamberhurst

Southampton

Rock Lodge

Avon

Stour

Breaky Bottom

Adgestone

of rather dubious repute. The great tragedy, in a sense, of UK winemaking is that Riesling - hero of the German vineyards - just won't ripen.

Notwithstanding that, some pretty torrid summers in the middle 1990s gave a tantalising glimpse of what English winemakers could achieve given half a chance. In years such as this, the autumnal weather has provided the right circumstances for the development of botrytis, and some outstanding dessert wines have been made.

Best prospects of all, however, lie in traditional-method sparkling wine, which has not so far received nearly enough attention. The soils in swathes of southern England are part of the same geological chalk deposits as are found in Champagne. A cool climate is auspicious for yielding just the kind of low-alcohol, high-acid base wine that good fizzes need. The omens could scarcely be better.

The single most important determining factor in the style of an English or Welsh wine is the grape or grapes that go into it. Regional characteristics are not sufficiently sharply delineated as yet, but the varieties do play an important part. Some of the most commonly planted are listed below.

Müller-Thurgau The most widely planted grape in Germany turns out also to rule the roost in England. Not unexpectedly, its wines are no more thrilling than they are in the Rheinhessen. Some producers add a little sweetening to it before bottling to create a more commercially appealing style. Those wines can be palatable enough.

PRODUCERS: Breaky Bottom, Staple St James, Wootton, Bruisyard St Peter.

Seyval Blanc Seyval is something of an albatross to the English wine industry in the sense that it is a hybrid variety. This means that it has some non-*Vitis vinifera* parentage, thus outlawing it within EU rules from any wine classified under the approved appellation system. As a varietal, it gives generally dull, thin, neutral-tasting wine, and is best blended with grapes that have a little more to say for themselves. Breaky Bottom in East Sussex makes about the best unblended Seyval.

Reichensteiner A three-way cross, Reichensteiner very often turns out rather lifeless wine, but can occasionally make a more scented (and often slightly sweetened) varietal. Some wineries, such as Northbrook Springs, have achieved partial success with it by giving it a period in oak.

Other better-quality, but not widely planted white grapes include Ortega, Schönburger, Bacchus (all three of which can provide attractively perfumed wines), grapefruity Scheurebe, a little Gewürztraminer, and increasing quantities of good old Chardonnay. Reds include the Pinot-like Triomphe d'Alsace, as well as increasing plantings of Pinot Noir itself, so far better at rosé and sparkling wines than reds.

Among England's better wineries are: Lamberhurst, Breaky Bottom, Chiddingstone, Wootton, Three Choirs, Biddenden and Adgestone. Nyetimber and Ridgeview make some of the more conspicuously successful sparklers to date.

Only a tiny amount of wine is made in the south of Wales, and most is consumed locally, but Monnow Valley has made some good, crisply refreshing whites.

Breaky Bottom, in Sussex (above). Frost and birds are two menaces facing growers.

CENTRAL EUROPE

Led by Austria, the wine regions of Central Europe - stretching from Switzerland to Slovakia - are becoming increasingly important in the international arena. Internationally familiar grape varieties will help them to compete.

This highly ornamental gateway (above) leads to the wine cellars of Gustav Feiler at Rust, in the Burgenland region of eastern Austria.

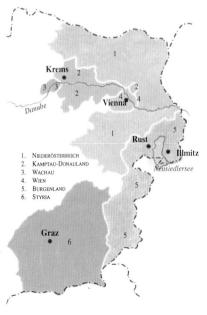

Krems

Danube

Vienna

Rust

Illmitz

Neusiedlersee

Graz

1. NIEDERÖSTERREICH
2. KAMPTAU-DONAULAND
3. WACHAU
4. WIEN
5. BURGENLAND
6. STYRIA

Austria's vineyards lie in the eastern half of the country (right), producing mainly full-bodied dry white wines, now being joined by some rapidly improving reds. Around the Neusiedlersee lake in Burgenland, the regular occurrence of noble rot provides some of Europe's best-value dessert wines.

THE CENTRAL EUROPEAN countries, some of them former constituents of the old Soviet bloc, were of only marginal importance to the international wine scene at one time, but with new trade agreements in the air and an influx of expertise in the shape of the so-called flying winemakers, things are changing fast. As elsewhere, the lesson has been absorbed that only the relentless quest for quality can equip unfamiliar wines with a fighting chance of survival in the jungle of today's market.

AUSTRIA

Undoubtedly the most exciting developments in central European wine are taking place in Austria. Its recent wine history is a tale of remarkable resurgence after an adulteration scandal in the mid-1980s that made its wines commercial poison for a decade. It takes time to recover from that sort of setback, but the country's many conscientious wine-growers are now being rewarded for their efforts as Austrian wine keeps winning international awards.

The vineyard regions are all concentrated in the eastern half of the country, along its borders with the Czech Republic, Slovakia, Hungary and Slovenia. Germanic as well as French grape varieties are grown, but being that much more southerly than most of Germany's wine regions, Austria's climate allows for a wider spectrum of wine styles than is the case in Germany.

The local grape made good in Austria is a white variety called Grüner Veltliner; it occupies more vineyard land than any other. The wine it yields is quite unique, mediumweight on the palate, but with an extraordinary dry spice like white peppercorns that may almost remind you of an Alsace wine.

Otherwise among whites, there's Müller-Thurgau (slowly being abandoned), Riesling, Gewürztraminer, Pinot Gris and a sprinkling of Chardonnay and Sauvignon Blanc. Welschriesling, which is nothing to do with the real Riesling, has achieved some improbably tasty results in parts of Austria. It crops up in Italy and Hungary too where its wines are mostly deadly dull. Then there are Rotgipfler and Zierfandler, the Rosencrantz and Guildenstern of the grape world: together, they go into a peculiarly heavy wine called Gumpoldskirchner, made just south of Vienna.

Red varieties are led by the indigenous Zweigelt, which gives an often purple-hued wine with a Dolcetto-like taste of blueberries. The German varieties Portugieser and Blaufränkisch also appear, as well as some impressive Cabernet Sauvignon and Pinot Noir, the latter known as Blauer Burgunder. St Laurent is a central European grape gaining a reputation for itself. Once used to produce lightweight quaffing material, it is now making some slightly spicy, raspberryish wine not a million miles from the style of classic meaty burgundy.

The crown jewels of Austrian wine, though, are its botrytised dessert wines. These are mostly produced around the Neusiedlersee, a large, shallow lake on the border with Hungary. Conditions for the development of noble rot are so obliging most years that they enable Austria to sell its sweet wines for much less than the top German examples. The categories for dessert wines are essentially the same as Germany's, including Eiswein, though with one extra classification - Ausbruch - inserted between Beerenauslese and Trockenbeerenauslese. A speciality is *Strohwein* (meaning "straw wine") made from naturally overripe grapes that are dried on straw mats, as in the production of Spanish *mistela* or the French *vin de paille*.

Prädikatswein is the designation for the top-quality wines, although - unlike Germany - it excludes wines classified as Kabinett, the sweetness category below Spätlese. A small amount of regional wine, made from specified grape varieties, is labelled as *Landwein*, and the basic stuff is *Tafelwein*, which means in practice the majority produced in any given year.

The northernmost wine zone is Niederösterreich or Lower Austria, north of the Danube. Its wines are predominantly dry or medium-dry whites from Grüner Veltliner, Riesling and Welschriesling. Kamptau-Donauland on the western fringe, north of Krems, makes some of the most richly intense Grüners of any Austrian region. Just to the south, in Wachau, some fine, sharply defined Rieslings (some botrytised) are rivalling those of the Rhine valley.

The capital city, Vienna (Wien to the Austrians), is a little wine region in itself, not a claim that any other European capital can make. Grüner, Riesling and Pinot Blanc are the best wines, and are almost exclusively snapped up by the Wieners, not surprisingly. Traditional taverns, known as *Heurigen*, in which much of wine is drunk are cheery hostelries in the city's outskirts where growers' families sell the wines of the new vintage, many of them unclarified and still cloudy from the tank.

Burgenland, on the Hungarian border, is the region that includes the Neusiedlersee. A versatile range of dry table wines is made here as well as fabulously opulent dessert wines from grapes such as Welschriesling, Gewürztraminer, the local Bouvier and so on. Whites take in some firmly textured Pinot Blanc and Welschriesling, as well as creamy oaked Chardonnay and gooseberryish Sauvignon, while Zweigelt and

Blaufränkisch reds are often packed with savoury spice and are increasingly being barrel-matured. One or two growers have attained astonishing levels of concentration in Cabernet Sauvignon wines.

The southernmost viticultural sector is Steiermark or Styria. It is predominantly white-wine country and, while geographically extensive, only accounts for a modest fraction of Austria's total output. The style, whether for Sauvignon, Chardonnay (often known by one of its rarer pseudonyms, Morillon), Gewürztraminer or dry Muscat from Gelber Muskateller (Muscat Blanc à Petits Grains), is extremely dry, often tart, with sharply emphasised acidity. In the west, around Graz, a red grape called Blauer Wildbacher makes Schilcher - a highly regarded rosé.
NOTABLE PRODUCERS: Opitz, Kracher, Moser, Stiegelmar, the Winzerhaus range from co-operatives in Lower Austria.

The imposing white church gives its name to the village of Weissenkirchen (above) in the Wachau region of Austria, source of some of the country's finest Riesling wines.

Trimly tended vineyards
cluster around the village
church at Conthey (above),
in the Valais, western
Switzerland.

Through the heart of Europe
stretches a band of cool
vineyards (right). Once
under the rule of empires
and some now emerging
from Communist control,
they produce mainly white
wines.

SWITZERLAND

The wine-growing areas of Switzerland are concentrated near the country's borders - with
France in the west, Germany in the north and
Italy in the south. Its wines are not exported in
any great quantity, and tend to be horrifyingly
expensive even in situ. Unless a path to better
value can be found, they are only ever likely to
have curiosity status in external markets.

Around the continuation of the river Rhône in
the west, the Valais and Vaud regions specialise
in French varieties, although the favoured white
grape, Fendant (Chasselas to the French), is not
much prized in its mother country, yielding a
thin, unassuming, sometimes minerally but not
conspicuously fruity white. Sylvaner does well
here, and there are isolated outposts of
Chardonnay and Pinot Gris.

Pinot Noir makes some reasonably tasty light
reds, sometimes in a blend with a smaller proportion of Gamay and labelled Dôle in the
Valais, Savagnin in the Vaud. With avoidance of
maceration, a white version of the Valais blend,
Dôle Blanche, is made. East of France's Jura is
Neuchâtel, where the local claim to fame is a
delicate Pinot Noir rosé, Oeil-de-Perdrix
("partridge-eye").

Ticino in the south is the Italian-speaking
section of Switzerland, interesting because its
production is overwhelmingly dominated by
Merlot reds. Some are light and grassy, others
have a bit of sinew to them, helped along by
judicious application of oak.

LUXEMBOURG

Müller-Thurgau (known here as Rivaner) and a
pallid-tasting variety called Elbling are backed
up by most of the Alsace varieties in Luxembourg's vineyards. Nearly all the wine is white,
with a little Pinot Noir for frail rosés, and is
labelled by variety. There is just one appellation,
Moselle Luxembourgeoise. Perhaps the most
interesting wine is Crémant de Luxembourg, a
denomination that came into effect in 1991 for
the country's champagne-method fizz, both
white and rosé. Quality is good, but you'll probably have to go to the Grand Duchy to taste it.

CZECH REPUBLIC/SLOVAKIA

Both halves of the former Czechoslovakia are
emerging, blinking, into the modern wine world
after decades of insularity under the state-controlled Soviet-bloc system. The Czech Republic
is the lesser of the two players as yet. Its vineyards are largely concentrated in the
southeastern region of Moravia, on the Austrian
and Slovakian borders, although an insignificant quantity of wine is made north of Prague.

International varietals to look for are Cabernet Sauvignon and Pinot Noir for reds, and
Sauvignon Blanc, Pinot Blanc, Riesling and
Traminer (Gewürz) for whites. Sporadic plantings of the Austrian Grüner Veltliner, together
with Müller-Thurgau, are responsible for quite a
lot of Czech white. St Laurent makes appetisingly rustic red, and the violetty Blaufränkisch
crops up as Frankovka.

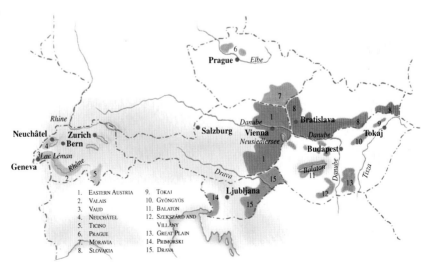

1. EASTERN AUSTRIA
2. VALAIS
3. VAUD
4. NEUCHÂTEL
5. TICINO
6. PRAGUE
7. MORAVIA
8. SLOVAKIA
9. TOKAJ
10. GYÖNGYÖS
11. BALATON
12. SZEKSZÁRD AND VILLÁNY
13. GREAT PLAIN
14. PRIMORSKI
15. DRAVA

Slovakia's vineyard regions extend in a virtually unbroken line along the country's southern borders, all the way from Austria to Russia. Varieties grown are mostly as in the Czech Republic. A local curiosity is the Irsay Oliver grape, which makes fragrantly graceful white wines, with more than a whiff of scented soap about them, especially in the Nitra region - strange but attractive. Pinot Gris does well too. As with its western neighbour, the principal impetus for Slovakia's improvement will be the visits of international wine consultants.

HUNGARY

Hungary was once famous only for Tokaji (previously spelt Tokay), occasionally great, often stalely oxidised, brown dessert wines that bore an uncanny resemblance to sherry. Produced in the northwest of the country, they are made in a range of styles, from basically dry to lusciously sweet. Tokaji is matured in large casks under a film of naturally formed yeast comparable to the *flor* of the Jerez region, hence the wines' similarity to sherry.

The sweeter styles, labelled Aszú, involve the addition to the base wine of rotted grapes pounded into a paste. They are measured out in custom-made hods called *puttonyos*; the label states the number added (from 3 *puttonyos* up to a sticky-sweet 7). Tokaji Essencia, sweetest of all, appears only in occasional vintages, and is made from free-run juice cask-aged for at least five years. Inward investment in the Tokaji region in the last few years, including French and German interests, has gone a long way to restoring the wines to their former exalted reputation.

As well as Tokaji, Hungary's table wines are gaining ground, again because of the input at key wineries by foreign producers. Hugh Ryman, born in Britain, trained in Australia, has introduced a range of good dry white varietals, including Chardonnay and Sauvignon from Gyöngyös in northeast Hungary. The Balaton-boglar winery, near Lake Balaton in the west, is under the watchful eye of Kym Milne, one of the most imaginative of the whole troupe of flying winemakers.

Most of the major varieties of Burgundy, Bordeaux and Alsace are now planted in Hungary, and are yielding encouraging results. Native white grapes include the Furmint and Hárslevelü used in Tokaji, but also in some straight dry whites, and the crisp but unremarkable Ezerjó. The principal red is Kadarka,

which makes beefy reds in the southern regions to the west of the Danube such as Szekszárd and Villány. (It is also the backbone of Bull's Blood, once thought the height of racy sophistication in Britain.) Blaufränkisch is successful as well; it is known in Hungarian as Kékfrankos.

SLOVENIA

The northwestern province of the old Yugoslavia became an independent country in 1991, neatly escaping the ravages of the war further south. It was from here that one of the biggest-selling wine brands of the 1970s came - the palatable but undistinguished Lutomer Laski Rizling, made from the Welschriesling grape common throughout central Europe. These days, Slovenian wine production is trying hard to enter the international quality league with a range of classic varietals. Expertise and influence are being absorbed from neighbouring Italy and Austria, in the Primorska and Drava regions respectively. Sipon (Hungary's Furmint), Sauvignon Blanc, Cabernet Sauvignon and Merlot are all doing well, while the best of the Muscat family - Muscat Blanc à Petits Grains - can make refreshing, simple sweet wines.

Vineyards at Nova Gora in Slovenia (above), one of central Europe's emergent wine nations.

Checking on the development of sweet Tokaji in the mould-coated cellars of the Tokaji Wine Trust, Hungary (above).

EASTERN EUROPE

Through the great empires of the Greeks, Byzantines and Ottomans who crossed Eastern Europe, the vine has flourished and faded. Centuries on, winemaking is again enjoying a new momentum.

AS WE MOVE TOWARDS the eastern fringes of Europe, we are nearing the birthplace of wine itself, the first homeland of the winemaking grape *Vitis vinifera*. If history ever paid lip-service to the notion of precedence, then Greece would have been the pre-eminent wine country in Europe ever since classical antiquity.

But it didn't happen that way. The Greeks took their expertise into Rome and parts of southern Europe, and the Roman Empire carried it on northwards and westwards. In time, the native varieties of what was to be France became the most highly prized of all wine grapes; the vineyards in which they grew were painstakingly selected for the most sympathetic matches of soil and climate, and French wine ascended to greatness.

In the Middle Ages, Greece became part of the Byzantine Empire. At this stage, it still had a thriving viticultural tradition, particularly on certain of its islands in the Aegean. One single piece of administrative short-sightedness in the

The swathe of Eastern Europe, crossing Bulgaria, Romania and Moldova, Turkey and Greece (below), offers a vast range of styles and native grape varieties.

11th century, however, was to undermine it for centuries to come. The Emperor Alexius decided to grant Venice, long since detached from Byzantium, favourable trading status in certain key cities of the Empire. From 1082, the Venetians were exempted from paying duties on commodities they exported to the east. As Greek wine, along with everything else, was thus deprived of the ability to compete, the entire economic edifice of the Empire came clattering about its ears.

When an enterprise becomes obsolete because others are able to practise it more cheaply, the inevitable decline is accompanied by a critical loss of skills and knowledge, even where they have been possessed for many generations. So it was with Greek wine. As the collapsing Byzantine Empire was overrun by the Ottoman Turks, its fate was sealed. The nation that had, in large measure, taught Europe how to make wine saw its viticulture regress to a helpless infancy that was to endure until the period after the Second World War.

In the eastern countries formerly in the Soviet sphere of influence, a quality wine industry was not seemingly viewed as anything approaching an economic necessity when the agricultural sector as a whole was so perennially fragile. The one exception was to be Bulgaria, where an experiment in flooding western markets with heavily subsidised state-produced wines was to be one of the more conspicuous economic successes of the Soviet era.

Today, eastern Europe is struggling somewhat to keep pace as wines from the southern hemisphere have caught the imaginations of British consumers in particular. Bulgaria and Romania are dedicated to the cause, however (the former still trading to some extent on its success in the 1970s and '80s), while Greece - with a little help from western friends - is learning all over again how to make good wine.

GREECE

When Greece joined the European Union in the 1980s, it had put in place an appellation system so devotedly modelled on the French that the

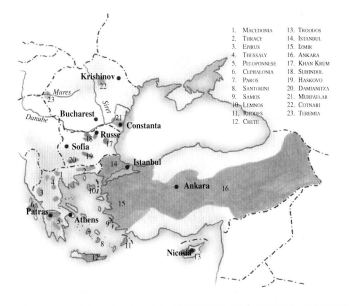

1. MACEDONIA	13. TROODOS
2. THRACE	14. ISTANBUL
3. EPIRUS	15. IZMIR
4. THESSALY	16. ANKARA
5. PELOPONNESE	17. KHAN KRUM
6. CEPHALONIA	18. SUHINDOL
7. PAROS	19. HASKOVO
8. SANTORINI	20. DAMIANITZA
9. SAMOS	21. MURFATLAR
10. LEMNOS	22. COTNARI
11. RHODES	23. TEREMIA
12. CRETE	

French terms *appellation contrôlée* and *vin de pays* are often seen on labels. As in other countries, the better wines that have been treated to prolonged ageing in cask are named Reserve wines, again in French - Réserve or Grande Réserve. Table wines, including branded wines of dubious repute, make up the rest. There are now approaching 30 appellations throughout the country, from Macedonia in the north down to the island of Crete.

Macedonia and Thrace The northern regions are especially noted for red wines. Xynomavro is the main indigenous red grape, making intense, oak-aged, raisiny reds in Náoussa and Goumenissa. One of the first reds to be taken seriously in the early stages of the renaissance of Greek wine was Château Carras, from the slopes of Mount Meliton on the Thracian peninsula. Here, the great Bordeaux wine professor Emile Peynaud played a part in creating an authoritative Greek version of classic claret, based on good Cabernet Sauvignon. The result has been a new appellation, Côtes de Meliton, and subsequent feverish experimentation with blending French and local grape varieties. Prospects look extremely healthy.

Epirus and Thessaly Vineyards are rather thinly spread over the central regions of Greece. In the west, not far from the Albanian border, a local variety called Debina makes a slightly pétillant white wine at Zitsa. On the Aegean coast, the Xynomavro grape crops up again, this time in a blended, cask-aged red, Rapsani, made in the shadow of Mount Olympus. Further south, Ankhíalos is a crisp dry white made from native grapes Rhoditis and Savatiano, a combination also much favoured in retsina (see below).

Peloponnese The southern peninsula is home to more of Greece's appellations than any other zone. The extensive vineyards of Patras in the north produce wines that span the stylistic spectrum, from Patras itself, a light dry Rhoditis white, through fortified Muscat of Patras (made in the same way as Beaumes-de-Venise), to the fairly widely known Mavrodaphne, Greece's answer to port. Mavrodaphne is the name of the grape that plays the greatest part in the blend, and the vinification is the same as that for port. Extended cask-ageing is the norm, although the wine tends to retain its deep red colour. The best, such as those from the Kourtakis company, are a match for a good LBV.

At Nemea in the northeast, another good red grape - Agiorgitiko - comes into its own, mak-

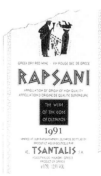

ing full-bodied, concentrated, oaky reds at high altitudes. Some of the less good wine from this region is made slightly sweet.

On the central plateau of Mantinia, some of Greece's more arresting original wine is made from Moscophilero, one of the rare varieties of grapes that may accurately be classed as pink, rather than red or white. Most of the wine is a highly scented, viscous white full of musky orange aromas like a heavier version of dry Alsace Muscat. The pigmentation in the skin, however, means that a period of maceration can yield a full-fruited rosé.

Hot and dry, Cephalonia, in the Ionian Sea (left), makes both fortified and varietal white wines.

Picking Cabernet Sauvignon on the slopes of Mount Meliton, in Thrace (below), for the Château Carras red. Styled on claret, this wine marked the birth of Greece's modern wine industry.

Pruning vines (above). Old-fashioned methods still rule in many of Cyprus's remote hilltop vineyards.

Almond trees in blossom among the vines in the foothills of the Troodos mountains (below), home of Cyprus's legendary fortified sweet wine, Commandaria.

Greek islands In the Ionian Sea off the west coast of Greece, the island of Cephalonia makes its own versions of the fortified wines of Patras, as well as a strong-limbed, heavy-going varietal white from the northern Italian Ribolla, here called Robola.

The Cycladean islands of Paros and Santorini each have their respective appellations, the former for a red wine curiously blended from the red Mandelaria grape with some white Malvasia, the latter for a dry, refreshingly acid white made from the local Assyrtiko.

Greece's most celebrated fortified Muscats, from the top-flight Muscat Blanc à Petits Grains, come from two islands in the Aegean. Muscat of Samos, from the island just off the Turkish coast, is the better-known, and comes in a variety of styles from gently sweet to an almost unbearably concentrated nectar, made from fully raisined grapes. The version most often seen abroad is somewhere in the middle, a *vin doux naturel* like Beaumes-de-Venise. Further north, the island of Lemnos makes a similar style of sweet wine, as well as a small quantity of dry wine for local consumption and a resinated Muscat made like retsina.

Rhodes has a trio of appellations, representing different wine styles. The dry white is made from a grape called Athiri, the red is from the

Mandelaria seen on Paros, and there is also the inevitable dessert Muscat.

Crete, which has been making wine since early antiquity, has a good showing of native grape varieties. Peza, in the centre of the island, is the principal appellation, making both red and white wines from grapes such as red Liatiko and white Vilana.

Retsina The wine that was entirely synonymous with Greece in the early days of mass tourism was, for many, the very definition of the phrase "acquired taste". The style is based on techniques that date back to classical times, when the stone jars known as *amphorae* were lined with pine resin in order to preserve their contents. Today, however, retsina is a simple dry white wine that has had lumps of resin, specifically from the Aleppo pine, infused in it during its fermentation. It is made all over Greece, but principally in the area immediately around Athens to supply the tourist industry.

Retsina's improbable popularity among the first influx of tourists was perhaps based as much on its challengingly foreign nature as any genuine appreciation. It became well enough known to sell in the UK, however. Served extremely cold, in sherry-like quantities, it can be an interesting alternative, but a little does go a very long way.

CYPRUS

Winemaking on the island of Cyprus leaves much to be desired. Production is virtually cornered by four large industrial concerns whose installations are located near to the port of Limassol for easy export. That, of course, means that the vineyards themselves, mainly up in the hills, are far enough away to require temperature-controlled transportation, but this is a luxury not deemed entirely necessary in the cash-strapped Cypriot wine industry. There are very tentative signs of improvement, but Cyprus has no ready market for its wines since the end of its trade agreements with the old Soviet bloc.

Two indigenous grape varieties dominate the vineyards. Both could make reasonably good wine given half the chance. The red is Mavro, at its best when the wine is still fairly young and fresh; the white is Xynisteri, a bit of a rough diamond but certainly capable of giving wines with at least some aromatic personality. Southern French grape varieties, as well as the inevitable Chardonnay, are being tried, with reputedly encouraging results.

Melnik, in the torrid south-western region of Harsovo, Bulgaria (left). The native Melnik grape makes characterful, dark reds for ageing.

The only commercially visible Cypriot wines on the export markets were traditionally its sherry equivalents. Even they have had to contend with the banning in the EU from 1996 of the term "sherry" for anything other than the produce of Jerez. The sweet brown liquor was never going to win any prizes for subtlety, but there is some fino-style wine matured under *flor* and aged in a *solera* system, exactly like the best examples of the real thing. For those visiting the island these are worth seeking out.

As in other Mediterranean regions, Cyprus has a legendary, now little-known dessert wine. Commandaria, a fortified sweet wine made from sun-dried Mavro and Xynisteri grapes, is made in the foothills of the Troodos mountains. It is aged for a minimum of two years - often much longer - in casks, arranged in some cases into a *solera* system. After years of decline and abuse, the name was at last finally protected in an edict of 1993 that defined its geographical origin and method of production within strict guidelines. As other European fortified wines flounder, Commandaria could just be poised to make a well-deserved comeback.

TURKEY

Turkey's viticultural history goes back at least to Biblical times, when - as the story has it - Noah established the first vineyard on Mount Ararat after the Flood. Excavations in this area have lent strong support to the theory that some

of the very earliest systematic wine-growing did indeed arise here. Today, it is mostly very basic state-controlled slosh for the tourists that accounts for Turkey's efforts. There are plantings of some of the southern French grapes, and even Riesling and Pinot Noir, in the west of the country, while Anatolia produces wines from mainly indigenous varieties that can withstand the climatic extremes.

The privately owned Doluca company makes some half-decent reds and whites, but for the time being there is nothing like the level of expertise, or indeed will, to get Turkey off the ground as a significant producer. It will have to wait until the travelling circus of international winemaking consultants discovers its potential, at which point grape names like Papazkarasi and Oküzgözü may be on all our lips.

BULGARIA

Bulgaria's phenomenal export success in the 1970s and '80s was built on a winemaking tradition among the most venerable in the world. The Ottoman interdiction on alcohol consumption during the period that Bulgaria came under its sway contributed to a certain decline, but it was undoubtedly the investment in state-owned vineyards that communist Bulgaria initiated in the years after the Second World War that set the ball rolling once again.

A combination of uprooting and neglect, coupled with the economic upheaval following the

A truckload of freshly picked Chardonnay at Blatetz (above), in the sub-Balkan region of Bulgaria.

At Cernavoda, east of Constanta in Romania, the vineyards lie alongside the canal (above right).

reforms of the *Perestroika* era in the former Comecon countries, has led to troubled times for Bulgaria's wine industry. As the vineyards have been sold back into private hands, many smallholders cannot readily afford to ship their grapes to the central vinification plants established under the old state system. The result has been a considerable setback in terms of the quality of exported wine.

The equivalent of *appellation contrôlée* in Bulgaria is *Controliran*, denoting specific vineyard sites that may only grow approved grape varieties. There were getting on for 30 such designated areas by the 1990s. The varieties with which Bulgaria shot to prominence were classic French reds led by Cabernet Sauvignon and Merlot, together with a small amount of Pinot Noir (blended bizarrely with Merlot at the central Sliven winery). Whites included Chardonnay that could occasionally be good, in a fairly cheesy sort of way (from wineries like Khan Krum in the northeast), Sauvignon Blanc that tended to lack aromatic definition and rather flabby Riesling.

These are supplemented by some good native red grapes such as Mavrud and Melnik, which both give appetisingly meaty wines, and Gamza, which turns out to be the same as Hungary's grape Kadarka. Native white grapes are less inspiring, and include a variety called Dimiat of no noticeable character, which has

been crossed with Riesling to produce Misket, but still contrives to be resolutely tasteless. Welschriesling is there too.

The country divides into four basic regions, the eastern (including the Khan Krum and Schoumen wineries), northern (Suhindol, Svischtov, Russe), southern (Haskovo, Stambolovo, Assenovgrad) and southwestern (Damianitza, Harsovo). There are considerable climatic variations between them, the northern having the most temperate climate while the southwestern, bordering Greece, is pretty torrid. Some of the central wineries have, over the years, established reputations with particular varieties, such as the often distinctly claretty Cabernets of Russe and Svischtov, the voluptuously plummy Merlots of Stambolovo and the fiery Mavruds of Assenovgrad.

ROMANIA

Romania's vineyard regions are comprehensively scattered across the country, from Teremia in the west to Murfatlar on the Black Sea coast. The vast majority of the wine produced - even after the breaking of the economic deadlock with the fall of the Ceausescus - is still consumed within its borders, however.

There is now a drive to transform this picture by the accepted strategy of seeking western investment, which has begun to flow, and planting international varieties. In time, runs the

current consensus, Romania could become the most reliable producer of quality wine of all the old Comecon countries. Its climate is far more dependable than that of Bulgaria, for example, and it does have some excellent indigenous styles of wine.

Cabernet Sauvignon has established an extensive base all over the country, far more so than in Bulgaria, and there is some already famed Pinot Noir, together with Merlot, Welschriesling, Burgundy's Aligoté, Sauvignon Blanc and Pinot Gris. Two versions of a white grape called Fetească represent the most widely planted varieties of all, and are used in some of the sweet wines in which Romania has a long and distinguished tradition. Tămâioasă and Grasă are the two native ingredients of Cotnari, Romania's greatest and most assertively flavoured botrytised dessert wine, which is made in the northeast of the country, near the border with Moldova.

North of the capital Bucharest, the Dealul Mare region has made waves with its often sensational Pinot Noirs. At their most carefully vinified, they can be uncannily close to the style of good rustic burgundy. Cabernet and Merlot, meanwhile, have made some hearty reds in Babadag and Istria nearer the Black Sea. Lower down on the coast, Murfatlar also has a dessert wine tradition, but its wines are almost invariably less opulent than those of Cotnari, being much less prone to noble rot.

MOLDOVA

Moldova was an integral part of Romania until the USSR took a large bite of its eastern sector during the war. It is now an independent state, but one that retains strong cultural ties with Romania and speaks its language. Moldova's vineyards are hugely extensive and, like its western neighbour, it looks set fair to ascend the quality scale in time. A very catholic range of grape varieties is grown, including most of the major French names, some Russian varieties such as the white Rkatsiteli and the red Saperavi, plus a few of its own. Cabernet, Chardonnay and Sauvignon have inevitably been the first successful Moldovan wines seen in the west.

As well as promising table wines, Moldova also makes sparkling wine, together with some high-potential fortifieds similar both to sweet sherry styles and to the Liqueur Muscats of Australia. A small splash was made in the UK in the early 1990s with the importation of some deeply traditional, extensively aged red from the 1960s - Negru de Purkar and Roshu de Purkar. The wines were pretty oxidised and heavily browned, but some thought they detected in them something of the faded splendour of long-matured claret.

OTHER CIS

Wine is still of great commercial importance in the sections of the former Soviet Union that now comprise the Confederation of Independent States. As well as Moldova (see above), Russia, Belarus, the Ukraine and Georgia are the major producing areas. Rkatsiteli and Saperavi are the two principal indigenous varieties (white and red respectively), but there are also widespread plantings of Cabernet Sauvignon, Riesling and the Aligoté of Burgundy. Crimean reds were once celebrated far beyond the boundaries of the Ukraine, and may come to be once again if the investment currently flowing in begins to pay dividends.

Visitors to the old USSR may remember the great quantities of Soviet sparkling wine, fancifully referred to as *champanski*, that were available. Despite the name, the fizz was made by a technique known as the Russian Continuous Method. The yeast-boosted base wine was passed through a series of connected tanks over several weeks, depositing dead yeast cells as it went, until it emerged clarified and sparkling at the end. It is still produced in gargantuan quantities, the quality generally quite acceptable.

Hay-making in the Tîrnave region, in central Transylvania, Romania (left). The high, cool vineyards produce mainly white wines.

Gigantic fermentation tanks at the bulk-producing Sliven winery, Bulgaria (above), typify the large-scale postwar investment the country conferred on its wine industry.

MIDDLE EAST, NORTH AFRICA *and the* FAR EAST

Israel and Lebanon are extending their reputation with classic grape varieties, while the wines of North Africa and the Far East remain little-known beyond their borders.

Historic barrels outside the Carmel winery (right), a huge co-operative that produces most of Israel's wine.

B EYOND THE CONFINES of Europe is a handful of countries that have been making wine for centuries, small amounts of which may find their way into the export trade. In Israel and Lebanon, western know-how has contributed enormously to the creation of quality wines, while the north African countries, by and large, await the arrival of the flying winemakers.

ISRAEL

The modern Israeli wine industry was effectively founded by Baron Edmond de Roth-schild, owner of Château Lafite in Bordeaux, in the late 19th century. He conferred on the returning Jewish settlers a huge endowment for agricultural purposes, including the establish-ment of vineyards for the production of kosher wine. For most of the 20th century, that was the industry's main concern: it was exported to Jewish communities worldwide. Since the beginning of the 1980s, however, Israel has moved to capitalise on its favourable grape-growing climate to produce an expanding range of wines for general consumers.

Carmel is the label most often seen on the export markets. The fairly basic wines come from the first co-operative winery founded with the Rothschild money in the 1880s. Perhaps the most exciting development to date was the establishment of the Golan Heights winery in northern Israel. It makes a number of good international varietals - Cabernet Sauvignon, Chardonnay, Sauvignon Blanc and Riesling among them - under the brand names Golan, Gamla and (best of all) Yarden.

Lebanon's Bekaa Valley and Israel's Golan Heights (below), in the Middle East, offer especially favourable climes for grape-growing.

Beirut

Tel Aviv
Jerusalem

1. BEKAA VALLEY
2. GOLAN HEIGHTS
3. GALILEE
4. SHOMRAN
5. SAMSON
6. JUDEAN HILLS
7. NEGEV

LEBANON

The story of Lebanese wine in recent times has basically been the story of the Château Musar winery in the Bekaa valley. Owner and wine-maker Serge Hochar trained in Bordeaux and makes what is undoubtedly the region's most celebrated red wine, exporting virtually every bottle produced. A blend of Cabernet Sauvignon and Cinsaut, it is matured in both barrel and bottle for several years before release, and is a ferociously dark, intensely spicy and cedary wine with plenty of alcohol and a haunting, savoury character that lingers on the palate.

It is all the more remarkable for being made in the gruesome circumstances of invasion and civil war that, until recently, dogged the region. Hochar's winery has been shelled and, in one year, used as a bomb shelter by local villagers, but his tenacity is legendary and it is only in very occasional vintages that he has been pre-vented from making a wine altogether. He also makes small quantities of oaky white wine from a mixture of Chardonnay, Sauvignon and a local grape called Meroué. Ksara is another Bekaa winery exporting to western Europe.

Ploughing a young vineyard at Enfidaville, Tunisia (left). Most of the country's vines are southern French varieties.

NORTH AFRICA

Algeria's vineyards are principally concentrated on the Mediterranean coast in the northwest of the country. It was once a hugely important bulk producer, sending much of its wine north to the former colonial power, France, where a lot of it undoubtedly ended up in bottles that bore impeccably French labels. Algerian viticulture is now declining, largely as a result of the onward march of Islamic fundamentalism. This may well reduce its industry to an export-only business, in which case it will collapse the more rapidly since external markets will be very hard to find.

Not since the launch in the 1970s of the colourfully named brand Red Infuriator has anyone paid much attention to Algerian wine. Its winemaking goes back to antiquity, although it has suffered in the modern era from under-investment. One of its better inland regions, the Coteaux de Mascara, makes cheerfully abrasive reds from a fistful of southern French grape varieties.

Morocco's wine industry benefits from intensive tourism, producing a fairly broad range of French varietals, including Cabernet Sauvignon, Syrah, Chenin Blanc and Chardonnay, for the holiday crowds. To show it means business in the quality stakes, it has devoted the most assiduous effort of all the north African countries to honing its nascent appellation system (AOG, or *appellation d'origine garantie*) to approximate to European standards. Low-priced raisiny reds, typified by the palatable Domaine de Cigogne seen recently in British retailers, are the norm, and there is a little Cinsaut rosé as well. The honeyed fortified Muscat de Berkane could well turn out to be an eye-catcher in the future.

Tunisia also has tourists' thirsts to slake, and does so with pretty rough-and-ready red and rosé wines, again made largely from southern French grape varieties. Whites include a rather leaden dry Muscat (made from the less good Muscat of Alexandria). For the time being, it probably needs to be sipped ice-cold in order to taste good, but if vinification practices improve, it may win converts abroad.

INDIA, CHINA AND JAPAN

India's repute as a wine producer rests solely on the sparkling wine of Maharashtra, Omar Khayyam, launched with expertise from the champagne house Piper Heidsieck. It can be appetisingly full, dry and nutty but has been too variable for commercial comfort.

China is awash with native grape varieties and has plenty of good vineyard land, but so far not much in the way of solid viticultural knowledge. The state wineries produce sweetened-up plonk for a country that naturally prefers grain wine like *shaoshing*, made from rice. However, French and Australian money is coming in, and enterprises like the Huadong winery at Qingdao are testing the international waters with varietal Chardonnay, Riesling and the like.

Japan makes grape wine on three of its four islands (with northern Hokkaido having the largest plantings), although local predilections have only recently made it a viable industry. Japanese investors have in recent years discovered a taste for the finest wines of France, in the sense that some are actually drinking them now rather than merely buying and selling them. Giant industrial concerns such as Suntory have been responsible for much of the investment to date. The country's own vineyards are, for the time being, hampered by the fact that they are largely planted with north American hybrid grape varieties, which can give some very peculiar flavours, but tastebuds weaned on *sake* may not mind that.

Vineyard worker thinning out grape bunches in early summer (above) in Suntory-owned vineyards, Japan.

AMERICAS AND REST OF THE WORLD

Vine leaves reddening with the onset of autumn in the Napa Valley, California (above).

The dramatic landscape of Marlborough, New Zealand (below).

No single factor has done more to change the world of wine in the modern era than the advent of wines and winemakers from North America and the southern hemisphere. These are the countries that comprise a great unwieldy region called the "New World" in many European minds.

For a time, the presence of wines from California and Australia in the major wine markets of Europe was blithely ignored by winemakers in the old countries, especially the French. What have we to fear, they asked themselves, from the products of wine cultures invented no more than 150 years ago in some cases, when we've been at it for centuries? The answer, as always, lay in the bottle.

In the end it wasn't sheer novelty value that induced wine consumers, the British in particular, to turn to the wines from these new countries so enthusiastically. That would have worn off in time in any case. It was the fact that the wine tasted so exuberant.

Australia led the way with its Chardonnay and Cabernet. Whether it was the staggeringly rich, sunny, butterscotch flavours of the one or the velvet-soft, creamy blackcurrant essence of the other, no European wine had ever tasted like this. And not only were the wines largely free of the tart, unripe acidity or the hard, mouth-furring tannins of the European run-of-the-mill

offerings, their fruit flavours were so appealingly easy to understand.

To capitalise on that instantly recognisable taste profile, the new wines were varietally labelled. Consumers came to see that Chardonnay meant lemon and butter and maybe vanilla, Cabernet was blackcurrants and plums and perhaps some melted chocolate, Pinot was raspberries and cherries, Sauvignon was gooseberries, and so on. By emphasising those fruit characteristics, the so-called New World wines did a valuable job in educating people in one of the essential factors that influences the way wines taste - the grape types they are made from.

Although the term "New World" may understandably have offended the sensibilities of American winemakers who didn't see the logic in bracketing them with Australians and vice versa, the concept did in one sense do everybody a favour. Consumers came to believe there was such a thing as a New World style, one that was in direct contrast to anything they might find in Europe. This led them to try the wines of far more countries than they would otherwise have done had the style had been fixed as, say, Australasian. The common identifying factor was that varietal labelling.

In this way, the non-European winemaking countries kicked down the door and started to rewrite the rules. It wasn't simply that many of these wines came from places that had good, reliable climates in which the annual vintage was usually nothing like the lottery that the French have to contend with. There were new approaches in the vineyards and wineries that were playing an integral part in shaping the flavours of the wines: cold fermentations, artificial yeast cultures, stainless-steel tanks instead of huge age-old casks, cold maceration of red grapeskins in the juice before fermentation to extract maximum concentration, sterile bottling conditions.

Some of these techniques were in use among quality-conscious European winemakers, to be sure, but the generality still worked exactly as their forebears had done, by picking the grapes at a predetermined time, pressing as much juice as possible out of them and closing the lid on the cask to let nature get on with it.

Nowadays, the once entrenched opposition between old and new ways is becoming a meeting of minds. Château Lafite's Gilbert Rokvam winters in Chile, South Australia's Geoff Merrill does Teroldego in Trentino, his compatriot Peter Bright works wonders in Portugal, while

Moët et Chandon - one of the biggest wine names of all - now makes bubbles not just in Champagne, but in California, Australia and Spain. The world of wine is becoming a global vineyard.

There are some who regret this and seek to blame the New Worlders for what they see as the creeping internationalisation of wine. If it hadn't been for them, hallowed traditions would have remained undisturbed.

What the complaint about standardisation is in danger of ignoring, though, is that the greatest individual wines of old Europe were the very ones that most people never knew because they couldn't afford them. What they were left with was the mediocrity and the outright dross. If California Chardonnay and Australian Cabernet helped to elbow aside the likes of the ropiest St-Véran and the bitterest Bordeaux Supérieur, then they did us all a good turn. But more than any of us, they did the Burgundians and the

Bordelais a favour because they put a bomb under the complacency that was steadily crushing the life out of those regions.

Today, the countries that are explored in the following pages are each establishing their own identities in the wine markets of Europe. Their best wines may owe something to the various classic antecedents of European wine. But the days when every Chardonnay wanted only to be either a Chablis or a Meursault, every Cabernet a Château Latour, are long gone.

Most audaciously of all, winemakers in the United States and Australia particularly are trying their hands at grapes that have previously only enjoyed minority acclaim in their birthplaces. Napa Valley Barbera, Oregon Pinot Gris, Barossa Grenache and Victorian Marsanne represent the strongest evidence to date that the new countries are awash with confidence. Exciting times lie ahead.

California poppies, the state flower (above), provide a splash of colour beneath the wire-trained vines of Kenwood Vineyards, Sonoma County.

South Australia's Clare Valley (left), splashed with spring flowers and newly planted vineyards.

UNITED STATES

Enthusiasm and the willingness to experiment has brought great success to the winemaking states of North America. Led by California and the Pacific Northwest, America's vineyards have made a great impact on wine-drinkers around the world.

ALTHOUGH THE contemporary wine industry in the USA dates back only to the first half of the 19th century, Nature always intended the States to be a wine producer. Exactly whose ship made the earliest landfall at precisely which spot may never be known, but the Norse settlers who discovered the North American continent a millennium ago christened the place Vinland, after the wild vines that luxuriantly carpeted the lands on the eastern seaboard.

The first permanent European settlements were not established until the late 1500s, and it was to be fully two centuries later before anything like an embryo wine industry could be identified. By this time the settlers included Germans, Spaniards, Italians and Greeks. What dogged the early attempts was the realisation that the vines that grew wild in America were not *Vitis vinifera*, the European wine grape species, but a collection of weird and mostly unwonderful native species, such as *Vitis labrusca*, *Vitis riparia* and *Vitis rupestris*. Wines made from these are nothing like *vinifera* wines; they often have a strangely animal smell to them, for which the common coinage for many years was "foxy".

The US's top winemaking regions are centred on the west coast, in California, Washington and Oregon, but other areas are gaining reputations for fine wines.

Once the problem was identified, colonists from the wine countries decided that all they needed to do was to ship over some of their good old *vinifera* vinestock from home, and start again. They reckoned without a whole host of pests and diseases that were at that happy time unknown in European viticulture. Various forms of mildew and rot, as well as the devasting phylloxera vine louse, which feeds on sap in the vine's roots with fatal consequences, visited the first *vinifera* vines in America like the ten plagues of Egypt. And as if all that weren't enough, many decades of trial and heartbreaking error went into finding the right climatic zones in which the European varieties could survive.

Initially, the answer seemed to lie in cultivating hybrid mixtures of *vinifera* and one of the American species, the hybrids first occurring by chance cross-fertilisation, and then as a result of deliberate botanical engineering. Such magical names of 19th-century American viticulture as the Catawba, Isabella and Concord grape varieties, hybrids all, might have remained the whole story of wine in the USA, were it not for the annexation of the Spanish colonies in the south and west. The Spanish had been practising relatively trouble-free *vinifera* cultivation in what is now New Mexico, and to a lesser extent California, for generations.

One of the key pioneers of the period was a central European entrepreneur, Agoston Haraszthy, who arrived in California just in time to grab a piece of the Gold Rush action. Although not quite the undisputed godfather of California wine that some of the histories have portrayed him as, Haraszthy did undeniably exert a seminal influence in the expansion of winemaking in the state. Apart from anything else, he was responsible for shipping cuttings of many European grape varieties into the region, then struggling to make the best of less than brilliant performers such as Mission, an indigenous South American grape brought northwards by the Spanish to provide the California monasteries with communion wine. (It is still widely grown in Chile, where they call it País.)

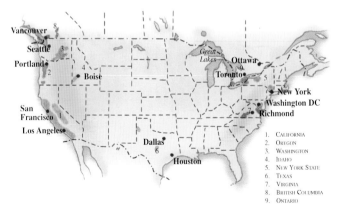

1. CALIFORNIA
2. OREGON
3. WASHINGTON
4. IDAHO
5. NEW YORK STATE
6. TEXAS
7. VIRGINIA
8. BRITISH COLUMBIA
9. ONTARIO

The flat valley floor of Salinas in California's Monterey County (left). Monterey is cool, yet one of the state's most prolific grape-growing areas.

In the 20th century, the emerging American wine industry was dealt a near-fatal blow by the advent of Prohibition in 1920. Although vineyards were kept going for the production of grape concentrate, used to make non-alcoholic juice, the expertise the winemakers had acquired withered on the vine. The banning of alcohol lasted just long enough - 13 years - for the bare bones of the US wine industry to have crumbled to virtually nothing. As a result, it was to take another four decades before first California, and then the United States as a whole, assumed its rightful place as a major player on the world wine scene.

Even now, American winemakers are not without their problems. Falling sales in recent years have meant that their quality wines have become increasingly expensive, both at home and abroad. On top of that, phylloxera - the old enemy - has once more inundated the vineyards of California. It is a very difficult pest to detect in advance, both because it is microscopically small and because it mainly lives underground, sucking on the vines' roots, and so the first you tend to know about it is when your vines start looking brown and shrivelled. Once things have gone that far, there is no alternative but to pull them up and replant at great expense.

Perhaps most perniciously of all, there is a new mood of Prohibitionism abroad in the States. It is more virulent and hysterical than anything seen in Europe, where even France has succumbed to controls on alcohol advertising. The hidden agenda of the anti-alcohol campaigners, who have already won the battle to label winebottles with health warnings, is to stop others from exercising freedom of choice.

Hope, however, springs eternal in the winemaker's heart, as any European grower studying the summer weather forecasts can attest. The economy will turn around as the wineries' prices moderate to keep pace with the foreign competition. Phylloxera will be vanquished once more as the new vines are grafted on to hardier, more resistant rootstocks. And when American TV showed a documentary programme about the findings of Dr. Serge Renaud, the Lyon cardiologist who has established that wine plays a definite part in reducing the risk of coronary heart disease, consumers all over the country turned back, albeit briefly, to drinking red wine in healthy quantities.

A further sign of the increasing maturity of the industry came in 1983, when the United States began to implement a sort of appellation system consisting of geographically defined American Viticultural Areas (AVAs). Although that wording does not as yet appear on the labels, the system decrees that wines using the individual AVA names must be made from no less than 85 per cent of grapes grown in that area.

There are many who say that the USA is probably foremost among the non-European winemaking countries now: for the diversity its regions are capable of, its willingness to absorb the lessons of that old French concept *terroir* in choosing the best grape varieties for each specific site, instead of just planting cash-crop Cabernet and Chardonnay everywhere, and in terms of the sheer dynamism its winemakers are driven by. There appear to be no vinous challenges these days the Americans are unwilling to take on, and if that isn't the authentic pioneering spirit, I don't know what is.

Modern technology in the vineyard and winery includes sterile winemaking equipment such as this crusher-destemmer (above).

California's own red grape variety, Zinfandel, arriving at the winery (above).

California's wine country (below) stretches the length of the state. Vineyards are planted on cool, hillside sites, in hot, inland valleys and close to the ocean.

CALIFORNIA

To say that the state of California is at the epicentre of the United States wine industry would be something of an understatement. Nine out of every ten bottles of American wine come from there. From Mendocino County north of San Francisco to the San Diego and Imperial Valley areas on the Mexican border, it's wine country practically all the way. Cross the Golden Gate Bridge heading north out of San Fran, and you soon enter the Napa Valley, California's Bordeaux, where it's difficult to find anybody growing anything other than vines. From world-class champagne-method sparklers to idiosyncratic fortified Muscats and even brandy - if it's possible to make it, California does.

For a long time, all the European markets ever saw was pretty basic stuff, known as "jug wine" in its homeland for the inelegant flagons it used to be packaged in. Paul Masson was one of the more visible brands in the UK, as often as not sold in de-alcoholised versions that didn't win many friends. E & J Gallo of Modesto was another large brand. Founded by two brothers in

the wake of Prohibition's repeal, it had become the largest wine producer in America by the middle of the century, and is now the biggest on the planet. Gallo now has some ambitious wines, but the backbone of its commercial success was unashamed jug wine.

The revolution began in the 1970s, in 1976 to be precise, when, at a comparative tasting in Paris, two California wines - a Chardonnay and a Cabernet - beat all comers in a scrupulously blind taste-off. They were Chateau Montelena Chardonnay 1973 and Stag's Leap Cabernet Sauvignon 1973, their names forever deserving to be invoked because they sparked the tidal wave that swept California wine into Europe. What was so indigestible to the French was that, quite apart from the fact that many *cru classé* clarets and *grand cru* white burgundies were relegated to runner-up status, it was the French themselves that did it. There were no American judges. There could be no greater plaudit.

Since then, California has gone from strength to strength. It is beyond any doubt one of the most innovative wine-growing regions on earth and is now set fair to startle us all - not just the French - with what it can do.

As in most of the wine regions outside Europe, California is making the running with international, largely French, grape varieties. The rollcall includes Chardonnay and Cabernet Sauvignon, of course, the hugely fashionable Merlot (which has established a varietal reputation for itself as a sort of Cabernet without tears), some of the finest Pinot Noir anywhere (including Burgundy), cool, crisp Riesling, some often ill-defined Sauvignon Blanc and small amounts of jet-black Syrah.

Its one peculiar claim to fame is a red variety called Zinfandel. In recent years, the cautious theory that the grape was the same as a southern Italian variety seen in and around Puglia, where they rather unfeelingly call it Primitivo, seems to have firmed up into confident fact. It could very well have been brought over by Italian settlers as early as the 18th century, and was certainly in currency at the onset of modern California viticulture in the mid-1800s.

Styles of Zinfandel wine vary. There is a lot of deeply coloured purple-red wine of high alcohol and tremendous fruit concentration, displaying ripe berry flavours like blueberries, together with something strangely herbal (sometimes even compared to fresh tea leaves). Some is much lighter, made in a quasi-

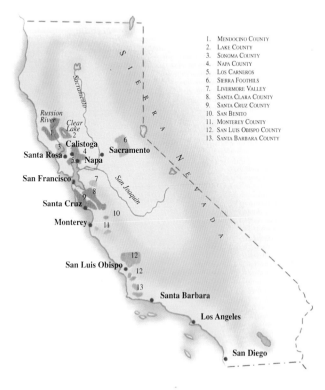

1. MENDOCINO COUNTY
2. LAKE COUNTY
3. SONOMA COUNTY
4. NAPA COUNTY
5. LOS CARNEROS
6. SIERRA FOOTHILLS
7. LIVERMORE VALLEY
8. SANTA CLARA COUNTY
9. SANTA CRUZ COUNTY
10. SAN BENITO
11. MONTEREY COUNTY
12. SAN LUIS OBISPO COUNTY
13. SANTA BARBARA COUNTY

Beaujolais idiom, and not generally as impressive. Then there is a usually slightly sweet pink style called "blush", which can be as refreshing as raspberry-ripple ice-cream, and just as sickly taken in quantity.

Enterprising growers are trying their hands at almost anything that takes their fancy, from native Italian and Spanish varieties to Rhône-style Viognier and the aromatic grapes of Alsace.

Mendocino and Lake Counties These two counties, through which runs the Russian River, lie at the northern end of California wine country. Mendocino, on the Pacific coast, encompasses a very broad range of micro-climates as it extends inland, meaning that the styles of wine produced take in everything from delicately spiced Gewürztraminer and lightly leafy Sauvignon to big, meaty Cabernets and Zinfandels. As far as defined AVAs (American Viticultural Areas) go, there is one large catchall designation for the whole of Mendocino, within which are three valley areas - the coastal

Anderson and inland McDowell and Potter.

In Lake County to the east, Clear Lake is the main AVA, with the smaller Guenoc Valley, consisting of only one winery of the same name, founded around the time of the Great War. Lake County, being that much smaller than Mendocino, is climatically less diverse, but has built a reputation for pleasantly green-fruited Sauvignons and soft, approachable Cabernets. MENDOCINO PRODUCERS: Fetzer (the biggest Mendocino winery, making a fistful of fine varietals, including nutmeggy organic Bonterra Chardonnay, juicy Barrel Select Cabernet, damson-rich Pinot Noir and gorgeously brambly Zinfandel), Jepson Vineyards, Parducci, Handley Cellars and Roederer (the last two producing fine champagne-method Chardonnay-Pinot fizz). LAKE PRODUCERS: Kendall-Jackson (whose fine, savoury Chardonnay comes from vineyards much further south in Santa Barbara), Konocti (good smoky Sauvignon), Guenoc (for Chardonnays and red and white Bordeaux blends called Meritage in California).

The herb garden at Fetzer winery (below), in Mendocino County, planted with hundreds of varieties of herbs.

Sonoma Sonoma is a coastal county north of San Francisco Bay, encompassing a valley of the same name that forms its main sub-region. For a long time, the Sonoma region existed in the shadow of its eastern neighbour, Napa County, but its growers and wineries have worked assiduously to define its undeniable potential for quality, now reflected in ten demarcated AVAs.

The Alexander Valley AVA has seen the most intensive programme of plantings in Sonoma in the last quarter-century. Grape varieties that grow nowhere near each other in France flourish here in happy proliferation. The Simi winery makes one of northern California's more diverting Chardonnays here, while Jordan Vineyards has hit the headlines with an elegant champagne-method sparkler called "J".

The Sonoma Valley AVA itself includes some of California's oldest wineries, such as Buena Vista (established in the 19th century by the pioneering Mr Haraszthy) and Sebastiani. Running north to south, the valley is blessed with subtle gradations of microclimate as it moves away from the cooling influence of the Bay. This means that a highly disparate range of grapes can be grown. At the southern end, it takes in a section of the celebrated Carneros region, which it shares with Napa County (see below).

One of the coolest Sonoma areas is the

Russian River Valley, which forms its own AVA within Sonoma County. The impact of the morning fogs that roll in off the Bay is most keenly felt here, with the result that Pinot Noir is notably successful (especially from practitioners like Williams-Selyem, Dehlinger, Iron Horse and Rod Strong). Chardonnay can be superbly balanced from the likes of De Loach, and there is fine sparkling wine too.

Dry Creek Valley AVA, formed around a little tributary of the Russian River, is making a name for itself with some sharply delineated Sauvignon from Preston and Dry Creek Vineyards, as well as one of the more memorable Zinfandels from Quivira. The other AVAs are Chalk Hill, Knights Valley, Sonoma-Green Valley, Sonoma Coast, Sonoma Mountain and Northern Sonoma (the last an important redoubt of E&J Gallo).

OTHER GOOD SONOMA WINERIES: Laurel Glen, Chateau St Jean, Arrowood, Ravenswood, Carmenet, Kenwood.

Napa If California is the premier state for American wine, the Napa Valley is its regional frontrunner. So much land has been planted with vines that the area is almost at capacity, forming a virtual grape monoculture. The Napa is the Côte d'Or of California, if such comparisons can mean anything. Like Burgundy's best

(Above) State-of-the-art sparkling winemaking at Domaine Chandon, in Napa Valley, owned by champagne house Moët & Chandon (right). The fertile valley floor of Napa Valley is considered by many to be the state's premier site for Cabernet and Chardonnay.

patch, it is barely more than 20 miles from end to end, but embraces a dizzying degree of climatic variation. As with Sonoma, the southern end near the Bay is relatively cool and foggy, while the northern end at Calistoga is fiercely hot.

The overall Napa AVA was, by the mid-1990s, being organised into a string of smaller appellations, based on the main towns along the valley highway. From north to south, they will be Calistoga, St Helena, Rutherford, Oakville, Yountville and Napa. Some of the very best Chardonnays, Cabernets and Merlots are made along this trail, varying in style as much because of their geographical location and altitude as because of the philosophies of individuals. A rollcall of the great and the very great would have to take in Robert Mondavi, Heitz Cellars, Niebaum-Coppola (owned by Francis Ford Coppola of cinematic fame), Beaulieu Vineyards, Beringer, Swanson and many others.

Other Napa AVAs are the qualitatively important Stags Leap District, just to the north of the town of Napa (including fine Cabernets and Merlots from Stag's Leap Winery itself, Clos du Val and Shafer), Howell Mountain in the east of the valley (where La Jota makes some sensationally concentrated Cabernet), Mount Veeder, between Napa and Sonoma (with the Hess Collection producing its most distinguished

Chardonnays and Cabernets), and the emerging Wild Horse Valley, east of Napa itself.

OTHER GOOD NAPA WINERIES: Newton, Silverado, Caymus, Joseph Phelps, ZD, Vichon, Grgich Hills, Silver Oak, Trefethen, Cuvaison, Duckhorn, Franciscan. Domaine Mumm's Cuvée Napa and Schramsberg are the two leading producers of champagne-method sparkling wine.

Carneros The Carneros district overlaps the southern ends of both the Napa and Sonoma regions and forms a distinctive AVA of its own. Being immediately to the north of San Francisco Bay, its climate is continually influenced by the dawn fogs that roll in from the Pacific, often not clearing until around mid-morning. They mitigate the ferocious heat of summer to such a degree that Carneros qualifies as one of the coolest areas on average in all of California.

It shot to prominence in the 1980s for a handful of exquisitely crafted Pinot Noirs and Chardonnays from wineries such as Acacia, Saintsbury and Carneros Creek. The quality of the Pinots in particular - angular in youth, but packed with deep red fruit and roasted meat intensity - served notice that the citadel of Burgundian Pinot was about to be stormed.

Carneros has developed a reputation as a good producer of sparkling wines as well, with the champagne house Taittinger (Domaine Carneros) and cava producer Codorníu (Codorniu Napa) representing the European vote of confidence.

Sierra Foothills The foothills of the Sierra Nevada mountain range that forms the border with the state of Nevada encompass some of the oldest vineyard land in California, dating from the Gold Rush that began in 1849. Within the overall Foothills AVA are a number of subdivisions. El Dorado County forms one, while Amador County to the south takes in Shenandoah Valley and Fiddletown. The usual diversity of grapes is grown, but the acreage of Zinfandel vines is among California's more venerable. The North Yuba AVA consists only of the Renaissance winery, famed for delicate Rieslings and Sauvignons and a totally contrasting Cabernet - a pitch-black study in rip-roaring tannins.

Livermore Valley East of the Bay in Alameda County, the Livermore Valley AVA was historically famed for its Bordeaux-style white blends, but has since followed the path of California diversity. One of the Livermore's oldest wineries is the 100-year-old Wente Brothers, acclaimed now for its best cuvées of Chardonnay as well as some tasty sparkling wines.

Clos Pegase, in Napa Valley (above). This striking modern building contains not only the winery but an art gallery too.

New vines waiting to bud against a stark California landscape at Au Bon Clinat, Santa Barbara (above).

Vineyards of Wente Brothers in Livermore Valley (above), east of San Francisco Bay in Alameda County.

Santa Clara Valley South of Alameda, the Santa Clara Valley is now rather more about micro-electronics than wine, although it was one of the first AVAs. Ridge Vineyards is the big name around here: winemaker Paul Draper makes succulent Montebello Cabernets and a show-stopping Lytton Springs Zinfandel, from Sonoma grapes. The Mount Eden winery is, among others, keeping the flag flying with top-notch bottlings of Cabernet and Chardonnay.

Santa Cruz A coastal AVA south of the city of San Francisco, the Santa Cruz mountain vineyards have been a notably dynamic contributor to the California scene. This was one of the first regions to try producing great Pinot Noir, the proximity to the ocean making its climate cool enough not to overstress that notoriously fragile variety. Now all sorts of grapes have moved in, many of them under the creative aegis of Randall Grahm at the Bonny Doon winery. His entertainingly off-the-wall labels and wine names announce some genuinely original wines. Plantings of Marsanne, Roussanne, Syrah, Grenache and Mourvèdre, just as everyone else was going hell-for-leather with Cabernet, earned him the nickname of the Rhône Ranger, and helped to blaze a particularly fruitful trail. If it's Cabernet you're after, though, Klein Vineyards and Ahlgren make some of the most opulent.

San Benito San Benito is a smallish inland wine region west of Fresno, whose brightest star is Calera Vineyards. Calera's Josh Jensen is the sole proprietor in the tiny San Benito AVA of Mount Harlan, where he produces hauntingly scented Mills Vineyard Pinot Noir, a lovely, buttercream Chardonnay and the most extraor-

dinary Viognier made anywhere in the world outside Condrieu. It sells for about the same sort of giddy price as Condrieu, but the aromatic intensity of the wine is powerfully persuasive.

Monterey County Monterey, on the so-called Central Coast, is marked by both coolness and aridity, so that grape-growing has always been something of a challenge. Notwithstanding that, the county is one of the more densely planted California regions. Cool-climate grapes such as Pinot Noir, Riesling and even Chenin Blanc are now doing well there. Within its all-encompassing AVA, there are three flagship zones with their own designations that represent Monterey's premier division: Chalone, Arroyo Seco and Carmel Valley. The first of those is home to Chalone Vineyards, maker of benchmark Chardonnay, surprisingly full Pinot Blanc and richly gamey Pinot Noir.

San Luis Obispo The next AVA along the coast south of Monterey is San Luis Obispo. The county covers the climatic extremes, with the most highly regarded wines tending to come from the cooler coastal areas such as Edna Valley, which enjoys its own AVA. The Edna Valley winery makes pace-setting Chardonnay here. North of Edna is the large, elevated plain of Paso Robles, where the fiercer conditions are better for Cabernet and Zinfandel. South of the Edna Valley, in the Arroyo Grande AVA, the champagne house Deutz has established one of its overseas outposts, Maison Deutz (the other is in New Zealand).

Santa Barbara The southernmost of the Central Coast wine counties is fog-shrouded Santa Barbara, not far north of Los Angeles. Its best vineyards congregate in the two valleys that constitute the AVA land: Santa Maria and Santa Ynez. Both enjoy the cooling influence of the ocean and make good showings of Pinot Noir and Chardonnay, much as Carneros does, as well as some crisply textured Sauvignon and Riesling. Au Bon Climat and Sanford wineries have set a tough standard with their effortlessly concentrated, raspberry-fruited Pinots, while Zaca Mesa has done improbably good things with Syrah and Byron Vineyards scores highly for Sauvignon and Chardonnay.

In the south of the state, three regions of no enormous viticultural significance are located: Riverside County (which includes the Temecula AVA), San Diego County (including the tiny San Pasqual Valley AVA) and the inland Imperial Valley.

PACIFIC NORTHWEST

Three states in the far northwest of the USA have emerged in recent years from the long shadow cast by California's status as the Number One wine region in America. Of the three, it is the challenging climatic circumstances of Oregon that have caused the most excitement so far, but Washington State and - to a much lesser extent - Idaho are now making strong showings as well. From here will come the next wave of American wines to break upon European shores in significant volumes.

Oregon Although *Vitis vinifera* vines were first planted in Oregon over a century ago, it is only comparatively recently that the state's potential as a quality wine producer has been taken seriously. Even then, it was in the face of considerable scepticism from their southern neighbours in California that a handful of indomitable visionaries put their state on the world wine map. The picture began to change when a vintage of David Lett's Eyrie Vineyards Pinot Noir wiped the floor with a few red burgundies in an international blind tasting.

Pinot Noir, the Holy Grail of aspirant winemakers everywhere at the time, became the Oregon buzz wine *par excellence*, so much so that there are probably too many growers producing mediocre Pinot reds when they could be giving a better account of themselves with something easier. Alsace varieties have done remarkably well, providing some dry, spicy, fragrant wines from Riesling, Gewürztraminer and - most successfully of all - Pinot Gris.

One long valley area dominates Oregon production - the Willamette Valley. It occupies a northwestern corner of the state, near the Pacific coast, and enjoys the kinds of cool growing conditions that are to be found in parts of northern France. All of the finest Oregon producers are located here. Adelsheim, Ponzi and Eyrie make full-blown, creamy Pinot Gris (Eyrie is also tops for Chardonnay with its subtle, baked apple-flavoured Reserve bottling).

As to the celebrated Pinot Noirs, Elk Cove, Bethel Heights, Ponzi, Argyle and Sokol Blosser all make state-of-the-art, sweetly cherryish but ageworthy wines. Burgundy négociant Robert Drouhin bought a piece of Oregon real estate after absorbing the Eyrie Vineyards lesson in the '70s. His daughter Véronique has been making Pinot at the Oregon Domaine Drouhin since 1991, and has propelled it into a sharp upward swing.

Washington State In volume terms, Washington's production of *Vitis vinifera* wine is second only to that of California, and some say it is also first runner-up for quality. The two halves of the state are, climatically, chalk and cheese. While the seaward side has temperate, dampish conditions, the eastern half has sweltering summers and unforgivingly cold winters.

Notwithstanding that, nearly all the vineyard land is in the east, where the overall Columbia Valley AVA accounts for most of the wine produced. An important sub-region of Columbia - the Yakima Valley AVA - is home to some of the state's oldest vineyards.

Cabernet, and particularly Merlot, have proved themselves adept at coping with the climatic torments of eastern Washington, and generally yield round, emphatically fruity wines that are drinkable quite early on. Riesling, perhaps surprisingly, does well, and can produce outstandingly graceful dry and medium-dry styles - it seems a shame that the variety isn't especially popular among American consumers.

The inevitable Chardonnay, however, sells like hot cakes, and good, gently buttery stuff it is too. Semillon, not previously much lauded in the USA, looks like becoming something of a fad in Washington; the style is somewhat similar to the minerally dry, unoaked examples of Australia's Hunter Valley.

Oregon's cool Willamette Valley (above) dominates the state's wine industry, with the top producers clustered at the northern end of the valley.

While Oregon's vineyards lie close to the ocean, Washington's major wine regions are in the east, where the temperatures are more extreme, as in neighbouring Idaho (below).

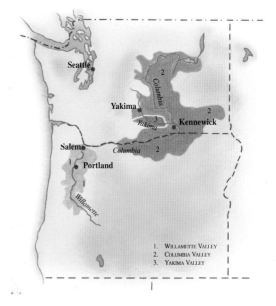

1. WILLAMETTE VALLEY
2. COLUMBIA VALLEY
3. YAKIMA VALLEY

Half of all Washington production is accounted for by one giant combine, Stimson Lane, which puts out wines under a number of labels such as Columbia Crest, Chateau Ste Michelle, Snoqualmie and so forth. Quality is good, if rarely idiosyncratic. Best of the smaller wineries include Hogue Cellars (which makes a beautifully subtle, lightly oaked Chardonnay), Staton Hills and Kiona (look for its delightfully well-made late-harvest sweet wines from the Alsace varieties Muscat, Gewürztraminer and Riesling).

Idaho Washington's eastern neighbour shares much the same climate as the Columbia Valley, except that Idaho's vineyards are planted at very high altitudes, making winter conditions here extremely severe. High-acid white varieties do better than Chardonnay, so Riesling and Chenin Blanc can be impressive. Against all the omens, Cabernet is beginning to yield some reassuringly ripe reds now. A single high-volume producer, Ste Chapelle, rules the Idaho roost, and its wines are generally good. However, most of the state's production doesn't travel much further than Washington State.

Riesling vines of Idaho's main producer, Ste Chapelle (above).

Vineyards spreading towards the water's edge in New York State's Finger Lakes AVA (right).

OTHER STATES

New York State Unlike the west coast states, in New York State the wine industry still relies to a significant extent on the native American vine species that grow wild in such profusion on the eastern side of America.

New York viticulture only really got under-way in the early years of the 19th century, not much before California's, although the eastern state had of course been settled for much longer. The principal growing region is the Finger Lakes AVA, a group of long, thin bodies of water in the centre of the state, south of Rochester. Long Island also has fairly extensive vineyards, and a pair of AVAs in The Hamptons and North Fork.

Seyval Blanc is important in New York State, as is the red variety Concord. Best of the international grapes have been Chardonnay (particularly good from the Finger Lakes winery Wagner and Long Island's Bridgehampton), Cabernet and Merlot (Hargrave, one of the Long Island pioneers of *vinifera* grapes, makes pedigree Cabernet) and some classically steely Riesling.

Texas The Lone Star state develops apace, and now has six AVAs. Its wine industry is essentially a recent creation dating from the 1970s, when the Llano Estacado winery set the ball rolling, making fine Cabernet, Chardonnay and Sauvignon near Lubbock. Now there are also Pheasant Ridge, Fall Creek and the ambitious Ste Genevieve - a joint venture with a négociant company in Bordeaux. Fall Creek makes a particularly good fist of varietal Carnelian, a crossing of Cabernet, Grenache and Carignan that has yielded disappointing results elsewhere.

Virginia Despite the fact that it has an uncompromisingly hot climate, some are tipping Virginia as a forthcoming story in American wine. Unusually, given the pretty torrid conditions, it has proved itself most adept so far at white wines. The Chardonnays are luscious enough to give the best of California a run for their money, while Semillon and Riesling also look promising. Reds are faltering for the time being.

Other states that may soon be capable of causing a stir in wine circles are **Missouri**, **Maryland** and **Pennsylvania**.

A coming region is the state of Virginia (above), where new plantings of classic white varieties are proving successful.

CANADA

Canada first attracted attention for its award-winning Icewines. Now, with plantings of popular international varieties, the country's producers are surging forward with an impressive range of styles.

Harvesting frozen Vidal grapes (above) in winter for Canada's speciality, Icewine.

Canada's two important wine-growing regions are divided by the vast country itself, with Ontario on the east coast, bordering New York State, and British Columbia on the west.

WHILE OTHER EMERGENT wine countries have targeted European markets with huge sales drives and promotional campaigning, Canada has quietly been developing its own industry at a rate that suits itself. The first wines to be released in the UK were made from hybrid grape varieties similar to those found in the eastern United States. They found the going pretty rough, as those who bothered to try them at all found the weirdly pungent flavours of wines like Maréchal Foch red quite baffling, even repellent. The impression was given that Canada couldn't really be a serious wine-producing country.

Happily, Canadian wine is poised in the new century to begin definitively reversing that notion. The way forward, as it will turn out to be in New York State, is with *Vitis vinifera* varieties. That hasn't necessarily been an easy solution in the harsh northern climate of Canada. Its summers are perfectly benign, but the several degrees of frost that can be relied on year in, year out in the winter months can be highly dangerous for the dormant vines. Nonetheless, patient perseverance has identified the most

suitable sites for a clutch of international varieties, and early results - many of these vines only came into full production in the last decade - are encouraging indeed.

At least one of the hybrids may still have a role to play in one important respect. The white Vidal grape has yielded some of the most lusciously concentrated examples of Icewine, which is rapidly turning out to be Canada's major speciality. After all, if you have sub-zero winters as a matter of course, you may as well put them to good effect. Canada's Icewine is made in exactly the same manner as Germany's, from grapes that are left to overripen on the vine and then freeze as night-time temperatures start to plummet with the onset of winter. When the frozen berries are harvested, they are quickly pressed so that the ice-pellets of water remain behind in the presses, and the sweet, concentrated juice runs free.

So favourable are the conditions for making Icewine that Canada has become the foremost world practitioner of the frozen arts. Most of it is made from either the hybrid Vidal or from Riesling. It easily attains the kind of sugar

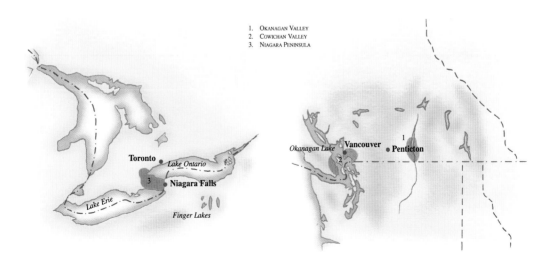

1. OKANAGAN VALLEY
2. COWICHAN VALLEY
3. NIAGARA PENINSULA

concentration (or "must weight", to give it its technical term) found in all but the very sweetest German and Austrian versions. Good acidity balances the apricot-syrup sweetness of the wines, so that, although irresistibly easy to drink on release, they are also capable of ageing in the bottle.

Dry table wines from hybrid grapes are not a noticeably attractive proposition. As well as Vidal, there is some of the Seyval Blanc grown in New York State and England, while the red grape Maréchal Foch is supported by the even less lovely Baco Noir. These varieties are the legacy of Canada's early wine pioneers in the 19th century. It is only since the 1970s that grapes more familiar (and more acceptable) to international tastes have been planted on anything like a significant scale.

Chardonnay and Riesling are the best whites so far, though some of the Alsace varieties are showing promise. Pinot Noir and a certain amount of light-textured Cabernet Sauvignon show progress among the reds. Cabernet Franc, with its naturally more delicate profile, may yet prove a better bet than its Cabernet cousin, making cranberryish Loire-style reds.

To demonstrate the seriousness of their endeavours, Canadian winemakers instituted a rudimentary appellation system in 1988, the Vintners Quality Alliance. To make the VQA grade, wines have to be sourced entirely from grapes grown in the defined regions and to have achieved minimum levels of ripeness. As plantings increase, so should the number of wines made under the auspices of the VQA system.

Canada's vineyards are located in four of its provinces. Of these, the first two listed below are by far the most important for quantity.

Ontario The province that borders New York State has similarly cool, marginal growing conditions. A degree of natural protection is afforded by a high ridge overlooking the main vineyard area that mitigates the worst effects of the climate. Riesling is a star performer here, from crisp dry styles to the celebrated Icewines, and Chardonnay too achieves good things in the style of steely Chablis and softer, gently oaked examples. Pinot Noir grown in these cool climes may very well turn out to be among North America's finest.

It was in Ontario's Niagara peninsula that the modern Canadian wine industry got going, with the innovative Inniskillin winery's first plantings in the 1970s. Its standard bottlings of

Chardonnay and Riesling are well-made wines, and - for those with a sense of gustatory adventure - Inniskillin does still make a Maréchal Foch varietal. Henry of Pelham is another of the more dynamic producers.

British Columbia Whereas most of Canada's vineyards lie in the Atlantic east of the country, the western province of British Columbia, way out on its own Pacific limb, is also participating in the quality wine movement. The Okanagan Valley in the southwest of the province is where the vineyards are found. Good varietals have been produced from Alsace grapes such as Pinot Blanc and Gewürztraminer, as well as Riesling of course, although some of the delicate Chardonnay has tended to be rather smothered with oak. Mission Hill is a name to look out for.

Quebec and Nova Scotia The other two eastern provinces to make wine have only a sparse scattering of vineyards. So far they are largely dedicated to the production of wines from hybrid grape varieties, although there are tentative plantings of Chardonnay.

The beautiful Okanagan Valley in British Columbia (above) is carving a name for itself for Alsace grape varieties.

SOUTH *and* CENTRAL AMERICA

Led by the great successes of Chile and Argentina, South America has become an important player in the southern hemisphere. Mexico, from where vines initially headed south with the Spanish, is also enjoying a revival.

ALTHOUGH WILD VINES flourished in Central America just as they did in the north, there is no indication, archaeological or otherwise, that winemaking was practised on the continent in pre-Columbian times. It took the arrival of the Spanish and then the Portuguese to develop systematic viticulture in Central and South America. The progress of vine cultivation occurred in a rapid southward march from Mexico, down through Peru to Chile and Argentina. Today, organised wine industries are to be found in around ten Latin American countries, from the major production of Argentina, whose export efforts are gathering momentum, to the very minor cultivation of mostly native species in Venezuela.

Climatically, Chile and Argentina offer the best wine-producing conditions in South America (below). There are also pockets of vineyards in Brazil and Uruguay.

For the purposes of the export markets, however, the flagship of South American wine so far has been Chile. Although its annual production is smaller than that of either Argentina or Brazil, Chile's wine industry moved up a gear in the 1980s. It won renown with its Cabernets and Chardonnays of course, and to a lesser extent with some Sauvignons and Merlots. Chile was proud not only to be producing wines that could hold their heads up in the best international company, but also to be attracting some big European names into the country. However, not the least powerful card in its hand was that Chile was virtually the only wine producer in the world never to have been invaded by phylloxera.

The worldwide epidemic of phylloxera began in the 1860s when it was carried to Europe on cuttings of North American vines. Within a very few years, it had swamped the continent, devastating vineyards, and forcing many growers beyond the limits of commercial survival. The antidote was eventually found in grafting new plantings of European varieties on to roots from American vine species, which had become immune to the louse. What was also observed, however, was that the one type of soil where it doesn't survive is sand. Those vineyards planted in coastal areas, where sandy soils predominate, tended to find the attack passed them by.

Chile's main protection lay in the circumstances of its geography. Since the country is, in essence, one long, narrow strip of Pacific coast, nearly all of its soil is sand-based. Furthermore, the natural bulwark of its border with Argentina, the Andes mountains, prevented what limited outbreaks of phylloxera arose in Argentina from spreading westwards. Chilean vines have, as a consequence, never had to be grafted, so that the wine being made today should still resemble - at least in theory - the wine of a century ago. (The fact is, of course, that modern viticultural and vinification practices mean that it would be very odd if it didn't taste considerably better.)

It can only be a matter of time before Argentinian wine starts making the same sorts of

1. BAJA CALIFORNIA
2. SONORA
3. HERMOSILLO
4. QUERETARO
5. ACONCAGUA
6. CENTRAL VALLEY
7. MENDOZA
8. RIO GRANDE DO SUL
9. CARPINTERIA
10. CERRO CHAPEU

New vineyard plantings of Cabernet in Chile (left). Vines do not need grafting on to phylloxera-resistant roots as the pest cannot thrive in the sand-based soils.

headlines as Chile did in the 1980s. Unlike Chile, the country has not significantly benefited from foreign investment, and the leaders of its wine industry are wary of straying into the new-kid-on-the-block trap that saw Chile fawned over and then dropped as the global wine circus moved on in search of the next novelty.

What will ultimately help Argentina is that it isn't entirely hidebound as to the varietals it produces. Malbec, one of the minor varieties in red Bordeaux, is accorded a status that it doesn't quite enjoy anywhere else outside Cahors (see southwest France). The perfumed white variety Torrontés, a relative of the one grown in Galicia in northwest Spain, is very widely planted and can make intensely fragrant wines with cleanly defined acidity.

The Andean mountains provide the vineyards of Mendoza in western Argentina, as well as the wine regions of central Chile, with one important viticultural advantage. In the searing, arid climates of South America, vines may very often be deprived of water at the point in the growing season when they most need it. There is sufficient rainfall in most of Europe for irrigation to be forbidden under EU wine regulations (although there are ways around the ban for the truly determined), but the hotter, drier countries couldn't manage without it.

The Spanish colonists and Jesuit missionaries bequeathed to the winemakers of Argentina and Chile a complex but highly efficient system of channelled irrigation, using the water that ran down from the mountains when

the snowcaps melted. To this day, it flows through the vineyards in carefully laid trenches, providing measured relief to the vines' roots.

The large Brazilian wine industry is, despite its scale, not geared for export at all, other than to one or two of its neighbours. That is mainly because it relies to such a far-reaching degree on hybrid grapes, principally Isabella, once common in California. With the steady increase in plantings of *Vitis vinifera* that recent years have seen, this could eventually change dramatically. Certainly, the volumes are there, although finding the right sites - even within the colossal Brazilian interior - is not the most straightforward of operations, owing to the enervating heat and humidity most of the country endures. Nearly all of the vineyards have been established in the relatively mild southern regions.

Mexico, the only other wine producer of significant scale on the continent, is where the whole American wine story started. Planted by Spanish *conquistadores* in the 1500s, the country's vineyards had gone into a seemingly terminal decline by the beginning of this century. Fiery spirits like mescal and tequila were for a long time the staple alcohol of the Mexicans, but in the last 30 years or so they have rediscovered an enthusiasm for wine, perhaps as a result of migrant workers who went to labour in the California vineyards coming back with a taste for it.

The revival is a happy event, as Mexico has provided ample proof within just one generation that it can make some superlative wine, especially from the southern French red varieties.

All over central Chile, new vineyard holdings are being established, making the country currently the most dynamic in South America (above).

Ploughing the old-fashioned way (above) in Argentina.

(Right) Three-quarters of Argentina's wines, and the finest, come from the western province of Mendoza, in the foothills of the Andes. Of the other four regions, Salta is producing the most notable wines.

1. MENDOZA
2. SAN JUAN
3. LA RIOJA
4. SALTA
5. RIO NEGRO

ARGENTINA

The vast majority of Argentina's vineyard land is in the western province of Mendoza, in the foothills of the Andes. The earliest vines were established here by Jesuit monks in the mid-16th century. It is a very dry region, and depends greatly on irrigation from melting mountain snow to prevent the vines from becoming terminally parched.

In the past, wine quality suffered from the fact that the slow, manual harvest was followed by an often arduous, hot journey to the nearest central winemaking plant, by which time the grapes were in less than prime condition. As elsewhere, the chief priority in bringing the country's viti-culture into the modern era has been investment in new technology that can speedily and hygieni-cally process the grapes at wineries constructed much nearer to the growing areas.

For many years, the mainstays of the Argen-tinian wine industry were a clutch of pink grape varieties that represent the hoi-polloi of South American winemaking: two variants of a grape called Criolla - Grande and Chica (the latter, known as País in Chile, was the important early Californian variety Mission) - and another called Cereza, whose name means "cherry".

These grapes can be vinified to produce a heavy, flat-tasting white wine with a distinct pinkish tinge or they can be blended with some-thing a little darker to make a still fairly bloodless red. They are the typical locally con-sumed wines that potential importers from abroad prefer to draw a veil over, and the grapes that make them will inevitably continue to yield ground in the vineyards to the international stars.

White grapes are dominated by an undistin-guished variety called Pedro Giménez (not to be confused with the Pedro Ximénez of Jerez) and the humdrum Muscat of Alexandria, which makes rather leaden sweet wines. The promising, aromatically citric Torrontés is accompanied by Chardonnay and Semillon for top-quality whites.

Malbec leads the field among reds, and is responsible for many of Argentina's most sophisticated, ageworthy red wines. Italian red grapes from Piedmont and Tuscany do well in this climate, as does Spain's Tempranillo. Cabernet and even a little speculative Syrah add to a rollcall that would make up most people's lists of pedigree red varieties.

Mendoza This is where about three-quarters of all Argentinian wine is made, and where all of the companies that have so far come to notice in the

export markets are based. The much-favoured Malbec heads the list of grapes planted, and is supported by Barbera, Sangiovese, Tempranillo and Cabernet. By and large, Mendoza Malbecs are rich, opulently damsony reds, with pronounced but controlled tannins and fairly overt oak influence. The Cabernets can be denser and darker still, often reminiscent of good *cru bourgeois* Médoc. White wine exports are, not unexpectedly, dominated by Chardonnay - fine, lightly buttery Chardonnay with beautifully weighted oak, in the case of Trapiche's top bottling - and there is even a little Sauvignon.

The Trapiche label is owned by a giant combine called Peñaflor, but its various cuvées offer both quality and value. Other good producers include Cavas de Weinert, Norton, Esmeralda, Lopez and Cateña.

San Juan The area north of Mendoza is important in terms of volume but not of the quality to balance it. With a much less forgiving climate to contend with than the Mendozans, San Juan's wineries have contented themselves with supplying the domestic market only.

La Rioja The scattered vineyards of La Rioja lie to the northeast of San Juan. Although this is where Argentinian wine probably started, there isn't much to stimulate the imagination now. There is not much call for flabby Muscats.

Salta The northwestern province of Salta is currently producing the best Argentinian wine after Mendoza. Here, some convincingly ripe Cabernet is produced, and the speciality Torrontés comes into its own. Etchart makes a fine example at Cafayate in the Calchaquies Valley, all orange-blossom and cinnamon on a crisp, appley base.

Rio Negro This southern region, as yet largely untapped, looks to have the best potential of all. Its cooler climate and more propitious soil types should make it a happy hunting-ground for new investors when the bandwagon starts to roll. White varietals such as Torrontés, Sauvignon, Chenin and the obligatory Chardonnay could well be among Argentina's finest, while sparkling wine production has been given a substantial fillip by the arrival of a posse of Champagne VIPs with money to spend.

Irrigation channels in a Mendoza vineyard (below). The water is sourced from the melting snowcaps of the Andes mountains.

Huge old oak fermentation vats at a vinery in Rio Grande do Sul, Brazil (above).

BRAZIL

Brazil's viticultural history fits the general pattern of most of the Americas. Colonists (Portuguese in this case) and missionaries planted the vine, slow vineyard expansion led to hybrid grapes churning out basic plonk by the 19th century, foreign investment arriving in the 20th century transformed the scene with sprinklings of Chardonnay and Cabernet and a splodge of Welschriesling.

In Brazil's case, the progress has been more lumbering than most, despite the fact that it is now one of the top three South American producers. Most of the country is simply too tropical for *vinifera* vines to cope with. Raging humidity and extremely high rainfall are not what even Chardonnay is used to, but in Rio Grande do Sul in the deep south of the country, conditions are more temperate. In the regions of Serra Gaucha and Frontera, the latter near the intersection of the borders of Brazil, Uruguay and Argentina, the best results so far are being achieved.

The greater part of the Brazilian vinescape is still planted with native species and hybrids, pre-eminent among them being Isabella (she once hung around California's vineyards, before

the smarter *vinifera* set moved in). As well as Chardonnay, most of the Bordeaux grapes, red and white, are planted, as well as a little optimistic Pinot Blanc and Gewürztraminer. Sparkling wine is made, mainly to cater for local tastes, although Moët has enough faith in it to have a commercial interest here, just as it does in Argentina.

Consumers availing themselves of one of the rare opportunites to taste Brazilian wine in the export markets may be surprised to find it all rather light and delicate - not at all what the climate would lead you to expect. That is because most of the winemakers are currently overcompensating by picking their grapes while they still have plenty of acidity in them. The theory is that they thereby retain fruity freshness; the unkind way of looking at it is the wines simply taste unripe. In the case of the reds, the lightness is of almost Bardolino proportions.

The Palomas company is about the most intensive exporter as far as Europe is concerned.

CHILE

The meteoric rise of Chilean wine in both European and North American markets in the late 1980s was one of the more sensational (and also more salutary) tales from the world of wine in latter times. Just as the consumer craze for southern-hemisphere wines was taking off, first and foremost within the UK, the prices of wines from Australia particularly were suddenly given a stiff hike. California wine has never been especially cheap in the first place, but bargain Chardonnays full of oak and sunshine from the valleys of South Australia were very much the name of the game. As prices elsewhere rose, Chile was poised to step into the breach.

With the exception of Shiraz, the Chilean industry had most of the big-name varietals that Australia produced, the fruit flavour was strong and convincing, and the national economy - working hard to emerge from its embargoed isolation under Pinochet - needed hard currency. Furthermore, not to be outdone by the Americans, Chile had its own French-bashing story to trail before the international wine press.

One of its premium Cabernet Sauvignons, from the Los Vascos winery in Rapel, went to Bordeaux, muscled in among the top châteaux and set their annual winefair alight. Breathless notices in the French press called it "Chile's *premier cru*". And so Chile found itself hailed as the hot new property.

Certain members of the international wine aristocracy had, to be sure, been convinced of the potential of Chile's vineyards as far back as the 1970s, when the Torres family of Catalonia bought some land. Château Lafite now has a stake in Los Vascos, flying winemaker Hugh Ryman helps out with the Discover company's Montes wines, while Napa Valley winery Franciscan is a force in Casablanca. In some ways, however, the stampede to Chile was a case of too much, too soon.

It wasn't that Chilean wine turned out to be disappointing, exactly. It was more the case that it proved initially more limited in stylistic range than Australia, to which it was unfairly being compared. What is fascinating now is to see the meeting of North and South that, between them, Chile's top Cabernets and Chardonnays represent. Many are made in a distinctly French style, the red wines with austere, backward tannins in their youth, the whites showing tantalisingly subtle oak seasoning and taut acidity. Others have nailed their colours to the southern-hemisphere mast, with voluptuous, essence-of-blackcurrant Cabernets and galumphing, wood-driven Chardonnays with plenty of attitude.

As to other varietals, Chile is now emerging as a producer of world-class Merlot (with the best wines showing enveloping aromas of black fruits and well-hung game à la Pomerol) and some vastly improved Sauvignon. In the latter case, one problem lies in the fact that what many growers have is not the noble gooseberries-and-asparagus Sauvignon Blanc, but a kind of country-bumpkin cousin called Sauvignon Vert or Sauvignonasse. The difference is apparent to even a relative beginner's tastebuds, but nothing on the label will warn you because the claim (largely emanating from the Sauvignonasse people, one suspects) is that you can't really tell them apart in the vineyard.

Chile has oodles of Semillon, but that has traditionally gone into the roughly made bottom-rung stuff the domestic market is happy with (or was, until home consumption started dropping like a stone in the 1980s). There are small quantities of Riesling, but that doesn't do too well in the baking climate. The latest success story, though, is much-improved Pinot Noir (outstanding from Cono Sur), which could give California Pinot Noir a hard time in Europe if enough growers master it. Speculative plantings of Syrah could be very exciting in time, sparkling *champaña* probably not.

Cabernet grapes arriving at the Santa Rita bodega (left), in Chile's Maipo Valley.

PRODUCE OF CHILE
1993
VILLA MONTES
Sauvignon Blanc
CURICO
Alc 12% vol   CHILEAN WHITE WINE   75 cl

A long narrow strip of land caught between the Pacific and the Andes, Chile (below) is blessed with sandy soils. The vineyards lie mainly in the centre of the country, where the climate is benign.

Valparaiso
Aconcagua
Santiago

1. ACONCAGUA
2. CASABLANCA
3. MAIPO
4. RAPEL
5. MAULE
6. BIO-BIO

Curicó

The most widely planted grape of all, however, is País, the feeble pink variety that is equally widespread as Criolla Chica in the vineyards of Andean neighbour Argentina. It produces precisely the same sort of thin, tasteless semi-red here as it does in Argentina, but is deeply traditional, and will thus take a generation or two to die out.

Most of Chile's vineyards lie in the climatically benign central section of the country, immediately south of the capital, Santiago. The smouldering heat of summer is mitigated to a significant degree by the proximity of the vineyards to the cooling influences of the Pacific Ocean, and irrigation is virtually as widely practised here as it is in Argentina. And no description of Chilean viticulture would be complete without mention of the celebrated fact that these mountain-protected, sandy vineyards are a no-go zone for the dreaded phylloxera.

Stainless-steel tanks at Montes winery, in Maule's Curicó area (above), symbolic of the investment in and influence of modern technology in Chile.

one of Chile's most far-sighted winemakers, Ignacio Recabarren. Casablanca's Sauvignons and Chardonnays are masterpieces of tropical fruit intensity, and there is also a Gewürztraminer that veers from forgettably dilute in one vintage to gorgeously aromatic and *alsacien* in the next. The Cabernets are cool-climate giants, stuffed with brooding tannins and chewy damson fruit.

Central Valley South of Aconcagua, the vineyards of the Central Valley and its various sub-regions are concentrated midway between the Andes and the Pacific. At the northern end is Maipo, just south of the capital. Cabernet is king once again, but there are some improving Sauvignons too, and the Chablis grower William Fèvre has also set up shop.

Recabarren of Casablanca makes more everyday wines here, under the Santa Carolina label. Viña Carmen is a promising new enterprise of the long-established Santa Rita winery. (Santa Rita itself makes one of the few recognisably good Rieslings in Chile.) Canepa has made a splash with a boldly fruity ground-breaking Zinfandel, while the house of Cousiño Macul is a bastion of tradition with its Antiguas Reservas Cabernets that can age for 20 years to a gamey, claret-like venerability.

Next south is Rapel, comprising the two valley districts of Cachapoal and Colchagua. The latter has been more important for export wines so far, the distinctive Cabernets of Los Vascos setting the pace, along with the innovative Pinot Noirs of Cono Sur. In Cachapoal, California's Clos du Val has invested in a winery called Viña Porta, which is making some world-class Cabernet and Chardonnay.

The Maule area is cooler again than Rapel, and includes the important wine centres of Curicó and Lontué, both of which are good for white wines, crunchy Sauvignons as well as lightly creamy Chardonnays. In Maule itself to the south, Merlot is beginning to show some real class as a varietal, particularly from the Terra Noble winery in Talca. Terra Noble's winemaker is from the Loire and, not surprisingly, makes a good Sauvignon Blanc too.

Bio-Bio The largest wine region, Bio-Bio, south of the Central Valley, is also the least interesting to date. It is considerably cooler and damper than Maule to the north, and is mostly carpeted with País. Undoubtedly, though, there is potential for the classic grapes, as soon as the big companies venture this far south.

Aconcagua/Casablanca The northernmost region for export wines is the Aconcagua, north of Santiago. It is named after both a river and the highest peak in the Andes. Cabernet Sauvignon is the grape best suited to the arid, broiling conditions here, where it achieves massive, pitch-black concentration in the premium wines of Errazuriz.

Southwest of the Aconcagua, nearer to the coast and the city of Valparaiso, the Casablanca district has been the main talking-point of Chilean wine in recent years. Here, the climate is much cooler, so much so that frosts in the spring are not at all uncommon, and the summer swelter is constantly mitigated by ocean breezes. Concha y Toro, which has a good range of Cabernets and Chardonnays (the Don Melchor Cabernet is the top cuvée), is located here, as is the Casablanca winery itself, brainchild of

MEXICO

When the *conquistadores* arrived from Spain in the wake of Columbus's voyages of discovery, Mexico was where they started their long triumphal sweep through Central and South America. Wherever anyone settled, vineyards were planted, so that something like the life back home could be replicated in the brave new Spanish world. The wine may not have tasted much like the produce of the motherland, but at least it was wine.

Wine production has always taken a back seat to distillation in Mexico, and the cactus spirits tequila and the originally hallucinogenic, now sanitised mescal were supplemented by brandy. Mexico actually produces one of the world's largest export brandies, Presidente, and much of its vineyards' yield is destined for the stills. However, faint flickerings of domestic interest, followed by the usual sporadic foreign investment, have created the bare bones of a modern wine industry.

Since the Spanish also once occupied what is now California from their Central American base, it comes as no surprise to find most of the vineyard land concentrated in the north of the country near the United States border. The Mexican state of Baja California is its premium growing area; along with the other main northern region, Sonora, this is where most of the wines with any chance of competing internationally will come from.

Southern French red varieties make up much of the vineyards, together with outposts of California grapes both old and new, including the historically significant Mission (Chile's País), a variety called Petite Sirah (nothing to do with Syrah, but actually another dark-skinned French grape Durif) and a spot of Zinfandel. Petite Sirah

has shown particular promise in producing a thick, savoury red at the L. A. Cetto winery, which also makes excellent Cabernet. Plantings of white grapes have not so far been of the more distinguished varieties. Sparklers may one day get a foot in the door, if the presence of the Spanish cava company Freixenet is anything to go by.

URUGUAY

If Brazil doesn't emerge to join Chile and Argentina as the next big South American wine country, then Uruguay could well be in the frame. The usual drawback of widespread hybrid vines is present, but a very broad-minded range of international *vinifera* varieties now supplements them. Just as Argentina has its Malbec, so Uruguay has made something of a speciality of one of the other lesser-known southern French grapes in Tannat, the often brutal red menace of Madiran. Uruguayan Tannat, however, seems better suited to its surroundings, and the Castel Pujol bottling, which spends several productive months in oak barrels, is a beauty - full of ripe purple fruits and dark chocolate richness.

Vineyards are planted in most parts of Uruguay, with those at Carpinteria in the centre of the country and Cerro Chapeu near the Brazilian border showing the most exciting promise. The industry has a long way to go before it can think seriously of exporting in any quantity, and a lot more investment is needed, but given the current outside interest in South America, that should certainly come.

Other South American wine producers, of no real significance outside their own national boundaries, are Peru (which was once the dominant source of wine on the continent), Bolivia, Ecuador and Venezuela.

An old timber-roofed wine bodega at Ensenada, Baja California, Mexico (above).

Traditional low-trained vines in Uruguay (left). Viticulture is practised all over the country.

SOUTH AFRICA

After a century of political strife, the South African wine industry is developing fast. The potential for quality wines is vast, and exciting times lie ahead for the country's winemakers.

VITICULTURE WAS among the very first enterprises of the Dutch settlers who arrived on the Cape of Good Hope in the mid-17th century. We don't know what grapes they brought with them, though it seems likely the cuttings would have come from Bordeaux. Early results were not immediately seized on with glee when they found their way back to the settlers' homeland, but a start had been made. What first put Cape winemaking on the map was the creation of one of those legendary dessert wines with which vinous history is littered.

Constantia was the name of an estate near Cape Town planted by colonial governor van der Stel barely 40 years after the new territory had been claimed by the Dutch. It made sweet wines in both colours from grapes that were left to overripen and then dry out on the vine. There is some uncertainty as to whether they were fortified, although analysis of the contents of antique bottles opened a few years ago suggests not. Perhaps some of the wine exported by sea was fortified to preserve it, as indeed was the developing practice at the time.

However that may be, the wines took Europe by storm. In the 18th and 19th centuries, they enjoyed a reputation so exalted that higher prices were paid for them than for any of the classic dessert or fortified wines of Europe. In

1861, Great Britain was the colonial power in the Cape. The Whig government of William Gladstone abolished the tariff relief that imported goods from outposts of the Empire had, until then, qualified for. This forced South African wines to compete on the same terms as those from suppliers much nearer their target market. It then only took the advent of the vine pest phylloxera, swinging through the Cape 25 years later on its triumphal world tour, to smash what was left of Constantia's edifice.

As South African wine found itself unable to compete in world markets, a colossal wine lake began to accumulate. Corporate action to deal with the resulting chaos and wastage was taken in 1918 with the establishment of the Ko-operatiewe Wijnbowers Vereniging, or KWV (Co-operative Winegrowers Association). This huge organisation exercised swingeing powers over the industry. It declared what could be planted where, how much of it could be produced and what the growers could sell it for. The initiative worked, but at the cost of steamrollering diversity. For many years, the only wines likely to be seen in export markets were bottled under the auspices of the KWV.

Excess production was sent for distillation into brandy, or was fortified to produce a range of wines - some with a resemblance to port, others more like madeira - that became something of a Cape speciality. The table wines were generally based on grapes that didn't enjoy

The Cape of Good Hope has always been the focus of wine-growing in South Africa (below). Even so, inland from the cooling Atlantic and Indian oceans, the climate here can still be hot and humid.

1. OLIFANTS RIVER
2. SWARTLAND
3. PAARL
4. DURBANVILLE
5. CONSTANTIA
6. STELLENBOSCH
7. ELGIN
8. WALKER BAY
9. WORCESTER/TULBAGH
10. ROBERTSON
11. KLEIN KAROO

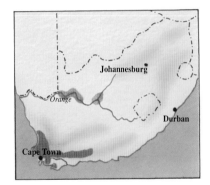

huge cachet in knowledgeable circles. Acidic Chenin Blanc (known in South Africa as Steen) and thin red Cinsaut were not really anybody's flavour of the month. The chance to branch out was now stymied by two factors. One was the stranglehold that the KWV still had over all Cape production, and the other was the world-wide trade boycott of the apartheid era.

Boycotts are never wholly effective. The longer they persist, the more holes are punched in them by those determined to make money where others refuse to tread. But the boycott of South African goods was unusually tenacious. While European governments declined to take part, individual consumers shunned Cape pro-duce almost as an article of faith. The effect, on the wine industry in particular, was crippling. It was unable to attract any significant outside expertise and, although it was powerful enough to export its wines at prices that should have enabled them to compete with the very humblest of European rustic slosh, they basically failed to sell.

With the political settlement of the early 1990s came the long-awaited denuding of the powers of the KWV. Small private growers began to plant the varieties they chose, inward

investment started to flow and South Africa is consequently poised to move in among the giants of the southern hemisphere and ruffle a few feathers. The current picture is one of happy confusion, with growers going off at their own tangents all over the place, but some of the wines reaching Europe - Chardonnays, Gewürztraminers, Merlots and even Pinot Noirs - are evoking gasps of astonishment that so much has been achieved in such a short time.

The appellation system that South Africa inaugurated in 1973 remains a very imprecise one. It is broadly geographically based, and involves certification of wines by panels of tasters, but doesn't make any imposition as to yields. Vintage-dated wine is generously allowed to contain up to 25 per cent of wine made in the years immediately before and after that stated on the label.

Regional definitions are often so loosely drawn as to be meaningless. If a wine entered for classification is passed, it receives a special seal that proclaims it to be a Wine of Origin (WO). As the industry gets into its stride, this system will presumably be tightened up, and something more closely analogous to the *appel-lation contrôlée* system will be formulated.

Harvesting Sauvignon grapes at Klein Constantia (above), in the Cape.

The manor house at Klein Constantia (below), the smallest of the three producers that make up the small, yet famous, Constantia wine region.

Looking out across the stunning Paarl region from Fairview Estate (above). Paarl produces the full range of South African wine styles.

It is quite plain that the century-long nightmare that South African winemaking suffered has been put firmly behind it. Producers may be forgiven for regretting the fact that their chance to shine has come at a time when there are more competitors in the field of wine than at any other period in viticultural history. That a resurgence of Cape wine is in the offing is not in any doubt.

In a country whose climate is so propitious for the production of concentrated, rich red wines, it may come as some surprise to learn that no less than 85 per cent of the vineyard land is planted with white varieties. The South African preference, however, beyond the speciality fortified market, was for light white wines to quench the thirst, rather than complex reds for ageing in the bottle. It is expected the balance of red to white varieties will gradually change as the Cape begins to win plaudits for its Bordeaux-style blends and Shiraz.

Chief among the whites is Steen (what most of the rest of the world knows as Chenin Blanc). It is encouraged to perform with as much versatility as it does in France's Touraine. Its repertoire ranges from almost excruciatingly sharp, young dry wines, through the ever-popular off-dry style (like demi-sec Vouvray) at which the grape excels, all the way up to honeyed, liquorous dessert wines made from grapes picked after the main harvest. Colombard, a French import from the Cognac region, was traditionally important in South Africa's brandy industry too, and is often used to make light dry whites. As a varietal, however, it has little character other than a waxy coarseness not designed to endear it to the Chardonnay set.

Chardonnay itself is spreading like wildfire, as is Sauvignon Blanc which, in some of the cooler areas, is turning out some superbly complex, smoky Loire-style whites. Crouchen is a French variety the French have long since forgotten but that South Africa found a place for in its history; they confusingly call it Cape Riesling. The real Riesling is here as well, generally known as Weisser (White) Riesling. Ugni Blanc (Italy's Trebbiano) is just the sort of neutral grape beloved of brandy producers, but only contributes to diluting any character in a blended white wine. Both of the two main Muscats are used for producing sweet and fortified wines. Most promisingly, some growers are achieving highly impressive results with Gewürztraminer, especially in the Paarl region.

devices, it doesn't amount to much, but it was one of the minor components of Constantia, and is still grown on part of the old estate in readiness to play a role in the wine's resurgence.

Most of South Africa's wine regions are located in the southwest of the country, where the vineyards benefit to greater and lesser degrees from the cooling maritime influence of both the Atlantic and Indian Oceans. Most of the interior is too hot for successful viticulture, although there are some recently established vineyards around the Orange River in the centre of the country. Although winters are usually damp and windy, the growing season is characterised by prolonged hot and arid weather conditions. Irrigation is routinely practised by most Cape vineyards, although not quite to the extent that South American growers have to resort to.

Vergelegen's highly functional cuvier (below), in Stellenbosch, where viticulture dates right back to the Dutch colonists' arrival in the 17th century.

As to red grapes, the most widely planted variety traditionally was Cinsaut, one of the less distinguished southern French reds. The pedigree gang are all here, though: Cabernets Sauvignon and Franc, Merlot, Syrah (given its Australian name, Shiraz, on the Cape), Pinot Noir and even a little Gamay. There is even a smattering of Zinfandel.

South Africa's equivalent of Zinfandel, a grape they can call their own, is Pinotage. It is a crossing of the ubiquitous Cinsaut with Pinot Noir. If that sounds a rather clumsily arranged marriage, many would agree. Like Zinfandel, there are three Pinotage styles: simple rosé, light, Beaujolais-like red and a deeper, often barrel-aged version. At its most basic, it has a hard-to-pin-down fruit flavour veering towards little pippy berries like cranberries or redcurrants. Made in the more lavish idiom, it can be almost Rhône-like, with lush raspberry fruit and sinewy density of texture, reflecting at least one half of its parentage.

The Cape pantheon of red grapes includes a French variety long since abandoned in its homeland. Pontac, named after one of the more illustrious families in Bordeaux history, is actually rather a rustic grape. Left to its own

La Concorde (below), head-quarters of the KWV (Co-operative Winegrowers Association) in Paarl.

The following guide to the regions moves anti-clockwise around the Cape.

Olifants River Primarily a source of bulk wine for distillation, the mountainous Olifants River area is home to several of the major Cape co-operative producers. The biggest of these, Vredendal, is actually one of the better practitioners, with some appetising Chardonnays and Sauvignons. Its Goiya Kgeisje is an early-bottled fruity-fresh Sauvignon-based white, its flavours presenting considerably less of a challenge to European tongues than its name. Sweet Muscat wines are locally popular. Red wine production is only a marginal activity.

Swartland The blackish scrubland of this large, mostly very hot region gives the area its name (meaning "black land"). Notwithstanding the heat, Sauvignon Blanc is curiously one of its best varietals, as in the smoky and nettly Reuilly or Quincy lookalike from the Swartland co-operative for example. Pinotage does well, achieving some of its more concentrated results here. A measure of how promising this sort of climatic context is for thick-skinned red varieties that can take more ripening than most is the

success of Tinta Barocca. One of the mainstay grapes of port production, it makes an intriguing, plums-and-pepper varietal at the Allesverloren estate.

Paarl With Stellenbosch, this is one of the Cape regions that has made the headlines in the export trade in recent years. It is where the once all-powerful KWV is based, and still represents the epicentre of the whole South African wine enterprise. One of the hotter regions as a result of lying completely inland, Paarl nonetheless produces the full range of South African wine styles, from crisp, light dry whites and sparklers to full, long-lived reds and excellent fortified wines, as well as some of the country's premium brandies.

All of the major varietals are made in Paarl. The Nederburg estate is one of the largest private producers, making some succulent Chardonnay and some not-so-succulent Pinotage. Fairview Estate is representative of the modern South African outlook, making an impressively diverse range of top varietals. These include cherry-fruited Gamay rather like a young Brouilly, minerally Semillon, steely Chenin Blanc and a particularly well-crafted Gewürztraminer that, sometimes seasoned with a dash of Riesling, comes close to the fullness and weight of Alsace versions.

Villiera also does good Gewürz, as well as sensationally intense Sauvignon (sometimes with as much exuberant fruit as New Zealand growers typically obtain), while Backsberg makes creditable Chardonnay and Shiraz. The Glen Carlou estate is notable for one of the Cape's best Pinot Noirs to date, with a headily perfumed Turkish Delight quality, as well as persuasively Burgundian Chardonnay.

In the southeast of the region is a valley enclave called Franschhoek (meaning "French corner", after its original settlers). It could be that some of Paarl's best wines will come from here in future, or perhaps that it will simply come to be seen as a region in its own right. High flyers so far have been Dieu Donné, whose superb Chardonnay is in the buttered-green-bean Côte de Beaune mode, La Motte with its brambly Shiraz, and the big-scale Boschendal operation, renowned for plump Merlot, richly oaky contemporary Chardonnay and crisp, well-made sparkling wine. Clos Cabrière is a specialist in champagne-method fizz.

The KWV still makes its sherry-style fortifieds in Paarl, maturing the dry ones under a *flor*-style yeast layer and putting them through a *solera*

Meerlust Estate in Stellenbosch (left), with the Helderberg mountain beyond.

Modern equipment and new oak barrels (above) at Klein Constantia.

system. Its portfolio doesn't stop at wine, however, but goes on to encompass several spirits, as well as the once-popular Van der Hum, a kind of South African Grand Marnier whose name translates as something like Thingummyjig.

Durbanville Like many another small vineyard region that lies in the shadow of a major city, Durbanville's existence is being threatened by the urban expansion of Cape Town. It won't consequently play a significant role in South Africa's wine renaissance.

Constantia The old, sprawling estate where South Africa's greatest wines were made was eventually broken up and divided among three proprietors, the largest of them - Groot Constantia - state-owned. The result is that Constantia is effectively now a little wine region, rather than a single property. Of the two privately owned portions, one is in German hands, while the smallest of them all, Klein Constantia, has so far proved itself the most visionary. As well as producing splendid modern varietals in the shape of Sauvignon and Chardonnay (together with a less than compelling Cabernet), it has been the first to make a serious attempt to revive the fortified Constantia of blessed memory. The early efforts - rechristened Vin de Constance - are hugely encouraging.

Stellenbosch Viticulture in the coastal Stellenbosch region, south of Paarl, dates back to the first generation of Dutch colonists. Today, it is home to more of South Africa's first-division wine estates than any other district. Benefiting from their proximity to the ocean, the vineyards of Stellenbosch regularly produce the best-balanced red wines of the Cape. At the heart of the region is the town of Stellenbosch itself, headquarters of the Republic's principal viticultural research institute.

Blended red wines, often using all three of the main Bordeaux varieties, are usually a better bet than varietal Cabernet, which characteristically lacks the class of other examples from the southern hemisphere. Warwick Farm's Trilogy bottling is a good blend, in the unashamedly austere Bordeaux vein, as is the Paul Sauer cuvée from Kanonkop. The latter estate also makes one of the more charming Pinotages. Neetlingshof is an enterprising producer, making a couple of aromatic Alsace varietals as well as expressive late-picked sweet wines.

Sauvignon Blanc from the Uitkyk estate is impressive, while Thelema has won plaudits for its rounded, golden Chardonnay and a voluptuously silky Merlot of great power and presence. Avontuur's Reserve is one of the more convincing varietal Cabernets. Mulderbosch's Sauvignons are everything good Sauvignon should be - either oak-fermented or *au naturel* - and Stellenzicht makes an enterprising, though fairly tart, light Zinfandel, plus some lusciously intense dessert wines, including a botrytised Sauvignon-Semillon labelled Noble Late Harvest.

PRODUCE OF SOUTH AFRICA

THELEMA
1991
Cabernet Sauvignon
Merlot

WINE OF ORIGIN STELLENBOSCH
Grown, produced and bottled by
THELEMA MOUNTAIN VINEYARDS,
HELSHOOGTE, STELLENBOSCH
750 ml   15% Alc. Vol.

Clearsprings
Cape White

Produced and Bottled by Simonsvlei
Co-op Winery, Paarl

Barrel cellar of Graham Beck Winery in the Robertson region (above), renowned for its Madeba Sauvignons.

Elgin One of South Africa's newer wine regions, following the recent trend to plant vineyards at higher altitude in order to benefit from cooler growing conditions. Elgin may turn out to be a good source of varietals from northern French grapes such as Sauvignon, Chenin and especially Pinot Noir.

Walker Bay Further east along the coast, near the town of Hermanus, Walker Bay is already ahead of Elgin in the race to produce cool-climate varietals, and with greater subtlety than has been the norm hitherto. Chardonnay and Pinot Noir are both looking good, and one of the larger Burgundy négociant houses has entered into a joint venture, Bouchard-Finlayson, to bring a little piece of the Côte d'Or to the Cape. Their wines, as well as those of Hamilton Russell, show what can be done. Not all of the vintages to date have been spot-on, but the potential is indisputable. Bouchard-Finlayson also makes a clean, snappy Sauvignon. The Wildekrans estate weighs in with some highly typical Pinotage.

Worcester The Worcester and Tulbagh regions lie well inland, northeast of Paarl, and are largely occupied by volume-producing co-operatives making old-fashioned fortifieds. The Muscat and Muscatel varieties (the latter may be red or white) are responsible for producing sweet wines in a number of styles. Jerepigo is made either from red or white Muscatel, the production method similar to that used in Moscatel de Valencia and certain Portuguese equivalents. Intensely sweet, fresh grape juice is fortified with the addition of grape spirit before it has had a chance to ferment, resulting in a not unexpectedly grapy sweet wine at around 17 per cent alcohol. The whites are lightly refreshing, the reds more seriously blood-warming.

The Tulbagh sub-region, to the northwest of Worcester, has produced one of the most admirable sparkling wines yet with the Krone Borealis Brut from the Twee Jongegezellen winery, despite the fact that this is not theoretically the right sort of climate for fizz.

Robertson Robertson is another of South Africa's up-and-coming wine regions. Located well back in the hinterland, it is hot and steamy, its vineyards heavily dependent on irrigation. Nonetheless, it has emerged as a premier-league producer of white wines rather than red. Pre-eminent among these are Chardonnays, with plenty of fleshy, chunky Colombards and more of that super-ripe, eminently fortifiable Muscat and Muscatel.

De Wetshof has worn the yellow jersey so far in the Tour de Chardonnay, its Danie de Wet cuvées aged on their lees to produce an indulgently rich, buttercream style with powerful appeal. Van Loveren's are almost as good. Sauvignons from this region are now exhibiting plenty of lush tropical fruit, and the Madeba bottling from Graham Beck is replete with pretty convincing gooseberry character. Beck also makes fine Chardonnay called Lone Hill and one of the region's more conspicuously successful sparklers, Madeba Brut. Among the rare reds of any note is a Shiraz from the Zandvliet estate.

Klein Karoo Sprawling landlocked region where fortified Muscatels are best suited to the indomitable heat, though a few producers are chancing their arm with dry varietal table wines.

Mossel Bay Like Walker Bay and Elgin, this easterly coastal area is a newly established wine region designed to benefit from the ameliorating sea breezes, in this case blowing in from the Indian Ocean. Cool-climate varieties are what the growers are putting their faith in, with Pinot Noir at the pinnacle of ambition as usual, supplemented by Riesling and Sauvignon Blanc. Given time to find a foothold, the wines should be excellent.

Orange River To the west of the landlocked state of Lesotho, the Orange River region is South Africa's climatically fiercest wine area, its riverside vineyards further from maritime influence than any on the Cape itself. Volume production is the chief activity; since the vines have to be so intensively irrigated, the amount of fruit they bear is correspondingly far too high for quality. Nobody is going to make great varietals around here.

SPARKLING WINES

South Africa is continually growing in confidence as a producer of sparkling wines, and has come a long way in the few short years since all it could really offer was KWV Mousseux. So important has the current generation of Cape fizzes become that a new country-wide term, Méthode Cap Classique (MCC), has been instituted to describe any sparkler produced using the traditional bottle-fermentation method of Champagne. A measure of the maturity of the nascent industry is that nobody tries to label their wines as "Champagne" for the domestic market, where the EU writ doesn't apply. (If only all non-European fizz producers could claim as much.)

Some of these sparkling wines are made from the classic Chardonnay-Pinot Noir blend, others may have a dash of something non-*champenois* like Chenin in them, but the overall quality is becoming frankly breathtaking. Indeed, we may not be too far away from being able to claim that they are the best such wines made anywhere outside Champagne itself. Given that the traditional method is literally only a product of the 1980s in South Africa, this achievement is highly commendable. There are now around 40 wineries making MCC sparklers, and the atmosphere of healthy competition is acting as a powerful impetus for excellence.

What has been notably striking about many of the early releases is the degree of yeast autolysis they display. Autolysis is the name for the biochemical interchange that takes place within the wine as it undergoes its second fermentation in the bottle. As the active yeasts die off, the dead cells impart a distinctive aroma and flavour to the wine, a kind of pungent wheat-grain character reminiscent of freshly baked biscuits. The more pronounced it is, the longer by definition the wine must have spent maturing on its lees before being disgorged. There is no surer indication that a sparkling wine producer means business than when it allows its wines a healthy maturation period before release. In the context of South Africa's fledgling industry, it is all the more impressive.

BEST OF THE EXPORTED FIZZES TO DATE: Krone Borealis Brut (from Twee Jongegezellen in Stellenbosch), Pierre Jourdan Brut and Blanc de Blancs (from Clos Cabrière in Franschhoek), Pongracz (made by the Bergkelder co-operative in Stellenbosch), Graham Beck Madeba Brut (Robertson), Boschendal (Franschhoek), Simonsig Kaapse Vonkel (Stellenbosch).

Look out also for a strange but eventually likeable sparkling Sauvignon Blanc from the Bergkelder. Not a grape variety normally noted for its contribution to sparkling wines, this ultra-fresh, grassy, bone-dry fizz makes a diverting summer aperitif.

Pressing Chardonnay grapes (above) destined for the Cap Classique sparkler, Madeba Brut, at Graham Beck Winery in Robertson.

This gleaming white, intricately gabled façade (left) belongs to the manor house of the Boschendal estate in Franschhoek, Paarl.

AUSTRALIA

Leaders in the triumphal march of the varietal movement, Australia's winemakers have taken Chardonnay and Cabernet Sauvignon, added Shiraz to the list, and recreated them in styles all of their own.

ONE NAME MORE than any other is responsible for keeping Europe's wine-makers awake at night. The shudders of apprehension that the mere mention of Australia evokes are not hard to understand. It isn't just the speed with which its wines went from a mere trickle in northern-hemisphere markets at the beginning of the 1980s to an unstoppable surge by the end of the decade. It isn't just the indigni-ty of having squadrons of Australian consultants arriving in the Midi, in Trentino, in the Alentejo, to point out how things could be done better. It is, at bottom, the fact that of all the newer non-European winemaking countries, Australia is the least in thrall to European ways of doing things.

Australia's wine industry is effectively scarcely any older than that of the USA and quite considerably younger than South Africa's. (In fact, some of the earliest vine cuttings to be brought into the country came from the Cape, including the all-important Shiraz.) Unlike North America, Australia had no wild vines, and nor has its industry ever had to go through the painful process of freeing itself from hybrid varieties like California's Isabella and the others.

By the early years of the 20th century, Aus-tralian wine was finding its way to Britain through the channels of the Commonwealth in significant quantities. There was a certain amount of unsubtle table wine, but the bulk of what was coming in was fortified - passable approximations of port that were long forgotten by the time the contemporary wine boom began. One of the first red wine brands to brave the British wine trade in the postwar era was market-ed as Kanga Rouge, exhibiting about the same level of self-esteem as Algeria's Red Infuriator.

What changed everything was the advent of Chardonnay and Cabernet Sauvignon. While California wines from those two grapes were winning prizes in French tastings, Australia's growers were just about planting their first experimental cuttings. But if Chardonnay and Cabernet have become the Esperanto of the

Australia's vineyards run in a swathe across the south-east of the continent, as well as popping up in enclaves in Western Australia and on the island of Tasmania.

modern wine-drinker, they have done so more as a result of their Australian manifestations than any of their rivals. Winemakers in the Barossa and Hunter Valleys, in the Adelaide Hills and Victoria, taught the non-specialist wine consumer varietal recognition by making the wines so easy to love. They took the red-hot, mouth-drying tannins out of Cabernet, and the steely acidity out of a lot of traditional Chardonnay, and marinated them both in the sweet vanillin of brand new oak, and the rest is history.

Fuelling this development was the importance within Australia itself of wine shows. All of the wine-producing states regularly hold their own regional competitions, in which wines are tasted blind and awarded medals, rather in the manner of the UK's International Wine Challenge organised by WINE Magazine.

The awards have a high profile within the domestic trade, with gold-medal bottles flying off retailers' shelves as fast as they can sell them. Consequently, many winemakers have come to fashion their wines in a style that will help them to command attention in a long line-up of other similar wines. These have become known, not always flatteringly in some circles, as "show wines" - big, brash, love-me-or-leave-me types designed to make an immediate impact but not always easy to drink in any quantity.

To some extent, there is justice in this case. Australia makes the richest, oakiest, yellowest, most upfront Chardonnays in the world, wines that have no trouble in attaining 14 per cent alcohol. But it would be entirely misleading to suggest that all Australian Chardonnay tastes like that. Revolutions need to be ushered in by some headline-grabbing act that stirs the hearts of potential followers, and the zeal with which those first wines were seized on by British (and even American) consumers told its own story.

The Chardonnays were followed by Cabernets and Shirazes and blends thereof. Those who are phobic about red wine because they associate it with harsh tannins and vinegary sourness were encouraged by these wines to abandon their prejudices. Then there were sparkling wines that tasted of ripe summer fruits, mango-scented whites and strawberry-perfumed rosés, selling in Britain for as little as a third the price of non-vintage champagne at a time when the champagne producers were having one of their collective dizzy spells.

Behind them came a phalanx of fortifieds, liqueur Muscats unlike any other *vins de liqueur* on earth, headily redolent of smoky tangerine and creamy milk chocolate. It all added up to a non-stop scattergun strategy, and it worked like a dream.

Opening the vintage (above) at the annual Barossa Festival, in South Australia.

Morning sunlight over the northern slopes of the Great Dividing Range (below), in Victoria.

Margaret River (above) is one of Australia's cooler wine-growing regions.

nearer the equator, have a correspondingly fiercer climate to contend with, in which the spring can bring virtual drought while the harvest season suffers torrential rains.

The vineyards are strung throughout a swathe of southeast Australia, from north of Adelaide in the state of South Australia, through Victoria and up to the Hunter Valley north of Sydney. There is a small outpost on a high plateau called the Granite Belt just into Queensland, as well as small but important plantings in the state of Western Australia. The island of Tasmania, in the Tasman Sea between Australia and New Zealand, has isolated vineyards, mainly on its northern edge.

There is a regulatory system in Australia's wine industry. It covers the expected three principal features of labelling: region of origin (a minimum of 85 per cent of wine so labelled must come from the specified area), grape variety (85 per cent again) and vintage (95 per cent). To an even greater extent than in California, however, Australian wine is often made from grapes that are grown in areas quite distant from the winery itself, with the produce of different areas being blended in the same cuvée. A rough-and-ready appellation system allows wines to be considered of GI (Geographic Indication) status if the 85% rule for grape sourcing is observed, but the process of mapping out the GI regions has been bedevilled by non-stop wrangling.

Australia's premium white grape varieties are led by Chardonnay, planted more or less wherever vines are grown. At best, it produces the broad-beamed, sunny, golden wines the world has come to adore, with subtle variations of style according to sites chosen and the vinification regimes of individual winemakers. Some is kept back for blending as a crowd-pulling component with other grapes such as Semillon and Colombard.

After Chardonnay comes Riesling (more often than not known as Rhine Riesling). In many ways the backbone of fine white wine, it is still top dog in South Australia, but has been overtaken nationally in the last few years by the vogue for Chardie. Riesling gives a fatter, riper wine here than in Europe, but one that is quite as capable of developing interestingly in the bottle. Semillon shares that characteristic, but is very much an Australian original in its dry, unoaked and unblended guise. Always popular in Australia itself, it has had to be patient in awaiting international recognition.

The result of Australia-mania has been that some commentators have tended to say the country's wine philosophy emphasises instant commercial appeal at the expense of traditional vinous complexity. The wines don't age, runs the line; they are all about primary fruit and oaky richness and not much else. Like all the old generalities, that statement is there to be shot at by a wave of practitioners intent on competing with the best the world has to offer. Perhaps we will after all see a more European orientation creeping in, especially for those varietals in which the first generation of export wines frankly did not excel - Sauvignon Blanc, for example, and Pinot Noir.

Whatever modulations may arise in the coming years, though, Australia has established itself a solid bridgehead into the global wine village, and it did so - however hard it may be for the French and others to swallow - more quickly and decisively than was achieved by any other emergent nation in wine history.

Most of Australia's regions experience reliably hot, dry growing conditions year on year. Within the overall pattern, however, there are cooler pockets where more temperate summers have a consequent effect on wine styles. They include the Margaret River area of Western Australia, inland regions such the Clare and Eden valleys in South Australia and much of Tasmania. By contrast, the vineyards of New South Wales and Queensland, being that much

Sauvignon Blanc is occasionally blended with Semillon, as in Bordeaux, but more is often seen on its own. It is a grape that many winemakers are only just learning how to handle, early examples often suffering from a lack of clarity or inappropriate and excessive oaking.

Other classic white grapes planted in small quantities include Gewürztraminer, the Rhône grape Marsanne, and Chenin Blanc.

In addition to those, there are widespread plantings in the irrigated Murray River region of South Australia of an indifferent white variety called Sultana. As its name implies, much of it ends up being processed as dried grapes, but a lot is still used for wine, often the bulk output of bag-in-box wines that account for an important proportion of the domestic market. Muscat of Alexandria, which goes under the local name of Muscat Gordo Blanco, also plays a role in volume production, and is not an ingredient of the premium liqueur Muscats. Colombard is grown too, but on nothing like the scale that it appears in South Africa.

Chief among reds is Shiraz (the Syrah of the northern Rhône), another grape that Australia fashioned in its own image. The reds of the northern Rhône are varietal Syrahs too of course, but the southern-hemisphere style is hugely rich, creamy and blackberryish, with little or none of the black pepper or sharp tannins of young Hermitage. It is best exemplified by the wines of Barossa. At its least sensitively vinified, Shiraz can turn out roaringly alcoholic wines with a blurred, cooked flavour like jam, the sweetness of which is then made the more cloying with extended oak-ageing. Thankfully, these wines are by no means the norm for exports.

Shiraz is frequently blended with Cabernet Sauvignon, generally forming the greater element in the mix. The effect can be to stiffen the sinew of the otherwise soft-centred ripe Shiraz, or to mitigate some of young Cabernet's severity where Shiraz is the minor partner. Cabernet is also valued as a varietal in its own right, though, and can offer incontrovertible evidence to those inclined to be sceptical about the winetaster's vocabulary that Cabernet Sauvignon really can taste intensely of blackcurrants.

Increasingly, if Cabernet is blended, it is with its traditional claret bedfellows, Merlot and Cabernet Franc. They are both currently grabbing themselves ever-increasing shares of vineyard land across Australia. One consequence may well be more varietal Merlot, not

hitherto - and unusually in the southern hemisphere - one of Australia's specialities.

Grenache looked until recently as if it might be doomed to die out as a humdrum variety used to bulk everyday reds. Just lately, however, it is beginning to hog a share of the limelight as certain winemakers discover it will make a hugely concentrated Shiraz-style red of undeniable pedigree. Pinot Noir is coming on apace as well. Much of it goes into premium bottle-fermented sparkling wines conceived in the champagne image, but there are doughty souls, as there are wherever quality red wine is made, determined to make world-class red varietal Pinot. The first signs of success are with us already, as suitable sites are identified for the famously unforgiving grape.

Minority red grapes take in the Mourvèdre of the southern Rhône and Languedoc - here usually known as Mataro - and Tarrango, a crossing of white Sultana with the port grape Touriga Nacional. It is vinified by some (notably Brown Brothers) in the style of a muscular Dolcetto.

The grounds of St Hallett's in Barossa Valley (below), where 100-year-old Shiraz vines still yield fabulous wines.

Red gum trees in Western Australia (above) flower at grape-harvest time, distracting birds from eating the grapes.

LEEUWIN ESTATE

Western Australia's vineyards lie at the southwestern tip of the state (right), with the top producers clustered in the Margaret River region close to the Indian Ocean.

WESTERN AUSTRALIA

Swan Valley One of the very hottest wine regions in a hot country, the Swan Valley was once the main growing area of Western Australia. It is now of declining importance as a result of the identification of cooler sites further south. Notwithstanding that, the Houghton winery still makes a range of decent generic wines here, together with improbable varietals bottled under the Moondah Brook label, such as Chenin Blanc and Verdelho (the latter one of the white grapes of Madeira). Evans & Tate makes a Semillon that bears a positively uncanny resemblance to smoky Sauvignon.

1. SWAN VALLEY
2. MARGARET RIVER
3. LOWER GREAT SOUTHERN
4. SOUTHWEST COASTAL PLAIN

Perth

Margaret
Margaret River

Frankland

3 **Mount Barker**

Albany

Margaret River One of the great talking-points of Australian wine lately, the milder climate of the Margaret River district has led to the production of some intriguing wines in a considerably less upfront style than is tradition-ally associated with Australia. Cooling breezes off the Indian Ocean exert a moderating influence here, in a country that doesn't generally receive the same maritime amelioration that, say, South Africa or the western US states do. Consequent-ly, the Margaret River's Chardonnays have an almost Burgundian profile and may require much less acid adjustment than those from South Aus-tralia, while the Cabernets are leaner and more closed in their youth. Sauvignons are briskly fresh and herbaceous, while the Semillons are crisp but healthily rounded.

Cullens is one of Margaret River's best estates, making nutty, savoury Chardonnay in a restrained style. Moss Wood makes a slightly richer version that, in some vintages, has the unmistakable waft of shredded cabbage familiar to lovers of Puligny-Montrachet. Cullens also makes a bench-mark toasty Semillon without oak (as well as one with) and impressive Pinot Noir. Cape Mentelle, the winery that founded the show-stopping Cloudy Bay in New Zealand, has its Australian base in this district, where it produces an apple-and-melon blend of Semillon and Sauvignon and even has some plantings of Zinfandel.

Leeuwin Estate is one of the most ambitious wineries in all of Australia. Its expensive but indisputably brilliant Chardonnay is an object-lesson to others. A varietally intense Cabernet and deep, resonant Pinot show its versatile abilities to the full. The long-established Vasse Felix winery's Shiraz is plump and rich, without slumping into jamminess.

Lower Great Southern Western Australia's largest wine area is situated a little to the east of the Margaret River. In the sub-regions of Mount Barker and the Frankland River, it is beginning to demonstrate its promise quite emphatically. An entire range of grapes succeeds here, including the finicky Pinot and Sauvignon. The potential for Rieslings in particular looks extremely exciting.

Mount Barker winery, Plantagenet, does all sorts of things well, including a meaty Cabernet to age, tropically juicy Riesling and lemon-butter Chardonnay. Goundrey, also at Mount Barker, has raised some eyebrows with its good-value bottlings of creamy Chardonnay and cassis-scent-ed Cabernet. Another sharply focused, lime-zesty Riesling is made by the Howard Park winery.

SOUTH AUSTRALIA

The most copious wine-producing state of Australia is home to many internationally famous wineries. Its vineyard regions are fairly widely scattered throughout the southeast of the state, with the result that pronounced differences between them can actually be tasted in the glass. In the southern district of Coonawarra, South Australia boasts one of the most distinctive growing regions anywhere in the southern hemisphere. Almost every major variety performs well, and botrytised dessert wines - from Semillon and Riesling - have lately become a notable South Australia speciality.

Clare Valley One of the cooler growing regions, Clare actually consists of four interconnected valleys, the Clare, Skillogallee, Watervale and Polish River. The premium varietal here has to be Riesling, which achieves diamond-bright, intensely defined lime-juice and petrol characteristics from the best growers. Semillon is good too, in the austere, minerally, unwooded style, while Chardonnays can be a little on the shy and retiring side, unusually for Australia. Reds are lean as well, often with pronounced tannins and acidity, but for that reason do perform well if bottle-aged.

Tim Knappstein's Riesling is indicative of the Clare style - smoky, full-bodied and zesty, and ageing to a delicious pungency. His Cabernet is good too. Skillogallee and Pike are textbook Riesling specialists (the latter also makes a first-division Chardonnay.) Another Tim, Tim Adams, makes spectacularly concentrated Semillon and deep, long-lived Shiraz. Jim Barry attracts followers for his crisp Rieslings and Sauvignons, as well as a hauntingly aromatic Shiraz labelled Armagh. The Leasingham label, owned by the Hardy conglomerate, is a good source of simple Clare varietals, including a ripely blackcurrant Shiraz.

Riverland The backwash area of South Australian wine, making bulk produce for the bargain end of the market, is located on heavily irrigated vineyard land along the Murray River. This is where plantings of the more mundane varieties such as Sultana and Muscat of Alexandria (Gordo Blanco) are concentrated.

The Berri-Renmano combine, owned by the godfather of Australian wine, BRL Hardy, pumps out tasty enough varietals. These are led by a powerfully vanillary, but often rather oxidised Chardonnay and light, approachable Cabernet. Angoves makes a lot of generic wine for supermarket own-labels and is probably more reliable. The greater part of Riverland production, though, goes into wine-boxes. By no means of unacceptable quality, these are best glugged back round the barbie rather than lingered over before dinner.

Spring-time scene (above) in the Polish Hill area of South Australia's Clare Valley, home to fine whites.

*Penfolds' space-age
Nurioopta Winery (right)
in the Barossa Valley,
South Australia.*

*The most prolific wine-
producer in Australia, South
Australia's vineyards extend
across the state (below),
offering distinctively
different styles of wine.*

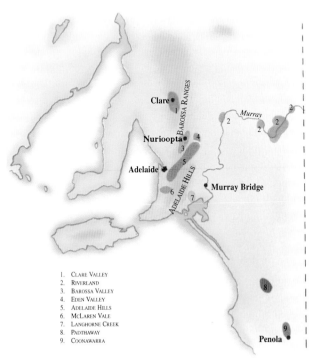

1. CLARE VALLEY
2. RIVERLAND
3. BAROSSA VALLEY
4. EDEN VALLEY
5. ADELAIDE HILLS
6. McLAREN VALE
7. LANGHORNE CREEK
8. PADTHAWAY
9. COONAWARRA

Barossa Valley Probably the first regional name in Australian wine that overseas customers came to recognise, the hot Barossa Valley, northeast of Adelaide, is in many ways the epicentre of the whole industry. It was settled and planted by Germans and Poles in the 19th century, and today is where much of the harvest from neighbouring regions finds its way to be crushed. A high proportion of Barossa's wineries, therefore, are not necessarily making exclusively Barossa wine.

The bottom of the valley has the hottest microclimate, and is the source of some of Australia's most intensely coloured and alcoholic reds. Shiraz from this region attains incomparable levels of concentration, the epitome of which is Penfolds Grange, the Barossa's legendary *grand cru*. Growers in search of cooler conditions for the Rieslings and Chardonnays for which the area is equally famed have latterly begun planting higher up on the valley hillsides.

Penfolds remains the pre-eminent Barossa name for a comprehensive range of varietals and blends to suit all pockets, as they say. From its simple, zesty Riesling and oak-driven full-on Chardonnay, to its versatile and splendidly crafted reds, quality exudes from every bottle.

Among the red highlights are the top-value Bin 28 Kalimna Shiraz, always a supple, brambly masterpiece, Bin 389 Cabernet-Shiraz and the sensationally concentrated, ink-black Bin 707 Cabernet Sauvignon. Grange (known at home as Grange Hermitage) is nearly all Shiraz, a colossal and yet immaculately graceful wine, full of the aromas of preserved purple fruits, soft leather and wild herbs, and capable of ageing in the bottle for decades. It isn't cheap, but it's still a fraction of the price of the Château Pétrus to which it is often compared. Penfolds' bottlings of Coonawarra wines (see below), especially the Cabernet, are more purely indicative of the region than virtually any others.

Other large-scale operators include Orlando-Wyndham, maker of the best-selling Jacob's Creek range, and Seppelt, whose extraordinarily diverse portfolio takes in premium sparkling wines such as the bone-dry Salinger and trailblazing sparkling Shiraz (like alcoholic fizzy Ribena), together with authoritative fortifieds, among which the sherry styles are tops (see below).

A list of excellent smaller wineries would have to include Grant Burge (appetisingly nutty Zerk Vineyard Semillon and a soft, plummy Hillcott Merlot), St Hallett (famously intense Old Block Shiraz from century-old vines), Peter Lehmann (minty, almost claret-like Stonewell Shiraz), Basedow (musclebound, unapologetically oaky Chardonnay), Rockford (idiosyncratic, smooth-contoured Basket Press Shiraz) and Wolf Blass (a comprehensive range including some musky, aromatic Cabernets).

Eden Valley A group of high valleys in the Barossa Ranges, Eden is properly speaking a continuation of the Barossa region itself. It is considerably cooler than the Barossa Valley floor, and those gentler conditions show up in the wines, especially in the significant quantities of Riesling the area produces.

One of the biggest names in Eden is Yalumba, which owns the Hill-Smith, Heggies and Pewsey Vale labels, as well as bottling under its own name. The Hill-Smith Sauvignon is an especially poignant wine, an eloquent riposte to those who claim that Australians don't understand the grape. Pewsey Vale and Heggies Rieslings both represent benchmark lemon-and-lime versions of that variety. Yalumba's own Family Reserve Shiraz is a triumph, a superbly complex red with a beguiling waft of coffee. The company's sparklers, such as its supremely quaffable Angas Brut wines and the more serious Yalumba D and Pinot-Chardonnay, and fortifieds like the chocolatey, caramelly Clocktower, are also to be reckoned with.

Hot, dry Barossa Valley (above) is South Australia's premier wine region.

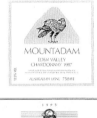

A camel sanctuary amid the vines (below) in the flat expanse of South Australia's McLaren Vale.

Henschke is another name to drop. It owns some of the oldest vineyard land for miles around, its shatteringly profound Hill of Grace Shiraz made from 100-year-old vines. Its Mount Edelstone is another top-drawer Shiraz, while Cyril Henschke is fine, concentrated Cabernet that demands ageing. The whites are good too, particularly the pungent, petrolly Riesling, another one to age.

Adelaide Hills The hill ranges east of the city are fairly sparsely planted, but represent another favourable microclimate for growers looking for relief from South Australia's heat. Petaluma is the most widely-known name around here, although its most celebrated bottlings come from Coonawarra fruit (see below). Bridge-water Mill is its alternative label, and includes a good, citrus-fresh Chardonnay. Pirramimma's Cabernet has an attractive eucalyptus note.

McLaren Vale South of Adelaide, this flat, expansive district is carving out a regional iden-tity for itself with wines that are increasingly being made in a much subtler style than was once the case. It is part of a wider, though not precisely enough defined area known as the Southern Vales.

The Chapel Hill winery is making the run-ning with some exquisitely honed reds from Cabernet and Shiraz. Chateau Reynella makes powerhouse Basket Press Shiraz here too under the auspices of the Hardy conglomerate, in whose crown this is the jewel. Among Caber-nets, Wirra-Wirra's Angelus bottling exhibits all the cassis intensity looked for in South Australia, while Ryecroft's Chardonnay is a curvaceous charmer. Wandering winemaker Geoff Merrill is here too, making a range of good-value varietals under the Mount Hurtle label, including a raspberryish rosé from Grenache and some melony Sauvignon-Semillon.

Langhorne Creek The Langhorne Creek district is east of McLaren Vale, but shares much the same characteristics. Too much of its production finds its way into blended Southern Vales wines at present, but as the inherent quality of the region comes to be appreciated, that will hopefully change.

Padthaway Padthaway is a sort of northern out-post of the more famous Coonawarra region. Lying in the southeast corner of the state of South Australia, it is nearly as cool as its neigh-bour and has a little of the sought-after *terra rossa* soil of Coonawarra. Whereas the latter has developed a reputation for red wines, Padthaway has become something of a white-wine enclave - specifically Chardonnay, Riesling and Sauvignon. Most of the vineyard land is owned by companies based in other areas, but who make special cuvées that carry the regional name on the bottle label.

Orlando, Seppelt and Penfolds all have interests in Padthaway. Penfolds Chardonnay from the region is one of the most richly buttery; the company also now owns the long-established Victoria winery Lindemans, whose Padthaway Chardonnay is almost as powerful.

Coonawarra Just south of Padthaway is the region that got everybody so excited about Australia in the first place. Declared a GI in 2001, Coonawarra's unique blend of cool climate and *terra rossa* soil - the paprika-coloured red loam that lends the vineyards such a striking appearance - is without doubt responsible for the obvious class of its wines.

Coonawarra's finest bottles provide the answer to that interminable rhetorical question that still fuels debates between the so-called Old and New Worlds: does vineyard siting or *terroir* make a difference outside Europe? Not all of Coonawarra's vines are planted on the red soil, and those that aren't do seem to lack that extra dimension of perfume and complexity boasted by those that are.

It is the reds, Shiraz and (most notably) Cabernet Sauvignon that best demonstrate the regional identity, although there are good Chardonnays and even some Riesling as well. The Cabernets are made in a positively French idiom, in that their youthful tannins can be decidedly severe and the aromatic components stubbornly refuse to show themselves. When they do open out, however, there is nothing remotely French about them. They have a pronounced savoury quality, often resembling mocha coffee beans, sometimes a deliberate slight volatility like Worcestershire sauce, but underlying them is that dry, subtly spiced dark fruit, with the odd date or prune thrown in with the basic blackcurrant.

There are a few more wineries actually based here than in Padthaway, but the headline-hitting wines have tended to be made by outsiders owning priceless Coonawarra land. Penfolds makes some of its most extravagantly beautiful Cabernet from grapes grown here; its range is as good a place to start as any. (Lindemans' bottling, now under the Southcorp umbrella with Penfolds, is also very fine, though.) Petaluma has long had a reputation for a hugely intense Cabernet-Merlot blend, simply called Petaluma Coonawarra. The premier-league Rosemount company from New South Wales has a well-made Coonawarra Cabernet too.

Among wineries located in the region, Hollick makes a glorious, challenging Ravenswood Cabernet, as well as a more immediately accessible Cabernet-Merlot blend and fresh, limey Riesling. Katnook Estate makes tobaccoey Cabernet and a big, fleshy Chardonnay, while Penley is a relative newcomer making dense-textured Cabernet and a brambly, gamey Shiraz. Wynns is a well-known name, now also under Southcorp's wing, and is an ultra-reliable producer of ripe-fruited unoaked Shiraz, smoky Chardonnay, a sweetly limey Riesling and a pitch-black, massively structured, top-of-the-range Cabernet called John Riddoch (it needs about ten years to come round).

The name that everyone recognises as uniquely Australian (above), Coonawarra is the most southerly of South Australia's wine regions.

VICTORIA

Victoria's vineyards are no longer as extensive as they were a century ago (they suffered badly in the worldwide phylloxera plague that South Australia managed to escape), but the cooler southern reaches of the state are now producing fine varietals and sparklers to compete with the best. In the northeast, Australia's celebrated fortifieds reach their apogee.

Drumborg Very cool western region, dominated by Seppelt, which uses grapes from here to make one of its extensive range of sparkling wines, Drumborg Brut.

Great Western The area known as Great Western is further inland than Drumborg, and consequently somewhat warmer. It too has a sparkling wine tradition, immortalised in the name of Great Western Brut, yet another fizz from Seppelt. Increasingly, though, it is becoming clear that the potential for Australia's best two red grapes, Cabernet and Shiraz, is most exciting of all. Chardonnays tend to be fashioned in the rounded and richly oaked style.

Mount Langi Ghiran is one of the high flyers of this region, with a Shiraz in an intriguingly restrained style and Cabernet with plenty of extract. Its Riesling has long been one of the best, and is structured for ageing. Cathcart Ridge makes a particularly lush, chocolatey Shiraz, while the Best's winery has a portfolio of cheap and cheerful varietals with good, lemon-meringue Chardonnay but thinnish reds.

High-altitude cool vineyards of Victoria's Great Dividing Range (above), source of delicate Riesling and subtle Chardonnay.

From the cooler coastal areas, to the hot inland regions, the smaller state of Victoria (right) produces a wide range of wine styles, including the famous liqueur Muscats made in the northeast.

1. DRUMBORG
2. GREAT WESTERN
3. GEELONG
4. YARRA VALLEY
5. MORNINGTON PENINSULA
6. GOULBURN VALLEY
7. GLENROWAN-MILAWA
8. RUTHERGLEN
9. MURRAY RIVER
10. LAUNCESTON
11. BICHENO
12. HOBART

Geelong First of a ring of small regions surrounding Melbourne (Geelong is just west of the city) that are home to some of the more far-sighted and ambitious of Australia's current generation of winemakers. The winemaker at the Bannockburn estate doubles as a Burgundy vigneron during Australia's winter months, so it comes as no surprise to find him a dab hand at Chardonnay and Pinot Noir. Nor does his Cabernet lack for anything in varietal richness. There are eloquent Cabernets and Chardonnays too from the Idyll winery.

Yarra Valley The temperate Yarra is Victoria's answer to South Australia's Coonawarra, a prime site for highly individual winemaking and superlative cool-climate varietals. This is one of the most promising areas in Australia for Pinot Noir, with Green Point, Coldstream Hills and Tarrawarra leading the pack. Mount Mary's is coming up fast on the inside. There was a tendency in the past to overoak the wines, which is now thankfully being resisted. Green Point (the export name for Moët's Domaine Chandon) also makes a very fine, lightly buttery, nut-meggy Chardonnay - not a million miles from the Sonoma County, California, style - as well as its much-praised fizz. The Cabernets and Shirazes of Yarra Yering winemaker Bailey Carrodus are idiosyncratic creations fully worth the high asking price. St Huberts makes a deep, satisfying Cabernet to last.

Mornington Peninsula There are not far off 100 wineries crowded on to this little peninsula southeast of Melbourne. Like the Yarra, it is a region of stylistic pioneers who are making waves. Dromana is a winery with a versatile portfolio, including a soft, strawberryish Pinot Noir and plushly textured Cabernet-Merlot. Its soundly made cheaper range is bottled under the Schinus Molle label. Stonier's Merricks has textbook Chardonnay and Cabernet in the full-blown opulent style.

Goulburn Valley North of the Yarra, Goulburn is an expansive valley region that contains some of the oldest wineries and vineyards in Australia, whose vines miraculously escaped the worst of the phylloxera wave. Château Tahbilk has some 100-year-old vines, its Private Bin bottlings of Shiraz and Cabernet bursting with venerable class. This is one of the properties that pioneered varietal Marsanne in Australia. The Mitchelton winery produces both oaked and unoaked versions of Marsanne. It certainly has a style all of its own, but its clinging, top-

heavy, buttery banana quality is too much for some. Delatite offers a more broad-minded range from its high-altitude vineyards. Snappy Riesling, delicately scented Gewürztraminer and rose-petally Pinot Noir supplement the excellent Shiraz and Cabernet.

Glenrowan-Milawa As you head into the northeastern sector of Victoria, you are heading towards fortified country (see below). At Milawa, though, table wines are made in quantity, the most important producer being Brown Brothers, one of the vanguard companies that blazed the trail for Australian wines in the UK. Its range is wide and fairly stolid, but some wines stand out: buttery King Valley Chardonnay, the juicy-fruited Dolcetto lookalike Tarrango, deliciously peachy late-picked Muscat, and hazelnutty Semillon.

Rutherglen Pre-eminent for liqueur Muscats and Tokays (see under Fortified Wines).

New vineyards planted by Brown Brothers (below), one of hotter, inland Glenrowan-Milawa's top producers of table wines.

Vineyards of the Lower Hunter (above) suffer more from tropical rain storms than those in its more northerly partner, the Upper Hunter.

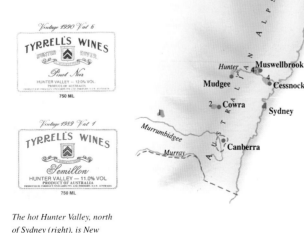

The hot Hunter Valley, north of Sydney (right), is New South Wales' finest wine region.

NEW SOUTH WALES

Although it contains the Hunter Valley region of worldwide repute, New South Wales only accounts for a relatively tiny fraction of Australia's annual wine production. Its climate is as hot and hard for growers to contend with as parts of South Australia.

Murrumbidgee Irrigation Area (MIA)
The world's least attractively named wine region is responsible largely for volume output destined for boxes and own-brand bottlings. Botrytised Semillon is an unlikely exception to the humdrum rule, and is especially distinguished from de Bortoli.

Cowra Small region supplying much of the Hunter Valley's raw material. Hunter winery Rothbury makes an impressive regional Cowra Chardonnay, though.

Mudgee The Mudgee district is sufficiently proud of its regional pedigree to have invented its own appellation. A pity then that much of the produce of this hot, dry district goes to beef up Hunter's wines when their harvests are hit by rain. Firm Cabernet and stout Shiraz are the baseline (Botolobar's Shiraz is a stunner), but gathering potential is being observed in Chardonnays too.

Hunter Valley Divided into the Upper and Lower Hunter, this hot, extensive valley is the premium wine region of New South Wales. The Upper section is quite a way to the north of the Lower, and manages to escape the tropical rains that can disrupt the Lower Hunter vintage. Dry Semillon, practically an indigenous Hunter style of great lineage, is the proudest boast. It's usually fairly low in alcohol, austerely hard and minerally and famously takes on a burnt-toast quality as it matures in the bottle. This has fooled many a blind taster into thinking it has been aged in charred oak, when it may very well be entirely innocent of the stuff. Red wines can be a bit muddy - a lot of that sweet plum-jam style of Shiraz comes from the Hunter - but they are improving.

Good Semillon producers include Rothbury, Rosemount, McWilliams Elizabeth, Tyrrell's Vat 1 and Brokenwood. Rothbury also make a slim but beguiling Shiraz, Rosemount a show-stopping, vegetally Burgundian Roxburgh Chardonnay, Tyrrell's an exciting, offbeat range sold under Vat numbers (such as the famed Vat 6 Pinot and the butterscotchy Vat 47 Chardonnay) and Brokenwood a reverberating Shiraz sombrely called Graveyard Vineyards.

QUEENSLAND

Right on the border with New South Wales is a an area unromantically known as the Granite Belt. Only its altitude makes it a propitious place to grow grapes, and the wines don't tend to travel much further than Sydney.

TASMANIA

Led by the visionary and multi-talented Andrew Pirie at Pipers Brook vineyard, a small band of Tasmania producers intends to show the world that the island can make sharply defined varietals, especially Pinot Noir and Chardonnay, in a distinctively European (i.e. French) idiom. The two centres of production are Launceston in the northeast and Hobart in the south; they are delineated by an appellation system that Tasmania has drawn up for itself and its modest output.

Pipers Brook winery, in the northern region of the same name, makes exemplary Pinot Noir, hard in youth and needing time, a subtly steely Chardonnay and some crisp, zesty Riesling. Moorilla Estate produces good, beefy Pinot, and is trying its hand at Gewürztraminer. Heemskerk was traditionally known for big but fairly brittle-centred Cabernet, and is now set on making fizz after some initial input from champagne house Louis Roederer.

FORTIFIED WINES

There are two basic styles of Australian fortified wine. One derives from the days when the hot southern-hemisphere countries all had a shot at imitating the traditional methods and flavours of port and sherry. Indeed, those terms were until recently in widespread use in Australia itself, though they are now on the wane. Among the port-styles are some extremely sweet strawberry-jam-like wines made from fortified Shiraz; McWilliams, Seppelt and Montara offer typical examples, of which some are vintage-dated. Extended wood-ageing washes out the colour of some, which are then referred to - as in the Douro - as tawny. The sherry styles are not as widely seen on the export markets, but can be even better. Seppelt makes a comprehensive range of tangy, salty fino (labelled DP117), hazelnutty amontillado (DP116) and toffeeish oloroso (DP38).

The other styles are unique to Australia. Liqueur Muscat and Liqueur Tokay are breathtakingly rich fortified wines made from, respectively, the Muscat Blanc à Petits Grains (here known as Brown Muscat for the dun-skinned variant locally grown) and Muscadelle, the minority grape of Sauternes. The production area is mainly in northeast Victoria around the town of Rutherglen, although some Muscats are also made in Glenrowan, a little to the south.

Their production seems to combine a little of every traditional method for making liquorous dessert wines. Firstly, the grapes are left to overripen and partially shrivel on the vine. They are then pressed and the viscous juice partially fermented but fortified with grape spirit long before the piercing sweetness has even begun to soften. After that, they are aged and blended from a barrel system something like the *soleras* of Jerez.

The Muscats, especially, are shockingly intense. Pure orange marmalade on the nose, they dissolve in the mouth into a glutinous amalgam of milk chocolate, sticky dates and candied orange rind, with a finish that persists on the back of the palate for minutes on end. There are many fine producers, the more notable of whom are Stanton & Killeen, Chambers, Morris, Yalumba and Campbells of Rutherglen.

Heemskerk Vineyards in the Pipers Brook region of Tasmania (above), makers of notably well-built Cabernet and elegant sparkling wines.

NEW ZEALAND

In just 20 years, New Zealand's winemakers have taken the world by storm to become the fastest growing wine country in the world. Undaunted by geographical isolation, they have established a strong regional identity.

THIS IS WHERE the global wine tour makes its final stop, at the world's most southerly vineyards on the North and South Islands of New Zealand. Any further, and we would be trying to make Icewine in Antarctica.

Australia may be a relative junior in the international wine industry, but New Zealand really is the new kid on the block among the major producing countries. Its potential for fine winemaking only began to be taken seriously in the 1970s but, undoubtedly helped to a great degree by the successful rise of its ambitious northern neighbour, it now has one of the most rapidly growing viticultural sectors anywhere. Although winemaking will never be as

The world's most southerly vineyards operate in a damp, cool climate. Except for South Island's Central Otago, New Zealand's wine regions (below) lie on or close to the coast.

important to it as sheep- or dairy-farming have famously been, there is nonetheless an infectious and widespread atmosphere of experimentation, such as overtook California in the 1960s and Australia in the 1970s.

It has to be said that the domestic market in New Zealand has not, until very recently, been a conspicuously favourable one in which to sell wine. At about the same time as it was introduced in the United States, New Zealanders briefly experimented with Prohibition. National licensing laws have, for most of the century, been the most restrictive in the English-speaking world. High-street wine shops are a post-war phenomenon, while supermarkets have only been allowed to sell the country's home wine produce since the beginning of the 1990s.

Viticulture was tentatively practised in the 19th century. Its earliest pioneers were British settlers, led by the enterprising James Busby. He created a thriving little vineyard in the north of the country that lived off sales to the local garrison. Phylloxera, the vine louse that built an empire of destruction in the world's vineyards in the closing decades of the 19th century, was careful not to pass New Zealand by. The whole-sale replanting that followed was of hybrid grape varieties of mixed *vinifera* and American vine parentage, so that, until well after the Second World War, the dowdy Isabella held sway over both islands.

What eventually catapulted New Zealand into the limelight was, of course, Sauvignon Blanc. There is an oft-expressed feeling among wine commentators that Sauvignon is not quite a major-league grape variety, owing to its brash and relatively unmalleable character. If any region is likely to persuade consumers to come down on the other side of the argument, it will be the Marlborough district of New Zealand's South Island. There is more uplifting, happy fruit flavour in New Zealand Sauvignon than in any other dry white wine on earth.

Sauvignon was followed by fruit-fuelled Chardonnay and Riesling. Reds lagged behind for a while, the varieties not carefully enough matched to the planting areas; much of the

1. AUCKLAND
2. GISBORNE
3. HAWKES BAY
4. WAIRARAPA
5. NELSON
6. MARLBOROUGH
7. CANTERBURY
8. CENTRAL OTAGO

Auckland
Gisborne
MT RUAPEHU *Hawkes Bay*
Napier
Wellington
TASMAN MTS *Cook Strait*
Blenheim
SOUTHERN ALPS
Christchurch
Queenstown
Dunedin

Cabernet Sauvignon was excessively light and herbaceous, its inescapable whiff of green pepper skin complaining bitterly in the glass of climatic indignities in the vineyard. Producers have addressed that problem now with better site selection, and some wineries are achieving even faster improvements with Pinot Noir, always a likelier bet than Cabernet in a cool climate. The latest development is the appearance of that other cool-climate classic, fine *méthode traditionelle* sparkling wine, promptly followed by a Champagne delegation looking to invest.

At the moment, the New Zealand wine industry is still very much in a state of germination. It has proved that it can make a range of commercially successful varietal wines, whites especially, but not necessarily, as yet, that they can achieve internationally acknowledged greatness. There is certainly a small clutch of wineries ahead of the field, whose wines (Cloudy Bay is the most prominent example) are sufficiently sought-after that export allocations have to be severely restricted and the proprietors have only to name their price.

The country's wine infrastructure, however, is still in its infancy in the sense that much of the annual harvest still has to travel unconscionable distances to reach the winery at which it will be pressed. The journey may very well include a rough crossing of the Cook Strait, the body of water that separates the two islands. While that is being addressed, party-pooping phylloxera is on the march again, gnawing its way through precious Marlborough vinestocks.

Preferential duty rates for home produce do not prevent the Australians from selling a healthy quantity of wine in New Zealand, and then there is the problem of how to get the world to beat a path to your door when you are so off the beaten track. For the time being, the industry's ruling body, the Wine Institute of New Zealand, has sensibly decided to target the greater part of its export effort at the UK, but that does mean that the influential American wine constituency remains largely sceptical or completely ignorant of what the country is capable of.

Eventually, all of these problems will be resolved. Investment in new installations is increasing faster than ever before, so that a greater percentage of each vintage will be processed close to the vineyard where it was grown. The replanting that the latest bout of phylloxera will entail should be on resistant American rootstocks. Home consumption will

The love-affair with Marlborough Sauvignon Blanc began with the wines of Montana. Machine-harvesters at work (above) picking Sauvignon grapes at Montana's Brancott Estate, Marlborough, North Island.

Stunning landscape of inland South Island (left), on the shore of Lake Wanaka in Central Otago.

increase as the industry's overall capacity grows. As to the preference for the UK market, it is currently paying dividends, so why upset the applecart?

The next step is an appellation system to cover New Zealand's widely dispersed vineyard regions. A start was made in the mid-1990s with the identification of regional names, although at the outset, any wine that was composed of grapes from more than one region, rather than being denied a regional designation, was simply allowed an amalgamated one. That of course

Ngatarawa Winery and vineyards (above) in the well-established Hawkes Bay region of North Island.

defeats the object of having an appellation name in the first place (imagine the French allowing two growers in the Loire to pool their Sauvignon and officially call the resulting wine Ménétou-Sancerre) and should be tightened as soon as practically possible.

When all is said and drunk, though, New Zealand has no greater asset than the fact that its wines have recognisable national identity. And it is that irresistible factor on which the repute of any wine-producing region, old or new, is inevitably founded.

Not only does New Zealand have a cool climate, it also has a damp one. Annual rainfall is plentifully distributed throughout the year, with the result that vines often yielded too vigorously, giving low-quality fruit, or that the grapes were diluted by water penetration during the all-important ripening phase. New techniques in vineyard management introduced during the 1980s have widely rectified those particular problems. This allows many growers to harvest earlier, leading to riper, fuller and more concentrated flavours in the glass.

The growing regions are scattered throughout an extensive stretch of the North and South Islands, for all that the total acreage is still very limited compared to that of Australia, which annually produces about ten times more wine than New Zealand. With the exception of southerly Otago, they are all situated on or near the coast, mostly on the Pacific side. The whole show began in the far north of the North Island, in area now logically enough known as Northland, just about the warmest section of the country. Although most of the recent activity has been in vineyards much further south, there

are moves afoot to re-investigate Northland as a possible site for warm-climate varietals.

Müller-Thurgau once occupied pole position in the vineyards, but has now been put in its place rather decisively by Chardonnay and Sauvignon spreading like wildfire. The former achieves more overt fruit quality in New Zealand than it does seemingly anywhere else. Aromas of peach, banana and pear are quite common, and not especially disguisable by oak treatments. Some wineries are attempting to capture a more Burgundian ethos, with buttery richness as opposed to fruit-salad freshness, but they are not yet the norm. Müller can, surprisingly, yield a soft, gently fruity wine from the best exponents but its poor reputation elsewhere means that it is likely to continue declining here.

Sauvignon Blanc is the great white hope of New Zealand wine - better here than in the Loire, many think, for sheer fruit-powered dynamism. There are quite dramatic stylistic differences between wineries, some emphasising the green, herbaceous flavours of gooseberries, asparagus and freshly-washed watercress, others plunging headlong into tropicality with mango, passion fruit, pineapple and musky Charentais melon. I have tasted Marlborough Sauvignons that smelt of red peppers, grated carrot, the purest blackcurrant juice, even glacé cherries. It is one exciting wine when it wants to be.

Riesling achieves classical steeliness, without quite the petrolly pungency of Australian versions. Then there's a dash of Chenin Blanc, which should enjoy the climate, some delicate but recognisable Gewürztraminer and limited plantings of so far rather unremarkable Semillon, better blended than made as a varietal.

Cabernet Sauvignon, once the most widely planted red, now plays second fiddle to Pinot Noir. Those vegetal flavours that have dogged its image are still too easy to find, but some offerings are showing much deeper, plummier concentration than before, so there is hope. Pinot itself could be potentially as thrilling from here as it is from Carneros or Oregon, once the variety is fully mastered; for the time being, there are a handful of ageworthy wines from Pinot that display good solid fruit profile as well as a distinctly Burgundian reluctance to charm in their first flush. Merlot is striking out on its own in some parts, while playing its historically sanctioned role of chaperoning Cabernet in others.

NORTH ISLAND

Auckland The area in the immediate vicinity of Auckland was at one time in decline as a wine region, as attention was resolutely turned to more fashionable districts further south. In the last few years, it has started gaining in status as the most auspicious region for well-built reds. It is warm, but prone to harvest rains, which means that fruit from other regions often has to be bought in to beef up the blends, but in the kinder years Auckland reds are looking good. The region includes a subzone called Matakana, north of the city, as well as Waiheke Island, situated in the harbour.

Persuasive Bordeaux-blend reds come from Te Motu, Goldwater and Stonyridge. Kumeu River makes a profoundly Burgundian and quite atypical Chardonnay as well as a striking red with more Merlot than Cabernet.

Gisborne On the east coast of the North Island, Gisborne has begun to find its feet as a quality region after years of languishing as a bag-in-box bulk area. Copious plantings of Müller-Thurgau still testify to that, but Gisborne has become so good at premium white varietals, and won so many awards, that it now styles itself - without a blush for modesty - Chardonnay Capital of New Zealand. As well as Chardonnay, Gewürztraminer has performed creditably, and the smart money is now on champagne-method sparkling wines. The town of Gisborne stands on Poverty Bay, sometimes used as an alternative name for the region.

New Zealand's two biggest wine companies, Marlborough-based Montana and Corbans from near Auckland, both have footholds in Gisborne. Millton Vineyards is a partially organic producer, making some of its wines according to the biodynamic principles followed by Nicolas Joly in Savennières (see Loire section). Its Chardonnay is a thunderously rich, lemon-curd wine. Auckland family producer Nobilo makes a more restrained and smokily oaked Poverty Bay Chardonnay.

Hawkes Bay Further down the coast, in the environs of the town of Napier, Hawkes Bay is one of New Zealand's longer-established vineyard regions. Like Gisborne, it has a high reputation for Chardonnay, as well as some subtler, gentler Sauvignon than is commonly met with on the South Island. There is plenty of Müller still, as there is in Gisborne, but red Bordeaux blends are improving significantly in what is one of the country's sunnier vineyards.

Hawkes Bay winery Te Mata makes what is probably the most authoritative range of wines in the region, taking in soft, gooseberryish Sauvignon (Castle Hill), discreetly buttery Chardonnay (Elston) and full-frontal, muscular Cabernet-Merlot (Coleraine). To indicate the measure of the ambition, Te Mata has also planted some Syrah. The Villa Maria conglomerate, which owns both the Vidal and Esk Valley labels, makes some tasty Sauvignon and modest, approachable red blends. Ngatarawa (the "g" is silent) makes ripely expressive Cabernet-Merlot and, in some years, a good stab at dessert Riesling from noble-rotted grapes. Auckland's Babich winery makes a regional Hawkes Bay Chardonnay (Irongate) in the oaky buttercream mould.

The damp climate encourages vines to grow too vigorously. Pruning and leaf-trimming help control their growth here at Esk Valley vineyards in Hawkes Bay (above).

Wairarapa At the very southern tip of the North Island, near the New Zealand capital of Wellington, Wairarapa is home to some of the country's best small wine-growers. Reds are the declared speciality, whether from Cabernet or Pinot Noir, and the challenge has been taken sufficiently seriously that the export wines, at least, have been hugely impressive. A sub-region within Wairarapa, Martinborough, has emerged as particularly promising for Pinot Noir, and is being mentioned in the same breath as California's Carneros by some.

Martinborough Vineyards, having taken its name from the region, does the area proud by producing its most celebrated Pinot Noir, a clean, raspberry-fruited, deeply complex wine with Burgundian levels of acidity and - perhaps - longevity. Its Chardonnay and Riesling are also finely crafted. Ata Rangi's Pinot is another resonant performance, subtly spiced and meaty; this is another winery with a bit of Syrah, which it uses to plump its fine Cabernet-Merlot blend. A slightly lighter, more cherryish Pinot is made by Palliser Estate, whose bold Sauvignons and Chardonnays have plenty of guts.

Vines were only planted in Marlborough (below) as recently as the 1970s, by big producer Montana. The region is now synonymous with fruit-rich Sauvignon.

SOUTH ISLAND

Nelson A hilly region on the fringes of the Tasman mountains, Nelson is Chardonnay country *par excellence*. Only a handful of wineries have made their homes here, in a damp but otherwise promising cool-climate district, but the quality of the white varietals is very persuasive. Neudorf makes a finely honed Chardonnay and some pretty good, positively flavoured Pinot, while Seifried (aka Redwood Valley) has crisp Riesling in both dry and lightly sweet versions and a heartwarming, bright golden Chardonnay with overtones of banana.

Marlborough Over the last decade and a half, Marlborough (centred on the town of Blenheim at the northern end of the South Island) has emerged as the greatest of all New Zealand regions. Little matter that it doesn't have a particularly elevated reputation for red wines, it is the origin of many of the country's most sharply definitive white wines, with Sauvignon Blanc at the head of the pack. The region is cool but relatively dry, and its misty autumns mean that botrytised wines from Riesling are a possibility in most vintages. Chardonnay plays an important role too.

Montana, the New Zealand wine colossus, basically invented Marlborough as a wine region in the 1970s when it planted the first vines here, and its top-value benchmark Sauvignon has become a contemporary classic wine. For all that it may wax and wane from year to year, it is never less than riotously fruity. Montana's Chardonnay is a peachy little number, there's good botrytised Riesling, but the Cabernet is stuck in the old school (light but greenly tannic).

Cloudy Bay was the second winery to startle the world with its Sauvignon from Marlborough. Those in the know fight over the limited quantities. It is expensive, but profoundly eloquent wine, thrown into relief by a little Semillon. Its Chardonnay is deep and complex, and the Cabernet-Merlot a damson-rich powerhouse of long, refined flavour.

Hunters Estate is another great name for opulent Sauvignon and Chardonnay, Jackson Estate makes soft, biscuity Chardonnay and an emphatic, explosive Sauvignon, Vavasour (and its alternative label Dashwood) has high-octane Sauvignon and Chardonnay, Delegats' Oyster Bay range from Marlborough includes a smoky, peachy Sauvignon, Matua Valley's Shingle Peak label offers gooseberry-crammed Sauvignon, Wairau River has a taut, orchard-fruited

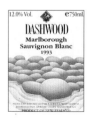

Sauvignon and melt-in-the-mouth Chardonnay... but you get the picture.

Marlborough is also where most of New Zealand's champagne-method sparklers are being made, often with expertise and investment from champagne houses such as Veuve Clicquot and Deutz. Pinot Noir and Chardonnay are the grapes used, and the examples so far released show just how distinguished sparkling wines can be when made in a cool climate.

Pelorus is the Cloudy Bay fizz, undoubtedly the best to date, for its limpid, toasty richness derived from maturation on the yeast lees. Deutz Marlborough Cuvée, released by Montana, is extremely crisp and dry, a touch more knowing than its everyday Lindauer fizz (though the Lindauer rosé is expressive enough). Cellier Le Brun, a sparkling specialist, could yet outstrip them all.

Canterbury Centred on the city of Christchurch, Canterbury's vineyards are cooler still than those of Marlborough, with the Waipara zone north of the city producing the most elegant wines to date. Chardonnay and Pinot Noir are the varietals of choice, but there is good Riesling too. Waipara Springs offers an ample-fleshed Chardonnay, as does Giesen, which also makes noble-rotted Riesling when the weather performs. Pinot Noir looks ostentatiously good from the recently established Mark Rattray winery. Innovative St Helena has planted Pinot Gris and Pinot Blanc.

Central Otago East of the town of Queensland, on South Island, Central Otago is New Zealand's smallest, and most southerly, wine region. It is also the only inland region, with a handful of producers. The vineyards are only at a tentative stage of development as yet. The two foremost grape varieties so far are the intriguing duo of Pinot Noir and Gewürztraminer.

CONCLUSION

Wine has never been as diverse, as confident or as expansive as it is today. It would be fascinating indeed to see how much bigger a book like this will have to be in, say, 20 years' time, when we find ourselves drinking wines from places we never even imagined could grow grapes. There will be more South American countries to consider. There may well have to be a chapter on Dutch and Belgian wine. I do know a man who makes wine in the Republic of Ireland (and it's not bad wine either).

Viticultural historians to come will, I believe, identify the last decade of the twentieth century as one of the crucial turning-points in the age-old story of wine. Our generation has seen more cross-fertilisation and more productive interaction between the wine-growing areas of the world than any other before it.

Slowly but surely, winemakers in the most insular regions of Europe, those who have always made wine just as their grandparents did, are starting to see that they can't afford to live within the confines of their own little patches of vineland any longer. They can't afford to because, sooner or later, nobody will want the kind of wine they make. It's all very well preserving your granny's recipe for *cassoulet* through the generations, but wine has to progress, and your grandad's recipe for Corbières doesn't have quite the same charm.

It has, above all, been a technological revolution, an extended demonstration of the simple point that, if nature has endowed you with a harvest of exquisitely ripe and disease-free grapes, you are letting yourself and your customers down if you don't treat them well once you get them to the winery.

That means, for example, letting your light white wines ferment at controlled temperatures in clean stainless steel instead of fizzing themselves into a tumult in grubby old casks. It means ensuring that all your vinification equipment, from storage tanks to the bottling chain, is hygienically maintained.

Some people say that, because a lot of these lessons are being absorbed into Europe from North America and the southern hemisphere, there is a real danger that all wine will end up tasting the same. Others dismiss that as reactionary nonsense, and say that there can be no going back to the bad old days of sloppy practices and high-handed indifference to the consumer.

The resolution of the current debate will emerge, as it often does, from some sort of compromise between old and new. Yes, we want wine to be made with respect, both for the raw materials and the sensibilities of those who are being asked to buy it and drink it. But we don't want winemaking philosophies to become so dully standardised that all wine is made in the image of those pleasant but characterless Chardonnays that could actually have come from anywhere. Then there are the Chardonnays made in France by South Africans or Australians that taste as if they have been pushed and pulled into a shape they don't feel comfortable with.

By the same token, those French growers and co-operatives who airily dismiss wine in which their southern hemisphere counterparts have had a hand as merely "technological wine", an artificial construct with no soul, will come to realise that their days are numbered unless they can enthusiastically offer people who want wine the wine they want. There is no great sentimental attachment among today's consumers to traditional European wines. And anyway, whatever became of all that junk that flowed into the wine lake? Ah yes, that's right. It was processed into fuel for the Brazilians to put in their cars.

The most important development of all, though, is one in which the Europeans *have* been able to influence the newer countries. It is the model of the *appellation contrôlée* system. Nothing may be more baffling for newcomers to wine to grasp than those rules and regulations that seem designed only to keep bureaucrats happy. Why not abolish the whole show and do as the Californians and others do?

Except that the Californians and others are all venturing cautiously and reflectively into some sort of appellation approach themselves. The reason is simple and irresistible. It is that one fine day in one fine vintage, you find that the Pinot Noir you have made from that little sheltered patch of vines halfway up Crooked Hill is the best damn wine you ever made in your life. So in future, you will avoid blending those grapes with grapes from your other Pinot plots, and you will send it out into the world proudly labelled Crooked Hill Pinot Noir. And, stripped of all the mystification, that's all an appellation is.

If you kick down the pillars of the temple, you won't get better wine. In fact, in the short term, you'll get the very opposite. You'll get wildly unbalanced, pretentiously priced stuff from growers who, ignoring the precedent of centuries, decide they want to plant Cabernet Sauvignon in cool, damp, high-altitude vineyards, or Riesling in arid, flat dustlands because it might sell better than the wine they were originally obliged to make.

It is indeed hard for the time being on those who are stuck with names like Madiran or Bairrada or Aglianico del Vulture when all the world seems to want is Chardonnay, but the first flicker of a yawn as the next bottle of smoky, vanillary, golden wine is opened is the first flicker of hope for those others. And if we want to preserve that diversity, the appellations are the best chance in town.

In the mean time, just enjoy. That's what wine has been there for ever since it slopped around in great stone jars in biblical times. And so it always will be.

INDEX

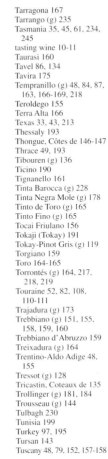